MBA Basics

Third Edition

by Tom Gorman

ALPHA

A member of Penguin Group (USA) Inc.

ALPHA BOOKS

Published by the Penguin Group

Penguin Group (USA) Inc., 375 Hudson Street, New York, New York 10014, USA

Penguin Group (Canada), 90 Eglinton Avenue East, Suite 700, Toronto, Ontario M4P 2Y3, Canada (a division of Pearson Penguin Canada Inc.)

Penguin Books Ltd., 80 Strand, London WC2R 0RL, England

Penguin Ireland, 25 St. Stephen's Green, Dublin 2, Ireland (a division of Penguin Books Ltd.)

Penguin Group (Australia), 250 Camberwell Road, Camberwell, Victoria 3124, Australia (a division of Pearson Australia Group Pty. Ltd.)

Penguin Books India Pvt. Ltd., 11 Community Centre, Panchsheel Park, New Delhi—110 017, India

Penguin Group (NZ), 67 Apollo Drive, Rosedale, North Shore, Auckland 1311, New Zealand (a division of Pearson New Zealand Ltd.)

Penguin Books (South Africa) (Pty.) Ltd., 24 Sturdee Avenue, Rosebank, Johannesburg 2196, South Africa

Penguin Books Ltd., Registered Offices: 80 Strand, London WC2R 0RL, England

Copyright © 2011 by Tom Gorman

International Standard Book Number: 978-1-61564-071-3
Library of Congress Catalog Card Number: 2010915377

13   12   11   8   7   6   5   4   3   2   1

Interpretation of the printing code: The rightmost number of the first series of numbers is the year of the book's printing; the rightmost number of the second series of numbers is the number of the book's printing. For example, a printing code of 11-1 shows that the first printing occurred in 2011.

Printed in the United States of America

Publisher: *Marie Butler-Knight*

Associate Publisher: *Mike Sanders*

Executive Managing Editor: *Billy Fields*

Senior Acquisitions Editor: *Paul Dinas*

Senior Development Editor: *Phil Kitchel*

Production Editor: *Kayla Dugger*

Copy Editor: *Krista Hansing Editorial Services*

Cover Designer: *Rebecca Batchelor*

Book Designers: *William Thomas, Rebecca Batchelor*

Indexer: *Johnna VanHoose Dinse*

Layout: *Ayanna Lacey*

Proofreader: *John Etchison*

Contents

Introduction

M-B-A. These three letters spell success in business, and for good reason. In reality, just having a Master of Business Administration degree doesn't make anyone a master of business administration. That takes years of on-the-job experience. But the course of study that leads to an MBA prepares you extremely well for a business career by giving you several things that (until now) have been hard to get elsewhere.

First, an MBA teaches you the key principles of how to manage a business. A business can be managed either by the "seat of the pants" or professionally, and business school teaches you the professional way. Professional management calls for setting goals that motivate people, allocating resources to activities that move the company toward those goals, monitoring progress, and making any necessary adjustments. These principles, and others taught in an MBA program, usually lead to success.

Second, an MBA gives you exposure (at least, classroom exposure) to the departments—the functions—that you'll find in most businesses. These include management and operations, finance and accounting, and sales and marketing. You learn about the roles these functions play in a business and how to get these areas to work together. All of this prepares you to deal effectively with the various people working in a company.

Third, an MBA program gives you sophisticated ways of approaching business problems. It gives you methods, which often involve simple calculations or diagrams, to enable you to clearly see the parts of the problem, develop potential solutions, choose the best course of action, and present your case to others in a winning way.

Finally, MBAs know the language of business. Like any profession, business has its own lingo and jargon. Some MBAs seem to get a kick out of throwing around these words for the heck of it (or to confuse the uninitiated), but most management, financial, and marketing terms do refer to important business concepts. If you understand the words, you understand the concepts. If you understand the concepts, you can apply them in your business.

The Complete Idiot's Guide to MBA Basics, Third Edition, gives you all these advantages—an overview of business, an understanding of the various functions, a set of analytical tools, and knowledge of the language of business, just like an MBA program would.

Well, it's not exactly the same thing. For one thing, this book costs a tiny fraction of the price of even one course at a business school. For another, it cuts right to the core of each item it covers. In the tradition of *The Complete Idiot's Guide* series, this book makes the material clear and applies it to the kinds of situations that you'll run into on the job. It also leaves out what you don't need: the heavy detail that most MBAs either forget or never use.

This third edition of *The Complete Idiot's Guide to MBA Basics* reflects a number of key developments in MBA programs and in the business environment. The basic subjects covered in an MBA program have remained essentially the same, particularly in areas such as accounting, financial analysis, and marketing. But even those areas needed to be updated, given business developments.

MBA programs keep pace with the times. Many B-schools now offer courses on risk management and classes on managing the health, safety, and environmental impacts that a business generates. You'll find new chapters on these topics in this edition (Chapters 24 and 25, respectively), as well as new material on the economic and business cycle (see Chapter 6), given the recession of the late 2000s. I've included new information on marketing and advertising, in light of the Internet's impact on these areas (see Part 4). Chapter 4, on leadership, now presents a proven method of managing change, and Chapter 10, on productivity and quality, explains Six Sigma and other formal quality-improvement methods.

Elsewhere and throughout the book, I've updated the material with recent examples, new information, and (wherever necessary) even clearer explanations.

This book actually amounts to a "mini-MBA," and it will prepare you to manage a business of any size, even a start-up. If you work (or plan to work) for a large company, the knowledge and skills you'll get from this book will prepare you to compete and succeed. In fact, a management position in a large company typically demands an understanding of these business concepts.

If you manage (or start) a small company, it will run much more smoothly and be far more competitive if you allocate your resources properly; understand budgeting, finance, and accounting; and use sophisticated sales and marketing techniques.

Having earned my MBA over 20 years ago at New York University, I have benefited as a corporate manager, small businessman, and citizen. Most of all, the broad business knowledge, the grounding in finance and marketing, and the decision-making tools I gained in B-school enabled me to be comfortable and effective in any business situation. That's the major benefit I want you to get from this book.

Here's the approach I take:

Part 1, Managing People, shows you ways of getting things done through other people. It also covers leadership and shows how it differs from management, and explains how to manage change in an organization.

Part 2, Making Decisions About Resources and Operations, covers the workings of both economics and operations, along with the principles that determine how a country or a company wins or loses the money game. In this part, you learn about the business cycle of recession and recovery, methods of quality improvement, and decision-making techniques that will help you succeed in any environment.

Part 3, Managing Money, Accounting, and Finance, takes you into the world of accounting systems and financial statements. Here you learn how a company keeps track of sales, expenses, and profits, and how it makes budgeting and investment decisions. This part also examines the financial markets and the major securities bought and sold on those markets.

Part 4, Managing Marketing for Maximum Sales, shows how companies learn about their customers' needs, develop products and services to meet those needs, and use marketing strategy to focus on the customer and outsell the competition. The Internet has transformed marketing and advertising, and this part of the book shows how to deal with that.

Part 5, Steering the Business into the Future, deals with strategic planning, which is the major tool for managing longer-term aspects of the business. One key long-term challenge is sound risk management, because without it there *is* no long term. That is also true of sustainable business practices, which are necessary for the survival of not only the business, but the planet as well. This part also covers managers' legal and ethical responsibilities, and explores entrepreneurship and how to write a business plan.

Extras

In addition to the text, throughout the book you'll find the following signposts that highlight information I want to be sure you catch.

MBA LINGO

These sidebars give you definitions of words and business concepts that might not be familiar to you.

MBA MASTERY

Read these hints to find out how to boost your—and your company's—performance to higher levels with insider tips and lessons from the current best practices in business.

CASE IN POINT

These sidebars provide real-life examples that illustrate and expand on the material.

MBA ALERT

Here you'll find examples of how to deal with problems you'll face on the job.

Acknowledgments

Many thanks to everyone who helped to make this book possible. For assistance on the third edition, I'd like to thank Paul Dinas, acquisitions editor; Phil Kitchel, development editor; Kayla Dugger, production editor; and Krista Hansing, copy editor. Thanks also to Mike Snell, my agent; my wife, Phyllis, and my sons, Daniel and Matthew; my professors and instructors at New York University's Stern School of Business; and all of my past employers, employees, colleagues, and customers.

Trademarks

Managing People

Management has been defined as "the art and science of getting things done through people." Of course, there are other areas of management: these include making decisions about plant and equipment, and managing the organization's money and investments.

However, most managers find managing people to be the most challenging aspect of the job. Those who succeed at it understand their role in a business and know a bit about organizational structure. They also know the difference between management and leadership, and they know when leadership is called for and how to exercise it. They consistently practice certain managerial skills and use proven procedures for hiring the right people and guiding them toward their goals.

These areas of management are all covered in Part 1 because most of what a manager gets done, gets done through others.

The Meaning of Management

In This Chapter

- A (very) brief history of management
- A manager's responsibility and role
- The Essential Six principles every manager must know

Imagine an army with no general, a team with no coach, or a nation with no leaders. How could the army beat the enemy? How could the team win games? How could the nation avoid anarchy?

They couldn't. Similarly, an organization can't succeed without managers. Managers make sure that an organization stays, well, organized. Organizing and directing the work of the people in the organization is the work of managers. People need organization and direction to work effectively, and managers provide just that.

This chapter introduces you to the development and role of management and covers the key principles of managing any business.

What Makes a Good Manager?

Management is generally defined as "getting things done through others." This definition emphasizes that a *manager* plans and guides the work of other people. Some (cynical) individuals think this means that managers don't have any work to do themselves. As you'll learn in this book (if you don't already know it), managers have an awful lot of work to do.

Organizing and directing the work of others is known as administration. In a business, it is called business administration. (In a hospital, it is called health-care administration. In a government agency, it is called public administration.) Thus, *business administration* means managing a business, and an *MBA*—Master of Business Administration—degree prepares a person to manage a business. In a graduate-school MBA program, you learn about the structure, parts, and purpose of a business, and about the skills and tools you need to manage the business. The skills include planning and leadership skills, and the tools include budgets, financial statements, and methods of analyzing business decisions.

 MBA LINGO

Management is the art and science of getting things done through others, generally by organizing and directing their activities on the job. A manager is therefore someone who defines, plans, guides, assists, and assesses the work of others, usually people for whom the manager is responsible in an organization.

Business administration means organizing and directing the activities of a business. An **MBA,** or Master of Business Administration, degree is a postgraduate degree from a university with a business school (or B-school, for short). Essentially, the program covers the structure and purpose of a business and its various functions, and the skills and tools needed to manage these functions— just as this book does.

As in politics or sports, some people seem more naturally suited to being managers than others. In our society, people often believe that men and women with a certain personality or appearance are best qualified to be managers. Often, however, it doesn't work that way. Management isn't about personality or appearance. I've known many managers with the so-called right image who were "empty suits."

It takes dedication to avoid being an empty suit, someone who enjoys being a manager but shirks the actual work. And it *is* work. A manager must think ahead several moves; planning is central to good management. A manager must deal skillfully with people, giving positive feedback for solid performance, helping those with performance problems, and, occasionally, terminating those who cannot improve their performance. Managers must keep financial considerations, as well as customers' needs, front and center, because a business exists to make money by serving a customer need.

Nonetheless, despite these "musts," some managers try to avoid stepping up to all the responsibilities of managing. Some managers fail to plan realistically, don't develop their interpersonal skills, or lose sight of financial considerations and customer needs. Such managers not only make it tough for their employees, superiors, and customers, but they also give managers a bad name. They give people the idea that a manager is someone paid to do nothing—who "watches while others do the work." Managers who are worthy of the name take their responsibilities and roles seriously.

A manager has an area of responsibility, an activity or a function that he or she is responsible for running. A financial manager is responsible for some area of finance. In sales, an account manager is responsible for a set of accounts. A departmental or regional manager is responsible for a specific department or region.

A manager's role is to run his or her function properly. It may be as large as the entire company, as is the case for the chief executive officer (CEO), or it may be as small as the mailroom. Whatever the area of responsibility, management comes down to doing a specific set of tasks well and consistently. Before we look at these tasks, let's view the role of the manager in historical context.

The Professional Manager

How can "being the boss" be a profession? A profession has its own principles, practices, and standards, and it requires a course of study. (Think of the traditional professions: medicine, law, engineering, architecture, and accounting.) Does management share any of these characteristics?

The answer is yes, and it has been since the early 1900s. When factories became large and complex enough to demand skills beyond those of a simple owner-boss, management grew out of economics and engineering to become a distinct discipline.

The need to apply concepts from economics and engineering became apparent as businesses grew beyond relatively small, simple craft operations and farms into larger, more complex operations capable of higher production. Economics enabled managers to analyze ways to drive down costs and increase profits. Engineering helped managers develop ways to optimize the physical (as opposed to financial) aspects of production. These include decisions regarding factory layouts, division of labor, and methods of distributing products.

The need for professional management arose when businesses built larger factories and adopted the new machines of the Industrial Age. A mere "boss," in the sense of someone who mainly told others what do, could not manage such operations. Therefore, the professional manager stepped up to the task.

In the early 1900s, the professional status of management got a boost from the concept of *scientific management*. Frederick Taylor was the Father of Scientific Management. (It's on his gravestone.) Taylor believed that managers could improve the productivity of factory workers if they understood workers' tasks and then properly planned each task for each worker.

"Taylorism," as scientific management came to be called, led to legions of *efficiency experts* doing *time-and-motion studies* in organizations. These studies led to the redesign of factory work. Some experts credit Taylorism with helping the United States win the Allied victory in World War II. U.S. factories were able to quickly gear up production of arms, ammunition, vehicles, airplanes, uniforms, and equipment needed for the war effort, and to establish and maintain high levels of quality while doing so. This was largely thanks to modern management methods, many of which were introduced by Taylor or others who extended his work.

MBA LINGO

Scientific management applies scientific tools (such as research, analysis, and objectivity) to business to improve productivity. A **time-and-motion study** breaks down work into subtasks to discover how long each task takes. The goal is to understand the job and improve the way it is done, to improve efficiency.

An **efficiency expert** is an outdated term for someone who uses scientific management principles to improve business processes. Today this work usually falls to management consultants, who work either as hired independent professionals or as employees within the company (as internal consultants).

The professional standing of management was enhanced when management associations and business education flourished in the first half of the 1900s. Of course, graduate schools offering MBA degrees also boosted management as a profession.

Scientific management advanced further in the 1950s with the work of W. Edwards Deming and Joseph M. Juran in the areas of product quality. These were two students of Walter Shewhart, who, at Bell Labs, pioneered the use of statistics to analyze process and product performance. Deming worked with Japanese engineers in the 1950s as their nation rebuilt after World War II. Juran published articles and books on quality improvement in the 1950s and 1960s, and the work of these two men did much to foster "the quality movement" in Japan, Europe, and North America from the 1960s to the present day.

Today the quest for better management practices continues with as much intensity as ever. Business now occurs on a more international scale than in the past, so competition is tougher than ever. Customers around the world become more sophisticated and demanding with each passing year. Technology creates (and destroys) companies and even entire industries more quickly than ever. So managers face challenges as great as or greater than they did in any other time.

CASE IN POINT

The Japanese quickly adopted the ideas of Edwards Deming and Joseph Duran, which formed the basis of quality-improvement efforts in the Japanese auto industry. Toyota most famously adopted quality-improvement methods, which apply statistical methods and scientific investigation to production processes. Using those methods, managers can discover and correct problems that cause defects in products. Typically, problems include defective materials, mistakes by workers, poor design of work processes, and poor maintenance of machinery. Specific methods of improving quality, which I discuss in Part 5, include total quality management, kaizen, and Six Sigma.

Managing Knowledge Workers

Among the greatest challenges is the changing nature of work and workers in many companies. In Western Europe and North America, and particularly the United States, much manufacturing work has been sent to nations with lower production costs, such as Mexico and China, India, and other Asian nations. At the same time, service industries have expanded along with "knowledge work" and the number of "knowledge workers."

By "service industries," I don't mean only retail and restaurants, but also professional services firms, such as accounting, engineering, law, and consulting firms—and the financial services industry and high technology, particularly software. In those industries, most workers don't use machinery to produce a product; rather, they use their minds to produce analyses, reports, plans, software, legal cases, and other forms of *intellectual property.*

MBA LINGO

Intellectual property refers to plans, blueprints, publications, films, software, video games, advertising and brands, and formulas and processes used to produce products and services. Intellectual property is usually the product of knowledge workers, and companies work to protect that property through copyrights, trademarks, patents, and security measures.

Managing these knowledge workers differs from managing employees who produce tangible products. Often the workers are more expert in their specializations than their managers. Their work is more difficult to evaluate in terms of quality, and the time it takes to produce can be difficult to control or even to measure. The workers don't have to be onsite, and they carry many company secrets in their heads. They can also be difficult to motivate—and to keep—and it can be hard to assess their productivity.

Managers have risen to the challenge of managing knowledge workers, but much work remains undone. For example, most managers now understand that a knowledge worker can be productive from home. But companies still struggle with ways to evaluate the quality and value of knowledge work and to best develop and use the skills of knowledge workers. I discuss these challenges in greater detail throughout this book.

Regardless of the workers they are managing, professional managers, like other professionals, understand certain principles, perform certain tasks, and uphold certain standards. These elements are what makes managers professional.

The Six Business Principles Every Manager Must Know

The following six concepts are central to business and are the reasons business needs managers:

- Value for customers
- Organization
- Competitive advantage
- Control
- Profitability
- Ethical practices

I describe each concept in more detail over the following pages.

Value: What Customers Pay For

A business exists to create value of some kind. It takes raw materials or activities and increases their value in some way, transforming them into products or services that customers will buy. Value is what customers pay for—customers buy things that they value.

For example, McDonald's creates value by setting up places where people can eat inexpensively away from home. The company builds restaurants, hires cooks and counter employees, buys food, and prepares meals. The customers value the convenience of location (you don't have to go home to eat), the speed of service (it's not called "fast food" for nothing), and the tastiness of the meals (most people like hamburgers, chicken, soft drinks, and fries).

A business—and its managers—must create value for customers. This can be done in almost limitless ways because human desires are limitless. But a single business cannot serve limitless desires. Instead, it must create a specific kind of value in a specific way. This is often called "the value proposition"—the manner in which a product or company proposes to deliver value to the customer. Once management decides what the value proposition of the business is, it must organize the business accordingly.

Let's Get Organized

An organization must have goals and the resources (human, material, and financial) to meet those goals. It must keep track of what it does and how well it does it, hence the saying in management, "If you can't measure it, you can't manage it." Each department has to perform its function properly. Employees must be assigned specific tasks that move the business toward its goals.

Management is responsible for keeping the company organized. The employees— human resources—and all other resources, such as equipment, floor space, and money, must also be organized.

Managers achieve organization by means of *structure*. The overall structure can be represented in an organization chart like the one you'll see in Chapter 3. But managers have other structures for achieving organization. For example, the company's financial structure organizes the way it uses money. The sales force can be structured into sales teams by geography, products, types of customers, or some combination of these.

MBA LINGO

Structure refers to the way a company or department is organized. A company's structure includes elements such as the corporate hierarchy, number and kinds of departments, number of locations, scope of operations (for example, domestic or international), and job descriptions.

Companies achieve organization in various ways. Some take a highly structured, almost military approach, with strict hierarchies, sharply defined duties, and formal protocol. Others take a more informal approach, which allows people greater leeway and creates a more unstructured environment.

The nature of the business can determine how structured or unstructured a company is. For example, smaller firms (those with fewer than 50 to 100 employees) tend to be less structured than large ones. Companies in heavy manufacturing are usually more structured than those in creative fields, such as advertising or entertainment.

Regardless of how tightly or loosely structured a company is, managers must keep it organized. Even a highly structured company will become disorganized if management fails to manage properly. And even a very loosely structured company will be organized as long as management does its job.

Competitive Advantage: The Winner's Edge

To succeed in a particular market, a company must do something better than other companies in that business. Doing something better creates a competitive advantage. That "something" may be only one aspect of the product or service, as long as customers value it highly. For example, a company can gain a competitive advantage by offering the widest selection of products. Or rock-bottom prices. Or high quality. Or great service. But it can't do all of those things.

Managers decide what basis the company will compete on, and they must be quite clear about this. For example, despite advertising claims, no company can really provide both the highest quality and the lowest price, at least not for long. (It can offer the highest quality in a certain price range, but not at the lowest price.) So management must decide whether it wants to compete on quality, price, or service.

CASE IN POINT

The grocery chain Whole Foods has a very clear value proposition and competitive advantage. It provides a wide selection of high-quality organic (and nonorganic) produce, dairy, and other products, and excellent service—but at a high price, relative to other grocery chains. Starbuck's has achieved similar clarity with its attractive cafés, addictive coffee, and hospitality—again, at high prices.

By this, I mean that a company must consistently present a certain advantage to its customers. A "big-box" store does not pretend to be a luxury retailer, and vice versa. Big-box stores compete on price and pull in bargain hunters. Luxury stores compete on quality and service and attract customers motivated by those considerations rather than price concerns. If big-box stores displayed designer clothing and $400 fountain pens, customers would laugh. If luxury stores carried no-name clothing and Bic pens, customers would turn up their noses.

Customers who can afford high quality will buy from the high-quality company; those who want low prices will buy from the low-price company. Customers can figure this out. But sometimes managers cannot.

Control Means Never Having to Say You Lost It

After management decides how to create value, organize the business, and establish a competitive advantage, it must control the company. This does not mean ruling with an iron fist (although some managers believe it does). Rather, it means that everyone must know the company's goals and be assigned tasks that will move everyone toward those goals. It also means having the right information on the various production, distribution, and financial processes (those that ensure that the company pays its bills and gets paid by customers), and that the company complies with all relevant laws and regulations.

Controls ensure that the right manager knows what's going on at all times. Controls are based mostly on information. For example, every company needs financial controls. Managers have budgets so they can control their department's spending. They receive regular information about the amount their department has spent and what it was spent on. Financial controls ensure that the company spends what it needs to spend—no more, no less—to do business and meet its goals.

A business is made up of many processes, so "process control" is something you may hear about. A manufacturing process, a hiring process, and a purchasing process all require controls. In these examples, the controls ensure, respectively, that product quality is maintained, that the right people are hired at the right time, and that the right materials are purchased at a reasonable price.

Controls, and the information and information systems that support them, enable managers to manage.

Profitability: The Purpose of the Business

A business is set up to make money. As you will see in Part 3, the money a business earns can be measured in various ways. But no matter how it is measured, a business has to make money—earn a profit—on its operations.

If, during a certain period of time, a business takes in more money for its products than it spends making those products, it makes a profit for that period. If not, it has a loss for the period. Losses cannot continue for long, or the company will go *bankrupt*.

MBA LINGO

A company may go **bankrupt** when it is continually unable to pay its bills for an extended time. After a company declares bankruptcy, it goes through a legal process either to reorganize itself so it can become profitable or to close down completely.

The most basic goal of management is to make money for the business owners. Regardless of how well they do anything else, managers who lose money for the owners will not keep their jobs for long. Whatever else a business does, its overall goal must be profitability.

Practicing Ethical Practices

In 2002, a series of business scandals in the United States came to dominate the news. Senior managers at Arthur Andersen, WorldCom, Adelphia Communications, and Imclone Systems faced criminal charges brought by the U.S. Justice Department. Executives at AOL, Computer Associates, Enron, Global Crossing, and Qwest were under criminal investigation. The charges involved securities fraud, *insider trading* and other illegal transactions, and obstruction of justice, as well as improper accounting procedures.

Then, in 2007 and 2008, the banking industry underwent turmoil due to irresponsible mortgage lending to *subprime borrowers* and reselling of those mortgages throughout the financial system. Governments had to step in to support the international banking system to head off a worldwide depression. While borrowers, regulators, and bond rating agencies also behaved badly, lenders are responsible for their lending policies. The parties who originated those mortgages did so without proper documentation and without caring whether the borrowers could repay the loans.

Today's competitiveness and the drive for profits have been blamed for an upswing in bad behavior in business. However, dishonesty and greed have been around as long as business itself—longer, in fact. Although the vast majority of businesspeople are honest, managers, in particular, must engage in and tolerate only completely ethical practices.

MBA LINGO

Insider trading occurs when a manager, employee, or other person "inside" a company uses information not known to the public to profit from a purchase or sale of the company's stock. **Subprime borrowers** are those who do not meet lenders' normal criteria or, in the U.S. mortgage market, those who do not qualify for loans under certain government agency guidelines.

This is true for four reasons. First, managers (especially senior managers) hold a position of trust as stewards of the company for the stockholders, employees, customers, and community. Second, managers have the most opportunity to enrich themselves at the expense of the company's investors, employees, customers, and community. Third, managers set the standard for the entire company. If they are fudging their numbers, how can they expect honest numbers from their subordinates? Fourth, and finally, managers are responsible for managing the risks that the company incurs in the course of doing business. Unethical practices expose the company and its investors and employees to risks that are both high and unnecessary.

Chapter 27 more fully covers the role of ethics and integrity in business, and Chapter 24 covers risk management. Yet it is worth noting here that integrity has always been a fundamental principle of business, if for no other reason than that the lack of integrity destroys companies.

Remember the Essential Six

Remember the six concepts summarized in this chapter. Think of them as the Essential Six, because they underlie everything a manager does. That is, all the activities of management have one collective aim: to make these principles real for the company and its employees and customers.

The Essential Six are guiding principles, as opposed to skills. Skills, which you will learn about in the next chapter, enable managers to make sure that these principles are realized at the day-to-day level in the business.

The Least You Need to Know

- Managers must monitor the Essential Six business principles: value for customers, organization, competitive advantage, control, profitability, and ethical practices.
- A business—and its managers—must create a specific kind of value for customers.
- Management is responsible for keeping the company organized.
- Managers decide what basis the company will compete on.
- Managers are responsible for control. They must know the company's goals and assign tasks that will move everyone toward those goals.
- The most basic goal of management is to make money for the business owners.
- Managers must hold themselves to the highest ethical standards.

The Seven Skills of Management

In This Chapter

- The importance of proper planning
- Developing your decision-making skills
- The secrets of effective delegation
- Communicating with your employees effectively

Management skills and tasks all have one purpose: to help you get things done through others. Management theories and fads come and go. Most of the theories (and even some of the fads) have something useful to say about management. But the skills and tasks we examine in this chapter have always been, and always will be, essential to managing others.

Managers should spend their time focusing on these seven main skills and tasks of management:

- Planning
- Goal setting
- Decision making
- Delegating
- Providing support
- Communicating
- Controlling to plan

In this chapter, I show you how to use each of these skills to get things done.

Proper Planning Prevents Poor Performance

The Five-P Rule—Proper Planning Prevents Poor Performance—represents the starting point in management. A manager must have a plan. The pervasive need for planning underlies the many kinds of plans you'll find in large outfits: strategic plans, financial plans, marketing plans, and production plans, to name a few. (I talk about these plans in more detail in later chapters.)

The need for planning is equally important, although more often ignored, at smaller companies. The lack of a plan leads to reactive, seat-of-the-pants management, which you find more often in small firms. We examine business planning (and management) for small companies in Chapter 26.

A plan must be in writing. At times you may hear people say, "I have a plan—it's right here in my head," as they tap their noggin with a forefinger. They don't have a plan. They have an idea. An idea can be in one's head. A plan must be on paper.

Planning incorporates many of the other six managerial tasks discussed later in this chapter. Goal setting and decision making are integral to planning. A plan must consider delegation—who will do what—and, of course, a plan must be communicated to others. Controlling to plan, or following up to monitor progress, assumes that you have a plan in the first place.

MBA MASTERY

Planning is not just for companies and departments. As an individual, you need daily, weekly, monthly, and yearly plans for your success. A long-term study of college graduates revealed that the major determinant of their level of professional success was whether they had written plans for themselves.

There are various plans in business, but they all share the goal of creating order, discipline, and improved chances of success. A plan does this by enabling you to bring the future into the present. This lets you imagine a certain future and then take steps to create that future. Those who dislike planning often cite the unpredictability of the future as the reason for not planning. Yet despite the murkiness of the future (or perhaps because of it), planning—thinking about the future, getting resources in place, taking certain steps, and developing *contingency plans*—has proven its worth.

MBA LINGO

A **contingency plan** is a Plan B, or a backup plan you can adopt if Plan A fails or conditions change.

Most plans share these elements:

- A goal and a measure of the distance from the goal

- An assessment of the environment

- An assessment of the company's Strengths, Weaknesses, Opportunities, and Threats (SWOT analysis)

- An assessment of existing and needed resources

- A series of tasks that will move the company toward the goal

- A mechanism for measuring progress

I show you these steps in detail in Chapter 23, which concerns strategic planning (that is, planning for the entire company). At this point, you need only understand that planning is essential to progress.

Goal Setting: Where To?

I've always liked the saying, "Ready! Fire! Aim!", which humorously describes so many business situations in which things go wrong. You have to have an aim, an objective, or a goal before you act. Equally important, it has to be the right goal.

Goals can be stated in a variety of ways:

- **Business goal:** To be the world's largest exporter of automobiles to Canada by the year 2020

- **Financial goal:** To increase our net profit to 8 percent of sales next year

- **Marketing goal:** To increase our share of the soft-drink market by 1 percentage point in each of the next three years

- **Individual goal:** To be head of the marketing department within five years

Each of these examples exhibits the three characteristics of a good goal. Each one is ...

- Specific.

- Measurable.

- Time-limited.

A *specific* goal goes beyond shooting to be "the biggest," "the best," "the highest quality," or some other nice-sounding adjective. It is sharper and expressed more precisely. Even the size-related goal—to be "the largest exporter of autos to Canada"—is specific (and measurable).

A goal must be *measurable* so you know whether you achieved it. Whenever possible, devise goals expressed in numbers—that is, in dollars, percentages, or a numerical increase or decrease. (Some goals cannot be measured numerically, but they can still be clear, as in the case of "to be head of the marketing department.")

A *time-limited* goal has a deadline. Personally, I don't consider a goal to be a goal unless it has a deadline. A deadline motivates those who must reach the goal. It creates urgency and energy. Deadlines are also important because most plans specify that certain tasks must be completed by certain dates. These interim deadlines, often called milestones, help you measure progress toward the goal well before the final deadline.

CASE IN POINT

Many companies, including some large, well-established ones, invest heavily in programs without having a clear goal. This often happens when a new technology comes along or a new need is recognized.

For example, when the World Wide Web first came along, many companies invested heavily in websites without having any clear goals beyond just … having a website. More recently, some companies invested in social media with a similar lack of focus.

Similar problems can occur with a new need, such as risk management or environmental responsibility. Just hiring a senior risk manager or starting a corporate responsibility program is not very useful. There has to be a clear goal for a person or a program, and that goal must be in keeping with the strategic and business goals of the organization.

These three characteristics add up to the one characteristic that any useful goal must have—clarity. The "Ready! Fire! Aim!" approach comes from having a fuzzy goal as often as it does from having no goal.

Goals should be the right size—that is, big enough to inspire people, but small enough to be achievable. Tiny goals won't inspire anyone, but big goals capture the imagination. Big goals create a sense of mission, and a sense of mission creates motivation. Motivation calls forth people's energy and commitment.

Keep in mind, though, that even large goals must be basically achievable, or employees will see them as manipulative or just plain silly. A company that sets unattainable goals sets itself up for failure.

> **MBA MASTERY**
>
> A manager has to keep his or her people aware of company goals. This means breaking big goals into smaller ones that relate to the employee's day-to-day job and can be completed in a relatively short time. To motivate your people, give them tasks related to the overall goal and short-term deadlines for completing them. Also, always be sure they see how their goals support the company's larger goals.

The right-size goal depends on your business. For a fast-growing company in a new industry, it might make sense to try to grow sales volume at 25 or even 50 percent a year. For a company in a mature industry, growth at perhaps the rate of the industry's growth plus a few percentage points might make sense. One way to target ambitious goals for sales and profit growth is to pick a solid competitor and try to match or exceed that growth rate.

Be aware, however, that no goal can be permanent. According to many economic forecasts, after the Great Recession at the end of the 2000s, growth in most nations was expected to fall far short of levels forecasted earlier in that decade. In that case, companies that geared their plans to high growth conditions had to at least consider the new economic reality and redo their plans, if necessary.

A Professional Decision-Making Process

You've probably heard managers referred to as "decision makers." A good manager is exactly that. However, some managers dislike decision making, which is sad, since it's a key part of their job.

Most managers who "pass the buck" are afraid of being wrong. They see any mistake as major failure. Usually they either lack confidence (or backbone, if you prefer) or work for superiors who can't tolerate failure. However, some people simply don't know how to go about making a good decision. They lack a framework for decision making. So here's a six-step process for making business decisions (and personal ones, for that matter) in a rational way:

1. **Define the problem.** Most decisions relate to a problem or can be framed as a problem. This means that making the right decision depends on first

defining the problem correctly. If your sales are falling, the problem could be low quality, high prices, poor performance by the sales force, or new competition. Each problem calls for a different solution. So start by asking, "What's the problem?" Answering that question may require exploration.

2. **Gather information.** Good business decisions are based on good information. Once you define the problem, gather all the relevant facts. This often requires research, such as studying competitors, talking with suppliers, examining historical data, or hiring a knowledgeable consultant. However you go about it, get the facts!

3. **Analyze the information.** Having information is not enough, because different people can draw different conclusions from the same facts. Therefore, you may need to apply analytical tools to the facts. These tools, formal ways of analyzing information, often involve making calculations or setting up charts showing the connections between facts. You may even have a *decision-support system*. However you go about it, analysis helps you understand the facts and what they mean. (You'll learn about ways of analyzing information in Part 2.)

MBA LINGO

A **decision-support system** is a formal means of helping people make decisions. These often-computerized systems usually help in the analysis phase. This may consist of guidelines in a policy manual (for example, for employee discipline cases), checklists (such as the ones bank employees use when making lending decisions), or computerized models that help forecast future business conditions. As the name indicates, these systems support, rather than replace, the decision maker.

4. **Develop options.** When you have a decision to make, you need choices. For example, to increase sales in the face of new competition, you could improve quality or cut prices. You could hire more salespeople or pay your current salespeople differently. Options like these give you a basis of comparison and a better chance of finding a real solution instead of doing what seemed like a good idea at the time. In some instances, you may have only one option, but they should be rare if you carefully consider all possible solutions.

5. **Choose and use the best option.** Now comes the moment of truth: you must decide. If you followed the first four steps, you will probably make a good decision. And be sure that you do make a decision. Avoid "analysis paralysis"—that is, analyzing a problem forever instead of acting. Decision makers make decisions.

6. **Monitor the outcome.** You usually cannot just make a decision and then forget about it (much as you might like to). Generally, the only way to know whether your decision solved the problem is to follow up afterward. If your solution worked, great. If not, you may need to take corrective action; try another option; or even reexamine the problem to make sure you defined it correctly, gathered enough facts, and analyzed them properly.

> **MBA MASTERY**
>
> If you like to decide based on feelings rather than facts, this decision-making process will be especially useful for you. Look at the six steps as a supplement or an alternative to going with your gut. Either way, use it. Businesspeople value facts and like dealing with people who are comfortable with facts. This process will help you avoid a reputation for being in denial or shooting from the hip. What's more, it generally yields better decisions.

With experience, this six-step process can become second nature. For small decisions you need not launch a major fact-finding effort—you may need to write one e-mail or make one phone call. Nor will you always need a long list of options—two may be enough. But even when you're making day-to-day decisions in a fast-paced environment, this process will help you. And major decisions always require information, analysis, and clear thinking about options.

In various forms, this framework for decision making has stood the test of time. The process promotes rational business decisions that can be explained to others (meaning that even if you mess up, you'll at least be able to tell your boss what you were thinking at the time).

Delegate All You Can

Delegation is the act of assigning tasks to subordinates for them to perform. This is actually how a manager gets things done through others. The assignment may be verbal or written, long or short term, phrased as a request (usually) or an order (less often). Assigning tasks to others and ensuring that they perform them properly is essential to any manager's job.

Effective delegation goes well beyond merely telling people what to do. Good delegation calls for knowledge of the underlying principles: responsibility, accountability, and authority.

Responsibility means that every manager and employee has a specific function or activity to perform. This is called the *area of responsibility*. In a corporation, the CEO is ultimately responsible for the entire company. He or she has a *big* area of responsibility. But the CEO delegates the actual work to everyone else in the company through the *chain of command*.

MBA LINGO

Delegation means passing along responsibility for performing a task to a subordinate—that is, to someone who reports to you, the manager. An **area of responsibility** refers to the scope of someone's job. This generally includes a set of functions (such as matters relating to finance or marketing), tasks (such as preparing budgets or advertising programs), goals (such as accuracy and timeliness or increased sales), and subordinates, if people report to you.

The **chain of command** refers to the system by which directives come from above and are transmitted downward in an orderly manner through layers of management.

The principle of responsibility implies that a manager must respect the chain of command by delegating work only to people in his or her area and by not going over the head of the manager above or below him or her.

Accountability ensures that everyone in the organization answers to someone else and is held accountable for performing his or her responsibilities. The CEO is accountable to the board of directors (who represent the owners of the business), and everyone else in the organization reports, directly or indirectly, to the CEO.

Authority means that someone has been empowered to do a job. If you have a budget, you have budgetary authority. If you can hire someone, you have hiring authority.

Essentially, your *responsibility* is what you usually think of as your job. You are held accountable for doing your job by the manager above you. The organization, through the manager above you, gives you the authority necessary to do your job.

MBA LINGO

Accountability refers to the fact that people with certain responsibilities are held to account for performing them. Their superior will make certain that these responsibilities are properly handled. **Authority** is the power to do something. The company gives the president of the company the power to run the organization, and he or she shares that power with other managers lower in the organization. **Responsibility** refers to the work that a member of an organization is supposed to do and the standards for that work to be considered properly accomplished.

Ignoring these principles causes real trouble ...

- When managers ignore the chain of command. When Bob, who manages Sue, goes over Sue's head and tells Leo, who reports to Sue, what do to, Bob undermines Sue's authority.

- When a manager holds a subordinate accountable for completing a task without extending the authority necessary to complete it, that subordinate has been placed in an untenable position. For instance, if Mary holds Jim accountable for expenses on a project when she did not give him authority over spending, she's treating Jim unfairly.

- When someone is given two managers to report to, when someone is not given clear job responsibilities, or when a manager leaves the company and no one tells his or her people who they now report to, the business cannot run properly.

Sadly, anyone who has been in business for several years has seen most of these things occur. Good delegation—orderly, sensible, consistent delegation—requires effort.

Everyone should have clear job responsibilities, be held accountable for them, and have enough authority to carry them out. Everyone should report to one, and only one, superior. Everyone should understand and respect the chain of command. When someone in the chain leaves, people should be informed about what happens next.

Here are proven guidelines for effective delegation:

- Carefully consider the task and its deadline and importance. Weigh the employee's strengths and weaknesses. Try to give your people a mix of assignments so they can capitalize on their strengths and overcome their weaknesses.

- When you give someone an assignment, be very clear about the results you expect and when you expect them. Clarify the assignment in an e-mail or a memo. If you give the assignment verbally, be sure to double-check that the employee understands your expectations—preferably in a confirming e-mail.

- To the extent possible, let the person who is doing the work decide how to do it.

- Understand that even though someone may not do a job exactly as you would, it can still be done to a high standard. If the work is not up to your standards, have the employee do it correctly rather than correct it for him. That way, employees learn your standards.

- Delegate all the responsibilities that you can, and delegate them to the lowest level of employee who can accomplish them. Don't withhold responsibility *or* authority from your people.

- Follow up both informally and formally at agreed-upon points in time or in the project. Don't think you can assign it and forget it. Following up and providing guidance are part of good delegation.

- Understand that you are delegating the work and the authority needed to get it done, but you cannot actually delegate your accountability. If something goes wrong, you, as the manager of that area, are ultimately accountable. Blaming your subordinates is extremely bad form.

> **MBA MASTERY**
>
> The word *empowerment* is often bandied about—and often misunderstood. Proper delegation *means* empowering employees to do their jobs. Empowerment is not about making employees feel good or raising morale. It's about giving them clear responsibilities and the resources (including training) and authority they need to do the job, and then assessing them fairly. Empowering employees makes management's job easier, but the employees must be properly trained and motivated.

Support Your People

A manager's work doesn't end with effective delegation. In fact, the toughest work lies ahead. A big part of getting things done through others is supporting them.

Employees need support because barriers usually stand between them and the desired result. These barriers exist inside the company in the form of bureaucracy and limited resources, and outside the company in the form of competition and customer resistance.

Employees also need support because they're human. They need correction, pointers, encouragement, and humor, particularly when the going gets tough—for example, on a big push to meet a tight deadline or during a series of layoffs.

> **MBA ALERT**
>
> Ignoring employee complaints can create financial and legal exposure for your firm. A manager I know ignored complaints from a worker, who claimed she had wrist problems from doing a heavy amount of word processing. The company wound up paying for the woman's wrist surgery and time off, plus compensatory damages to keep her from pursuing the matter in court.

The best way to support your employees is to remove barriers to their success, help them improve their performance, and treat them fairly. Here are some ways to do these things:

- Be an effective advocate for your employees with your superiors and the rest of the company. Lobby for their interests. Be loyal to them. Try as hard as you can to get them the resources—the equipment, staffing, money, and time—they need to do their jobs well.

- Take your employees' concerns and complaints seriously. The "stop whining" approach will get you only so far, and it can backfire horribly when employees have legitimate concerns.

- If your employees need correction, do it in private. When they deserve praise, give it in public.

- Keep your employees aware of how their efforts support the company's goals and benefit the entire outfit.

- Help your employees develop and advance. Most people want increased responsibilities, advancement, and a chance to gain new skills. I've found this to be true even of employees who pretend otherwise. Give everyone ample opportunity to prove themselves—and allow for failures now and then.

- Don't play favorites. This should go without saying, but you are human and you are going to like some employees more than others. If you don't treat people with equal fairness, you will create serious morale problems.

Supporting your employees involves leadership, which is covered in Chapter 4. Leadership and support are the opposite of what I call "wave-of-the-wand" management, which I've seen some managers try. They act as if they can merely assign a job and it will magically get done. Often these managers seem shocked or upset when it doesn't work out that way.

Think of management as a contact sport, which brings us to the next task.

Communication: Important Beyond Words

Communication skills consistently top the list of desired qualities in a manager. This includes written and oral communication. Business demands that you communicate clearly, accurately, honestly, and persuasively. Several techniques encourage effective communication in business. (Here I focus on oral communication. See my book

The Complete Idiot's Almanac of Business Letters and Memos, Second Edition, for more information on written communication.)

Listening skills are the starting point in good communication. So few people are used to someone who actually listens to them, with full attention and without interrupting, that the technique can be downright disarming. It's tempting, even natural, to use the time when someone is talking to think about your response or whether you agree.

Instead, try to listen with the goal of understanding the other person. Over time, that understanding forms a bond between two people. Not listening undermines that bond. People know whether someone is really listening to them. (You do, don't you?)

Whether you are talking or listening, be aware that the message sent may not be the one received. That's because each of us has his or her own *frame of reference* through which we filter what we say and hear.

MBA LINGO

A person's **frame of reference** is the set of facts, ideas, and concerns that make up that person's viewpoint. For example, the word *charge* means different things to a foot soldier, a retail clerk, and a defense attorney, due to their different frames of reference.

In American culture, businesspeople generally get the best results by speaking directly rather than indirectly and in concrete rather than abstract language. That way, your message has the best chance of fitting your listener's frame of reference. In some other cultures, however, people tend to be less direct and less informal than in the United States. Being too direct or informal on the job can alienate people. With business becoming more international with each passing year, every manager must be acutely aware of cultural differences and allow for them when communicating.

However, it pays to be precise when managing others so that they know what you expect. Here are some examples of both vague and precise language in some common business situations. The statements are from a manager to a subordinate, and in general, the more precise ones will get better results.

Too Vague	More Precise
"I'd like you to complete this project quickly."	"I'd like you to complete this project by noon this Friday."

Too Vague	More Precise
"Please get in touch with somebody about that."	"Please call Jim in Marketing about those missing pages."
"I can't talk now. Please catch me later."	"I'm sorry, I'm too busy to talk now. Please call back after 4:00, or tomorrow morning."
"You've been arriving late to meetings a lot recently."	"I've noticed that you arrived late to our last three staff meetings. Is anything wrong?"
"I believe your performance is dropping off."	"Your analysis of our markets left out some key points, and you seemed poorly prepared for last Tuesday's meeting."
"You've been doing good work lately."	"Thanks for your good work on the Acme project and for staying late last Monday."

Much on-the-job communication between managers and subordinates aims to guide and assist the subordinate in getting his or her tasks accomplished on time and up to standards. Vague, imprecise language leaves room for misunderstanding regarding what is expected and when it is expected. However, being a manager and speaking precisely does not mean that you should issue orders or "boss people around." The best communicators view their subordinates—and, for that matter, their superiors— as colleagues focused on the same thing: getting the job done well.

Finally, be sure to share information with your employees to the greatest extent possible. Most employees resent it when they're not "in the loop." You cannot usually tell every employee everything you know and cannot compromise others' privacy, but you should keep your people informed about anything that directly affects them.

MBA MASTERY

Cultivate an objective attitude toward people on the job. Think of them as you would fellow players on a team. The key is to work well together on your common goals. If you become friends, great. But it's more important to respect one another and work well together. Of course, truly thorny performance problems do arise. I discuss ways to address them in Chapter 5.

Don't practice "mushroom management," which says, "Keep them in the dark and feed them fertilizer."

Controlling to Plan

There's a wonderful saying in business: "Plan your work and work your plan." In other words, have a plan and stick to it. This is more formally known as controlling to plan, which means managing your resources—your people, time, equipment, and money—as planned to reach the goal. A good plan helps you every step of the way toward a goal.

A plan is not a document to write and then throw in a drawer and forget. It's a road map, to be consulted as you move forward. Sometimes you need to change what you're doing or speed things up to keep to the plan. Other times you may find that the plan, rather than your activities, needs to be adjusted. That's fine. But to adjust your plan, you have to have a plan—and refer to it regularly.

Over time, success in business, as in any endeavor, comes from diligent, daily execution of the basics. In management, "the basics" are the seven managerial tasks of planning, goal setting, decision making, delegating, supporting, communicating, and controlling to plan. Master these, and you will be a master of business administration.

The Least You Need to Know

- Management begins with planning and goal setting, and ends with controlling to plan. You must have a goal and a plan for reaching it, and use the plan to move toward the goal.
- Use a decision-making process instead of operating by the seat of your pants. Start by defining the problem; then gather related facts, analyze them properly, develop alternative courses of action, and choose the best one. Then follow up to see if it was the best choice.
- Good delegation is the only way to get things done through others. Pick the right people for a task, then let them do the job. Delegate all that you can, and delegate to the lowest level at which it will be properly done.
- Support your employees in the organization and remove barriers to their success.

The Moving Parts of a Business

In This Chapter

- The major departments of a business
- How finance and accounting control and track money
- How marketing and sales sell products and services
- The role of management information systems
- How support functions serve the rest of the business
- Understanding the org chart and company hierarchy

A business of any substantial size has to be divided into departments, each with its own job to do. One department may oversee the company finances, another may handle marketing, and still another may handle sales. The job of the manager is to run his or her department so that it makes its contribution to the entire company. This chapter introduces you to the different parts of a business and the role managers play in running them. This chapter also examines the basic forms in which a business can be organized.

Note that, in this chapter, I deal with businesses large enough to warrant having different functions and departments. This includes many small businesses, some with as few as 10 or 20 employees, right up to those with 50 to 100 (still considered small businesses by most banks and larger companies), and on up to giant enterprises.

Forms of Business Organization

A business may be organized in four basic ways: proprietorship, partnership, corporation, or limited liability company.

A *proprietorship* (also known as a sole proprietorship) is a business owned by an individual. That person, the proprietor, has the right to the profits generated by the business and is personally responsible for its debts. Most small businesses are organized as proprietorships, and any self-employed individual is essentially a proprietor. Although there is no legal limit on how large a proprietorship may become, most large businesses are organized as partnerships or corporations so that multiple owners have a share in the profits. Only a corporation can use the term *incorporated* in its name.

A *partnership* is a business owned by two or more individuals who enter into a formal agreement to contribute their funds and other resources to the business and to share its profits. A limited partner (sometimes called a "silent partner") contributes money to the business but does not make management decisions or participate actively in the business. A general partner contributes money, makes management decisions, and participates actively in the business. Many consulting firms and professional-services firms, including large accounting, law, and architectural firms, are organized as partnerships.

General partners are personally liable for the financial obligations of the business. However, the liability of limited partners is limited to the amount of their investment (hence the name "limited partner"). Also, a decision or action by a general partner binds all the partners to that decision or action.

A *corporation* is a legal structure in which the owners are not personally liable for the financial obligations of the business. They can lose only the money they invest in the corporation. That investment occurs when they contribute money to fund the start-up of the business or, later, when they buy stock in the company. A share of stock represents a share in the ownership of the company.

Although the owners are not personally liable for its obligations, a corporation is often referred to as a "legal person." This means that the corporation has some of the characteristics of a person. For instance, it can own property, initiate lawsuits, and be the object of lawsuits. In fact, the U.S. Supreme Court ruled in 2010 that banning political campaign spending by corporations (and labor unions) is unconstitutional, due to the First Amendment, which protects the people's right to free speech.

A corporation is usually chartered by a state and can raise capital in the public financial markets (as discussed in Chapter 16). It is the only form of business permitted to use the terms *Inc.*, *Incorporated*, or *Corporation* to identify itself. (In everyday discussions, the term *company* can refer to any sizable business.) Although most people think of large, publicly held companies when they hear the term, a corporation need not be large. In fact, many privately held corporations are as small as or smaller than many proprietorships and partnerships.

Limited liability for the owners and access to the financial markets are two major advantages of the corporate form of organization. Two others are that an owner can sell part or all of his or her stake in the business simply by selling his or her stock, and that the business exists apart from the owners and thus can easily be passed on to future owners.

A *limited liability company* (not corporation) is a relatively new form of business organization that's become quite popular. A limited liability company, or LLC, provides some of the benefits of both partnerships and corporations. As in a partnership, the company itself pays no tax. Instead, the earnings flow through to the owners, who are taxed at their personal tax rates. This does away with the "double taxation" that occurs when a corporation pays its income tax and then the owners pay personal income taxes when the earnings are distributed to them as dividends. (Dividends are discussed in Part 3.)

MBA MASTERY

Note that, for small corporations, the owners' limited liability from lawsuits may not be complete. In a number of cases, the courts decide to "lift the corporate veil" and hold owners liable for decisions that have negatively impacted others. This has not occurred in any cases of a major corporation, although stockholders can, of course, be affected by legal decisions that affect the stock price. An example would be a major product-liability award.

Owners of an LLC are granted the limited liability that owners of a corporation enjoy. LLC owners are not personally responsible for the debts of the company, nor are they liable for debts arising from lawsuits. In addition, an LLC is much easier to administer because there are no requirements to hold quarterly meetings of the owners and to keep minutes of the meetings, as there are for corporations.

LLCs have been permitted in all 50 states since 1988. Although the state laws vary, essentially they all allow the owners—who are called members, rather than partners or shareholders—to agree among themselves on how the company will be operated. That contract will then be upheld in court.

Note that an LLC cannot issue stock or bonds in the public markets. They can raise money from private investors and lenders, and, because of the limited liability, they can do so more easily than proprietorships and partnerships. Many professional services firms have chosen to organize (or reorganize) themselves as LLCs during the past 15 years.

Most of the discussion of the parts of a business in this chapter refers to corporations. However, a sizable business organized in any of these four ways will have most of these functions in some form or other.

CASE IN POINT

Some companies are famous for a specific functional area that performs particularly well. Proctor & Gamble, the largest advertiser in the United States and the maker of Tide detergent, Crisco shortening, Comet cleanser, and Zest soap, is legendary for its marketing capabilities. Southwest Airlines and Disney have reputations for operations that deliver first-rate customer service. General Electric has long excelled at finance, and indeed now owns substantial financial services businesses.

The Parts of a Business

Numerous activities must take place for a company to successfully create, sell, and profit from its products or services, and each activity is handled by a specific department.

Let's take a closer look at each of the departments most large companies have and what they do.

Finance Controls the Money

A business generates a flow of money. Money flows into, out of, and through each department in the company. The *finance department* (or, more simply, finance) makes sure that the company has the money it needs to operate. This includes the money to buy or lease property (such as office space) and equipment, purchase raw materials, and pay employees. Finance also ensures that the company continually has good investment opportunities and the money to pursue them.

MBA LINGO

The **finance department** is responsible for controlling the funds that come into and go out of a company. The tools for control include financial and investment plans, sales and expense budgets, records supplied by the accounting department, and procedures regarding who can sign and cash checks for the company.

Finance helps the other departments in the company prepare their *budgets* and consolidates them into one company budget. Finance works with senior management to set the company's sales and profit goals for the following year and designs controls to keep the firm's finances in order.

In a large company, finance includes the treasury function, which manages the company's cash and deals with banks. Many of the people in finance and the treasury are financial analysts, professionals who deal in budgets and investments and generate financial reports for the managers of other departments.

MBA LINGO

A **budget** is a set of estimates for sales, expenses, or both for a specific period of time. These estimates represent limits or targets and are thus key financial controls. In most businesses, every department has its own budget. Within those departments, individual projects and activities (such as training) may have budgets. One of a manager's main responsibilities is *making budget:* hitting his or her sales targets or keeping expenditures within the budgeted amounts.

Accounting Counts the Money

The *accounting* department works closely with finance, mainly by tracking the flow of money the company generates. Within accounting, you'll find an *accounts receivable* department that tracks the money that the company is owed and paid. *Accounts payable* tracks expenditures and authorizes checks to be cut or funds to be transferred so the company can pay its bills to suppliers. The *payroll* department ensures that employees get paid.

MBA LINGO

The **accounting** department keeps the company's financial records by tracking sales, expenses, and receipts and disbursements of cash. Accounting also calculates the taxes that the company owes. The **accounts receivable** department tracks money that is owed to the company for sales made on credit. The **accounts payable** department makes sure that the company pays its bills to suppliers. The **payroll** department tracks employee wages and salaries.

Accounting also usually includes the *credit department*, which decides how much *credit* (also called trade credit) the company will extend to a customer. If you've ever groaned over a Visa bill, you are already familiar with the concept of credit. Customers (which may include other companies) with good payment records can buy thousands or even hundreds of thousands of dollars worth of goods on credit, meaning they are given an extended amount of time in which to pay the bill. Most businesses that sell expensive goods (say, pricey automobiles) or services (extensive consulting work) do this because it makes it easy for customers to buy, and thus easier for the company to make sales.

Customers or companies that do not have good payment records must buy *COD*, meaning cash on delivery.

MBA LINGO

Credit decisions are made by the company's **credit department.** A company may extend **credit** (or trade credit) to a customer with a good payment record, which allows the customer a certain extended period of time—usually 30 days—to pay the bill. Customers who are denied credit usually must pay **COD** (cash on delivery).

Finally, accounting includes the *tax department*, which calculates the company's taxes and manages the timing of its federal, state, local, and foreign tax payments.

The accounting department is staffed mainly by accountants, logically enough. Accountants are trained in accounting practices and accounting and tax law. Since the practices and regulations are complex and change often, and because substantial amounts of money are at stake, these professionals spend a lot of time keeping up-to-date on practices and regulations. In most accounting departments, accountants are dedicated to a certain area, such as accounts receivable, accounts payable, tax, and so on, and can move among these jobs to enrich their careers. Finally, a company's accountants work with any outside accounting firms or *auditors* that the company uses. (I talk about the accounting function in more detail in Part 3.)

MBA LINGO

In a very large company, the **tax department** calculates the company's federal, state, and local taxes, as well as taxes on any foreign operations, and works to find ways of minimizing the company's taxes. **Auditors** are certified public accountants who certify a public company's financial statements as fairly representing the company's financial performance and position.

Operations Makes What the Company Sells

In a *manufacturing company* (one that produces goods, such as widgets, rather than one that sells services, such as loans), *operations* includes the factory where the company makes its products. It also includes departments such as shipping and receiving, where the company ships products to its customers and receives materials from its suppliers. The purchasing department buys the company's materials and supplies. Operations is often called the production function.

In a *service organization* (one that sells services, such as a bank or a brokerage firm), operations includes the employees who serve the customers and the places where they work. For example, in a bank, operations include the branch locations.

MBA LINGO

A **manufacturing company** produces a product from raw materials or parts and components made by another manufacturer, or both, and sells it. In any company, the term **operations** refers to the area that actually creates and delivers the product or service.

A **service organization** delivers a service such as meals (restaurants), insurance and banking services (financial services), haircuts or massages (personal services), transportation (bus lines and trucking companies), or hotel accommodations (hospitality services), among many others.

Operations also includes back-office functions in a service organization—that is, activities that the customers don't see but that relate to customer transactions. Let's take the bank example again. You may have no idea what happens when you write someone a check. In fact, once the bank gets it, that check travels through a series of steps before it is eventually deposited into someone else's account and deducted from yours. Those check-processing functions are an example of a back-office function.

The managers and employees in operations are directly responsible for employee productivity (how many widgets an employee can make in an hour), cost control (how much it costs to assemble a widget), and quality (ensuring the correct form and function of the finished widget).

In most companies, people who work in operations are those who do what most of us think of as the actual work of the company. In a manufacturing business, they are the production workers and their managers. In a service firm, they usually work directly with customers to deliver the service.

Marketing Sells to Groups

It's useful to think of marketing as selling to groups of people or businesses (as opposed to selling, which is done one-on-one). The *marketing department* works to get the story of the company's products and services out to customers and potential customers, known as *prospects*. Marketing does this through advertising, promotions, direct mail, special events, and other ways of creating awareness. (I cover these terms in more detail in Part 4.) Marketing's key job is to help the salespeople sell.

MBA LINGO

The **marketing department** prepares strategies, plans, programs, and messages that get out the word of a company's products and services—and the benefits they deliver—to customers and potential customers. Potential customers are called **prospects.**

The marketing function often includes *market research*, which studies customers and prospects to learn about their needs, motivations, and buying behavior (for example, the age and educational level of the average widget buyer). Marketing can also include *product development*, which devises new ways of serving customer needs (for example, a faster, more powerful widget), and public relations (or corporate communications), which prepares written material on the company and its products.

MBA LINGO

Market research conducts surveys among a company's customers and prospects to learn about their attitudes and buying behavior. **Product development** conceives, plans, designs, and develops new products and services for the company to sell. In firms that sell complex products, such as chemicals or medical instruments, research and development (R&D) has scientists and engineers who work on new products.

People in marketing either are specialists in a certain area within marketing or are marketing generalists. Specialists tend to work in market research, product development, public relations, direct mail, telemarketing, web-based marketing, or product literature. Specialists typically work for large companies with large marketing departments or for marketing consulting firms. Generalists tend to do a bit of everything (but usually not with the sophistication of a specialist) and can work for either large or small companies.

In today's competitive environment, marketing can make or break a company. A firm can have a wonderful product, but unless it spreads the word, gets shelf space, prices its products properly, and induces customers to buy, the company won't generate sales and profits.

Moreover, while the Internet is affecting every area of business, it is arguably having the greatest impact on marketing. On the one hand, it is changing television viewing and newspaper and magazine reading habits; on the other hand, it is changing the ways people make buying decisions. The web's interactivity, immediacy, and information intensity have changed the dynamics not only of advertising, but—in conjunction with *social media*—also of customer targeting, relationship building, and selling. We look at these dynamics more in Part 4.

MBA LINGO

Social media employ Internet and telecommunications technologies to enable people to communicate with one another individually and collectively. These media—such as Facebook and Twitter, to name two among many—feature user-generated content, instant communication, wide reach, and mobile accessibility. Most of these characteristics differ sharply from the broadcast and print media that dominated marketing in the past century.

Sales Brings in the Money

The *sales department* includes the men and women who sell the company's products or services. Salespeople may work on the telephone, in person, or both. They may sell to distributors or retailers who resell the product. They may sell directly to customers. They may sell to individuals or to businesses, to one-time buyers or to *national accounts* (a major account with a nationwide business). However, wherever and whatever they sell, salespeople bring in the money.

In most companies, the sales force is the most critical part of the business. Salespeople persuade customers to actually pull out their wallets and checkbooks and pay for a product or service, which is not an easy thing to do.

MBA LINGO

The **sales department** includes the men and women who sell the company's products or services. In most companies, a **national account** is a major account with a nationwide business. For example, Sears is a national account for power-tool maker Black & Decker.

In many companies, the sales function includes *customer service*, which works with customers after the sale is made. Customer service ensures that customers are truly satisfied with what they've bought, and helps with any problems that arise after the sale.

Many companies think of themselves as sales driven. These outfits have a sales force that aggressively presents products to customers, does all it can to please customers, and thinks creatively and competitively about ways to make every potential sale. For all its technology, IBM has always been famous for its sales force, which views selling for IBM as a mission.

MBA LINGO

After a sale is made, **customer service** works with the company's customers to maintain a link between the company and the customer, and to answer customer questions, resolve complaints, and, for some products, provide instructions for proper use and maintenance.

Sales departments are staffed mostly by salespeople, people who work to find new prospects and to turn them into customers. Customer service personnel usually work on the phone and via e-mail with the company's customers and may be headed for sales jobs or use the experience to move into marketing.

I discuss sales in more detail in Part 4.

Information Systems Keeps Everyone Informed

The *information technology* function, or *IT*, runs the company's computer systems. Computers have become so essential to running a business that the importance of this department has increased more than that of any other in the past 20 years. No longer does senior management view IT, which used to be called *data processing*, as a backwater remote from the company's "real business." IT is now integral to most businesses, especially large service businesses.

MBA LINGO

The **information technology,** or **IT,** function defines the company's requirements for computers, software, Internet, and related items; purchases, installs, programs, and maintains them; and uses the system to provide reports to managers throughout the company.

IT deals with the purchase, programming, maintenance, and security of the company's computers. Recently, companies have focused on using information for competitive advantage, as opposed to just tracking things. (Competitive advantage was covered in detail in Chapter 1.) As the value of information has increased, so has the value, and status, of IT.

Contrary to some early predictions, the proliferation of the Internet has only increased the importance of the IT function in most businesses. The web has formed the core of tens of thousands of companies, such as Amazon, Google, and YouTube, which means that those companies essentially operate on the basis of IT. The web has also transformed even most long-established industries, such as retailing, publishing, music and other entertainment, education, and financial services. In addition, the Internet has exposed companies' IT systems—and, thus, their information—to new types of cybercriminals, who can seriously damage a company's finances and reputation.

The IT department is mainly staffed by systems analysts, programmers, and networking experts. Systems analysts work to define and meet the company's hardware needs, programmers work on software needs, and networking experts deal with the Internet.

Support Functions Do the Rest

Any other area of a company not already discussed (aside from the board of directors) can be called a *support function*. The key support functions in a large company include these:

- Human resources
- Legal department
- Risk management
- Investor relations
- Facilities management

The *legal department*, staffed mostly by attorneys, ensures that the company remains in compliance with laws and government regulations. Legal, as it is usually called, also deals with lawsuits, whether they are brought by the company or against the company. The legal department is also known as house counsel (as opposed to outside counsel, which refers to an independent law firm). Most large companies use independent counsel for more complex legal situations.

Human resources (usually referred to as HR) works with managers in other departments to attract, hire, retain, and train employees. Because this department works closely with managers throughout the company, we'll examine human resources in detail in Chapter 5.

MBA LINGO

Support functions basically support all the other departments that are making something, selling something, or dealing with money. One support function is the **legal department** (also known as house counsel), which consists of attorneys employed by the company to handle its legal affairs.

The **human resources** department (also known as HR) works with the managers of other departments to attract, hire, retain, and train employees, and to ensure that the company is in compliance with government employment regulations. Human resources also sees that employee benefit programs are in place.

Risk management is a relatively new function dedicated to identifying, assessing, and managing all of the various risks a company faces in the course of its business. This function used to concern itself mainly with the types and amounts of insurance the company needed. More recently, particularly in financial services, it has employed risk-management specialists and deployed many risk-management tools apart from insurance. Risk management has become so important that I cover it separately in Chapter 24.

In many companies, *investor relations* is part of marketing or corporate communications or reports directly to senior management. Investor relations communicates with the company's shareholders, the owners of the company, and organizes the annual meeting of shareholders. (Investor relations exists only in publicly held corporations.)

Facilities management (or the facilities department) may be part of operations, particularly in a service company. Facilities deals with real estate matters and the maintenance and upkeep of the company's buildings. For example, facilities maintains the heating, air conditioning, and other systems in buildings. Related functions that may be part of facilities include telecommunications, which runs the telephone system, and security, which prevents crime on the company's premises and in its IT systems.

Above All: The Board of Directors

The board of directors is not considered a department or a functional area in the sense that marketing and finance are functions. However, the board of directors, often simply called the board, serves an important function.

A board consists of the CEO, who is typically also the chairman of the board, and usually other senior executives of the corporation. These are the inside directors. The outside directors are chosen from other businesses, academe, and the community to bring a broad, objective, external viewpoint to the company.

The directors are elected by the corporation's stockholders (who are its owners), usually at the shareholders' annual meeting, and are paid for their work as directors. The board represents the interests of the owners, oversees the senior managers of the company, and advises management on matters of policy. This oversight and policy function is known broadly as corporate governance.

Unless the chief executive officer owns all the stock of the company, he or she reports to the owners (and, through ownership of stock, may also be an owner). The CEO reports to the owners through the board of directors. As the owners' representatives, the board of directors has a serious duty. They hire and fire the CEO and advise the CEO on filling the other key senior management positions. They set broad policies, exercise corporate governance, and represent the interests of the community and the larger society, as well as those of the owners. For example, directors—particularly outside directors—advise management on the effect that certain policies and decisions may have on the larger community and society.

The board is not responsible for day-to-day operating decisions; the CEO and other senior managers are responsible for those. This, however, is where responsibilities can become unclear, because broad policies and matters of corporate governance are played out in day-to-day operations. For example, if the board insists on honest accounting practices, what is their responsibility if the senior sales manager for European operations, who works in Frankfurt, overstates the company's European revenues by $12 million?

There is no easy answer. Technically, they are responsible, and so is the CEO, the corporation's senior sales manager, and any other managers on the chain of command between the board and the senior sales manager for Europe. In practice, a strong board that insists on full and detailed accounting reports from the CEO stands the best chance of creating an environment that discourages dishonest accounting and catches and terminates those who practice it.

Members of lax boards may say that there is no way they can know about every decision that occurs in their company. However, lax boards are the very kind that encourage improper and illegal behavior. In that sense, if a board is lax and gives management a completely free hand, it has not really fulfilled its responsibility to the shareholders or to society.

MBA MASTERY

Since the corporate scandals of the early 2000s and the financial crisis later in that decade, the issue of corporate governance has increased in importance. Many management teams and boards used to have a cozy relationship rather than one based on true oversight. Since then, various regulations have made boards (and management) more accountable for their decisions and have increased the level of board scrutiny over management.

It is in a company's best interests—not to mention its shareholders'—to have a board that is seriously engaged in advising and overseeing management. After all, the board represents the shareholders, who have the ultimate authority over management. I cover corporate governance in Chapter 27.

Putting It All Together: The Org Chart

The following chart, an organization chart (or org chart), shows how the departments I've just discussed are organized in many companies.

As you can see, every department ultimately reports to the chief executive officer (CEO), usually the chairman of the board or the president. In a corporation, the CEO reports to the board of directors. In most companies, the titles of CEO and chairman of the board are both held by one person who has ultimate responsibility for the company. The president and chief operating officer (COO), also usually one person, oversees day-to-day operations.

Note that each division is run by managers, who in turn report to vice presidents, who in turn report to the president and COO. This organization chart is representative because *reporting lines* in companies follow fairly standard patterns.

MBA LINGO

On an organization chart, **reporting lines** refer to the relationships between employees and their managers, and between managers and more senior managers. A direct line links a manager with his or her immediate, primary boss. In some businesses, a dotted line in the org chart indicates a secondary, less formal reporting arrangement in addition to the primary one. For example, Accounting could report directly to the CEO but have a dotted line to the chief financial officer (CFO).

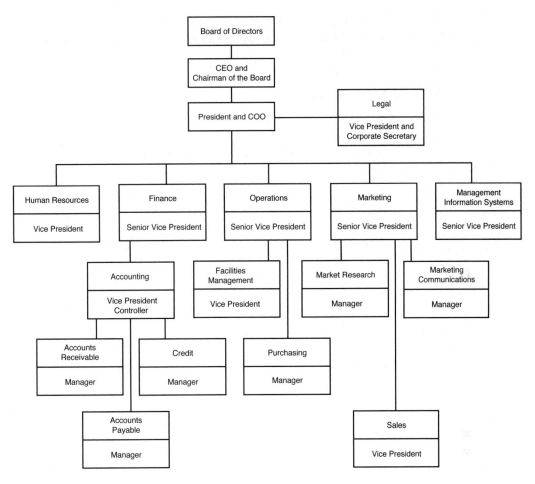

Organizational chart (or org chart) for a large company.

The Least You Need to Know

- Each part of a business has a specific function to perform. It is the manager's job to make sure that each part performs that function well.
- Finance and accounting control and count the money.
- Operations makes and delivers the products or services.
- Marketing and sales do the selling that brings in the money.

- Information technology has become extremely important in most organizations. This reflects the fact that computer-generated information is now a key resource in most industries.

- The board of directors advises management on policy and represents the interests of the shareholders.

- The organizational chart, or org chart, reflects the company structure.

Lessons in Leadership

In This Chapter

- The difference between a manager and a leader
- Leadership skills that really work
- All about coaching and mentoring
- Why managing change is so important

Leadership—as opposed to pure management—has become essential in business because, as pointed out in Chapter 1, many companies now employ mainly well-educated knowledge workers. Their work demands motivation, creativity, and flexibility, and you cannot simply ask (let alone order) people to be motivated, creative, and flexible.

Leadership has also come to the fore because most companies have moved away from so-called command-and-control management. They realize that a "traditional" manager directs people to do what they should do, but a leader gets people to do what they should do—and more—with less direction and greater efficiency.

Management and leadership are different but related. A manager's job is more defined than a leader's. Management skills, such as planning and delegation, are concrete compared with leadership skills, which are more abstract. A leader relies more heavily on influence, inspiration, and collaboration than on directives, policies, and procedures. Yet the two sets of skills overlap.

Management skills and leadership skills work together to boost the effectiveness of both managers and employees. For example, the management skill of goal setting is related to the leadership skill of sharing a vision. If a leader can share a compelling vision of what the organization could accomplish *and* can set goals and define tasks that move people toward that vision, everyone will achieve more.

Not every leader is a good manager, nor is every manager a good leader. But the best executives have mastered both management and leadership skills.

Style or Skills? Role or Position?

For many people, the word *leader* conjures a mental image of a famous leader, a George Washington or Winston Churchill. For some people, these famous leaders, and portrayals of leaders in popular culture, create the idea that leadership requires a confident, charismatic personal style. But even though confidence and charisma don't hurt, they don't by themselves make someone a leader.

The term *leadership style* actually refers to the way in which a leader interacts with his or her followers. Leaders may project authoritative or collaborative, energetic or low-key, rational or emotional styles, which reflect their personalities and the organizational culture. However, please know that becoming a leader does not mean developing any particular style or mimicking leaders portrayed in popular culture. Extremes of behavior seen in leaders in the movies and on television—the Mafia don's icy calm or the newspaper editor's bluster—simply don't work in real life, particularly if you don't happen to be naturally calm or blustery.

Yet effective leaders *are* playing a role. They know that, although they must be themselves, playing a leadership role in an organization demands that they practice certain skills and interact in ways that meet people's expectations of leadership behavior. For example, people expect a leader to hold him- or herself accountable and to hold them accountable for doing their jobs. If a leader fails at some aspect of her job but won't admit it, she will not be seen as an effective leader. Similarly, if an employee fails to do his job and the leader promotes him to a job with even more responsibility, she will not be seen as effective. Instead, the leader will undermine her other employees' morale and motivation.

Leadership depends on sending strong, consistent messages—through words and actions—that demonstrate that the leader cares deeply about the organization and its people and purpose. This kind of caring is almost impossible to fake, because people watch leaders closely and judge them constantly. They will tolerate foibles and even failure (up to a point). But they will not bestow the mantle of leadership, which is theirs to bestow, on a manager who is lazy, unfair, inconsistent, unsupportive, or otherwise uncaring about the organization and its people and purpose.

The best leaders focus on developing their personal and interpersonal skills, such as their ability to cope with stress and to communicate effectively, and on developing their self-awareness and their awareness of their effect on others. They also do this in the context of the organization or their mission within it, or both. In other words, they lead with a purpose instead of for the sake of leading others or simply having power.

CASE IN POINT

History's great leaders are all strongly associated with achieving a purpose, usually against opposing forces. Martin Luther King Jr. fought for racial equality, Franklin D. Roosevelt for government assistance for the unemployed, and Susan B. Anthony for women's suffrage. The best business leaders, such as Henry Luce (*Time* magazine), Bill Gates (Microsoft), David Packard (Hewlett-Packard), and Jack Welch (General Electric), engage people to aim for high quality, satisfied customers, and excellence as an end in itself.

So although leadership does not depend on personality, it does depend on the person.

People need leaders. That is why, in a leadership vacuum—for instance, in a badly managed department—a group will often recognize an unofficial leader. An unofficial leader doesn't officially head the group, yet people look to him or her for information, guidance, and decisions. Why? Because people trust that person. A leader has people's trust. Building trust is first among the leadership skills we examine.

MBA MASTERY

One good way to think about the difference between a leader and a manager is that leader is a role, while manager is a position. You can be promoted to a management position, but you must earn and grow into a leadership role.

Leadership Skills

Effective leaders motivate people to adopt the organization's purpose as their own and to do their best to fulfill that purpose. They inspire people to achieve more than they ever thought they could. They generate loyalty to the organization and get people to work together rather than against one another.

How do effective leaders do these things? Essentially, they …

- Build trust.
- Share a vision.
- Focus people on the right tasks.

- Create accountability.
- Maintain alignment.
- Coach and mentor.

These skills are more complex and more difficult to learn than management skills. Yet they *are* skills, and that means that you can learn them, practice them, and use them.

Lay a Firm Foundation

Trust is the foundation of the relationship between leader and follower (as it is in every human relationship). Therefore, effective leaders consciously build trust between themselves and their people.

They build trust by considering the good of all *stakeholders* when making decisions. They do not allow one stakeholder or group of stakeholders to benefit at the expense of another. Leaders also build trust by using their power properly. As noted in Chapter 1, leaders are the stewards of the organization and are in a position to enrich themselves at the expense of others. If they do, they destroy trust.

> **MBA LINGO**
>
> A **stakeholder** has a tangible interest in an organization or project. Stakeholders benefit if the enterprise succeeds and incur losses if it fails. In a company, typical stakeholders include employees, customers, suppliers, investors, lenders, and the community.

Effective leaders build trust by fostering collaboration. Some managers believe that internal competition strengthens a company. Giving a department some competition can work—for example, General Motors allowed its production managers to purchase parts from outside the company if GM parts were inferior. But pitting people within a company against one another or allowing "turf battles" undermines trust in the leader and within the company.

Trust is so important because business is among the most collaborative of human endeavors. To collaborate well, people must trust one another. They will share information openly, contribute their best effort, and support one another only when they trust one another. It is management's job to create that trust. Fair, principled behavior is the only way to create it.

> **MBA ALERT**
>
> Trust in senior executives has eroded in the past 20 years, among the general public and within business. A major cause is senior executives who focus mainly on enriching themselves. In the United States, executive compensation, which has grown far out of proportion not only to employee compensation but also to executive achievements, is among the main problems that must be addressed if trust in business leaders is to be restored.

Trusting someone is not the same as liking them. Trust is based on respect and expectations, not on personal affection. Members of a football or basketball team do not have to like one another. But they have to trust one another on the field or court if they are to win games. Similarly, a leader does not need to be liked by all stakeholders, nor does he or she have to like all of them. But a leader and those whom he or she would lead must trust one another, or there can be no leadership.

Share a Vision

Effective leaders usually have a vision of what they want the organization to stand for and achieve. When they share that vision with their stakeholders, everyone knows what he or she holds a stake in. (Arguably, even leaders who say they have no "vision" are sharing a vision, which is, "We don't envision—we act!") A vision is broader than a goal. It articulates the underlying values and sets the context in which goals are selected and pursued.

How do you articulate a vision when business is mainly about making a profit? By understanding that the greatest long-term profits come not by seeking money directly, but by serving a strong customer need in an effective, efficient manner. Of course, as a number of Wall Street investment banks have proven, you can make money while providing relatively little value (for instance, by moving money around in speculation or selling risky mortgage securities without disclosing the risks). But some of those banks went out of business, and others needed help from the government to survive.

Businesses that truly succeed in the long term meet a real need. They are often led by executives who envision new ways of meeting those needs, and who can articulate that vision and enlist others in seeing it as worth bringing into reality.

The best leaders are students of human nature. They know that people want more from their work than a paycheck. They understand that people want a sense of purpose, that they want to be given a mission they can believe in.

MBA MASTERY

Don't be afraid to envision something revolutionary for your business and its customers. A vision goes well beyond "making a profit" or "increasing market share." Those things are important, of course, but they often are achieved most spectacularly when a leader envisions a breakthrough to a new level of technical innovation, product quality, or customer service.

These leaders also understand the business reasons for creating a shared vision. People with a vision will work harder and longer and with a greater sense of achievement than they ever would for just a paycheck. But they need to be doing the work that the company exists to accomplish. Therefore, although it incorporates values, the vision must be a business vision. It must be rooted in the reasons for the organization's existence. And it must include the customer, because a company exists to serve its customers.

Creating a shared vision calls for two-way communication. Many people don't adopt a leader's vision immediately. They need to ask questions, grasp the underlying values, interpret the vision, and see their role in achieving it. Smart leaders allow this process to occur. They realize that it is the way some people make the vision their own.

Focus People on the Right Tasks

As managers, leaders must get things done through others. This means focusing people's attention on the most important tasks. Those are the tasks that will move the organization toward fulfillment of its vision and achievement of its goals. Effective leaders first identify the key tasks that will create the results they want to achieve. Then, through training, coaching, and incentives, they get people to perform these few tasks to the very best of their ability.

This leadership skill overlaps with the management skill of delegating, but even here leaders do things differently. They accept the fact that a company cannot do everything well. With this in mind, they consciously decide what the organization will do well and get people focused on those tasks *and not on other tasks.*

The typical manager lacks the laserlike focus on the few key tasks that leaders develop and impart to the troops. The manager lacks this focus not because he can't identify the key tasks, but because he can't keep himself and his people focused on them as intensely as the leader can.

CASE IN POINT

MBNA, the world's largest independent credit card company, has become so efficient at marketing cards, making credit decisions, and servicing customers that other banks now turn over those tasks to MBNA. The other banks keep their names on their MasterCard or Visa but pay MBNA to do the operational tasks, which are MBNA's core competencies. In handling so many other types of banking business, those other banks cannot match MBNA's efficiency or profitability in credit cards.

Effective leaders do not distract people with a flavor-of-the-month activity. Yes, if costs must be cut, they will get people to focus on cutting costs. If customer service slips, they will have people focus on improving customer service. However, the basic tasks that people in a given position must perform remain few in number and consistent in character.

In leadership literature, these tasks are often referred to as *core competencies.* Core competencies are the things that the company does extremely well to create value for the customer. For instance, in Disney's entertainment division, animation is a core competency. Disney has a history of making excellent animated films, does them extremely well, has created brands around animated characters—most famously Mickey Mouse—and attracts talented animators and technicians.

MBA LINGO

A **core competency** is a task, activity, or skill that a company does extremely well and that adds value for customers.

Who Does What? Creating Accountability

As you learned in Chapter 3, a corporation's owners entrust management to organize human and other resources to do certain things for customers and to make a profit doing them.

The owners hold the board of directors accountable, the board holds the CEO accountable, the CEO holds his or her senior managers accountable, the senior managers hold their managers accountable, and those managers hold their employees accountable for accomplishing certain things profitably.

Accountability is often the "missing link" in the management process. It is difficult, even unpleasant, to hold people accountable. They make excuses and cite reasons beyond their control. Or they admit that they screwed up but can't explain how they will prevent it from happening again. Or they hide their failures so that they cannot be held accountable in the first place.

MBA MASTERY

Hold people accountable for achieving results *ethically.* When people feel they must achieve a result no matter what, they will find a way to achieve it no matter what. Many things aside from the result—such as building trust and staying out of jail—also matter.

Effective leaders hold people accountable by allowing for mistakes and failures and realizing that they are part of the process, particularly when people are pursuing difficult goals. That way, people will admit their mistakes and failures and accept accountability. Effective leaders also have developed the ego strength to confront people about their failures and the skill to help them improve.

Finally, effective leaders hold themselves accountable for the things they say they will do and deliver. A leader undermines his credibility and trust if he doesn't hold himself to the same level of accountability as he holds his people.

Maintain Alignment

A leader must ensure that the organization's resources are aligned with its vision and goals. Alignment means that "everyone is driving in the same direction."

On an operational level, alignment refers to consistency in strategy, structure, and resource allocation. For instance, if a company decides on a strategy of growth through new product development, it must put structures in place that support the strategy and allocate resources to implementing it.

On an interpersonal level, alignment means that the leader's actions are congruent with his or her words. When a leader says one thing and does another, people stop trusting management and become cynical. For instance, when senior management announces a cost-cutting effort and then continues to fly first-class, they are throwing the organization out of alignment.

Organizational alignment demands that strategy, structure, resources, beliefs, words, actions, and goals all line up logically and fairly. If the CEO says, "People are our greatest asset," but allows (or encourages) high employee turnover, the company will go out of alignment. Likewise, if the CEO states that growth in sales will come from new products and then cuts the new product development budget, there will be lack of alignment.

MBA ALERT

Every member of management must be aligned in the messages they send to employees. It's fine for managers to hash out among themselves the message that they want to send to people. But once the message has been defined, every manager must accept it and communicate it clearly throughout the organization.

Consistency and congruence generate organizational alignment. The messages from management and the commitment of resources must be aligned with one another and with the company's goals and strategies. Effective leaders work hard to achieve this alignment, even to the point of firing people who cannot align themselves with the company's goals and strategy. These leaders know that an organization that's out of alignment will soon wind up in the ditch.

CASE IN POINT

Certain companies have executive compensation plans that continue to reward senior managers lavishly even when profits plummet and employees are laid off. This throws the company way out of alignment (and undermines trust and accountability).

Coaching and Mentoring

A true leader must also be a coach and mentor. Coaching and mentoring bring all the other leadership skills down to the person-to-person level. That is, coaching and mentoring are means by which a leader can build trust, share his or her vision, focus people on the right tasks, create accountability, and maintain alignment.

What's the difference between coaching and mentoring?

In general, coaching helps people do their current job better, while mentoring prepares them for their next job. Coaching helps people achieve results they are now accountable for achieving. Mentoring enhances people's *promotability* to greater responsibility.

MBA LINGO

Promotability refers to a person's readiness to assume greater responsibility within the organization. Factors that determine promotability include management and leadership skills, past and current performance, ability to collaborate, and knowledge of the organization as a whole.

Coaching essentially means giving people feedback on their performance in a specific area. The word *feedback* is both accurate and useful here, although *critique* might also be appropriate. Feedback is less judgmental than criticism, and that's what coaching should be. In business, a superior's comments about a subordinate's performance are often conveyed and perceived in negative ways. In sports, however, the coach assumes that the athlete wants to perform well and gives him information on what is working and not working in terms of his fundamentals, form, play, and approach to the game. Meanwhile, the athlete understands that the coach is commenting on his performance, not on him as a person.

A good leader offers feedback in the same spirit. She offers information—potentially helpful observations and advice on performance. She comments on what the employee is doing well and on what he could improve.

Coaching should occur both informally—for instance, after a meeting or presentation—and formally, in scheduled sessions. Without a formal program, many managers fail to practice these skills often enough with all of their people.

Comments should be specific. Saying, "You're doing a great job," isn't going to be as useful as saying, "You presented that material with all the right facts at the management meeting last week."

Coaching also involves setting goals for improvement in specific skills, developing a plan for improvement, and following up to ensure progress.

Mentoring involves similar types of communication. However, a mentor is often a level or two above the subordinate, while a coach coaches the people who report directly to him. A mentor exposes the subordinate to other functional areas of the company, explains how higher-level decisions are made, and helps the subordinate manage his career at the company. A mentor tells the subordinate where in the company he should think about working and what skills he should develop to get into that area.

Coaching and mentoring enable leaders to develop the organization's talent pool while showing people that the company cares about their development. Coaching and mentoring help a company keep good people. Also, the communication involved encourages people on both sides of the relationship to invest more of themselves in the organization.

Managing Change

Managing change has become an enduring topic in management because the continually changing business environment keeps presenting new challenges. Those challenges call upon organizations to change if they are to survive, let alone prosper.

Some observers maintain that the business environment has always presented the need to change, but the fact is that the paces of both technological and cultural change have accelerated rapidly in the past 20 to 30 years. From the technological standpoint, the proliferation of personal computers, mobile devices, and the Internet has given birth to multiple industries and revolutionized most others. From the cultural standpoint, high divorce rates and eroding "traditional values," lack of political consensus, erosion of middle-class incomes, increased household debt, shifting of risk from companies to workers, and globalization of markets have made change the only constant in the business landscape.

Why is managing change a discipline unto itself? Because, amid constant change, people have less context in the form of reliable signposts and frames of reference. They thus have less to depend upon, which can make them more fearful and distrustful, and less flexible and predictable. Under those conditions, they see change as threatening and may naturally resist it. That makes a leader's job tougher when the organization and the people in it must change.

A Five-Step Approach

View managing change as a specific activity, which is what it is. Change brings the new and unfamiliar into employees' working lives and demands new skills, new behaviors, and new attitudes of them. Worst of all, change often creates new and potentially negative effects on their incomes.

The change I'm discussing here usually involves new jobs or positions that may require new skills and new organizational structures or reporting arrangements, which employees may view, often justifiably, as negative. In situations involving these types of change, many leaders have had success with the following five-step approach:

1. Assess the nature of the change.

2. Explain why the change is occurring.

3. Explain what must change.

4. Explain how people will be expected to change.

5. Manage the change process.

Management cannot manage change unless it understands what needs to change and why, and how people in the organization will be affected. Changes typically come about when the organization adopts a new IT system; merges with another organization; reduces, increases, or reorganizes the workforce; or significantly alters its basic value proposition.

Many executives focus only on the positives for themselves, shareholders, and the larger organization, and forget that many or most employees will have strong negative feelings about the change. Others recognize those feelings and dismiss them, which can hurt the organization and undermine the change process. So management must understand the change and all the effects it will have on all stakeholders in the organization, including suppliers, customers, investors, and the media and community.

Be sure to communicate the need for the change clearly and in different ways. It's easy for management to see the need for a change—a new IT system, a merger, or a layoff—as almost self-evident. But it's unlikely to appear that way to most employees. Never mistake issuing a memo or making a speech for managing change. Instead, plan a series of communications to explain the change and then do so through managers, supervisors, and key employees at various levels and in all areas of the company. Also, honestly explain the actual *business case* for the change. People can distinguish truth from lies and will accept bad news more graciously when they feel that their leaders respect them enough to tell them the truth.

MBA LINGO

The **business case** for a decision or initiative is the financial rationale for a change. Usually, this case rests upon increasing revenue or reducing costs over a specified period of time. The business case provides sound reasons for change, as opposed to "Everyone is doing it" or "The consultants say we should do this."

To make people comfortable and to set the right expectations, leaders must describe what is going to change. In most organizations, people feel that management generally gives them only part of the story. One good way to portray this is by describing the current state and the desired future state. If the company is adopting a new IT system or merging with another company, describe the current capabilities and organization and the desired ones after the system is fully adopted or the merger is completed. If you're not sure about some things that may or may not change, mention that. It's best to minimize the number of unpleasant surprises. Be sure to genuinely encourage and welcome questions and to answer them as honestly as you can. Also explain the schedule for the change.

Be sure to tell people how they will be supported in learning their new jobs, developing new skills, and interacting in new ways. This is the most important explanation because it describes how people will do their jobs differently, what skills they will need, and how their communications and interactions will change. Again, do not believe that change occurs when you issue a memo or make a speech. In advance, assess their readiness to change in these ways, and develop ways to improve that readiness. People need to understand what they are supposed to do differently, and they need support in learning how to do it. Much of this work occurs between employees and their immediate superiors.

Managing change involves planning, goal setting, delegating, and following up to control to plan. (I covered controlling to plan in Chapter 2.) Expect resistance to change and plan accordingly. Realize that some people will be unable to change and to adapt to the new system or environment, and may have to leave the organization. Once the new direction is set, no one can be permitted to hamper or derail it. Most people are able to adapt, however, and when they understand the business case and believe that they are being treated fairly (even when they are negatively affected), they can typically accept and support the change.

A major difficulty in managing change is failure to understand how much work it takes. As I've emphasized, change is a process rather than an event. It does not come about by executive order. People usually need incentives to change, which can range from a vision and purpose that motivates them, to the prospect of increased income and advancement opportunities. Managing change means building such incentives into the program as part of the five-step approach.

Leadership Lessons of Life

The greatest management fallacy is to believe that employees will do things because they are told to do them. Executives who believe this will often ask questions like, "Why aren't people cutting costs? Didn't they read the memo we sent them last month?"

Most people will work hard in pursuit of their company's goals. But they must believe that the work and the goals are worthwhile. The company's leaders—and everyone in a management position—must instill those beliefs in their people.

The only way to accomplish this is to build an organization that holds to high product and service standards and treats all stakeholders fairly. Leadership skills won't work in the absence of high standards and fairness to all stakeholders. With those elements in place, leaders still have challenging roles to play. Yet with diligent practice of leadership skills, they can reach their business goals while enriching the lives of everyone their organizations touch.

The Least You Need to Know

- The basic leadership skills include building trust, sharing a vision, focusing people on the right tasks, creating accountability, maintaining alignment, and coaching and mentoring.

- Coaching, which helps an employee improve current performance, and mentoring, which prepares an employee for promotion, are leadership skills most managers must be encouraged to practice.

- Managing change is a distinct discipline and entails understanding the nature of the change, explaining why the change is occurring and what must change, telling people how their jobs will change and how they will be supported, and following up to ensure that the change is occurring.

The Nuts and Bolts of Managing People and Teams

In This Chapter

- The role of human resources
- Hiring and firing employees
- Dealing with difficult employees
- Types of teams and how to manage a team

In Chapter 2, we examined the everyday activities of management, such as planning, setting goals, and delegating. In Chapter 4, we covered the fundamentals of leadership, such as building trust and sharing a vision. To be successful in their own right, managers must also be able to guide their people to success. I call skills required to do this the nuts and bolts of management, but they could also be called the administrative side of managing people: hiring, firing, conducting performance appraisals, and working with difficult employees.

Fortunately, these aren't things you'll have to do every day, because most sizable companies have a human-resources function (more simply, HR) to help managers deal with them. HR professionals also take care of a lot of other nuts and bolts so that managers are free to manage their day-to-day operations. These other administrative matters include setting policies and pay scales, ensuring company compliance with employment regulations, assisting in employee growth and development, promoting diversity in the organization, and negotiating with insurance firms and other providers of employee benefits.

In this chapter, I explain how human resources does its job and helps you do yours. If your company is too small to have an HR department, this chapter briefs you about the administrative issues that every manager must understand and occasionally address. This chapter also covers managing teams, an activity that has grown in importance over the past several years.

What Does Human Resources Do?

HR helps managers hire, orient, and train employees, and establishes guidelines for employee compensation, performance appraisals, and disciplinary action. HR also helps a company comply with laws regarding employment discrimination and workplace safety. In companies with *unionized workers*, HR helps managers deal with the union's work rules.

MBA LINGO

Unionized workers are employees who have banded together to engage in collective, instead of individual, bargaining with management. The union negotiates a contract with management that applies to the workers, once the workers approve it.

Other key HR activities include the following:

- Recruitment
- Compensation analysis
- Benefits administration
- Training and development
- General employee administration

Recruiters develop a pool of candidates to fill open positions in the company. To do this, they post the job on employment websites and the company website, place ads in newspapers, work with employment agencies, and visit college campuses. They also screen candidates before they're sent to the hiring manager. (And, yes, HR is where those maddening individuals read and file—or throw out—all those resumés from people who want a job at the company.)

Compensation analysts define job functions and qualifications and write *job descriptions* for each position in the company. (A job description is an official definition of the responsibilities of a position.) Compensation analysts also set policies regarding how often someone in the job should be considered for a raise. They then decide what level of *compensation*—that is, wages or salary plus benefits—should go to people in that job. The wage or salary is usually defined as a range—for example, $33,000 to $38,000.

MBA LINGO

Recruiters are responsible for filling open positions in the company. Most companies have recruiters on staff in the HR department. Recruiters also work in independent companies set up to fill open positions in their client companies, usually at the executive levels—hence the name "executive recruiters."

A **job description** is an official definition of the responsibilities of a position. Every job in a company should have a job description, and every employee should have a copy of his or her job description. As a manager, you need copies of the job descriptions of everyone on your staff.

Compensation refers to an employee's pay plus his or her bonus (if any) plus the value of any benefits, such as company-paid health or life insurance. Total compensation refers to the value of all pay, bonuses, benefits, and what are known as perquisites, such as a company car or company-paid club membership.

Benefits administrators work with suppliers of health, retirement, and other benefit plans to see that employees have and receive benefits. Training and development professionals bring in outside training firms and develop in-house courses to ensure that all employees are trained for their jobs and prepared for advancement. General employee administrators handle employee communications, charitable efforts (such as blood drives), and employee grievances. In large companies, they may put out a newsletter or other regular publications. They also set policies regarding things such as smoking, office parties, and compliance with safety regulations.

Although the HR staff is there to answer virtually any question you may have about managing employees, its advice is particularly valuable when you are hiring new employees or dealing with problem employees.

Hiring the Right Person for the Job

In a large company, HR usually is involved in the hiring process. This is for your convenience and the company's protection, and it saves money.

For example, if you need an *employment agency*, HR knows reliable ones and can negotiate the best fees. The same applies to *executive search firms* and help-wanted advertising. HR also keeps some resumés on file, and a look through them might uncover a solid candidate still interested in joining the company.

MBA LINGO

An **employment agency** is a firm that other companies use to fill jobs. An **executive search firm** (or executive recruiter or headhunter) identifies, meets, and screens potential candidates, whether or not they are seeking a new job. When a position becomes available, the recruiter may then recommend a candidate.

Human resources ensures that the company stays within legal and regulatory guidelines governing employment. For example, a company cannot discriminate in hiring on the basis of ethnic background, gender, or age. Companies of a certain size must accommodate the handicapped. The manager of every department cannot be an expert on employment law, so the HR function has this expertise.

Interviewing Candidates

Interviewing job applicants calls for more preparation and effort than many managers devote to the process. Many job interviews are almost perfunctory, with the real agenda of assessing "chemistry." Unfortunately, chemistry alone isn't a good indicator of how well a candidate can actually do the job.

MBA MASTERY

My best advice on hiring: get strength in numbers. *Always* interview more than one candidate for a job and *always* have more than one person in your shop interview the candidates.

Before the interview, prepare questions in writing and be sure to get answers to them. After greeting the applicant and putting her at ease, gear your questions to the two major issues: *Can* this person do the job? *Will* this person do the job?

To get at the first issue—can she do the job?—ask questions related to the candidate's education, work experience, and (key point) past performance. Ask for specifics about her role and her accomplishments at past employers.

The second issue—will she do the job?—relates more to the candidate's character, motivation, and genuine interests. Probe deeply into what she liked and disliked about past positions and why she moved on. What seems to excite her? How does she see herself and others? How fully does she answer your questions? When you probe in a certain area, does she change the subject?

Finally, be aware that there are certain questions you cannot legally ask a job candidate. These include questions about health, religious and ethnic background, marital status, family plans, and age. Your HR department can give you a better picture of what you can and can't legally ask. Rule of thumb: don't ask any question that does not directly relate to the candidate's ability to do the job.

Checking References

Check references yourself, if possible. Otherwise, be sure HR does. If you check them, tell the person you've been referred to that this is an extremely important hire and that you need an honest perspective on the candidate.

It's not easy to get objective answers, but try. Many companies are wary about being sued by former employees if they give out negative information. Some will only verify that the person was employed there. However, you should still try to get an objective, useful reference from a former boss.

MBA MASTERY

When you ask a question, wait for the answer. Don't attempt to answer the question for the candidate or "lead" the candidate to make a particular response. If the answer is incomplete, wait for more. If you don't get more, prompt with a phrase like, "Can you be more specific?" or "In what sense?" or "Why is that?" The human tendency may be to let the interviewee "off the hook." Don't.

Extending the Offer

After you've interviewed what you consider to be enough candidates (I like to see five to eight for a professional position), you'll be ready to extend an offer.

Company protocol usually dictates how an offer is extended. Some outfits believe the offer should come from HR, while others believe the hiring manager should extend it. The latter may be warmer, but the former provides "distance" between the hiring manager and the candidate if negotiations ensue. If HR can act as a buffer, why not let them? Whoever does it, generally an offer is extended by phone and followed up with a verifying letter or e-mail.

MBA ALERT

A lukewarm or poor reference should raise a red flag but not necessarily end the candidate's chances. Personal animosity can fuel a poor reference, so ask for specific details about the employee's performance. If the specifics sound believable, beware. If instead you get vague negatives or descriptions of personality traits rather than specific behaviors, the poor reference may be "just personal."

Getting New Employees Oriented

After the candidate becomes an employee, HR provides materials that help him or her understand company policy, structure, benefits, and ethics. These materials include policy manuals, benefits handbooks, and so on. HR may also have worthwhile DVDs on the company.

Part of your responsibility as a manager is to develop your employees. This includes arranging for the training they need, as well as any they might request that is both relevant to their job and in the budget. If you have people reporting to you, you should have some money (even if it's just a few thousand dollars a year) budgeted for training. Or your area may have a share of a larger departmental or central HR budget for training and development. Employees interested in training or furthering their education should be encouraged to pursue it.

Dealing with Problem Employees

No one, and I mean no one, likes dealing with an employee who is performing poorly, slacking off, displaying personality problems, or undermining the outfit. Because no one enjoys the task, many managers try to "work around" problem employees rather than deal with them. As a manager, you owe it to your organization and to your good employees to hold problem employees accountable and, when necessary, fire them.

I'm defining a problem employee as one who is not performing or is disruptive, but whom you cannot or should not fire immediately. Few offenses warrant immediate firing. Most large companies limit these offenses to proven or admitted dishonesty (beyond stealing pencils), threatening language, violent behavior, on-the-job drinking or drug use, and gross *insubordination* (refusal to follow a reasonable request from a superior).

At most companies, virtually all other offenses (poor attitude, attendance, or job performance) require a formal termination process to give the employee time to improve. Note, however, that, in most companies, the employee's first 90 days on the job are officially a probationary period during which the employee can be terminated immediately. In addition, most companies now periodically lay off employees and use permanent layoffs as a way to "clean house" of poor performers. This does not mean that anyone who has been laid off was a poor performer, because in crunch periods companies lay off even competent people to save costs.

Large companies generally require managers to build a case before terminating a problem employee, partly out of fairness and partly because no company wants a *wrongful termination* suit on its hands. The HR department assists the manager during this termination process, while also giving an ear to the problem employee.

MBA LINGO

Insubordination is an employee's direct refusal to follow a reasonable, direct, job-related request from his or her superior. Repeated or vigorous refusal amounts to gross insubordination.

Wrongful termination is firing someone based on age, gender, race, or religion. Another example is firing a woman because she became pregnant or firing someone because he or she got a divorce. These are not legal because laws prohibit discriminating against workers on that basis. Valid reasons for terminating an employee are those relating to job performance.

The termination process gives the employee an opportunity to improve his performance or else be terminated. Typically an employee receives written notice of his failure to perform to the standards of the job. The notice mentions the specific areas in which his performance falls short, such as attendance or the quality of his work, and specific goals that the employee must achieve, such as perfect attendance or only 2 defects per 100 pieces of product.

It also usually mentions a time frame, usually 30 or 60 days, during which that improvement must be achieved. The notice is usually worded so that improvement must "be maintained thereafter" so that the employee does not improve temporarily just to keep his job and then fall off again.

Some problem employees do pull themselves together, but that's not the way to bet. Many simply refuse to change their behavior even after verbal warnings. By the time problem employees are given a formal written warning and are placed on probation, they are, in my experience, usually (although not always) on the way out.

CASE IN POINT

Some firms drag out the termination process unnecessarily. I've seen two cases in which employees (one mine, one another manager's) with disordered personalities were kept on the job for months because the managers were not permitted to terminate. One of these employees ultimately had to be escorted from the building by security after "losing it." Lobby hard for termination in such situations. Helping inefficient employees move on to the next stage of their lives is the best thing for them, as well as the fairest thing for their fellow employees.

HR can provide good advice on the legal and procedural aspects of termination. For example, when you write someone up, HR will help you focus on behavioral issues rather than personality conflicts. HR can also help you deal with the emotional dimensions of the situation, both yours and the employee's.

The best way to avoid problem employees is to hire carefully and do regular performance appraisals.

Take Performance Appraisals Seriously

Most companies require managers to give each of their employees a formal, annual, written performance appraisal. Unfortunately, not all managers follow through. But every manager should, for two reasons. First, employees deserve a periodic written record of where they stand. Second, appraisals document the employee's performance for future managers.

The HR department (and your superior) will have the necessary forms and advice on how to go about writing and administering performance appraisals.

The most common mistakes (aside from not doing appraisals regularly) are rating people too highly given their actual performance and not giving employees a clear program for improvement. I'm not encouraging negative performance appraisals, but I'm advocating balanced ones. I have seen perfect employees—exactly two in 20 years. Most of us (myself included) have strengths *and* weaknesses, and you must document both in the appraisal.

CASE IN POINT

A survey several years ago revealed that, in the average company, over 50 percent of employees rate their job performance in the top 10 percent of the outfit's employees. This is a practical, as well as mathematical, impossibility. Quite possibly, overly positive performance appraisals contribute to this situation.

If a poorly performing employee is due for an annual appraisal, use it as an opportunity to document the poor performance and give him or her an action plan and 30 or 60 days to improve. By the same token, an outstanding employee should be recognized and rewarded.

MBA MASTERY

One of the best techniques for appraising managers is the 360-degree evaluation. Usually administered with the help of external consultants, the "360" gathers very specific feedback on defined skills and behaviors from the manager's superiors, peers, and employees (hence the name). The feedback tends to be honest and fair, but it helps a lot to have an experienced consultant help the manager and his superiors interpret it. The manager also needs a plan and coaching to address areas that require improvement. For more on this, see *The Art and Science of 360 Degree Feedback,* by Richard Lepsinger and Antoinette Lucia (Pfeiffer, 2nd Ed., 2009).

Firing an Employee

When an employee has been given a real chance to improve and has failed, she should be terminated quickly. (Of course, you will have input from HR as well as your supervisor before you actually terminate an employee.) I have found the following general guidelines useful:

- Meet with the employee in a conference room or an office other than yours or hers. That way, you are both on "neutral territory" and the new environment signals to the employee that the process has moved to a new and final stage.

- Give the person formal, verbal notice of termination and a brief, blandly worded letter that states that "the company no longer requires your services."

- Don't apologize. You can say you're sorry things did not work out, if you like, but it isn't your place to make a true apology.

- Deliver the news yourself, but have someone from HR at the termination. That way, you have a witness to this final conversation (or confrontation), as well as someone to back you up.

- Ask the terminated employee to leave the premises when the conversation is finished. If you prefer, you may give the employee until the end of the day to collect her things, but the sooner she leaves, the better.

Don't be shocked if the employee threatens you with a lawsuit. When I hear that, I say, "You have to proceed in the way that's best for you," and nothing else. Many companies forestall legal action by providing (often generous) *severance pay* to terminated employees. Senior managers may receive this as part of their employment contract. But by no means does every fired employee get severance pay.

MBA LINGO

Severance pay is a final payment made by the company to an employee who is being terminated or laid off. The company makes this payment partly out of fairness to the employee, to "tide her over" during the period of unemployment presumably ahead, and partly to assuage any hard feelings the employee may have.

When severance pay is given to a fired employee, he or she usually signs a letter agreeing not to sue and accepting the payment as full settlement. Often these employees are "allowed to resign" instead of being fired.

Take Your Time

Although terminating employees is often taxing, fortunately, it is not an everyday task. However, when you take over a department, you may well find that one or two people will either have to improve their performance radically or be asked to leave. Just don't make any snap judgments or try to move too quickly. It takes at least six months to a year to build or significantly improve a department. It takes time to size up people's performance, communicate your standards, and bring employees up to those levels or replace them.

When you take over an existing function, unless it's a disaster, resist any gung-ho urges you may feel. Get to know your people—and let them get to know you—before trying to make radical changes. Use a consultative leadership style until you know who's who and what's what. Then, if or when you do start directing and delegating, you will be positioned to direct and delegate with more knowledge and credibility.

Team, Team, Teams

Although the traditional departments, such as finance, marketing, and production, can accomplish most tasks, at times a company needs a small, specialized work group—a team—to address a specific situation.

Situations best addressed by teams include crises (such as disaster recovery); tasks that demand the expertise of several functions (such as product development); and complex, short-term projects (such as changing the company's structure). The most common tasks involve engaging in fact-finding, developing recommendations, and implementing a course of action, or some combination of the three.

A fact-finding team conducts research and gathers information—for instance, on the causes of employee turnover. That same team or another one may then develop recommendations, such as policies and procedures to reduce employee turnover. Then a team may be needed to implement the recommended course of action, perhaps by training managers in policies and procedures to reduce turnover.

> **MBA ALERT**
>
> Some companies call almost any department or area a team. This is meant to promote teamwork. It may even be accurate. After all, a department is a group of people working toward a common goal. And someday, they won't be working together. However, true teams are specialized groups with a specific mission to accomplish within a certain time. Referring to standing departments as teams may cloud the meaning of the term and reduce the impact that true teams can have on the organization.

Cross-functional teams, which have become quite popular, comprise members from various functions, such as sales, marketing, finance, and production, or perhaps various geographic locations across the company. Not every function in a company must be represented. But every area that can truly contribute should be represented.

Pros and Cons of Teams

The advantages of teams stem from their nature. Small work groups often can accomplish a task faster than a traditional department because they are small, focused on a specific task, and less tied up in "red tape." Teams work especially well when the expertise of several functions is required or when a decision or course of action will affect multiple functions. Having the contribution and buy-in of those functions (on a cross-functional team) heightens the chances of success.

A team appointed by senior management has the authority to get things done where "business as usual" would be slow or ineffective. In fact, the very act of forming a *task force* to deal with a problem often signals to the organization a serious commitment to fixing it.

MBA LINGO

A **task force** is a temporary work group under one leader formed to accomplish a well-defined, often urgent project and then disband.

So teams can tap the right people, move quickly, bring together disparate functions, generate buy-in, and solve problems. Yet teams have some disadvantages. They pull high performers off their regular jobs. If a team places additional demands on employees, they won't be able to devote as much time and energy to their regular jobs.

Teams are also tricky to manage. Sometimes they are not given a well-defined goal and enough authority to achieve the goal. Even teams with a goal can get derailed if a strong personality takes over the team and clouds its aims or skews the results of its work. Teams have limited time to get up and running and to demonstrate effectiveness. Therefore, they must be disciplined and task-oriented. This means that even when members don't know one another well, they must quickly develop trust and start collaborating effectively. Representatives of a team must also act with diplomacy as they navigate the organization, or they will alienate others (who were not asked to join the team).

MBA ALERT

Scrutinize requests to join teams, particularly if you work for a large company. If you have the option of not participating, you may want to consider gracefully declining if the costs to you or your department would outweigh the benefits of your participation. (But don't alienate senior management or create the impression that you're not a team player.)

Also be wary of task forces formed to make it appear as if management is solving a problem it has no intention of addressing. The people on that type of team are, at best, wasting their time and, at worst, being set up for failure.

Managing Teams

Most businesspeople like "teams" but hate "committees." They believe that teams get things done and committees do nothing. Worse, a committee is apt to come up with a complex, unworkable solution to a problem. (You've probably heard the saying "A camel is a horse put together by a committee.")

How do you keep your team from turning into a committee? By considering the following questions and guidelines:

- **What must the team accomplish?** Decide at the outset whether the team is gathering information, making recommendations, implementing a course of action, or some combination of these tasks. Define the scope of the team's project carefully.

- **Is a team really necessary in this situation?** Sometimes one or two people can get more done in less time. Or perhaps hiring a consulting firm would be more effective.

- **Who should be on the team?** Include only the people the team really needs. Stakeholders who can't contribute but who will be affected, for example, should be kept informed and asked for input, but they should not be on the team.

- **How are we going to accomplish our goals?** At the outset, the team must define its tasks, who will complete them, at what cost, and by when. Each member must have a role, tasks, deliverables, and deadlines.

- **Who is leading the team?** A team should have a leader. Although the leader can think of him- or herself as a facilitator, someone must guide the team's efforts and be accountable for its results.

- **What are the team's resources?** A team usually needs a budget and other resources, such as meeting facilities and the time allocated by team members. The resources must be equal to the task that the team is expected to accomplish.

MBA MASTERY

A team should consist of people at similar management levels. If one member is far senior to the others, he or she may alter the group dynamics for the worse, for instance, by suppressing contributions, even unknowingly. It is the rare executive who can say to subordinates, "I am just another member of this team," and be believed.

A team leader must build trust, share a vision, focus on the right tasks, create accountability, maintain alignment, and coach and mentor the team members. In other words, a team leader must employ leadership skills.

Most of this chapter's material depicts the way things are done in large companies. Large companies can be bureaucratic and conservatively managed, but for all their faults, they are generally professionally managed. They have had the time and applied the resources to at least get the basics of management right. For that reason, it can be very useful for a small company to employ similar methods of hiring, reviewing, terminating, and managing employees.

The Least You Need to Know

- To build or improve a department, you must get to know your employees, communicate your expectations and standards to them, and guide them to that level of performance.
- Hiring carefully and with the input of human resources, another interviewer, and former employers of the candidate will help you avoid problems later.
- Problem employees must be handled through a procedure designed to be fair to them and to the organization.
- Teams may be formed for fact-finding, to make recommendations, to implement a course of action, or to accomplish some combination of these tasks.
- Forming a team does not guarantee that an effort will succeed. Indeed, the team must be formed for the right reasons and must be properly constructed and well managed in order to succeed.

Making Decisions About Resources and Operations

Much of a manager's work comes down to making decisions. Most of these decisions have to do with how the company's resources are allocated to various operations. These decisions can range from small ones, such as whether a restaurant should schedule two or three cooks for Thursday evening, to large ones, such as whether a natural gas company should build a pipeline across Canada.

Management decisions occur in the context of the larger economy—specifically, the economic cycle of expansion and recession, known as the business cycle. The business cycle affects virtually every business. Therefore, Part 2 begins by explaining how the business cycle operates and how to read economic indicators so that you know where you are in the business cycle.

You'll also learn analytical methods and tools that can help you make the best decision in a given business situation. Finally, you'll learn how to read a budget and make decisions that help you stay within a budget.

The Business Cycle and Economic Indicators

6

In This Chapter

- Why the business cycle occurs
- Fiscal and monetary policy and what they do
- Where to find economic indicators
- What economic indicators mean to you

Although we would all like the economy to grow constantly, it goes through expansions and contractions and periods of rapid and sluggish growth. Cycles of expansion and contraction, or recovery and recession, are called the economic cycle, or the business cycle. (Sluggish growth is just called sluggish growth.)

The business cycle affects business decisions because in times of economic growth businesses want to expand, so they invest more, hire more workers, and produce more. Businesses also want to expand in times of recession or slow economic growth, but that is more difficult and risky. They fear they might expand too much and wind up with costs that are too high, with too many workers, or with products they can't sell. So they cut back. But that can make the recession worse.

I explain how all this works in this chapter. I also explain some economic indicators so that when you hear or read the business news, you will know where the economy is headed and can factor it into your decisions.

Why the Business Cycle Occurs

The *business cycle* exists because of fluctuations in demand, also known as spending, and mismatches between demand and business capacity and output. Those mismatches occur when businesses have too much capacity—too many employees, too much inventory, too much office space—for the amount of sales they have.

MBA LINGO

Business cycle is another term for the economic cycle, the pattern of periods of economic growth, or expansion, followed by periods of economic contraction, or recession. In a sluggish economy, there is growth but at rates too low to employ all new workers.

Their sales, what economists call demand, come from consumers (consumer demand), other businesses (business investment), and government spending (government demand). Consumer demand is funded by household income and consumer debt. Business demand is funded by business investment and spending, which comes from profits and loans. Government demand is funded by taxes and debt.

Here's what happens in a typical business cycle. During a recovery, things steam along nicely. Consumers are spending and demand is rising. To meet rising demand, businesses expand. They lease new space, buy new equipment, and hire new workers so they can increase their capacity and thus their production.

As long as consumers keep buying and businesses keep investing, the recovery continues. Yet, inevitably, demand eventually decreases. This can occur because consumers get to a point where they have enough goods and services, and cut back on spending. Or businesses may reach a point where they have enough capacity to produce what their customers need, so they cut back on investment. Or some event, such as a war or, in the case of the 2008–2009 recession, a financial crisis, can cause consumers, businesses, or both to cut spending and start saving.

When this happens, a downward trend begins. When consumers reduce their spending, businesses lay off workers and stop investing in new capacity. When businesses lay off workers, consumers have less money and reduce their spending. When consumers or businesses (or both) reduce their spending, the economy stops growing. If they reduce their spending enough, the result is a recession.

Yet eventually, consumers who had cut back decide they need new cars, clothes, and homes and start spending again. When they do, recovery begins and businesses start investing to meet this new demand—and the upward cycle begins again.

Booms and Busts

A boom occurs when demand increases sharply over a long period. A major upswing in demand, say, for technology products, can create a booming economy. Or a boom can be more specific. For example, a nationwide housing boom may be driven by a dramatic increase of adults in the population who are ready to become homeowners—or by artificially low interest rates.

A boom generally means good times for most people. But if a boom continues long enough, it can generate overexpansion by business or an increase in prices, known as inflation. If businesses overexpand, they wind up with overcapacity and too many employees. Then they cut their costs and lay off employees, who cut back their spending, too.

Again, if businesses and consumers cut their spending sharply enough for long enough, a recession begins. If economic conditions become bad enough, the result can be a bust, a prolonged recession, or both. (*Bust* is a slang term for a boom that ends abruptly.)

Economic Policy

In the United States (as in other nations), the government plays a big role in the economy because government spending is about 30 percent of the U.S. economy. However, that includes state government spending, and we're concerned mainly with federal government spending. States have their budgets to manage, but only the federal government can affect the whole economy through *economic policy*.

I don't detail the workings of fiscal and monetary policy here, but I do in *The Complete Idiot's Guide to the Great Recession* (Alpha Books, 2010) and in *The Complete Idiot's Guide to Economics* (Alpha Books, 2003).

MBA LINGO

Economic policy is the means by which the federal government stimulates or reins in economic growth. There are two kinds of economic policy: fiscal policy and monetary policy. *Fiscal policy* is the use of government spending and taxation to affect the economy. (The term *fiscal* refers to budgetary matters.) *Monetary policy* refers to measures aimed at affecting the amount of money in the economy. Governments use both fiscal and monetary policy to keep their economies growing. But these do represent two different schools of economic thought, and each school has its extremists.

Fiscal Policy: Taxing and Spending

Given both taxes and spending, the government has four tools of fiscal policy. It can raise or lower spending, and it can raise or lower taxes.

If the government raises spending, it will stimulate the economy. Why? Because it will increase total demand in the economy and contribute to growth. It is putting money in the pockets of businesses and consumers, who then spend it. Increasing government spending to encourage expansion is called *fiscal stimulus*. This is true whether the government spends money from taxes or borrows the money by issuing debt. If the government spends more than it collects in taxes, it is *deficit spending*.

MBA LINGO

An increase in government spending or a reduction in taxes that is aimed to ignite a recovery or encourage economic expansion is called **fiscal stimulus** because the increased government demand stimulates demand in the other sectors and thus the economy.

Deficit spending occurs when a city, state, or federal government spends more than it collects in taxes during a given period. Since the money spent during a deficit doesn't come from taxes, the government must borrow it, which it does by issuing bonds.

If the economy is overheating—that is, growing at an unsustainable pace—and inflation increases or might increase, the government can attempt to slow growth by doing the opposite. If the government cuts or postpones its spending, it decreases demand, and that slows the economy.

Taxes have similar effects. If the government wants to stimulate a sluggish economy, it can cut taxes instead of increasing spending. This leaves more money in the hands of consumers and businesses, which they tend to spend. On the other hand, if the government raises taxes, it takes money away from consumers and businesses. This slows economic growth.

Monetary Policy

An economy runs on money. The amount of money available therefore plays a role in the size of the economy. Monetary policy enables the government to affect the money supply and therefore the growth rate of the economy. Essentially, the faster the growth in the money supply, the faster the economy grows; likewise, the slower the growth in the money supply, the slower the economy grows.

Monetary policy works mainly through the mechanism of interest rates, which the government strongly influences. Low interest rates tend to increase the amount of funds that banks can lend and, thus, the supply of money in the economy. That tends to stimulate economic growth because businesses and consumers borrow money when rates are low. When they spend it, they increase demand and businesses expand.

High interest rates tend to decrease the growth of the money supply and thus the supply of loanable funds—and thus the growth in demand and economic growth.

The Federal Reserve

The Federal Reserve, or "the Fed," controls the U.S. money supply. The Federal Reserve System is the U.S. central bank. Think of a nation's central bank as a "bank for banks." The Fed replaces old currency with new currency, guarantees bank deposits, and governs the banking system. The Fed also conducts monetary policy.

I discuss the signals that help you judge the direction of monetary policy later in this chapter. In general, though, you need to keep in mind three points about the Fed and monetary policy:

1. The Fed can act without permission from the president or Congress, so monetary policy can be enacted more quickly than fiscal policy. Fiscal policy involves taxes and spending, which involve elected officials and voters, so it takes more time. This is not to say that the Fed is totally nonpolitical, but rather it is a lot less political and more economic in its policy decisions.

2. The Fed closely monitors the economy and regularly reports on economic developments. At times, the Fed may be a bit too rosy in its forecasts because it does not want to roil the financial markets, but it is still worthwhile to listen to the Fed's take on the economy.

3. Monetary policy cannot work miracles and force an economic recovery. That is especially the case when household or business debt is high or when interest rates are already low. In the 2008–2009 recession, household debt was high and rates were already low, so monetary policy could only do so much to stimulate economic growth. It wasn't enough to create conditions for rapid job growth.

Federal Reserve actions can create conditions that favor increased or reduced lending, business activity, and economic growth, but monetary policy cannot directly create demand. However, stimulative fiscal policy can create demand. If the government hires workers or purchases goods and services from businesses, it puts people to work, and that creates income and puts money in people's pockets. That stimulates demand and thus business activity.

Note that fiscal and monetary policy both have their limits in terms of effectiveness, and both have contributed to good times and bad times in the U.S. economy (and elsewhere). President Franklin D. Roosevelt used stimulative fiscal policy during the Great Depression of the 1930s, putting millions of people to work when business couldn't. However, from the 1970s through the early 2000s, except for some of the 1990s, deficit spending occurred even during expansions. This racked up hundreds of billions in debt when fiscal discipline would have left the nation better prepared to deal with the next severe downturn, which occurred in the late 2000s.

Fed Chairman Paul Volker used monetary policy to excellent effect in the early 1980s. He cranked up interest rates to record levels, which choked off inflation that had been undermining the economy. This, together with President Ronald Reagan's stimulative tax cuts, set the stage for the 1980s expansion.

Unfortunately, interest rates were kept relatively low for the next 25 years, even during expansions, which greatly expanded consumer debt and left U.S. households with little room to take on new borrowing after the 2008–2009 recession.

Understanding Economic Trends

To understand economic trends, you need to be able to understand and interpret economic data. However, you don't have to be an economist to do that.

Before I give you a tour of economic indicators, here are a few general hints about economic data in general:

Evaluate economic data critically. Economics is a social science, so the accuracy and predictability of economic data are lower than those of data in the physical sciences. Also, people often have agendas when they quote economic data and often cite only data that supports their opinions. But honest confusion can occur simply because of the complexity of the data and of the forces that produce it.

Understand the terms. Most economic data has technical definitions. For instance, the unemployment rate counts only people who have looked for work in the past four weeks, which omits many unemployed people. Fully grasping the definitions of terms can require detailed study. If you're curious, you can find the definitions at the sources, but the key is to understand that people can calculate data in various ways.

Always consider trends. Economic data can be inaccurate and bounce around from period to period. Often a single factor, such as a layoff at a large company or a leap in home prices in a single region, can alter a national value. Data from one month or quarter doesn't equal a trend. It's best to compare data from at least three periods (months, quarters, or years) to establish an upward or downward trend.

Distinguish causality from correlation. Just because two measures move in the same or in opposite directions at the same time and pace doesn't mean that one is causing the other. Causal links in economics can be hard to prove. For instance, interest rates and economic growth are well correlated, but causality is not guaranteed.

Go Directly to the Sources

Economic news is useful, but it can be better to consult the original sources of the data. These are the entities that compile and report the data, usually as news releases. Reports mainly repackage facts released by the sources, so why not go to the sources' websites?

I am not saying economic news in the media is unreliable. In fact, the media offer convenience because, at some sources' sites, getting the data you want can take some digging. Also, going to various sites for various data can be time consuming. Good sources for market indexes and general economic data and news are usually *The New York Times* and the *Wall Street Journal*. Just be aware that they, and other news outlets and commentators, are reporting and analyzing data developed by other sources.

Following are original sources you can go to for economic data and information.

Government Agencies

Bureau of Economic Analysis
1441 L Street, NW
Washington, DC 20230
Phone: 202-606-6900
www.bea.gov

Bureau of Labor Statistics
Postal Square Building, 2 Massachusetts Avenue, NE
Washington, DC 20212-0001
Phone: 202-691-5200
www.bls.gov

European Union
Delegation of the European Commission to the United States
2300 M Street, NW
Washington, DC 20037
Phone: 202-862-9500
Fax: 202-429-1766

Federal Reserve System
20th Street and Constitution Avenue, NW
Washington, DC 20551
Phone: 202-452-3000
www.federalreserve.gov

U.S. Agency for International Development (Information Center)
Ronald Reagan Building
Washington, DC 20523-1000
Phone: 202-712-4810
Fax: 202-216-3524
www.usaid.gov

U.S. Census Bureau
Postal address:
U.S. Census Bureau
Washington, DC 20233
Street address:
U.S. Census Bureau
4700 Silver Hill Road
Suitland, MD 20746
Phone: 301-495-4700
www.census.gov

U.S. Department of Commerce
1401 Constitution Avenue, NW
Washington, DC 20230
Phone: 202-482-2000
www.commerce.gov

U.S. Department of Labor
Frances Perkins Building
200 Constitution Avenue, NW
Washington, DC 20210
Phone: 1-866-487-2365 (1-866-4-USA-DOL)
www.dol.gov

United States Department of the Treasury
1500 Pennsylvania Avenue, NW
Washington, DC 20220
Phone: 202-622-2000
www.ustreas.gov

World Bank
1818 H Street, NW
Washington, DC 20433
Phone: 202-473-1000
Fax: 202-477-6391
www.worldbank.org

World Trade Organization
Centre William Rappard
Rue de Lausanne 154
CH-1211 Geneva 21
Switzerland
Phone: 41 (0)22 739 51 11
Fax: 41 (0)22 731 42 06
www.wto.org

Nonprofit

National Bureau of Economic Research, Inc.
1050 Massachusetts Avenue
Cambridge, MA 02138-5398
Phone: 617-868-3900
Fax: 617-868-2742
www.nber.org

Commercial and Investment Banks

A number of private, for-profit companies specialize in economic information and forecasting, notably IHS Global Insight and Moody's Economy.com. Also, many major banks have economists who interpret economic data and develop forecasts for management and for the bank's customers.

> **MBA MASTERY**
>
> You don't have to be a market geek to keep up on economic developments. Just listen to the business and economic news, and keep relating ongoing developments to the larger picture of the business cycle and economic policy goals—and to your business and career.

Do-It-Yourself Economic Watch

The Bureau of Economic Analysis (BEA) releases key economic data, including GDP growth, two or three months after a quarter. GDP growth (or the lack of it) is the key indicator of the health of the economy.

The BEA releases an advance estimate of GDP growth for a quarter about a month after the quarter ends, a second estimate about two months after it ends, and a third estimate three months after it ends. These estimates are subject to revision, which can be significant. The delays and estimated nature of the data reflect the difficulty of measuring the U.S. economy.

This section provides brief explanations of key indicators and cites the primary source for the data. Most of this data is widely reported soon after—usually the same day—it is released. Newspaper and media reports usually provide analysis regarding the causes and trends of the indicator.

Let's look at these indicators in more depth.

Economic Indicators

GDP growth measures the rate of expansion or contraction in the economy. It is reported on a monthly basis, but the quarterly releases are more accurate and the annual numbers still more accurate. As noted previously, this data is subject to revision. The long-term trend for U.S. GDP growth—and the rate traditionally targeted by the Federal Reserve and the federal government—is 3 percent annually, according to the BEA. If growth is under 2.5 percent, unemployment either persists at current rates or rises, so when growth is below that rate, expect fiscal or monetary stimulus. (Source: Bureau of Economic Analysis, www.bea.com)

The *unemployment rate* is widely reported, as is the number of jobs gained or lost. The target unemployment rate is about 4 percent, which basically accounts for people between jobs and laid-off workers who will soon find jobs. A U.S. unemployment rate above 6 percent causes concern, and a rate much above that causes serious concern. Also, the rate understates the number of unemployed because it omits people deemed to have stopped seeking employment. If unemployment is over 6 or 7 percent, expect fiscal or monetary stimulus. (Source: Bureau of Labor Statistics, www.bls.com)

Inflation is considered low if it is below 3 percent, which is where it has been over the past two decades. Inflation (and deflation) are measured by the consumer price index (CPI)—the usual reported inflation rate—and the producer price index (PPI)—which can be an indicator of inflation that will hit consumers later. If inflation rises to near or over 3 percent, expect the Fed to raise rates to try to slow the rate of economic growth and thus inflation. (Source: Bureau of Labor Statistics, www.bls.com)

Changes in interest rates indicate conditions in the credit markets and the direction of Fed policy. The most widely reported is the Fed funds rate, which is set by the Fed periodically. With reductions to interest rates, the Fed tries to stimulate lending, increase the money supply, and ignite or sustain growth. With interest-rate increases, the Fed tries to do the opposite. If the Fed leaves rates unchanged, it wants economic activity to continue on the current trajectory (or to improve). (Source: Federal Reserve System, www.federalreserve.gov)

The two main indicators of *consumer confidence* are the Conference Board's Consumer Confidence Index and the University of Michigan Consumer Confidence Index. These are "soft" indicators of consumers' optimism or pessimism, based on responses to survey questions about the economy and their finances. Each of these indicators is an index, in which the responses were compiled for a base year and then compared to that base year from month to month. Thus, it is important to watch for sustained increases or decreases in the indexes. (Sources: Conference Board, www.conference-board.org; and University of Michigan, www.sca.isr.umich.edu/main.php)

Housing starts measure economic growth and the potential for future growth, and so do new and existing home sales. This data also indicates the consumer's mood. A sustained rise in starts and sales generally indicates that expansion is underway. The national numbers on starts and sales can be misleading because home building and sales activity can be very local phenomena. Thus, the data for your state will probably tell you more than the data for the nation. Look for a rising (or falling) trend over three or more months. Total starts—the reported number—include single-family homes and multifamily dwellings, but you can find both at the source, along with discussions of regional patterns and forecasts. (Source: National Association of Homebuilders, www.nahb.org)

Monthly sales for retail and food services, issued by the Census Bureau (part of the U.S. Department of Commerce), are good measures of economic activity. Look at the month-to-month trends and year-over-year comparisons. This report breaks spending out into major categories, including motor vehicles, furniture, electronics, building materials, clothing, and other key areas so you can track spending on specific goods. (Source: Department of Commerce, Census Bureau; www.census.gov)

Vehicle sales are a good gauge of consumers' willingness to spend. Annual U.S. sales in the range of 13 million to 14 million can now be considered a good level (down from the peak of over 16 million in the 2000s). (Source: Motor Intelligence, www.motorintelligence.com)

Stock market averages—the Dow Jones Industrial Average, S&P 500, and NASDAQ (National Association of Securities Dealers Automatic Quotations)—indicate the mood of investors. Stock prices rise during expansions and fall during contractions, but by the time the market trend is established, the new economic growth trend is already in place. (Sources: Dow Jones, www.dowjones.com; and Bloomberg News, www.bloomberg.com)

Gold has long been viewed as a hedge against inflation and as the ultimate safe investment. The price of gold trended upward after 9/11 and with the bursting of the housing bubble and disorder in the financial markets in the late 2000s. In general, a rising trend in the price of gold indicates economic pessimism and a flight from securities; decreasing gold prices indicate economic optimism and movement of money into securities. (Sources: Dow Jones, www.dowjones.com; and Bloomberg News, www.bloomberg.com)

The Composite Index of Leading Indicators, generated by the Conference Board, is widely reported in the media and is at the Conference Board's website (www.conference-board.org). The website's monthly press release discusses the index and which of the individual indicators increased or decreased. As is the case for most indexes, this one is tied to a base year (1996, in this case) in which the value of the index is pegged at 100. These are called leading indicators because upward or downward movement in them—and in the index—occurs before movement in that direction in the economy (as measured by GDP growth). (Source: Conference Board, www.conference-board.org)

MBA ALERT

The Composite Index of Leading Indicators is not foolproof; indeed, there are no foolproof indicators of future economic performance. Even professional economic forecasters armed with sophisticated economic models have a very mixed record of success.

Watch the Data, but Think Long-Term

Although economists have a poor record of forecasting turning points in the business cycle, economic indicators provide a good picture of what's going on currently. The key, however, is to consider economic data and economic conditions, but not have them dictate your business or career strategy.

In other words, the economy is important, but other factors, such as your industry, your company's strategy and product line, and your skills and competitive advantages, will usually have more to do with your success or failure.

Yes, there are industries and companies that "fell out of bed" when the Great Recession hit, but a number of them, such as the mortgage origination and reselling business, had prospered way out of proportion to the economic value they were adding. Others, such as certain retailers (and the mortgage, housing, and housing-related industries), enjoyed boom times in the 1990s and 2000s, fueled mainly by debt. Those businesses were growing at unsustainable rates, and they should have known it.

The Least You Need to Know

- The economic cycle, or business cycle, is caused by mismatches in demand by consumers (and businesses) and in the capacity and output of businesses.

- When consumer and business demand falls, government tries to stimulate growth with fiscal policy (lower taxes, higher spending, or both) or monetary policy (lower interest rates to fuel lending activity). Most often the government tries both, although monetary policy requires less political consensus and is therefore easier to implement.

- Economic data is compiled and released by a number of sources, including the Federal Reserve, Bureau of Economic Analysis, and Bureau of Labor Statistics. The Conference Board, economic forecasting companies, and major banks also provide economic analysis and forecasts.

- GDP growth is the key economic indicator. The growth rate will rise and fall with the business cycle, but over the long term, GDP growth will average about 3 percent.

- The health of the economy is important, but it's just one consideration when you're making business decisions. Many industries and companies prosper in good times and in bad, and no business should depend on high economic growth (or high consumer debt) as its strategy for survival.

Getting Down to Business: Operations Management

In This Chapter

- The secrets of resource management
- Performing a cost-benefit analysis
- The difference between fixed and variable costs
- Understanding economies of scale
- Centralization versus decentralization

Managing a business operation calls for making dozens of decisions a day, some of them small, some large, some of them routine, and some extraordinary. For certain kinds of decisions—particularly those relating to the operations and resources of the business—analytical tools like the ones in this chapter will help you make the best decision.

Picture two people, each running a separate business. One is a trained manager; the other is not and operates by the seat of his pants. They are each going to face dozens of similar decisions every day. A supplier will call and ask how much he should deliver next week. The evening-shift supervisor will want to know if she should add another person to her team because it's getting busy after 7 P.M. A machine will break down and may have to be replaced or repaired, depending on which is more economical. Each business may need to add capacity, but the bosses must decide how much.

The trained manager will have ways of looking at these decisions that are unavailable to the guy who goes by his gut. He will have a more systematic and organized way of thinking about these situations than the other fellow. The trained manager has this more sophisticated view of business situations because he understands key concepts in operations management.

The concepts we examine in this chapter can make the difference between guesswork and a good decision.

Managing Your Resources

Many business decisions come down to figuring out how to allocate your resources, including money, labor, materials, and buildings and equipment. Every business operates with limited resources—a finite amount of money, labor, materials, and buildings—so the savvy manager must decide the best use of the resources he or she has.

Here are some tough calls a manager may have to make when it comes to allocating resources:

- How much money should a company invest in developing a new product?

- What is the best size for a business? How much staff and physical space is needed?

- How does a manager determine the best buys on expensive equipment (for example, computer networks, industrial ovens, or tractors)?

- When should a store open and close for business?

- How much time should a project take, and how should it be done?

- Given two or more potential locations to expand a business, which one should a company choose?

How do managers answer these questions? Since resources are limited, managers must put them where they will do the most good—that is, where they will earn the highest *return*, or profit.

MBA LINGO

Return, in this context, is the amount of profit the company earns. This can be expressed as a percentage. For example, if the owners have a total of $10 million invested in the company and the company has profits of $1 million for the year, then the return on investment is $1 million, or 10 percent.

Certain key concepts help managers determine the best ways to use resources to maximize returns:

- Cost-benefit analysis

- The law of diminishing returns

- Fixed costs and variable costs

- Economies of scale

- Centralization and decentralization

I cover each of these concepts in the following pages.

What's It Worth?

Everything in business—a piece of equipment, a facility, a campaign, an employee—has a cost associated with it. This cost is almost always measurable in dollars. Most things that have a cost also have an associated benefit. This benefit is usually (but not always) a return measurable in dollars.

You'll often hear a businessperson say, "You've got to spend money to make money." However, not every expenditure earns money. Among those that do, some earn more than others. Therefore, before spending money, most businesspeople do a *cost-benefit analysis*. There are various tools for conducting a cost-benefit analysis, and you'll learn about some of them, such as break-even analysis and crossover analysis, in Chapter 9.

MBA LINGO

Cost-benefit analysis is a way of measuring the benefits expected from a decision, measuring the costs expected to be incurred in the decision, and then seeing if the benefits exceed the costs. If they do, the analysis favors going ahead with the planned course of action.

For now, let's consider a small neighborhood copy shop. Like the owner of any business that serves the public, the guy running the copy shop has to figure out his hours of operation. He might consider several factors—for instance, the hours of his nearest competitor and the convenience of his largest customers. But his major concern is the cost versus the benefit of opening an hour earlier or closing an hour later.

Let's say that he long ago figured out that he has to open the shop at 7 A.M. because that's when people who are headed to work and school stop off on their way. However, he's been closing at 11 P.M. only because the previous owner did. He isn't sure the evening hours are worth it.

After sitting down with sales data from the past three months, he has the information he needs for a cost-benefit analysis. He knows the cost of staying open that last hour, and he knows the average amount of money he makes in that last hour.

He's figured out that it costs him $69 to stay open from 10 to 11 P.M. This includes the cost of electricity for the lights and equipment, the cost of heat, and the assistant manager's salary. If he closes at 10, he saves all this money.

In terms of the benefit, he's figured out the profit on the volume he does in that last hour. He makes an average profit of 5¢ a copy (this is based just on the cost of making the copy; it doesn't count the costs of electricity, heat, and labor). He makes an average of 1,460 copies in that last hour. Thus, he makes an average of $73 (1,460 copies times 5¢ per copy) in that last hour of operation. That's the "benefit."

Now the big question is, does the benefit outweigh the cost?

In this case, it does. If you take the benefit of $73 and subtract the cost of $69, you get $4. (This is also known as the *net benefit*—the benefit after deducting or "netting out" the costs.) So on a pure cost-benefit basis, it is worth it to keep the copy shop open that last hour.

MBA LINGO

The **net benefit** is the benefit after deducting (or "netting out") the costs.

Of course, other considerations may enter into the decision. For instance, if the assistant manager wants to start going home earlier or if late-evening crime is rising, the owner may decide that it's just not worth it to stay open the extra hour for $4. But on a pure cost-benefit basis, it is worth it.

There are various ways of doing cost-benefit analysis—even various ways of placing a dollar value on the costs and benefits. We explore some of them in this book. The key element at this point, however, is that a manager looks at most situations in terms of costs and benefits.

MBA MASTERY

Some people find it odd that a business or office manager will try to save a few cents on some small items (coffee, pens, office supplies) that the firm buys regularly. But in a high-volume operation, pennies add up. Cost control lowers costs, and lowering costs automatically increases the benefit.

What About Social Costs and Benefits?

Over the past 25 years, people have become more aware of the social costs and benefits generated by a business. Social costs are costs that are not directly borne by the company. Social benefits are positive effects that do not directly benefit the company. (Here, I am using "social costs" to include all environmental, health, safety, waste, and energy and other resource impacts. I examine these all more fully in Chapter 25, which covers corporate responsibility and *sustainability*.)

MBA LINGO

In the context of corporate responsibility and **sustainability,** the latter refers to business practices that make the opportunities that existing generations have for economic growth and overall well-being available to future generations. Ideally, sustainable practices have no negative impact on the environment and on future generations' opportunities for economic growth and overall well-being.

Environmental pollution is a social cost. The larger community bears the costs of pollution generated by manufacturing processes or inefficient vehicles. These costs take the form of illness, increased health-care costs, inconvenience to people confined to their homes on bad air days, and so on. The costs also include the expense of cleaning up a river or toxic waste site.

The trend has been for society, in the form of local, state, and federal legislation and the courts, to make social costs explicit and make businesses and their customers bear or defray those costs. This happens through legislation—for example, the establishment of the federal Superfund, which is financed by companies that contribute to environmental pollution to pay for the cleanup of specific sites, or taxes on industrial emissions. It also happens through liability lawsuits, such as those brought against tobacco companies by people with lung disease.

However, social costs can be difficult to assess and address in some cases. For instance, many communities have seen increased automobile traffic as a result of companies moving from cities to suburban office campuses. Even though public hearings on the matter are often held, little has been done to assess these costs and bill companies for them.

In part, that's because businesses also generate social benefits by creating jobs, paying taxes, and purchasing goods and services in a community or state. They also provide the social benefits of a minimum wage and reduced discrimination (although some companies have been forced to do so by law).

Again, Chapter 25 addresses the issue of corporate responsibility for health, safety, environmental and social impacts, and sustainability. Chapter 27 deals with the legal and ethical relationship between business and society. Social costs and benefits are mentioned here because it is useful to consider the potential for them as part of a cost-benefit analysis.

CASE IN POINT

Many businesses now see adopting sustainable practices as good business, not just good corporate citizenship. For example, furniture manufacturer Herman Miller has significantly reduced its water usage and emissions and solid waste in its processes—and thus its costs. Wal-Mart has demanded less packaging from the manufacturers of products that it carries, partly because consumers want less packaging. UPS eliminated left turns on most delivery routes to save fuel and reduce its costs.

Too Much of a Good Thing

The *law of diminishing returns* basically says you *can* have too much of a good thing. In other words, if you keep adding more resources to your company's existing resources, you will at first see an added return. But after a while, you'll see a falloff in the added return the resource brings.

MBA LINGO

The **law of diminishing returns** states that the marginal return—that is, the added return—produced by any resource will after a point decrease with each additional unit of that resource that is added.

Let's say our copy-shop owner decides to advertise—something he's never done. He wants to place ads in local newspapers and on the radio. The following chart shows what happens. At first, his sales increase rapidly as people hear about his shop and stop in for copies. Sales continue to increase, but each additional day or week of advertising will produce more sales at a reduced or diminished rate, hence the idea of diminishing returns. In other words, there is a limit on how many dollars of new sales additional advertising will add.

The law of diminishing returns pops up constantly. For example, in most situations requiring workers, you will get more work done, or get it done faster, with each worker that you add. Eventually, however, each added worker will add less additional production (unless you add more of another resource, such as machinery).

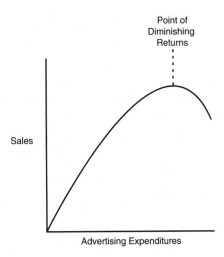

Diminishing returns are inevitable.

Estimating when returns will diminish can be tricky. There are no commonly used formulas or rules of thumb, because when the "law" will kick in depends upon the situation. For example, a logging operation selectively clearing a forest can keep adding new workers, and each added worker will at first be able to cut down more trees per day.

But at some point, an added worker is not going to be able to cut the same number of trees; there may be so many workers that they get in one another's way, or the trucks may not be able to haul away the logs fast enough, or some other factor will limit their productivity. In a sense, the only way to figure out when this will occur is by balancing your resources—for example, 2 loggers per saw, 10 loggers per truck—or through experience, or both.

Counting Costs

Most businesses have both *fixed costs* and *variable costs*. Fixed costs remain the same regardless of the amount of product the company makes and sells. For the copy shop, for example, the mortgage on the building and the cost of insurance are fixed. Some, but not all, fixed costs are considered *overhead* (costs not directly associated with production or sales).

Variable costs, on the other hand, change with the company's production and sales volume. For the copy shop, variable costs include the compensation of the copy clerks and the cost of copy paper and ink. One reason layoffs are common in troubled companies (and during recessions) is that, in most firms, labor represents the largest variable cost. (If the copy shop hits a drastic downturn in business, some of the clerks may be fired to save the owner money on their salaries.)

There's a saying in business: in the long run, all costs are variable. This means that, over a long enough period, the company can eliminate even a fixed cost; for example, the company can sell its factory or equipment. This is true, but the long run can be very long indeed, so it's wise to think of fixed costs as being fixed.

Some businesses, particularly in manufacturing, have inherently high fixed costs. Oil refining, automobile manufacturing, and printing are good examples. Other businesses, particularly service businesses, tend to have a high proportion of variable costs. Delivery services, temp agencies, and law firms fall into this category. Keep in mind, however, that almost every business has a mix of fixed and variable costs.

How Outsourcing Cuts Costs

One major way businesses have reduced costs is through *outsourcing*. Companies hire external suppliers to perform functions that used to be—or could be—performed within the company by employees. The goals of outsourcing are usually to …

- Reduce variable costs or keep them low by not hiring permanent employees to perform the work.

- Reduce fixed costs or keep them low by not purchasing or leasing the facilities and equipment needed to do the work.

- Gain flexibility, because it's easier to reduce the amount of work given to a supplier than it is to reduce staff, equipment, and facilities within the company.

- Improve quality and gain superior expertise, because the supplier is usually a specialist.

MBA LINGO

Outsourcing is hiring suppliers and vendors of services that have been or could be performed in-house. These can range from support functions such as accounting and customer service to core capabilities such as design and manufacturing.

In the past 30 years, U.S. manufacturers have outsourced millions of production jobs to less expensive foreign locations, particularly Mexico, South America, and Asia. In addition, companies in many different industries have outsourced millions of staff jobs. Some companies have been founded on an almost completely outsourced basis. Someone with an idea for a new shampoo can hire a company to formulate it, design the packaging, manufacture the shampoo, and get it distributed.

Then why doesn't every company operate that way? It's not that simple. For one thing, selling and distribution can be very difficult to outsource. Even customer service (as most of us know from personal experience) can be hard for a supplier outside a company to deliver at high quality. Intricate tasks calling for high employee motivation and tight managerial control are even harder to get right. Knowledge work can be particularly difficult to outsource, because it relies on intimate knowledge of the company's customer and ongoing collaboration.

Outsourcing works best with very structured tasks for which the specifications can be set and a process can be created and supported, preferably by computers, with minimal room for error. In fact, outsourcing customer service or support is not a particularly good idea unless you provide very clear instructions about when a customer with a nonroutine problem should be referred to an actual employee.

One other point: a lot of outsourcing has occurred in the form of employees being laid off and their jobs being outsourced to them, or to less expensive employees much like them. This can reduce costs, but it also reduces employee loyalty and shifts a lot of the risk associated with employment and economics from companies to workers—and perhaps ultimately onto society, in the form of social programs and slow or reduced demand during economic downturns.

When Is Outsourcing Right for You?

If you consider or actually undertake outsourcing, you need to answer four questions.

How critical is this function to the success of the company? If the activity is a core competency of the company and is essential to its success, outsourcing it might not be a good idea. If it's not essential, consider outsourcing.

What are the relative costs of keeping the function in-house and having a supplier do it? The costs of performing an activity in-house are usually clear. But be sure to consider the fully loaded costs of having a supplier do the work. These costs include any potential decrease in quality, time delays, poor communication, and negative effects on operations that remain in-house.

How good is the supplier you intend to outsource to? Thoroughly research any supplier that you will depend on for an important activity. Speak with current and, if possible, former customers in the same industry and size range as your company. Tour their facility and get to know them. Be sure you understand the ways they deliver their service, handle your activities, and make money.

What are the terms of the agreement with the supplier? Contracts with suppliers can be difficult to negotiate and manage, particularly for executives who lack experience in those areas. Be sure you understand the contract terms; the minimum, maximum, and likely costs; the types and frequency of reports; the quality of service or product you will receive; and the qualification of the people who will work on your account. Be sure the contract has an escape clause so that you can get out of it if certain conditions are not met, and be sure you have the right to audit records that pertain to the levels of activity you are purchasing.

Are we ready to outsource this and prepared to manage the relationship? Many managers see outsourcing as an easy solution to management and cost problems when in fact they have to actively manage the relationship. After a certain period of time, the supplier may develop bad habits, cut corners, or even start to enrich himself at your expense. You need not only the right to audit suppliers, but also the resources to hire an auditor to conduct the audit and to report back to you.

Outsourcing can be an effective way to reduce or control costs, but you have to handle it properly and not view it as a cost-free way of getting jobs done. As a manager, you must realize that you also must manage the suppliers to whom you outsource activities.

Size Matters: Economies of Scale

Economies of scale explain why many things are "cheaper by the dozen." Economies of scale make *volume discounts* possible because the average cost of making a unit of product decreases with each additional one you make. Economies of scale also make it possible for a supplier of, say, accounting, design, auto-fleet maintenance, or manufacturing services to perform the activity less expensively than a company that does not specialize in it.

Economies of scale occur as volume increases because fixed costs are spread out over more pieces, or units, of product. Each added unit absorbs a bit more of the fixed costs, and that lowers the amount of fixed costs that all the previous units must absorb. Thus, the average cost per unit falls. This occurs even though variable costs remain pretty much the same on each unit.

 MBA LINGO

Economies of scale refer to the lower costs that occur with higher production volumes. The cost per unit of manufacturing an item generally decreases as an operation makes more of them.

A **volume discount** occurs when you pay less per item the more you buy. Businesses give volume discounts to increase their sales. They take a lower profit on each item in order to make a greater total profit.

Let's go back to the copy shop example. Let's say the owner has a high-volume copier that costs $10,000 per year to lease. Let's also say that the variable costs, for paper and toner and so on, are 2¢ a copy.

Look at the difference in cost per copy at two levels of volume: 500,000 copies and 1,000,000 copies over the course of five years.

	500,000 Copies/Year	1,000,000 Copies/Year
Total variable costs (paper, toner)	$10,000	$20,000
Total fixed costs (annual copier lease)	$10,000	$10,000
Total cost of copies	$20,000	$30,000
Cost per copy	$0.04	$0.03

As you can see, although the fixed costs (the annual lease cost of the copier) and variable costs (the 2¢ cost per copy) are the same, the total cost per copy is lower at the higher volume.

Economies of scale mean that the more a company does something—that is, the greater the scale of its operation—the more economically it can do it. This can give a company a competitive advantage.

Consider this: in the copier example, the company that makes a million copies in a year could charge customers an average of 8¢ a copy and still make a profit of 5¢ a copy. The company doing half a million copies a year would have to charge customers 9¢ a copy in order to make a nickel a copy. The company with the higher volume could thus charge a lower price than the one with the lower volume. This could enable that company to pull in even more business and boost volume further.

CASE IN POINT

Many people decry the big commercial chains that dominate many businesses, but these megacompanies have been thriving for years. Long ago, chain businesses began to dominate markets like general retailing (Wal-Mart and CVS) and fast food (Pizza Hut and McDonald's). More recently, they've gone into, yes, photocopying (Sir Speedy and Kinko's).

Economies of scale often enable these operations to underprice local, single-site operators and ultimately make it impossible for the single-site shops to compete on price. They typically compete on selection and services.

Economies of scale are also the reason behind many corporate mergers. (A merger occurs when two companies combine their operations.) Most mergers consolidate certain functions to lower the costs of doing business. For example, the merged company does not need two accounting functions or two human resources departments. So they combine them into one (or just eliminate one) and then spread the fixed costs of the consolidated department over the larger, merged operation.

Come Together, Go Apart

Centralization and its opposite, *decentralization*, drive many business decisions. Centralization is an attempt to combine functions or operations. You centralize various functions by putting them together into one function. Often you seek economies of scale or some other form of efficiency.

Think of it this way: McDonald's is a huge franchise with thousands of separate restaurants all over the world. McDonald's could have each restaurant buy its own food, paper goods, and so on. However, by buying food and paper goods from one supplier—that is, by using a centralized purchasing function—McDonald's can give greater volume to suppliers and get volume discounts. Likewise, a magazine publisher such as Condé Nast, which puts out *Vogue*, *GQ*, and *Vanity Fair*, among others, can get better deals on paper and ink with centralized purchasing.

> **MBA LINGO**
>
> **Centralization** means placing a function or decision—such as buying office supplies, hiring workers, or pricing products—in one area for the entire company. This yields more control and more standardized decisions or results. **Decentralization** means allowing individual business units—for example, offices in various cities or countries—to handle functions and decisions independently. A middle ground is for headquarters to issue guidelines within which individual units can make their own decisions.

If you have all your buying done from one central function in the company, that increased scale gets you volume discounts. However, there are other reasons to centralize an operation. A major one is control. Having a centralized function, for purchasing or hiring, for example, provides greater control over costs or salaries than letting a bunch of smaller units make their own decisions. Centralization can also bring greater control over the quality of materials purchased or the qualifications of people hired.

The central function, whatever it is, should not meddle in decisions that it has left to the operating managers. It should either take care of those decisions completely for the smaller units or issue guidelines and let the operating managers make decisions within those guidelines. For example, purchasing can either deal with suppliers so individual operating managers don't have to, or it can issue a list of approved suppliers, supplies, and prices and let the operating managers decide how much of what they need and when.

How Much Centralization Is Good?

Managers repeatedly wonder how much centralization is good. As often occurs, where you stand depends on where you sit. Senior managers like centralization because it gives them greater control. Managers lower in the ranks prefer decentralization because they can make more decisions. They often feel positioned to make the best decisions because they're closer to customers and employees than "some guy back at headquarters." Plus, they need the authority to do their jobs.

A company has to balance the urges to centralize and decentralize. If decision-making authority is too centralized, people feel like automatons. They feel that they're not trusted to think. But if decision-making is too decentralized, there's a danger of lost control, particularly financial and quality control.

You'll See These Concepts, If You Look

The five key concepts discussed in this chapter come up often in business. Even when managers do not discuss them or refer to them directly, these notions underlie many business decisions.

A manager often makes decisions almost subconsciously based on one of these concepts. She may know that adding another worker would not be worth it, without actually thinking about diminishing returns or cost-benefit. Or she may squeeze more workers into the same space because she knows she can't buy a new facility and increase her fixed costs yet. A manager doesn't have to talk about economies of scale to understand volume discounts or group life insurance.

Nonetheless, understanding these business basics will help you know what's really at work in business decisions. They will also help you use the analytical tools we examine in the next chapter.

The Least You Need to Know

- A conscious or subconscious cost-benefit analysis underlies almost every decision a manager makes.
- Given societal trends, managers must consider the social costs (and benefits) of a decision, for business reasons as well as for ethical reasons.
- Every business faces both fixed and variable costs. Fixed costs do not change with the amount you produce and sell, but variable costs do.
- Economies of scale occur when a business produces high volume, which enables it to drive down the cost per unit. Economies of scale are the reason many large operations and chain stores are so successful.
- Be aware that the law of diminishing returns affects almost all new ventures or campaigns. When you first do something, you get a relatively high return, but over time, the return decreases.

Decisions, Decisions

In This Chapter

- The importance of break-even analysis
- Performing a crossover analysis
- Using planning and scheduling tools
- Making a decision tree
- Understanding basic business statistics

Having seen the concepts that can help you look at business situations like a pro, it's time to get hold of some tools that can help you in these situations. These analytical tools, as they are called, are structured ways of examining business situations and making managerial decisions. These tools all have one purpose: to help you make better decisions more easily.

Some of these tools, such as break-even analysis and crossover analysis, enable you to compare two or more choices in a standard manner. Others, such as planning and scheduling tools and decision trees, enable you to get the various parts of a complex problem "on the table" so you can see what you are dealing with. These tools are not a substitute for managerial decision making. Instead, they are designed to help managers in that process, and generally these tools do what they are designed to do.

This chapter also introduces you to basic business statistics. A course in statistics is required in most MBA programs because many managerial decisions in marketing, production, and finance are based on statistical information.

The Manager's Toolbox

Analytical tools have one purpose: to help you make better business decisions. We consider these four tools in this chapter:

- Break-even analysis

- Crossover analysis

- Planning and scheduling tools

- Decision trees

These tools apply to a wide variety of businesses and situations.

Break-Even Analysis

The break-even point for a product or service is the point at which the sales revenue equals the production costs. It is expressed in the number of units sold. Simply put, it is the point at which you start making money.

The importance of a break-even analysis is that when you are planning to offer a new product or service, you need to know how many sales you have to make to begin making a profit. Break-even analysis shows you that number of sales.

Calculate the break-even point with the following formula:

$$\text{Break-even units} = \frac{\text{Fixed costs}}{\text{Selling price} - \text{Variable cost per unit}}$$

Note that, to use this formula, you need to know both the fixed and variable costs of making the product or delivering the service (see Chapter 7).

Finding the Break-Even Point

Let's go back to the copy shop example used in Chapter 7. Remember that the shop uses a copy machine leased for $10,000 (which represents a fixed cost) and that paper, ink, and so on cost 2¢ a copy (which represents a variable cost). Let's say that the average copy sells for 8¢.

Plugging these figures into the formula gives us:

Break-even units = $10,000 ÷ ($0.08 – $0.02)

or

Break-even units = $10,000 ÷ $0.06

or

Break-even = 166,667 units

Another way of saying this is that the machine "pays for itself" after about 167,000 copies.

Break-even analysis helps in this decision because the manager can think about the volume he can expect to do in some period of time. Also, plugging other values into the formula shows what might happen in other circumstances.

For example, if the shop owner can lease a machine with total fixed costs of $5,000 per year, or 50 percent of $10,000, the break-even point will also fall by 50 percent, to about 83,000 units.

Break-even = $5,000 ÷ $0.06

or

Break-even = 83,333 units

Alternatively, if the business can raise the average price of a copy to 10¢, it can decrease the break-even point below 167,000 units even with fixed costs of $10,000.

Break-even units = $10,000 ÷ ($0.10 – $0.02)

or

Break-even units = $10,000 ÷ $0.08

or

Break-even = 125,000 units

You could also figure out the result of both raising the price to 10¢ a copy *and* lowering fixed costs to $5,000 (which lowers the break-even point to 62,500 units).

Break-even analysis is frequently used to make decisions about major purchases, investments, and leases involving plant and equipment. You consider the variables involved—aspects such as lease price, selling price, and variable costs—and then compare these from one machine to another. Of course, you also have to consider the machine itself, the volume it can handle, copy quality, and reliability. But financial aspects like the ones considered in break-even analysis are key to any decision.

MBA MASTERY

When you do break-even analysis, be sure to consider *all* fixed and variable costs. I've simplified the examples in this chapter for the sake of clarity, but you sometimes have to dig for all the information you need in order to factor every cost into the analysis.

You can plot the break-even point on a chart to help you visualize the break-even point, as well as the costs and profits, at various sales volumes. This chart doesn't precisely reveal costs and profits, but it does portray the relationship between them at various volumes.

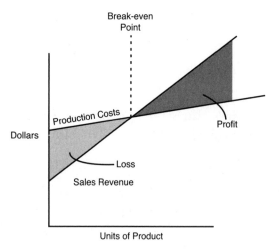

The break-even point.

The chart also implies that anything you do to shift the break-even point to the left—for instance, lowering your fixed or variable costs or raising your price—will get you into profits sooner. Conversely, anything that shifts the break-even point to the right will delay your profits.

Crossover Analysis

As a manager, you sometimes face the option of buying one of two comparable pieces of equipment. Usually each has its own set of fixed and variable costs. The question is, which machine should you buy?

Suppose that you're still the copy shop owner from our example in Chapter 7 and that you can buy one of two copiers. Machine 1 has fixed costs of $10,000 and variable costs of 2¢ a copy. Machine 2 has fixed costs of $5,000 and variable costs of 4¢ a copy.

Which machine you buy depends mostly on the volume of copies you expect to do. So the first thing to do is figure out the crossover point—that is, the unit volume at which the cost of the two machines is equal. *Crossover analysis* identifies that point.

 MBA LINGO

Crossover analysis enables you to identify the point at which you should switch from one product or service to another one that delivers similar general benefits but has different fixed and variable costs.

Here's the formula:

Crossover units = (Machine 2's fixed costs – Machine 1's fixed costs) ÷ (Machine 1's variable costs – Machine 2's variable costs)

Crossover units = ($5,000 – $10,000) ÷ ($0.02 – $0.04)

Crossover units = (–$5,000) ÷ (–$0.02)

Crossover units = 250,000 copies

At 250,000 copies (per year), the total cost of each of the two machines is equal. Above and below that volume, one machine is preferable to the other. To find out which one, calculate the cost of each machine at a unit volume just below the crossover point and just above that point. For instance, at 240,000 copies, the cost of each machine is as follows:

Machine 1	(240,000 × $0.02) + $10,000 = $14,800
Machine 2	(240,000 × $0.04) + $5,000 = $14,600

These two calculations tell us that Machine 2 is the cheaper one, at 240,000 copies.

At 260,000 units, the cost of each machine is as follows:

| Machine 1 | $(260,000 \times \$0.02) + \$10,000 = \$15,200$ |
| Machine 2 | $(260,000 \times \$0.04) + \$5,000 = \$15,400$ |

These two calculations tell us that Machine 1 is the cheaper one, at 260,000 copies.

So we see that Machine 2—the one with the lower fixed costs—is preferable below the crossover point, and Machine 1 is preferable above that volume.

Again, which machine should you buy? It depends on the volume you expect. If the volume will be above 250,000 units, you should purchase Machine 1. If the volume will be lower, you should purchase Machine 2.

Of course, this assumes that you can forecast the volume with some accuracy. Also, as with break-even analysis, these calculations ignore any differences in copy quality, speed, reliability, and so forth.

Planning and Scheduling Tools

Project management—planning, launching, and controlling a project—requires special tools, ones somewhat different from those needed when managing an ongoing operation. A project has a beginning, a middle, and an end. The project manager must plan and coordinate numerous activities, and keep them on track so that the project achieves its goal on time and on budget. In the following sections, I show you how you can best manage projects.

The Critical Path to Project Management

The Critical Path Method, or CPM, is a visual tool that helps you plan and control the tasks and activities in a project. CPM was developed by the chemical giant DuPont in the late 1950s for managing large projects, such as constructing huge production facilities.

Let's say you are planning to open a restaurant and have identified the following major tasks as the key ones in the project:

Task Code	Task Description	Predecessors	Time (Weeks)
A	Find location	None	6
B	Negotiate lease	A	2
C	Do renovations	A, B	8
D	Hire chef	None	8
E	Purchase fixtures	A, B	2
F	Plan menu	D	2
G	Hire and train crew	D, F	8
H	Install and test fixtures	A, B, F	4
I	Conduct a dry run	All	1
		Total time	41

Notice that, in addition to identifying the tasks, you must put them in order. You must identify predecessor tasks—that is, tasks that must be completed before others can begin. You must estimate the time each task will consume.

Notice also that the nine tasks in our restaurant example are not exhaustive. For simplicity, I've left out advertising, food purchasing, and so on.

Getting the Picture

The first step in CPM analysis is to chart the tasks visually so that you can see the relationships among them.

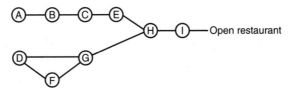

When you see the relationships, you realize that you can do certain tasks concurrently. In this example, you might think of the project as having two tracks: a Facilities Track and a Food Track. The Facilities Track (Tasks A, B, C, and E) involves getting the restaurant space ready. The Food Track (Tasks D, F, and G) involves hiring the chef and crew and getting the menu squared away.

CPM helps you see how to "collapse" the project and get it finished in less elapsed time than the total project will require. Here's how to set it up with estimated times included:

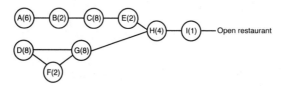

The longest path through the project is called the *critical path*. In our example, that path extends from point A to point I, and it will take a total of 23 weeks. This means that the total elapsed time of the project will be 23 weeks, even though the total project time is 41 weeks. That's because the Facilities Track will take 18 weeks, but the 16-week Food Track can be completed concurrently.

Note that the Food Track itself can be collapsed from 18 weeks to 16 weeks by planning the menu with the chef while also hiring the crew. This does not improve the total elapsed time, but there is no reason not to get whatever you can done in the most efficient way possible. After all, in business, Murphy's Law is always in operation.

MBA MASTERY

If you'd like to explore project-management software, you can find planning tools such as Critical Path Method in project-planning software packages like Microsoft Project.

Getting PERT

PERT, which stands for *Program Evaluation and Review Technique*, resembles the Critical Path Method. PERT was developed by the U.S. Navy and the Lockheed Corporation for the Polaris missile system project in the late 1950s.

MBA LINGO

Program Evaluation and Review Technique (PERT) is a project-management system that allows you to make an optimistic, pessimistic, and "best guess" estimate of the time it will take to complete a project. This system then lets you incorporate these three estimates into a unified analysis.

The major difference between PERT and CPM is that PERT enables you to make an optimistic, pessimistic, and "best guess" estimate of the time it will take to complete each task and the entire project. Then you calculate a weighted average by assigning a value of 1 to the pessimistic and optimistic estimates, and a value of 4 to the best guess. Then you plug the values into the following formula:

Estimated time = (Optimistic × 1) + (Best guess × 4) + (Pessimistic × 1) ÷ 6

(You divide by 6 because 1 + 4 + 1 = 6, and you are calculating a weighted average of the time estimates.)

Let's say that the best guess estimate of a task's duration is 10 weeks, the pessimistic estimate is 14 weeks, and the optimistic estimate is 8 weeks. The PERT formula calculates the estimated time as follows:

$$\text{Estimated time} = \frac{8 + (10 \times 4) + 14}{6}$$

Estimated time = 62 ÷ 6

Estimated time = 10.3 weeks

I am showing you a simplified version of PERT. The actual system can incorporate very sophisticated statistical techniques.

For your planning purposes, the real value of PERT is the idea of coming up with the optimistic and pessimistic estimates, and then seeing which way any deviation from the best guess is likely to go. In this case, since 10.3 is greater than 10 (the "best guess"), if you vary from the best guess, it is likely to be in the pessimistic direction.

In my own version of PERT, I figure pessimistic estimates for the large tasks that I can't directly control. When telling senior management about a project, I give them only the pessimistic estimates for these tasks (and thus the project) and pretend they're best guesses.

On a product-development project with a major company, I brought the project in eight weeks late from the best guess (due to "programming problems" beyond my control). But it was only two weeks late from the pessimistic estimate, which was the only one I gave management. And I had *doubled* the programming time estimate that Management Information Systems had given me!

Decision Trees: More Visual Aids

A *decision tree* is another visual tool to help you in decision making. Like PERT, a decision tree includes the element of probability by allowing three estimates.

MBA LINGO

A **decision tree** enables you to graphically illustrate potential decisions (or "scenarios") and the potential outcomes of these decisions. Essentially, this is a visual aid to decision making that incorporates probabilities.

Let's say that our copy shop owner has an opportunity to expand to the west side of his own city or into the next city. Of course, he also could choose not to expand at all.

He estimates his profits over the next five years at each of the two locations to be as follows:

Estimate	West Side	Next City
Optimistic	$6 million	$5 million
Best guess	$3 million	$4 million
Pessimistic	$2 million	$2 million

For both locations, he has a 60 percent likelihood that the best guess will occur and a 20 percent likelihood that either the optimistic or pessimistic estimate will occur.

Therefore, the decision tree looks like the following figure.

The decision tree lets you visually consider choices and risk. Putting probabilities on the estimates forces you to think carefully about what might really happen. When viewing an opportunity, it's easy for many of us to get carried away with optimism, so it's good to incorporate a pessimistic estimate into the analysis. The decision tree is one way of doing that.

Back to our example, what should our copy shop owner do? If he based his choice strictly on the decision tree, he should choose the alternative with the highest "expected value." In our example, that means he would choose to expand into the next city. The expected value of that choice is $3.8 million, while that of expanding to the west side is $3.4 million.

In actual practice, of course, he would use the decision tree as simply one more tool in his analysis. That's also what I hope you'll do.

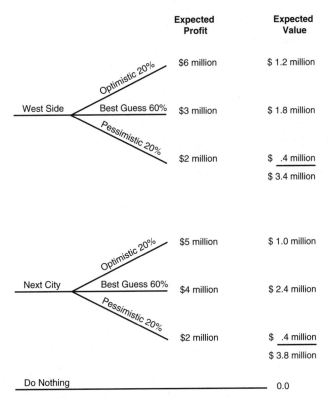

	Expected Profit	Expected Value
Optimistic 20%	$6 million	$ 1.2 million
West Side — Best Guess 60%	$3 million	$ 1.8 million
Pessimistic 20%	$2 million	$ .4 million
		$ 3.4 million
Optimistic 20%	$5 million	$ 1.0 million
Next City — Best Guess 60%	$4 million	$ 2.4 million
Pessimistic 20%	$2 million	$ .4 million
		$ 3.8 million
Do Nothing		0.0

A single decision tree.

Statistics for Business Decisions

The term *statistics* refers both to numerical data and to the discipline of analyzing numerical data. When data are analyzed, they can help you make decisions.

However, statistics can also be misused and misunderstood when managers pick and choose data that supports only their own point of view or slant an analysis to prove their point. As a manager, you must know when this is happening and know the right questions to ask so you can see the whole picture. You must also know how to conduct honest analysis of honest numbers so you don't fool anyone, including yourself. This knowledge comes with an understanding of basic statistics.

Suppose that a company conducted a survey of 50 former customers to learn why they had taken their business elsewhere. If the survey was well constructed and the responses were properly analyzed, the company's managers would know why those customers left. More important, they could infer that other former customers probably left for similar reasons. Then—and this is the reason for the whole project—management could decide which changes they needed to make to keep customers happy. (We look at the elements of good surveys in Chapter 18.)

Statistical analysis is used in science, health care, public policy, and many other fields. In business, it is used most often in marketing, finance, economics, and quality control.

Key concepts in statistics include these:

- Frequency distributions
- Measures of central tendency
- Measures of dispersion

Let's examine each of these concepts.

MBA MASTERY

Most quality-control methods, which I discuss in Chapter 10, attempt to minimize variability in a production or service delivery process. In other words, if a part is supposed to be a certain size or its performance is supposed to be at a certain level, quality-control methods aim to minimize variations from those targets. Quality control uses various methods to discover and minimize or eliminate causes of variation.

Frequency Distributions

A frequency distribution tells you how many times (that is, how frequently) a certain value occurs in an array of values. For example, here is a frequency distribution of the weight of 100 dressed chickens, to the nearest quarter pound, being shipped by a commercial poultry farm:

Weight	Quantity
3.00	3
3.25	8
3.50	10
3.75	16
4.00	28

Weight	Quantity
4.25	15
4.50	11
4.75	6
5.00	3

This frequency distribution tells us how many chickens were in each weight bracket. It shows the frequency of each weight (for instance, 16 chickens weighed 3.75 pounds) and shows how the frequencies were distributed.

Frequency distributions can also compile *classes* of *values*, expressed in ranges. The following is a frequency distribution for the amount spent per customer in a four-hour period in a supermarket:

Amount Spent	Number of Customers
Less than $20	18
$20–$39.99	18
$40–$59.99	44
$60–$79.99	23
$80–$99.99	11
$100 and over	33

MBA LINGO

A **value,** also called an observation, is a single, numerical instance of whatever is being measured. A **class** groups values into a range so they can be more easily handled and understood.

Classes are very useful for grouping values so that they are more manageable and easier to analyze, as shown by the six classes in the preceding table of customers' expenditures.

Displaying Distributions

It is often useful in business to display this kind of information in charts. The most commonly used are bar charts, histograms, and line charts. Charts are constantly used in business meetings and presentations to summarize and communicate numerical data.

A bar chart is useful for comparing values. The following chart depicts the weights of the chickens in the frequency distribution example:

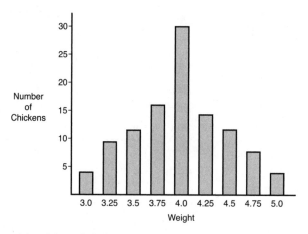

Bar chart: weight of dressed chickens.

Histograms are like bar charts, except that they depict classes of values rather than a single value. Following is a histogram of the amounts spent per shopper in the previous supermarket example.

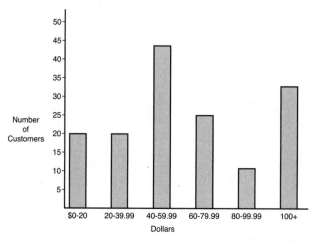

Histogram: amount spent by supermarket customers.

A line chart is best for showing the relationship between two types of data—for example, time and sales. The following line chart shows a company's annual sales for the years 2003 through 2010.

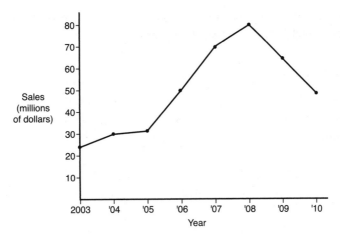

Line chart: annual sales 2003–2010.

Measures of Central Tendency

Measures of central tendency attempt to capture a set of values in a single statistic. The term *central tendency* means that the values tend to cluster around a central value. In any given situation, the values may or may not tend to cluster around a central value. But the measures of central tendency can still be calculated and compared. As you will see, in comparing them, you can learn a bit about how much the values tend to cluster.

The three key measures of central tendency are the mean, the median, and the mode.

The Mean

The mean is just a fancy word for the average. It is calculated by adding up each value and dividing by the number of values. For example, here are the hourly salaries of five consultants on a project:

Joe	$32
Helen	$40
Jim	$29
Stan	$46
Lee	$58
Total	$205

To calculate the mean, you add the values and divide by the number of consultants. In this case, the mean hourly salary is $41 ($205 ÷ 5).

Weighted Average

The weighted average accounts for the frequency of a value in a distribution. For instance, the weighted average of the 100 chickens in the previous example is calculated as follows:

3.00 × 3 =	9.00
3.25 × 8 =	26.00
3.50 × 10 =	35.00
3.75 × 16 =	60.00
4.00 × 28 =	112.00
4.25 × 15 =	63.75
4.50 × 11 =	49.50
4.75 × 6 =	28.50
5.00 × 3 =	15.00
	398.75 ÷ 100 = 3.9875

For practical purposes, the weighted average of the chickens can be rounded to 4 pounds.

The weighted average finds wide application in business. For instance, take our five consultants and put them on a project. Management estimates that it will take a total of 315 man-hours to complete the project, but each consultant will work a different number of hours on it. If you wanted to know the average hourly salary the consulting firm (not the client) will be paying the consultants on the project, you would use the weighted average.

Consultant	Hourly Wage	×	Estimated Total Hours on Project	=	Total Wages
Joe	$32		90		$2,880
Helen	$40		55		$2,200
Jim	$29		115		$3,335
Stan	$46		35		$1,610
Lee	$58		20		$1,160
			315		$11,185

The weighted average hourly salary on the project then is $35.50 ($11,185 ÷ 315).

Here the weighted average accounts for employees at different wage levels spending different amounts of time on the project. How could this information help the managers of the consulting firm make a decision?

CASE IN POINT

Most service firms, including consulting and legal practices, bill out their professional employees at some multiple of their hourly salaries. For most firms, that multiple is about four or five. In our example, we have a 315-hour project with a weighted-average hourly salary of $35.50. Thus, using the multiples of four and five, the price charged to the client for this project should range from $44,730 ($35.50 × 315 × 4) to $55,912 ($35.50 × 315 × 5).

First, in quoting a price to the client for the project, the managers of the consulting firm need to know two things: the number of hours the job will take and their cost per hour. The weighted average of the salaries of the consultants on the project is the cost per hour.

Second, the weighted average will help the managers adjust the human resources dedicated to the project before or during the project. In other words, if they add a consultant to the project who makes more than $35.50 per hour, they'll raise the hourly cost of the project. But if they add a consultant making less than $35.50, they'll lower their costs. If they raise their costs, they reduce the project's profitability. If they lower their costs, they increase the profitability.

Note that putting the lowest-paid employees on a client project is not always the best way to cut your costs. For some tasks, highly paid employees are more efficient and can complete the job in less time (and get it right the first time).

The Median

The median is the value in the center of an array. An array is an arrangement of values in their numerical order, either from highest to lowest (descending order) or from lowest to highest (ascending order). For example, if we arrange the hourly salaries of our five consultants in descending order, we find that $40, Helen's salary, falls in the center. That $40 is the median.

Lee	$58
Stan	$46
Helen	$40
Joe	$32
Jim	$29

In other words, half the values in an array fall above the median and half fall below the median. For instance, in an array of 15 values, the median is the eighth value. Seven values are above the eighth one and seven values are below it.

The median is an actual value only when there is an odd number of values in the array. If the array has an even number of values—six, for instance—the median position must be calculated by adding one to the number of values in the array and dividing the result by two.

For example, the median position in an array of six values would be 3.5 ([6 + 1] ÷ 2).

If the median position is 3.5, what is the median value? It is the average of the third and fourth values in the array (because 3.5 falls between the third and fourth values). Let's add a sixth consultant—Diane, who is a junior partner earning $95 an hour—to our team of five in the preceding example and calculate the median.

Diane	$95
Lee	$58
Stan	$46
Helen	$40
Joe	$32
Jim	$29

The median position is 3.5 in this array of six values. The third and fourth values are $46 and $40. So the calculated median is $43 ([$40 + $46] ÷ 2).

This means that half the salaries are above $43 and half are below $43, which you can see by looking at the array.

Note that, compared with the mean, the median is less affected by extreme values (known as outlying values) in an array. The mean of the six salaries, thanks to Diane, is $50 ($300 [the total of all six salaries] ÷ 6). But four people out of the six are earning under $50 per hour, and two of them, Joe and Jim, are earning well below that amount. Thus, in this case, the median is the better measure of central tendency.

The Mode

The mode is merely the observation in a data set that occurs most often. For example, in our example of the weights of the chickens, the mode equals 4 pounds because it occurs most often (28 chickens weigh 4 pounds).

Not every set of data has a mode. If no one value occurs more often than the others, there is no mode.

In practice, the mean, median, and mode are best viewed in the context of a measure of variability.

Measures of Variability

Two measures of variability are used most often in business. Here, *variability* refers to how much the values vary around the measure of central tendency. One measure of variability—the range—is quite simple. The other—the standard deviation from the mean—is rather complex, but it's presented simply here.

The Range

The range is represented by two values: the lowest in the array and the highest in the array. If possible, always consider the range along with one or two measures of central tendency. For example, let's look at the hourly salary ranges of our two groups of consultants, along with the mean and median for each group.

Case A (five consultants):   Range = $29–$58

Mean = $41

Median = $40

Case B (six consultants):   Range = $29–$95

Mean = $50

(Calculated) Median = $43

In Case A, the range is more tightly distributed around the mean and the median. At $41 and $40, the mean and the median are almost identical, and they both fall almost at the halfway mark between $29 and $58, which is $43.50).

In Case B, the range is more widely distributed around the mean and the median. At $50 and $43, the mean and the median differ significantly. The mean is higher than the median, which means that an outlying value is pulling it up. That value, of course, is Diane's $95-per-hour salary, as the range indicates.

Thus, we see that measures of central tendency and variability are best viewed together. Of course, it's not really necessary when you have only five or six values to keep track of, as used here to keep things simple. However, in business, these kinds of statistics can represent hundreds or thousands of values, and you need good measures to summarize that much information.

MBA ALERT

As Mark Twain famously said, there are lies, damn lies, and statistics. It's also been said that statistics will tell you that a man with one foot in a bucket of freezing water and the other in a bucket of steaming water will, on average, be comfortable. Clearly, we must view statistics critically and understand exactly what they are—and aren't—saying.

The Standard Deviation from the Mean

The standard deviation from the mean is just what it sounds like: a standard measure of how far the values in a set deviate from the mean. The underlying idea behind the standard deviation from the mean is the central limit theorem.

Stick with me here. The central limit theorem states that the mean of a sample drawn from a larger population will approach a normal distribution as the size of the sample becomes larger. In fact, a sample as small as 30 will begin to approach a normal distribution. What, you may be asking, is a normal distribution?

This is a normal distribution:

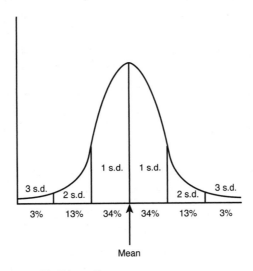

A normal distribution ("bell curve").

A normal distribution is one in which the values are distributed as follows:

- 34 percent fall within one standard deviation above the mean
- 34 percent fall within one standard deviation below the mean
- 13 percent fall between one and two standard deviations above the mean
- 13 percent fall between one and two standard deviations below the mean
- 3 percent fall beyond two standard deviations above the mean
- 3 percent fall beyond two standard deviations below the mean

The standard deviation is an amount calculated from the values in the sample. You can find the formula in any introductory book on statistics. But everyone who calculates standard deviations does so with software or a calculator.

The standard deviation from the mean for our 100 chickens would be about 6 ounces. (Take my word for it.) You may recall that the mean weight was 4 pounds. Thus, the farmer can say with some certainty that 68 percent of the dressed chickens he ships weigh 4 pounds, plus or minus 6 ounces. He can also say that 94 percent of the dressed chickens weigh 4 pounds, plus or minus 12 ounces. Only 3 percent weigh less than 3 pounds, 4 ounces, and only 3 percent weigh more than 4 pounds, 12 ounces.

Think of what this means for quality control. For instance, the farmer may not want to ship any birds weighing 3 pounds, 4 ounces or less. That means that those underweight chickens must be identified (before they are killed) and permitted to grow a bit heavier. The farmer will need a procedure for identifying these birds—or he will have to discard 3 percent of his chickens, which he certainly wouldn't want to do.

Here's what you need to know about the standard deviation and the normal distribution:

- The normal distribution applies to many characteristics found in nature, such as the weight of chickens, the width of rose petals, and inches of daily rainfall in a region. That is, when you calculate the mean and the standard deviation from the mean for the weights or widths or inches of rainfall, 34 percent of the values will be within one standard deviation above the mean, 13 percent will be between one and two standard deviations above the mean, and so on.

- By definition, 68 percent of observations will fall within one standard deviation above or below the mean, and 94 percent will fall within two standard deviations above or below the mean.

- This implies that the top or bottom 3 percent in any given sample or population are quite exceptional—exceptionally wealthy or poor, short or tall, likely to be watching television or unlikely to be watching it.

- The normal distribution has predictive value. For instance, the farmer knows that if he weighs a randomly chosen dressed bird, there is a 68 percent chance that it will weigh 4 pounds plus or minus 6 ounces. Therefore, if he pulled a sample of, say, 30 chickens and found that most of them weighed about 3½ pounds, he would want to check the birdfeed situation. After all, there's only a 13 percent chance that a bird will weigh that amount.

Statistics underlie many management decisions, which often depend on the validity of information and the probability of an outcome. Moreover, statistics are often bandied about in meetings and the media. Therefore, a grounding in basic statistics will help you develop better information and make better decisions—and keep you from getting snowed in meetings or by the media.

Use As Many As You Can

In this chapter, I've given you some MBA-style analytical tools. There are many more of these tools, but these are the most useful of the bunch.

These tools are here to give you an edge. So use all the tools that you can, because the risk of making a wrong decision is often greater than you think. Remember, though, that analytical tools and statistics are not magical: they are only ways to develop information and communicate about plans and decisions. In almost all situations, you have to decide based on what the tools and statistics tell you *and* on other considerations that they simply cannot incorporate into the analysis.

The Least You Need to Know

- Analytical tools are structured ways of examining business situations, and they help you make better decisions more easily.
- Break-even analysis tells you how many units of something you must sell in order to start making a profit.
- Crossover analysis helps you decide which of two competing prices of equipment you should buy or lease, depending on the amount of use the machine will get.
- Visual tools, such as the Critical Path Method and decision trees, can help you "see" solutions because they help you see the parts of the problem and your choices.
- Statistical information underlies many business decisions, and the better a manager understands that information, the better his or her decisions will be.

Budget Basics

In This Chapter

- Understanding budgets and variance reports
- The importance of staying on budget
- How to cut costs quickly
- The basics of credit management

Nearly every business decision must be considered in light of how it affects the budget. The budget itself is the result of management decisions regarding priorities, trade-offs, and the needs of the business. Future decisions that depart from those reflected in the budget must be made carefully and with sound justification. Also, problems may arise when a department deviates from its budget. In these situations, a manager has to understand budgets, variances from the budget, and cost control.

This chapter shows you how to understand a sales or expense budget and variance report. It also covers key steps in cost control and the basics of credit management.

What Are Budgets and Why Do You Need Them?

A budget is a financial plan and a means of control. A budget serves these planning and control functions in three ways.

First, the budget helps management allocate the company's resources. As you know from Chapter 8, some of a senior manager's key decisions concern resource allocation. Those resources are represented by expenses. In the *budgeting process*, management decides how much to spend on which resources.

> **MBA LINGO**
>
> The **budgeting process** occurs annually and creates the budget for the coming year.

Then management "works up the numbers" by adjusting last year's budgets upward or downward in light of the current economy, the goals for the year ahead, and the needs of the departments and the company. This is a balancing act in which nobody gets everything they want, but (hopefully) everyone gets what they need.

Second, managers at most levels have some budget authority. This authority may be given in various ways. One way is to allow managers to spend whatever amounts they feel are right, as long as they don't exceed their budget for that item. Another way is to give a manager "signing authority," which lets him or her authorize individual payments up to a certain amount, such as $500, $1,000, $5,000, or more. For control, most companies combine the two, allowing a manager to authorize payments up to a certain amount but requiring him or her to stay within an overall budget.

Third, if a manager feels it is necessary to exceed his or her signing authority or budget, he or she must get additional authorization to do so. This means that the manager above him or her must authorize the payment or the budget overrun.

Types of Budgets

A sizable business will have two broad categories of budgets: a capital budget and an operating budget. A capital budget governs significant expenditures on plant and equipment. This productive equipment will last for more than a year and therefore represents a long-term investment. These types of expenditures are often referred to as *capital* expenditures.

> **MBA LINGO**
>
> **Capital** is another term for plant and equipment. Money budgeted or spent on plant and equipment is called a capital expenditure, and a capital budget guides managers making capital expenditures. (And, yes, the word *capital* also means money to finance a business.)

In contrast, an operating budget covers the company's normal day-to-day operations and expenditures. The operating budget typically includes wages and salaries, materials and supplies, rent or lease payments, and so on.

Other types of budgets include budgets for special projects, meaning efforts that are neither capital expenditures nor part of normal operations. For instance, a business that must defend itself in a major lawsuit would allocate money to a legal defense budget. You will also hear about budgets that are actually subsets of the capital budget, such as the construction budget, or of the operating budget, such as the advertising budget or the travel budget.

However, our examination of budgets focuses on the two essential types of operating budgets: sales budgets and expense budgets. The sales budget sets forth the amount of revenue the sales force is committed to bringing in. Expense budgets apply to all areas that incur expenses (including the sales department).

Unfortunately, as often happens with plans, budgets do not always work out as originally foreseen. In other words, there is often a *variance* from the budget.

MBA LINGO

A **variance** is any deviation from the number originally planned for an item in the budget.

Sales Budgets and Variance Reports

In most companies, the sales budget represents a motivational tool, as well as a planning tool. During the budgeting process, the CEO goes to the sales manager and says something like, "Jim, we're looking to grow the bottom line by 15 percent next year. Can we count on you folks in sales to increase the top line by that amount?"

Now, if Jim says, "No," he's not being a team player. But if he just says, "Sure!" without really thinking about it, he's committing his people to growing sales by 15 percent. That might make sense sometimes, but other times it would be professional suicide.

So even though management always wants sales to increase, that could be hard to achieve for many reasons, including competitive products, good salespeople leaving for better jobs, and new taxes or regulations that hurt your product. So some back-and-forth about the sales budget takes place before management and sales agree on the numbers. Even then, variances will occur.

A Sample Sales Budget and Variance Report

Here's an example of a sales budget and variance report, usually just called a variance report. Incidentally, in these budgets and variance reports, a slash (/) means "or," since it gives this variance as both an amount and a percentage.

Acme Corporation—Office Products Division

Sales Budget Versus Actual, Six Months Ended June 30 (in Thousands of Dollars)

	June Actual	June Budget	June Variance $/%	YTD Actual	YTD Budget	YTD Variance $/%
Northeast	180	240	(60/25%)	1,530	1,800	(270/15%)
Southeast	160	160	0/0	1,140	1,200	(60/5%)
Central	180	200	(20/10%)	1,110	1,500	(390/26%)
West	220	200	20/10%	1,620	1,500	120/8%
Total	**740**	**800**	**(60/7.5%)**	**5,400**	**6,000**	**(600/10%)**

This variance report, like most, shows the actual sales achieved, the budgeted amounts, and the variances from budget—the difference between the actual and budgeted amounts. This report provides figures for both the month (June) and year-to-date (YTD). The numbers in the variance columns show both the dollar amount and the percentage of the deviation—upward or, in parentheses, downward—from budget.

As the table shows, Acme Corporation breaks down its sales budget by four major sales regions. Except in the Western region, things aren't going well for Acme in the first half of this year.

How to Read a Sales Variance Report

When reviewing variance reports, carefully read the column headers and *line items* so you know what you're looking at. You want to know who's "ahead of budget" (the regions exceeding their budgeted sales), who's "behind budget" (those not reaching their budgeted figure), and who's "on budget" (those meeting their figure).

MBA LINGO

A **line item** is an item with its own line in the budget—that is, its own row on the ledger paper or spreadsheet. In this example, each sales region has its own line.

Most variance reports show the most recent period—the week, month, or quarter—and year-to-date. This sample is a monthly report, but many companies use weekly sales variance reports. Managers receive these reports so that they know where they are and can improve areas that are behind budget.

Looking first at total sales in the fictitious sample variance report, you see that Acme's sales are off (meaning behind or below budget) 7.5 percent for the month of June and 10 percent for the year so far.

Turning to the individual regions, you see that the Southeast is doing fairly well: In June, they were on budget. For the year, they're behind 5 percent. Acme would probably see the Southeast as a region that can "make budget" if they push hard for the rest of the year. The West is in good shape, running 10 percent ahead of budget for the month and 8 percent ahead for the year.

The problems are in the Northeast and Central regions. The Northeast had a terrible June, missing budget by $60,000 or 25 percent. For the year, they're 15 percent behind budget, which is bad, particularly when you consider that the Northeast is the largest region—budgeted for 30 percent of Acme's January-through-June sales.

The Central region is an even bigger problem. June was bad enough, at 10 percent below budget, but the year-to-date is a disaster. The Central region is $390,000, or 26 percent, behind budget for the year so far. And they are budgeted for 25 percent of total sales, so this is bad news.

MBA ALERT

When you "miss budget"—that is, bring in sales below budget or costs above budget—you must have two things ready for your superior: reasons for the variance and a plan for improvement. By "reasons," I don't mean excuses, but rather a clear, honest analysis of what's wrong. By "plan," I don't mean vague promises that "we'll try harder," but rather a realistic program to address what's wrong. No good manager will settle for less. Nor should you settle for less from your people—or from yourself.

Year-Over-Year Variances

To save space, I have not shown year-over-year variances in this report. But they are important. Year-over-year variances show the actual values this year versus the actual values for the same period last year.

Year-over-year comparisons can be valuable if the budgets were unrealistic in the first place. If so, you may have a reasonable defense, particularly if you are doing better than last year but worse than the budget.

Any time you have budget responsibility, you want to know how you are doing against the budget *and* against last year's figures.

Expense Budgets and Variance Reports

Virtually all operating expenses go into expense budgets. The company expense budget is broken down into departmental budgets. Departmental expense budgets are prepared by the department managers with the financial staff during the budgeting process.

The following is an expense budget for a production department. (To keep this simple, I haven't shown the June figures as I did for the sales budget. Instead, I've shown just the year-to-date numbers through June.)

Acme Corporation—Office Products Division

Production Budget and Variance Report, Six Months Ended June 30 (in Thousands)

	Year-to-Date Actual	Prorated Budget	Variance $/%
Salaries & Wages	1,150	1,200	(50/4%)
Benefits	500	500	0
Materials	1,200	1,300	(100/8%)
Supplies	140	150	(10/7%)
Maintenance	70	80	(10/13%)
Transportation & Freight	420	500	(80/16%)
Training & Development	5	20	(15/75%)
Consulting Services	30	50	(20/40%)
Computer Leases	340	340	0/0
Utilities	140	150	(10/7%)
Depreciation	200	200	0/0
Miscellaneous	5	10	(15/75%)
Overhead Allocation	300	300	0/0
Total Production Expense	**4,500**	**4,800**	**(300/6%)**

This budget shows the expenses incurred so far this year and the prorated expenses for the first six months. These prorated expenses are just the annual amount budgeted for each line item divided by two to get the six-month figure.

How to Read an Expense Variance Report

This production budget tracks the expenses incurred in manufacturing Acme Corporation's line of office products. As you saw in Chapter 7, many production expenses are variable expenses that fluctuate with the level of sales. Others are fixed costs. In Acme's case, fixed costs include computer leases and depreciation. But most of the costs here are variable.

For example, wages (particularly those of production workers, as opposed to management) vary with production. When sales are slow, there will be no overtime and no new hires. There may even be layoffs. Materials costs vary quite directly with sales. If sales are slow, then production slows down, and purchases of materials (and supplies) also slow down. If fewer products are being produced, fewer will be shipped, so transportation and freight will decrease.

So if sales are behind budget, as they are in Acme's case, you should be reducing production activity, and thus production expenses. This is what Acme did. Year-to-date sales are 10 percent behind budget, and production costs are also below budget—but by 6 percent rather than 10 percent. This may indicate that Acme's managers should be cutting back production even more.

As with the sales variance report, people talk in terms of running "behind budget" or, more often, "under budget" or "over budget" for the month or the year. They also talk about the run rate, which is the amount they'll spend for the year if they keep spending at the rate so far for the year. In other words, for Acme Corporation, the run rate for the whole production budget is $9 million ($4.5 million × 2; the $4.5 million is what they've spent in the first six months, as shown in the preceding table).

Explaining Budget Variances

Budget variances are rarely self-explanatory. Therefore, the manager accountable for meeting a sales or expense budget must identify the causes of any significant variances. Then, within the scope of his or her authority, the manager must do whatever is possible to eliminate those causes.

The reasons for shortfalls in sales are among the most difficult to identify and address. Assuming that the sales budget was realistic and achievable, variances can usually be traced to one or more of the following factors:

- Competitors with better prices, products, service, warranties, advertising, or promotions
- Market *saturation*
- Loss of major accounts or high-performing salespeople (which still leaves the reason for the loss to be identified)
- Misallocated marketing and sales resources
- Inadequate training or support of salespeople
- Poor post-sale customer service and support
- Low morale among sales or customer service employees (again, why is morale poor?)

MBA LINGO

The market for a product is **saturated** when virtually all potential buyers have already purchased all they want or need of the product.

Identifying the correct factors is essential. For instance, if sales are being lost to a new competitor with a cheaper, more effective product, the sales manager cannot do much about that. However, the people in R&D or product development may be able to. Note also that if morale is poor or sales resources are being misallocated, the sales manager himself may be the reason for the variance. He may require coaching, additional training, or replacement. (Part 4 examines the entire subject of sales and marketing.)

Variances in the expense budget often can be identified and addressed more readily. In general, either the price or the usage of the resource has increased to levels beyond the budgeted amounts. First, the manager must identify which of these factors is at work, keeping in mind that sometimes both can contribute to a variance.

If the price of materials or supplies has risen, it may be necessary to negotiate a better deal with the vendor. Admittedly, this may be difficult, since you probably tried to resist the price increase in the first place. A search for a new vendor often turns up a better price, particularly if you haven't done any recent comparison shopping. Soliciting competitive bids for major purchases is always a good practice.

If the variance stems from higher-than-budgeted usage of a resource, first determine whether its usage varies with the volume of sales, production, or some other factor. For example, a department paying heavy overtime wages usually does so because of extraordinary demands on the staff. On the other hand, if the overtime was necessary to handle the normal workload, then either the budget was unrealistic or the department is understaffed.

In all cases, it's wise to identify short-term solutions and, whenever possible, long-term solutions to a budget variance. For example, it may take a year or two to deal with a competitor that has introduced a new and better product. That would be the long-term solution (provided it's worth pursuing). The short-term solution may be cutting your prices or *bundling* the product with other products of yours (or another company's) to create an appealing package that the competition cannot match.

MBA LINGO

Bundling a product with other products is a way of creating a system or a total solution for a customer, thus increasing the product's appeal. For example, most personal computer manufacturers bundle software with their computers, saving the customer the trouble of having to purchase the software separately (and increasing their profit on the sale).

In a sense, budgets are like flight plans. As conditions change and new information becomes available, a manager must respond, just as a pilot would respond to changes in weather or schedule.

Cost Control

At times, managers face a situation in which cost control extends beyond a few budget items. During an economic downturn or a sustained slide in sales, across-the-board cost cutting may be necessary.

For most companies, labor represents a significant, readily controlled cost. You can control labor costs by *not* doing certain things. You can not hire new employees, not replace workers who leave (a tactic called attrition), and not approve overtime. You can also reduce employees' hours or lay off workers.

How layoffs are handled can make the difference between a momentary dip in morale and the devastation of employees' spirits. Management must communicate honestly with employees and make the case for the layoff. Provided that the managers are not gutting the company out of executive greed, employees can understand the financial realities that lead to a layoff. Whether business is down or costs are up, or both, the reasons for the layoff, and the expected benefit to the company, must be described clearly. No company can guarantee lifetime employment in times of change, and today most people recognize that.

In the past—for much of the last century—many companies were slow to adjust to decreasing sales. However, with highly improved information systems, businesses have learned to respond much more quickly to changes in the business cycle, as noted in Chapter 6. For example, the prevalence of outsourcing has given businesses much more flexibility in matching their labor and other resources to the amount of work they have. Lower rates of union membership among workers has made it easier and less expensive for companies to lay off workers and to use fewer workers for certain tasks.

In fact, the movement of the U.S. economy to more employment in service industries and knowledge work and less in manufacturing has helped businesses respond more quickly to decreases in sales, whether they are due to economic conditions or to changing customer preferences or stronger competition. There is also far less loyalty between companies and employees than there was 30 or 40 years ago. Companies now make decisions to hire and keep employees mainly on the basis of financial considerations, and employees make their career decisions based mainly on similar considerations. In the past, personal considerations, including an employee's family situation or the company's history with the employee, entered more into employment and career decisions on both sides of the desk.

If you need to cut costs in your business or department, consider cuts in your travel and entertainment, new equipment, and publications budgets. You might also consider refinancing debt if interest rates have fallen below what you're currently paying.

These are piecemeal measures, but the pieces can add up. Yet sometimes you need to reduce costs drastically.

CASE IN POINT

I worked for a couple of companies that put a hiring freeze in place for the last quarter of almost every year. A hiring freeze can either allow no new employees to be hired or allow only replacements of employees who leave their jobs. A hiring freeze is often accompanied by a freeze on salary increases and promotions.

These companies did this because they were slow to react to underbudget sales (or overbudget expenses) earlier in the year. At times, they kept hoping for a "Big September" that never materialized. Consistent control earlier in the year would have been much less disruptive.

Radical Surgery

The decision to close down an operation is among the toughest a manager can face. People's livelihoods are at stake, and management's competence can be questioned. However, if a department, production unit, product line, or sales office consistently fails to contribute to income, it's best to shut it down or sell it.

How long a money-losing operation should be allowed to continue in business is purely a matter of judgment. However, decisions to close an operation are still often made too late. Management keeps hoping things will improve. They know that people in the money-losing unit are trying. But when the writing is on the wall and there's no clear path to growth and profitability, the best decision for the whole company is to end the operation.

MBA MASTERY

Often companies claim that they can't account separately for product lines or operations because certain costs are shared. In those cases, accounting must develop a way of allocating shared costs to the individual products or operations. Even if their system isn't perfect, if it is at least consistent, it will yield useful information over time.

Money-losing operations are a tremendous drag on a company. They suck up time, energy, and money, and deliver little in return. They divert resources from successful operations. You owe it to everyone—the shareholders, the employees in the winning units, and even the employees in the losing units (since they have no future)—to close operations that should be closed.

All of this assumes that you have the information that will tell you what is and isn't profitable. Some companies use accounting systems that combine operations in ways that make it hard to tell what's making money and what isn't.

As is the case in conducting a layoff, in closing down an operation, honest communication with the affected employees is essential. Management should explain why the unit must be closed and, if it is to be sold, tell employees as much as they can about the future of the firm under the new owners. Yes, some employees may become resentful or even confrontational, and that is why so many managers shy away from honest communication about these matters. However, managers owe their employees an explanation of why their place of business is being shut down or sold.

Take Credit Management Seriously

Good credit management can cut costs, boost income, and free up cash. The key to good credit management is to decide what your credit policy will be and then implement it consistently.

Credit policy should not be too tight or too loose. If it's too tight, the company will lose sales because *credit analysts* will be turning away customers or not approving them for all they would buy—and pay for—on credit. Overly aggressive *collectors* can alienate good customers in temporary trouble. On the other hand, if credit policy is too loose, the company will have difficulty collecting its money or, worse yet, have excessive bad-debt expense. Customers who don't pay their bills are useless.

MBA LINGO

Credit analysts decide how much trade credit customers should be extended. **Collectors,** or collection clerks, contact past-due accounts with the aim of getting them to pay up.

There's a natural tension in credit policy. Resolving it means deciding how much bad-debt expense you can accept as a cost of doing business and how quickly you want to collect your money from customers. This must be discovered over time, as you gain experience with your customers.

The Credit-Approval Process

The credit-approval process requires more information and analysis as the requested *credit line* (amount a customer can buy on credit) increases.

Many companies automatically approve any order under some amount, such as $250. For orders between this "automatic approval" figure and the next level (for example, $1,500), they would ask the customer to complete a form and provide credit references, and they would order a *credit report*.

MBA LINGO

A **credit line** is the amount of credit a customer is approved for by a company or bank. It's the total amount the customer can have outstanding with the outfit at any time.

A **credit report** is a record of how a company (or individual) pays bills from other companies. The largest source of credit reports on businesses in the United States is Dun & Bradstreet at www.dnb.com.

Beyond that next-level amount, credit will request financial statements of a company or client requesting credit and analyze them for creditworthiness—their ability and willingness to pay their bills.

When Things Go Wrong, Collections Gets Tough

If a company is paying slowly, use aggressive collection efforts, particularly if the amount owed is large. By "aggressive," I don't mean threatening to sue the company or even (necessarily) cutting off their credit. I'm instead suggesting that you get in touch, by phone, as soon as they are 30 days past due and ask (nicely) when you'll get paid.

Doing this has several benefits:

- Collection letters—letters "reminding" the customer to pay and then asking for payment in increasingly demanding tones—are easier to ignore than phone calls. (But use them, too, along with calls.)

- Personal contact creates personal relationships. Most people find it hard to not pay people they know.

- If you get promises to pay that turn out to be hollow, then you know the debtor either is in trouble or is defrauding you. In either case, it's time to limit your *exposure* (amount of money they owe you). Do not sell the debtor any more goods on credit until the company pays, or at least starts to pay, what it already owes.

 MBA LINGO

Exposure is the amount of money owed to you on trade credit or for borrowed money. A businessperson may say, "Our exposure on this account is $100,000."

Try to work out something with slow payers, but unless you see them headed for bankruptcy, be slow to accept some lower amount as "full payment" of what is owed to you. If you judge them to be viable in the long term and you can afford to wait, try to work out a payment schedule that will ultimately pay off the debt.

Getting Very Serious

At some point, aggressive collection means threatening to refer the account to a collection agency or attorney. Don't do this until the situation is hopeless. After two or three threats, refer the account.

Collection agencies are in the business of collecting past-due accounts. Generally, they charge one third of the money they collect, and if they collect nothing, you pay nothing. They use aggressive letters, phone calls, and threats of legal action; some may even visit the account in person.

A collection attorney will threaten to sue the account for the money owed, plus their fee and court costs—and then follow through on that threat. However, even if the attorney wins a *judgment* (court order) against the company, it must still be paid. If the company had money enough to pay the judgment, they probably would have paid the bill long ago.

MBA LINGO

A **judgment** is a court order for a company or person to pay a sum of money to a company or person. Judgments are shown on credit reports as either satisfied or not satisfied, meaning paid or not paid.

Uncollectable debts are a sad aspect of business. Credit is one area in which an ounce of prevention is truly worth a pound of cure.

The Least You Need to Know

- A budget is the most basic financial planning and control tool. Every department that makes sales or spends money needs a budget. Every manager with a budget needs to know how his department is doing in relation to that budget.
- Budgets must be fair and achievable if they are to be useful in the long run.
- Investigate budget variances and address the short- and long-term causes of the largest variances.
- To control costs effectively, look for significant expenses you can reduce, such as labor costs or a department or operation that's not earning its keep. Also scrutinize travel, entertainment, and telephone expenses, as well as new equipment purchases, publications, and consulting.
- Whenever interest rates decrease, look into refinancing any outstanding debt that has a fixed rate.

Managing for Productivity and Quality

In This Chapter

- How to measure productivity
- Ways to increase productivity
- Creating a "culture of quality" in your organization
- Formal methods for improving quality

In managing any business, two key considerations are productivity and quality. These factors relate directly to revenue and profits. The more productive a business is, the more it can produce and sell with a given set of resources and at a given cost. The higher the quality of its products and services, at a given price and set of costs, the more customers it will attract and the more it will sell.

For a company, department, or other operation, productivity is usually measured by how fast a given quantity is produced—how many units of product come off the assembly line per hour, how many hours it takes to build a car, how many tons of steel are produced by a mill in a year, how many customers a restaurant can serve per day—with a given level of resources. Productivity is about how long it takes to do how much and with what resources.

Quality is measured by how well something is done. It's about how many defects occur, how many products break down, and how many customers are satisfied rather than dissatisfied.

In this chapter, you learn about productivity and quality and ways of promoting them in your business.

What Is Productivity?

Productivity is the amount of output created by a person, machine, or organization (or a nation, when you consider an entire economy). Output can be measured in dollars of value, units of product, number of customers served, kilowatts, or any another measure that makes sense for a business. The more output, the greater the productivity.

Productivity is actually efficiency. An efficient worker or machine produces more output than an inefficient one. An efficient use of funds produces a greater return than an inefficient one. This last point is key: money itself must be put to the most productive uses available.

These elements—workers, machines, and money—are what economists call factors of production. It is management's job to make sure that each factor of production is used as efficiently as possible.

A wonderful saying in management says, "To manage it, you must measure it." Therefore, let's look at some ways of measuring and managing productivity.

Measuring Productivity

Productivity can be measured in various ways. Productivity as we are analyzing it here is not a total concept (as it is to an economist assessing a nation's productivity growth). Here we are concerned with productivity per worker or per machine. In a business, you increase productivity by increasing output per worker or per machine. If you increase the output of the business by simply adding more workers or equipment, you are not increasing productivity, but you are instead expanding your workforce or capacity. That may be desirable or necessary, but it is not increasing productivity.

Calculating Worker Productivity

You can use the following formula to measure worker productivity:

$$\text{Worker productivity} = \frac{\text{Output in units or dollars}}{\text{Worker hours}}$$

So if a staff of 15 production workers produces 9,000 gewgaws a week and the work week is 40 hours:

$$\text{Worker productivity} \quad = \quad \frac{9{,}000}{600 \, (= 15 \times 40)}$$

$$\text{Worker productivity} \quad = \quad 15 \text{ gewgaws per hour}$$

Each worker produces 15 gewgaws per hour. This is, of course, an average. As a manager, in many situations, you can also assess individual productivity. If some workers can produce more than 15 per hour, you can perhaps study their methods and try to apply them to other workers.

Calculating Machine Productivity

You can use a similar formula to calculate machine productivity:

$$\text{Machine productivity} \quad = \quad \frac{\text{Outputs in units or dollars}}{\text{Machine hours}}$$

Suppose you have five machines and each one operates 40 hours a week:

$$\text{Machine productivity} \quad = \quad \frac{9{,}000}{200 \, (= 5 \times 40)}$$

$$\text{Machine productivity} \quad = \quad 45 \text{ gewgaws per hour}$$

Again, this measure is an average and could be put to various uses—for example, to see how much more productive a newer machine may be, compared with an older one.

MBA MASTERY

However you measure productivity, be sure that you do measure it. In some businesses, this can present challenges, but even an imperfect measure of productivity will enable you to manage it, provided that you apply it consistently.

More, More! Faster, Faster!

Everyone wants to increase productivity. There are several ways to do this, including the following.

- Improving worker skills and motivation

- Improving the equipment

- Improving production methods

Each method involves an investment from management. You must invest time, effort, and usually money to increase productivity. Why bother? Because the greater the productivity of an operation, the greater the financial returns it produces.

Let's look at each of these ways of increasing productivity.

Boosting Employee Skills and Motivation

To improve worker productivity, you generally must invest in workers. This can entail hiring workers who have better skills, experience, and education, or training workers to become more productive.

To get higher productivity by investing in workers, you must invest in skills, experience, education, and training related to their jobs and day-to-day duties. Most companies with company-sponsored training or tuition-reimbursement plans use them only for courses that apply to the worker's current job. That's smart, because you don't want to train and educate people so they can leave your company for a better position elsewhere. On the other hand, to develop promotable employees, you may have to train them to handle increased responsibilities.

A number of companies see high employee turnover as a way to control labor costs by constantly replacing experienced workers with less experienced but cheaper ones. These firms tend not to invest much in training. But if you do invest in training, remember that you lose that investment when the employee leaves. So if you invest in training, try to limit your employee turnover.

Paying for Production

Another way to improve worker productivity is to provide incentives for them to be more productive. These incentives may be financial—perhaps you pay workers by the number of products they produce rather than the number of hours they work. Incentives can also be in the form of awards or special recognition, which tends to be less effective. You can offer productivity bonuses for individuals or teams, or provide awards or recognition on a team or individual basis.

You'll see in Chapter 21 that salespeople tend to be more productive when they have financial incentives. But financial incentives can also cause trouble. For production workers, they can cause quality to suffer. If you send workers the message that quantity is the overriding goal, you can wind up with more product—and a lot more defects, breakdowns, and returns.

Another problem with paying for high production is that, after a while, it doesn't work. There are usually very real limitations on how much workers can produce. A worker can physically go only so fast. A machine can pop out only so many units. So unless the *limiting factor* in your operation is the speed at which employees work, you simply can't increase productivity significantly with financial incentives.

MBA LINGO

The **limiting factor** in a situation is the element that will stop the process, even when other factors are still operating. For example, the limiting factor in the distance a vehicle can travel is the amount of gasoline it can carry.

What's the Motivation?

Worker motivation is a major determinant of worker productivity. As you learned in Part 1, motivating workers and teams calls for management and leadership skills.

To raise worker motivation to the highest possible levels, leaders must create and sustain a sense of mission in employees by building trust and sharing a vision of what the company could be. They must focus people on the right tasks (and have them stop performing unproductive tasks) and foster a sense of personal accountability in each employee. Effective leaders also coach their people to be more productive.

There is no perfect way to increase and maintain motivation. But companies that truly excel manage to create corporate cultures in which people are motivated to put forth their best efforts.

For a variety of reasons, once you have a skilled, educated, trained, well-paid, and motivated workforce, productivity comes down to managing well and requesting extraordinary time and effort from workers when the business demands extraordinary production.

CASE IN POINT

Companies with the most productive workforces tend to be rapidly growing companies with strong leaders and clear goals. Rapid growth creates an external demand (from customers) for high productivity. The leader creates an internal demand for productivity and sets an example. The vision and the goals—for example, to be the biggest, the first, or the best, or to reach a certain size by a certain time—bind everyone into a cohesive team. In this environment, unproductive people leave or are forced out.

Good examples include any number of firms that once experienced rapid growth with strong leaders and big goals, such as Apple Computer, Federal Express, and Starbucks. Unfortunately, that kind of growth does not last forever. So the challenge of managing to motivate people to stay highly productive never ends.

Improving Equipment

Perhaps the easiest and, in the long run, often the cheapest way to increase productivity is to give workers better equipment. This investment can boost productivity in several ways:

- New equipment is often more productive simply because it runs better.

- New equipment (for example, an improved or higher-end model) often offers more productive capacity.

- New equipment can often be run with fewer workers, thus enabling you to replace labor with capital.

- New equipment can improve quality (I cover this later in the chapter).

MBA MASTERY

Substituting capital for labor—that is, workers with machinery—is perhaps the oldest way of boosting productivity. In the long run, equipment is generally cheaper than employees. It requires less management and never gets sick or leaves for another employer. However, this substitution can be tougher to achieve in service businesses than in manufacturing.

Returning to our earlier example, recall that the average worker can make 15 gewgaws an hour. That's worker productivity. Recall also that the average machine can make 45 gewgaws an hour. That's machine productivity. There are five machines in the shop, and each machine requires three workers. The 15 workers operating the five machines produce 9,000 gewgaws per week, assuming a 40-hour week.

What would happen if we replaced one of those five machines with a new one that required only one worker and could produce 75 gewgaws per hour?

Productivity would increase. In fact, the five machines (which include the new one) could then produce a total of 9,000 gewgaws in a little over 35 hours rather than 40 hours. This would allow the company to reduce the workers' hours (thereby saving labor costs) while maintaining the same level of production.

Why?

Because in 35 hours, four machines producing 45 gewgaws an hour will make 6,300 gewgaws ($= 4 \times 35 \times 45$). And in 35 hours, one machine producing 75 gewgaws an hour will make 2,625 gewgaws ($= 1 \times 35 \times 75$). The total production of all the machines in 35 hours will be 8,925 ($= 6,300 + 2,625$).

CASE IN POINT

Many service businesses have harnessed information technology, and the energy of their own customers, to raise their productivity. For example, when bank customers use ATMs, they enable the bank to reduce the number of tellers. When Federal Express enabled customers to track the status of their packages on the web, they also reduced the number of incoming phone calls that employees had to field. Any company that enables customers to check the status of their accounts or troubleshoot their product problems on the web uses technology in the same way.

Ideally, this is a win-win strategy: it's more productive for the company and easier for the customer. However, reality often falls short of the ideal, for example, when customers can't reach a human receptionist or have no alternative to the technical manual on the website. Smart companies enable customers to serve themselves but give them the option of being served.

That 8,925 is only 75 gewgaws short of 9,000. You can get to the 9,000 by keeping one additional worker on overtime to run the new machine for one extra hour and produce the final 75 gewgaws.

Again, thanks to this productivity increase, you can reduce your company's work week from 40 hours to 35 hours. This reduction will save significant labor costs. In fact, new and improved equipment can often kick an operation up to a completely new level.

Improve the Processes

A final way to boost productivity is to examine the processes in your operation with an eye toward improving them. Process improvements are a major goal in *reengineering* a company.

Process improvements come from examining all the ways in which the work is performed and seeing how the tasks could be redesigned for greater efficiency—that is, for greater productivity. This can include examining and redesigning the type or number of tasks performed by a single worker, the way work gets to the worker (for example, conveyor belts versus handoff from another worker), and the layout of the work area.

Improvements can be realized by training workers in new methods and in the use of new equipment. Thus, a process improvement can include an investment in workers and in equipment.

You can identify ways to improve work processes by interviewing the people actually doing the work. These interviews should be conducted by outside consultants who grant "amnesty" to workers who cite inefficiencies. That way, you'll get honest answers. The interviews should focus on identifying waste in all its forms, including wasted time, equipment, effort, materials, heat, and electricity. Focus especially on the time that people spend waiting for something or someone, working on a task that does not really require their skills, or tracking down information that should be readily available. When properly conducted, these interviews usually identify easy ways to save time and other resources, and thus raise productivity.

Work studies are another way to understand your work processes. In a work study, some employees are asked to list all of the tasks they perform in an average week. Then, for about a month, they wear a beeper set to go off at random intervals. When the beeper goes off, they place a checkmark next to the task on the list that they were performing at the moment. (Few employees enjoy doing this, but dedicated people who realize that the work, and not their performance, is being studied will cooperate.)

Work studies break down processes and show how people actually spend their time. This enables management to eliminate waste by asking, "Why do we have people doing this?" Eliminating waste in a process is the surest way to increase the productivity of that process.

CASE IN POINT

Studies conducted in supermarkets by Conway Management Company, a consulting firm, show that the average chain can increase its overall productivity by 20 to 30 percent by reducing wasted resources, including time, produce, baked goods, heat, and electricity. For instance, one chain had all stores constantly rearranging their produce displays to convey an image of freshness. This practice wasted employees' time, damaged produce (with added handling), *and* irritated customers, who couldn't find what they wanted because it was never in the same place. Why were the stores rearranging produce displays? Because they had always done it that way.

At another chain, a program of preventive maintenance—in which a part for, say, a freezer, is replaced on a schedule rather than waiting for it to break down—saved tens of thousands of dollars annually. The program reduced the time employees spent responding to crises, overtime pay for repair crews, and wasted food.

What Is Quality, Anyway?

We usually think of quality as *goodness* or *excellence* or *superiority*. In business, it can mean these things and often does. However, it is best to think of quality as a decision and a goal.

First, let's consider quality as a decision. As mentioned in Chapter 1, you can have relatively low quality at a low price or relatively high quality at a high price. Customers know this, so a company has to decide what level of quality it wants to pursue.

That level of quality becomes the goal. For products, the goal is often best formulated in terms of the number of defects you can tolerate. These defects can be discovered by inspection or by the less desirable means of merchandise returns, warranty claims, and breakdowns. In service businesses, the goal may be formulated by calculating the average waiting time for customers in a store or restaurant, customer satisfaction, and number of complaints.

The decision about quality flows from your company's business philosophy, image, costs, target markets, and prices, as well as its human, financial, and other resources. Here we focus on the pursuit of quality, once you have decided on a level of quality.

Quality Assurance

Quality assurance (also known as *quality control*) has several meanings. First, it can encompass all the activities that go into achieving the level of quality that the company desires and customers demand. This can include everything from designing the product's specifications, to creating standards for suppliers of the materials used in the product, to conducting various inspections during manufacturing.

> **MBA LINGO**
>
> **Quality assurance** (or **quality control**) refers to policies, programs, and efforts to minimize product defects and ensure high quality, and to the formal function that conducts these activities within a company.

Second, quality assurance refers to the final inspection performed before a product is shipped. Note that this inspection can be performed by a human or through technology. For example, the manufacturing process can include running the product by a computerized scanner that is programmed to recognize any defects.

Third, quality control refers to mathematical tools involving statistics and probability that are applied in manufacturing for tasks such as sampling products and minimizing defects. For instance, in many situations, it would be too costly to inspect every product. So an inspector may pull a mathematically determined sample of each hour's or each day's production and use the results of that inspection to measure the quality of the entire production run. (Recall the example in Chapter 8 of chickens that had to weigh within a certain range.)

Finally, *quality control* can refer to the quality-control department that performs activities associated with maintaining product quality. Most operations have someone responsible for a quality check, while major manufacturers have large departments dedicated to the task.

How to Control Quality

Over the past 20 years, towering stacks of books and more conferences than you could attend in a lifetime have been devoted to the issue of quality. The wake-up call for U.S. manufacturers was Japan's success in the U.S. auto market in the 1970s. Before then, U.S. manufacturers of autos—and of many other products—had grown complacent about quality. Some even designed their products for *planned obsolescence*.

MBA LINGO

Planned obsolescence refers to the tactic of withholding a feature from a product so you can introduce a "new and improved" product later, or repeatedly making cosmetic changes to a product so that it constantly "goes out of style," or building the product so that it breaks down at some future point and requires replacement. The product becomes obsolete, but you planned it that way.

The quality-control process involves three practical steps:

- Developing quality standards
- Applying the quality standards
- Creating a corporate "culture of quality"

As you read about these steps, keep in mind that quality control has two basic purposes: first, to meet the customers' expectations and create satisfied customers, and second, to find cost-effective ways of fulfilling the first purpose.

Developing Quality Standards

One big issue in quality control centers on the number or percentage of defects that are acceptable. Traditionally, manufacturers believed that because manufacturing processes are imperfect—machines go out of alignment, people get tired, mistakes are made—you cannot eliminate defects.

With this approach, quality control means deciding what number and what types of defects are acceptable. These decisions amount to your standards, which must factor in customer expectations. For example, you might say that defects that affect performance are not acceptable, but that small defects in appearance are. Or you may say that you are willing to discard only 2 percent of the production run for defects, and you ship the rest.

Of course, you have important decisions to make regarding the number and type of defects you will accept. Too many defects will result in poor quality. And the wrong type of defects—for instance, those affecting customer safety—can bankrupt the company in product-liability claims.

What About Zero Defects?

Quality consultant Philip Crosby has made the quest for zero defects his cause. This clearly goes against the traditional approach of deciding which defects to accept. Crosby believes that a policy of knowingly accepting *any* defects will lead to accepting too many. The standard should be zero defects, because to have a standard that accepts *any* defects is to tell employees that defects are okay. A common side effect of accepting defects is a loss of focus on customer needs. After all, the customer wants zero defects.

Also underlying the zero-defects goal is the notion that it is easier to do something right the first time than to fix it later. Nevertheless, perfection is a tough—and, more to the point, expensive—goal to pursue. What's more, if you try to use it as a selling point, you may be going out on a limb. Customers may not believe it, and worse, it will amplify the impact of any defects or quality problems that do occur.

In the end, each company must define its own approach to quality standards.

What Are Quality Standards?

Whether you accept some level of defects or shoot for zero, the way you define and measure standards will depend on your operation and industry. For most manufacturing operations, you need standards in the following areas and of the following types:

Area	Type of Standard
Performance	Fulfills its functions
	Meets performance specifications
Appearance	Adheres to design specifications
	Exhibits uniform color
Workmanship	Displays a smooth finish
	Produces tight joints and fittings
Content	Passes tests for purity (for foods, drugs) and percentages of allowed content (for fat or other ingredients)
Safety	Resists fire or breakage that would endanger the user

Management, marketing, engineering, operations, and the design team must all be involved in developing quality standards. The product must be as safe as the company can possibly make it. But beyond that, the standards must be developed with a sharp eye on costs, target market, and company image.

Applying Quality Standards

Applying the quality standards is traditionally the work of the quality-control department. However, you must apply quality standards more broadly than that. You must apply them in the purchasing function, where the company decides which materials to buy and where to buy them. You must apply them in the receiving department so that someone checks to see that materials meet the standards. You must apply them in operations so that products are properly made at each step of production.

For most manufacturing processes, this constant quality control is more effective and less expensive than waiting until the product is completed before giving it a passing or failing grade. In fact, many companies go beyond issuing quality standards (although they do issue them) and emphasize that everyone in the organization is responsible for quality. These companies encourage employees and managers to think not only about the standards, but also about everything in the way they do their jobs that could affect quality, and to continually improve the way they work and the results they produce.

Aside from applying quality standards to materials and products at various stages of production, quality control faces the task of discovering the reasons for variations in quality. Discovering defects is good, but preventing them is even better. So when quality-control people notice a pattern of standards not being met, they must learn why and try to fix it.

Finding the Causes of Defects

Business analysts and academics take disciplined approaches to discovering the causes of defects, or poor quality. They generally seek root causes of defects, so their discipline is called *root-cause analysis*. The root cause of a defect is the factor or problem that, when eliminated, also eliminates the defect. The logic is simple: eliminate the problem and you eliminate the defect.

MBA LINGO

Root-cause analysis includes various methods for identifying the problem in a process that produces a product or service, which, when eliminated, will also eliminate a specific defect.

Two popular methods of root-cause analysis are the "Five Whys" and "Failure Modes and Effects Analysis."

The Five Whys were developed by Skaichi Toyoda. As the name suggests, you ask the question "Why?" five times (or however many times you must to get at the root cause). This tool is best applied to simple situations and processes. Suppose customers complain to a food company that deliveries of frozen foods are being left on loading docks and then thawing out and going to waste:

- Why are deliveries being left on the loading dock? Drivers are not being met by customers' employees.

- Why? Customers are unsure of when deliveries will occur.

- Why? Our drivers seem unable to stick to our delivery schedules.

- Why? Drivers say that our schedules are unrealistic.

- Why? They say they were made without input from drivers and realistic drive times.

Solution: Survey the drivers and accompany those on the most problematic routes. Revise the schedules and communicate new schedules to customers.

Failure Modes and Effects Analysis (FMEA) provides a structured way to identify all possible modes of failure in a process. The first part of the analysis is to identify all possible ways in which the process or product could fail to do what it is supposed to do. The second part is to identify the effects of each failure on other activities or results. Then you prioritize the potential failures and address them.

For example, defects in a vacuum cleaner could result in it being underpowered, being overpowered, or catching fire. The effect of each of these on the customer should be considered—and, obviously, a fire is to be avoided because the effects could include loss of life.

These admittedly simple examples cannot portray the richness or complexity of root-cause analysis when performed by quality-improvement professionals. However, these and similar methodologies have been applied in virtually every manufacturing industry and many service industries to improve processes that produce and deliver products and services.

Creating a Corporate "Culture of Quality"

Some people think of quality as something that applies only to high-quality, high-priced products. However, quality control applies to every company, because the real issue is maintaining the desired level of quality—the level of quality that the customer wants and is willing to pay for.

For any company, when it comes to quality, the real management challenge is to create a culture of quality. It begins with the goals, strategies, and plans presented by management. It goes on to hiring, training, compensation, and promotion practices. It includes the marketing and sales messages you send to customers. It must permeate the customer service function. It extends to your suppliers and distribution channels. All of this amounts to *total quality management.*

MBA LINGO

The term **total quality management,** or TQM, refers to every area of the organization being involved in creating quality. TQM means that everyone is responsible for quality. It also assumes that quality must be designed in and built in, rather than be added at the last step of production. TQM was something of a fad in the 1990s, but it became a permanent effort in some companies.

One way to create a culture of quality is to have everyone in the company think of themselves as serving customers. Everyone has internal customers to serve. For example, the accounting function delivers reports to other managers, who are its internal customers. The marketing department has the sales department as its key internal customer. The purchasing department has operations as its internal customer. And so on.

Thus, the notions of customer service and customer satisfaction can be used as motivators and standards in every area and for every employee.

In a culture of quality, everyone works to high standards within the context of the company's costs and values. They hold themselves and they hold one another to these standards. Those who cannot or will not join the culture, or those who undermine the effort of the larger group, eventually either choose to leave or are forced out—if they even get into the company in the first place.

Methods and Tools of Quality Control

In addition to the tasks of developing standards, applying standards, and creating a culture of quality, a few tools can assist you in the quest for quality:

- Lean

- Six Sigma

- Best practices and benchmarking

Let's talk briefly about each one.

Lean

Lean, also known as Lean Thinking, is a method of making a process more efficient. You "lean" a process by eliminating all waste within the process. Waste is defined as anything that does not add value for the customer (who can be either an internal or external customer). This includes wasted materials, motion, effort, energy, talent, and time. It also includes overproduction, underproduction, rejects, rework, and repairs. The more waste you remove from a process, the leaner and more efficient it becomes.

Lean focuses tightly on what customers really want and what they don't, and on doing more of the former and less of the latter. The method does recognize the need for supporting activities, such as accounting and human resources, which external customers actually don't care about. However, it recognizes that a number of things many companies do fail to add value in ways that customers will actually pay for. Lean tries to learn what customers value and will pay for, and to do only those things.

This focus on value helps management streamline processes and discover where to put resources. For example, going as far back as the 1970s, Japanese car manufacturers realized that many customers cared more about the reliability, durability, and economy of vehicles than about styling. So they made very few styling changes (especially relative to U.S. automakers) and focused on quality. They also applied this Lean Thinking to the entire production process—and to suppliers.

MBA MASTERY

For more on Lean, see the book *The Machine That Changed the World: The Story of Lean Production,* by James P. Womack and Daniel T. Jones (Harper Perennial, 1991).

Six Sigma

Six Sigma is a process-improvement methodology that takes a scientific approach to improving the effectiveness of a process. It does this by eliminating the causes of defects. The term Six Sigma is a statistical measure of quality that translates to 3.4 defects per million products. That translates to 99.99 percent defect-free products.

Six Sigma also refers to formal quality-improvement initiatives based on five steps: Define, Measure, Analyze, Improve, Control, or DMAIC (*da may' ik*). Here's a bit more on the process:

- **Define:** You define the problem—the defect or error—that you want to correct in a process. Let's say that you're trying to manufacture better windshield wipers.

- **Measure:** You measure the results of the process and the activities that make up the process. You measure the quality, durability, and performance of various materials, wiper holders, pressures, and so on—and all the activities in the manufacturing process that produce the wipers.

- **Analyze:** You look for variations in the performance of the wipers—how clean they get the windshields, how long they last without replacement, which factors cause wear and tear, which ones mar the windshield, and so on. You also analyze the process that produces the wipers, such as quality of materials from suppliers, quality of your molds, packaging and handling and installation instructions, and so on. At this point, you also come up with your solution to the problem, which might be to use more flexible material and instruct users to change wipers more often.

- **Improve:** You implement the changes. In this case, you work with your supplier to design a wiper with a more flexible blade and with your distributors and marketing personnel to get people to change their blades more often. Note that you would make this decision very carefully in real life, as you are making potentially expensive changes to your manufacturing process.

- **Control:** You continue to gather data—in this case, on the product's performance and on your ability to produce the product to the specifications you have defined. You also gather data on sales to distributors and end users on customer satisfaction and on product returns, complaints, and compliments.

This is a vast oversimplification of Six Sigma, which represents a world unto itself, populated by experts trained in the methodology (called "black belts") and with ever-evolving tools. In fact, Lean Six Sigma represents a combination of the two disciplines, in which you first "lean" a process to make it as efficient and free of waste as you can and then you apply Six Sigma to make it as effective as possible.

MBA MASTERY

For a great primer on quality improvement, see *The Complete Idiot's Guide to Lean Six Sigma,* by Neil DeCarlo (Alpha, 2007).

Best Practices and Benchmarking

The phrase *best practices* refers to the most efficient and most effective way of structuring and conducting a business process. Best practices in product development, for example, indicate the use of cross-functional teams. Best practices in a certain type of electronics manufacturing may indicate the use of printed circuits rather than wiring. Broadly, *best practices* means the best way of doing something. It means doing something the way those who do it best do it.

Benchmarking refers to a method of comparing your company's practices and performance with those of companies with the best practices that you want to employ. Benchmarking measures the results of best practices and describes how to get that performance in your processes.

For example, if another company can reduce the time it takes to develop a new product by using cross-functional teams or reduce the number of defects with the use of printed circuits, then you want to know the time that company needs to develop a new product or its number of defects. Those become the benchmarks, the targets you use in your business.

One way to get benchmarking going in your company is to have a task force drawn from key areas of the outfit to investigate best practices in their respective areas. This "best practices task force" can represent their areas and draw on the experience of their people (some of whom may have worked at companies with best practices) and direct their people to do some investigating as well. Much of the research can be drawn from news stories and articles about other companies.

Finally, you actually adapt the best practice to your needs. You begin using cross-functional product-development teams, or you start making printed circuits or getting a supplier to make them for you.

CASE IN POINT

The Baldrige Award, officially known as the Malcolm Baldrige National Quality Award, goes to companies judged to best meet the Baldrige criteria for quality. The U.S. Congress created the award to recognize companies that achieve extraordinary levels of quality and named it after Secretary of Commerce Malcolm Baldrige, who held the post from 1981 until his accidental death in 1987.

Companies that apply for the award are judged in seven areas: leadership, strategic planning, customer and market focus, information and analysis, human resources focus, process management, and business results. Applying for the award represents a significant project, and most companies that do so learn a lot about themselves from the process. Past recipients of the Baldrige Award include Ritz-Carlton Hotels, Motorola, Cadillac, AT&T, and Corning Telecommunications Products.

The Challenge of Global Competition

Global business competition means that productivity and quality are now the two most effective competitive weapons. A marketing strategy may or may not translate well overseas. Sales methods and distribution channels vary widely from nation to nation. Accounting and financial tactics may or may not work under another nation's accounting policies or financial system.

However, cost, price, value, and satisfaction are universal. A focus on productivity enables a company to control its costs by making the most of its resources. A focus on quality enables a company to deliver the best possible products to its customers. A company that offers good quality at a reasonable price can compete in any environment.

The Least You Need to Know

- Productivity is usually measured by how efficiently something happens. It is about quantity produced in a certain amount of time with a given amount of resources.
- To increase productivity, you can improve worker productivity, improve productive equipment, or improve production processes. Any of these moves involves an investment of time, effort, and (usually) money.
- Quality is measured by how well something is done. It's about how many defects occur, how many products break down, and how many customers are satisfied.
- To maintain or improve quality, you must develop quality standards, apply the quality standards, and, if at all possible, create a corporate "culture of quality."
- Specific methods of quality improvement include Lean and Six Sigma.

Managing Money, Accounting, and Finance

Some people find accounting confusing and finance frustrating, but I'm not sure why. It can't be the arithmetic, because if you can add, subtract, multiply, and divide—or use a calculator—then you can deal with the numbers in everything from basic budgets to major investments.

Of course, if the numbers don't give you trouble, then the words might. If you find terms like *depreciation*, *present value*, and *shareholders' equity* mysterious, don't worry: they're just words. And they have straightforward meanings, once they've been explained.

This part of the book explains all that and more, including how money flows through a company, where it comes from, and where it goes. It also shows you how to read financial statements—and once you can do that, you're on your way to real "business literacy."

Meet Your Balance Sheet

In This Chapter

- The importance of financial statements
- Assets and liabilities: how money flows through a business
- A tour through the balance sheet accounts

Money constantly flows through a company, and someone has to keep track of it. That's why God made accountants. Someone also has to make sure the company makes decisions that make money. That's where financial managers come in.

Accountants and financial managers have special ways of analyzing the health and growth of a company. They mainly use numbers, and they present these numbers in financial statements. Financial statements are the most important way you can understand and analyze a company. As a manager, you must understand these statements to know how your budgets, transactions, and decisions affect the company.

This chapter introduces the first of three main financial statements—the balance sheet.

Assets, Liabilities, and Owners' Equity: You Need 'Em All

To understand the balance sheet, you must first understand how money moves in and out of a company. Every transaction that a company conducts represents either an inflow or an outflow of cash. Most inflows of cash come from sales, but some come from loans or from the sale of stock. Most outflows of cash are created by expenses. When the company purchases materials, pays its employees, or pays interest on a loan, it has paid an expense.

In general, every single thing the company owns can be classified as an *asset*. The furniture, the inventory, the equipment, the building, even the cash in the bank and in the petty-cash drawer—all are assets. Assets have one thing in common: they are there to generate cash (unless they *are* cash, and even then, the cash should be invested). If an asset can't generate cash somehow, it doesn't belong on the books—the records kept by the bookkeeper or accounting staff.

Assets also include accounts receivable—money owed the company by customers who have purchased goods or services on credit. I explain accounts receivable in more detail later in the chapter.

A *liability* is an amount of money owed by the company to an organization or individual. Liabilities must be paid on or before some specific date and for a specific reason. Most liabilities are owed to the company's suppliers and creditors. One common exception is taxes payable, which are, of course, owed to the government. Liabilities arise from transactions that took place in the past. For instance, if someone sent you a keg of nails, they also sent you an invoice that you probably have 30 days to pay. That invoice is a liability.

Owners' equity is the amount left for the company's owners after the liabilities are subtracted from the assets. Put another way:

> Assets – Liabilities = Owners' equity

This simply means that the shareholders own the assets and owe the liabilities. After you subtract what is owed from what is owned, you have the actual stake the owners have in the company, and the actual value of the company. Owners' equity is also called *net worth*.

MBA LINGO

Assets refers to everything the company owns: the furniture, the inventory, the equipment, the building, and even the cash in the bank are all assets. A **liability** is an amount of money owed by the company to an organization or individual. Most liabilities are owed to the company's suppliers, creditors, and the government (in the form of taxes).

Owners' equity is the amount left for the company's owners after the liabilities are subtracted from the assets. Assets minus liabilities equals owners' equity. Owners' equity is also called **net worth.**

Meet the Balance Sheet

The *balance sheet* shows assets, liabilities, and owners' equity at a certain time, usually at the end of a quarter or *fiscal year* (the year that the company uses for budgeting and financial reporting).

MBA LINGO

The **balance sheet** shows assets, liabilities, and owners' equity at a certain time, usually at the end of a quarter or fiscal year. A **fiscal year** is the year that the company uses for budgeting and financial reporting. Most U.S. companies (about 70 percent) are on a calendar year fiscal year—that is, their fiscal year is from January 1 through December 31. Other companies use fiscal years geared to their particular season.

The formula for the balance sheet is:

$$\text{Assets} = \text{Liabilities} + \text{Owners' equity}$$

You'll notice that this version of the formula is a bit different from the calculation for owners' equity. This version expresses three things:

- The balance sheet presents assets on the left side of the statement, and liabilities and owners' equity on the right side. (For reasons of space or format, some balance sheets present assets on the top and liabilities and owners' equity below, but the concept remains the same: Assets = Liabilities + Owners' equity.)

- The balance sheet must balance. Assets *must* equal liabilities plus owners' equity.

- Assets are financed by liabilities and owners' equity. Liabilities and equity exist to finance assets. Assets exist to generate cash to pay off the liabilities, with enough left over to give the owners a profit.

This is how the money flows through a business. Owners invest money in the company, and banks and suppliers extend it credit. That creates owners' equity and liabilities. Management uses that money to buy assets. Assets generate cash that flows back to the right side of the balance sheet to pay off the liabilities, with money left over for the owners (which is profit or income).

The balance sheet is usually described as a snapshot of a company. That is true, because it is a picture of the company's accounts at a certain date. But the snapshot idea leads some people to forget the dynamic relationship of assets, liabilities, and equity. For reasons that will become clear later, it's also useful to think about the balance sheet as representing a flow of money through the business.

Let's look at a balance sheet and then take a tour of the various asset, liability, and owners' equity accounts.

A Sample Balance Sheet

To make the balance sheet clearer, take a look at the following sample balance sheet for a fictional company.

Balance Sheet for Sample Company, Inc.

	12/31/10	12/31/09
Assets		
Current Assets:		
Cash	$900,000	$600,000
Marketable Securities	$1,700,000	$920,000
Accounts Receivable (Less: Allowance for Bad Debt of $40,000 in 2010 and $38,000 in 2009)	$4,000,000	$3,800,000
Inventories	$5,400,000	$6,000,000
Total Current Assets	$12,000,000	$11,320,000
Property, Plant & Equipment:		
Buildings & Machinery	$9,700,000	$9,090,000
Less: Accumulated Depreciation	($3,600,000)	($3,000,000)
Land	$900,000	$900,000
Total Property, Plant & Equipment	$7,000,000	$6,990,000
Other Assets:		
Prepayments & Deferred Charges	$200,000	$180,000
Intangibles (good will, patents)	$200,000	$200,000
Total Assets	$19,400,000	$18,690,000

	12/31/10	12/31/09
Liabilities & Owners' Equity		
Current Liabilities:		
Accounts Payable	$2,000,000	$1,880,000
Notes Payable	$1,700,000	$1,800,000
Accrued Expenses Payable	$660,000	$600,000
Federal Income & Taxes Payable	$640,000	$380,000
Current Portion of Long-Term Debt	$400,000	$400,000
Total Current Liabilities	$5,400,000	$5,060,000
Long-Term Liabilities:		
Long-Term Debt	$5,000,000	$5,400,000
Total Liabilities	$10,400,000	$10,460,000
Owners' Equity		
Preferred Stock (6%, $100 par value, 1,200 shares authorized, issued, and outstanding)	$1,200,000	$1,200,000
Common Stock ($10 par value, 300,000 shares authorized, issued, and outstanding)	$3,000,000	$3,000,000
Additional Paid-in Capital	$1,400,000	$1,400,000
Retained Earnings	$3,400,000	$2,630,000
Total Owners' Equity	$9,000,000	$8,230,000
Total Liabilities & Owners' Equity	**$19,400,000**	**$18,690,000**

As you look at this balance sheet, keep a few points in mind:

- Remember that each dollar value on the balance sheet is a "snapshot" of the account, meaning its value as of the date of the financial statement (in this case, December 31 of 2010 and 2009).

- Total assets must equal total liabilities and owners' equity. It's called a balance sheet because it has to balance.

- Parentheses indicate a negative number, one to be subtracted from the column it appears in.

- Assets are listed in order of their liquidity—that is, how easily they can be converted to cash. Obviously, cash comes first; next come marketable securities (for example, Treasury bills, because the U.S. government is obligated to pay them). Then come accounts receivable, because your customers are obligated to pay them. Assets that are more difficult to convert or sell (buildings and land, for instance) come later.

- Liabilities and owners' equity are listed in the order in which they are scheduled to be paid (notice that the owners' profits come last!).

- Current assets are expected to be liquidated—that is, turned into cash—within one year of the date of the balance sheet. Current liabilities are payable within one year. Long-term assets are expected to be liquidated (if at all) more than a year from the date of the balance sheet. Long-term liabilities are payable more than a year from that date.

- You need balance sheets for two (or more) periods so you can compare the values in the accounts for the two periods. A balance sheet for one period offers no basis of comparison and is therefore of little value.

MBA MASTERY

Only by comparing balance sheets for two or more financial periods can you judge the financial health of the company. You analyze the year-to-year changes in the accounts to see what's going on.

A Tour of the Assets

I realize that a lot of terms and numbers in this balance sheet may be new to you. You've probably heard the old joke, "How do you eat an elephant?" Answer: "One bite at a time." So we are going to take these accounts line by line, a bite at a time.

Note that although our sample balance sheet and the following list are not exhaustive, they do present the assets commonly found on the balance sheet of a commercial or industrial company, such as a retailer or manufacturer. Financial services companies, such as banks, and companies in specialized industries, such as power generating or oil refining, have their own specific kinds of assets in addition to these. The assets we cover here are the standard ones you'll find in most companies.

MBA ALERT

Banks, insurance companies, and other financial institutions have special financial statements and asset and liability classes. For example, a loan, which is a liability to a manufacturer or retailer, is an asset to a bank. The loan represents money to be paid to the bank. Similarly, to a bank, a deposit is a liability because it is money that the bank must pay to a person or business—to whom the deposit is an asset!

Cash

Cash means the cash in the company's checking and savings accounts, and in petty cash. Often you see cash and marketable securities together on one line of a balance sheet.

Marketable Securities

Marketable securities are short-term investments, usually in U.S. government securities or the *commercial paper* of other firms. The securities have short maturities and stable prices. Because of their liquidity, these securities are referred to as *near-cash assets.* Companies put money in marketable securities because they often earn higher interest than checking or savings accounts earn.

MBA LINGO

Marketable securities are short-term investments, usually in U.S. government securities or the commercial paper of other firms. **Commercial paper** is the name for short-term promissory notes issued by large banks and corporations. The maturities run from 2 to 270 days. Marketable securities are often called **near-cash assets** because they are highly liquid.

Marketable securities are shown on the balance sheet at "the lower of cost or market," meaning at their original cost—the price the company paid for them—or the current market price, whichever is lower. This keeps the value shown for these assets conservative. Often when the securities are shown at cost and the current market value is higher, that current value is shown in parentheses or in a footnote to the financial statement.

Accounts Receivable and Bad Debt

Accounts receivable are amounts owed by customers who have purchased goods or services from the company on trade credit.

Of course, a small percentage of customers do not pay their bills. That is the reason for the allowance for bad debt that is noted on the balance sheet. This allowance is a contra account set up to accumulate an amount for those accounts receivable (or receivables) that will ultimately be uncollectible.

A contra account is an account created to offset potential future changes (usually losses) in another account. For example, retailers use a "Reserve for Returns" to offset their sales, because they know some customers will return the merchandise they bought. By deducting that merchandise from its sales figure, the store is stating sales realistically, because that money is returned to the customer. Contra accounts typically deduct a percentage of sales or accounts receivable (or whatever is being offset) based on experience or an industry average.

The company knows that some percentage (2 percent or so, in most lines of business) of accounts receivable will be uncollectible. At the time of the sale, the company sets aside this amount for bad-debt expense.

Inventories

Inventories are goods for sale to customers or goods in the manufacturing process at the time the balance sheet is prepared. A manufacturer usually has three kinds of inventory: raw materials, work in process, and finished goods. Raw materials are goods that the company purchased to make its products, while work in process is currently somewhere in the manufacturing process, as the name implies. Work in process is often called unfinished goods. Finished goods are goods awaiting sale.

A retailer has inventory and no raw materials or work in process because it buys and sells only finished goods.

Service companies typically do not sell goods (except as a sideline, such as when hair salons sell hair-care products), so they usually have minimal or no inventory on their balance sheets.

MBA ALERT

Be sure to keep your current assets moving. You want your inventories and receivables to keep flowing through the company (or "turning over") because you are then selling product and collecting money more quickly, and thus doing more business. Ways to speed up the flow of current assets through a company include stocking only fast-moving merchandise, discounting slow-moving items, taking deliveries of merchandise more often to keep inventories low, and collecting accounts receivable aggressively.

Property, Plant, and Equipment

Property, plant, and equipment refers to the buildings (offices, factories, warehouses, and so on) and equipment (machinery, furniture, and fixtures, such as lighting and display cases) owned by the company. Often you will see various elements of property, plant, and equipment broken out separately—for example, buildings and equipment, or buildings and fixtures and furniture.

Note that the property, plant, and equipment amounts represent the company's productive capacity and premises, not products the company is in business to sell. Thus, property, plant, and equipment are called *fixed assets*.

Accumulated *depreciation* is a contra account for tracking the depreciation of the value of fixed assets. Because the value of equipment and buildings generally decreases with age, the balance sheet must reflect the true worth of the fixed assets (as opposed to the amounts they were bought for). Depreciation, which I explain fully in Chapter 14, is a way of *allocating* the cost of a fixed asset to each year of the asset's life. In other words, the cost of the asset is charged against income over the life of the asset instead of all in one year.

MBA LINGO

Fixed assets are tangible property used in the operations of a business. They are not expected to be consumed or converted to cash in the ordinary course of business. **Depreciation** is a way of allocating the cost of a fixed asset with a life of more than one year. The cost of the asset is charged against income over the life of the asset instead of all in one year. **Allocating** a cost (any cost) means assigning portions of that cost to subsequent operating periods or to specific areas within the company.

By the way, in the sample balance sheet, I've shown depreciation as a separate line on the statement, while the allowance for bad-debt contra account was deducted as part of the accounts receivable line. Either presentation is correct.

You do not depreciate assets that are used right away or within one year (for example, paper or office supplies). But as I explain in Chapter 14, under tax law, you must depreciate assets with a longer life, such as productive equipment or company cars.

Land

Land owned by the company is usually carried at cost (the price paid for it) and listed separately from other fixed assets.

Prepayments and Deferred Charges

Prepayments and *deferred charges* are not really assets, in a sense, but rather prepaid liabilities.

MBA LINGO

Prepayments and **deferred charges** represent monies that have already been spent that will yield benefits in upcoming years. Prepaid insurance premiums and money allocated to research and development are examples of prepayments and deferred charges, respectively.

The best example of a prepayment is insurance premiums paid in advance. The company has paid the bill for, say, five years of insurance coverage in advance. That prepayment creates an asset that will be used up over the five-year period. Thus, it is carried as a long-term asset.

Deferred charges are similar. They represent money already spent that will yield a benefit in the coming years. For example, research and development expenses for a new product may be allocated over the life of that product. The company sets up an asset account for that amount so it can make that allocation.

Intangibles

Intangibles are assets that provide a business advantage even though they do not physically exist. Intangible assets include items such as trademarks, patents, and goodwill.

MBA LINGO

Intangibles are assets that provide a business advantage even though they do not physically exist. Intangible assets include patents, trademarks, and goodwill.

A trademark is a legally protected brand name, slogan, or design of a product or firm. A registered trademark cannot be used by another company, because the firm that owns it used its resources to develop and establish that trademark.

Patents give an exclusive right to a product or process to the holder of the patent. Like a trademark, this protects the company or person who developed the product or process from having the work exploited by others.

Goodwill is the amount of money paid for an asset—for example, a product line or another company—above the value it was assigned by the previous owner. Companies vary in their accounting for goodwill. In most cases, when one company buys another, it must write off any goodwill within 40 years.

The Major Liabilities

Like assets, the kinds of liabilities listed on the balance sheet are a bit different for companies in financial services and specialized industries. However, the following sections present the most common liabilities for most types of firms.

Accounts payable, or *payables*, are the amounts the company owes to its suppliers. (In other words, one company's receivables are another's accounts payable.)

Notes payable can include commercial paper or other promissory notes (meaning a written promise to pay) that represent short-term borrowings of the company, meaning those payable within one year.

The *accrued expenses* account sums up all the other money that the company owes to companies and individuals it does business with, including employees and independent contractors, attorneys and other outside professionals, and utilities such as the electric and telephone companies who have not been paid for services rendered on the date of the balance sheet.

Every business that makes a profit must pay federal income taxes and, where applicable, state and city income taxes. There are also real estate taxes, excise taxes, payroll taxes, other business taxes—you get the idea. Taxes are accrued on the books until they're due, and the accrued amount is shown in this account.

MBA LINGO

Accounts payable, or **payables,** are the amounts the company owes to its suppliers. **Notes payable** can include commercial paper or other promissory notes that represent short-term borrowings of the company.

Accrued means recorded but not paid, collected, or allocated. In the case of the balance sheet, **accrued expenses** sums up the money that the company owes to others (for example, employees, attorneys, and utility companies) who have not been paid for services rendered on the date of the balance sheet.

Remember the distinction between current (or short-term) assets and liabilities and long-term assets and liabilities? *Current liabilities* are those payable within a year, meaning within a year of the date of the balance sheet.

Thus, the current portion of long-term debt is the portion of long-term debt that is due in the coming year. For instance, if the Sample Company took out a three-year term loan on December 31, 2009, the portion of the loan that must be repaid in the first year (that is, 2010) would be shown in this account. The amount to be repaid in the other two years would be shown in the long-term debt account.

Long-term debt is all debt due after one year from the date of the balance sheet. This debt mostly represents financing from banks (including mortgages) and bondholders.

MBA LINGO

On the balance sheet, **current liabilities** are those payable within a year, meaning within a year of the date of the balance sheet. **Long-term debt** is all debt due after one year from the date of the balance sheet.

Owner's Equity

Owner's equity refers to the financial stake the owners have in the company. The business has assets, and after you subtract what the business owes to anyone it owes money to, what is left is the owner's stake. Note that this number can be zero or even negative if the company owes more than it has in assets. (That is, of course, a terrible situation that leads to bankruptcy if it's not quickly corrected with substantial and profitable growth in sales or an infusion of capital from the owners or investors.)

Any corporation can issue stock. This includes any incorporated business, from a one-person company to a giant outfit that employs thousands of people and issues stock to the public. A corporation will always have an account for stock on the balance sheet, as shown in our example.

An unincorporated business, such as a proprietorship or partnership, which you learned about in Chapter 3, will not have accounts for stock but will show the owners' equity in the form of capital contributions (money invested in the business by the owner or owners) and retained earnings (which is the same as retained earnings in our example—money earned by the business and then reinvested in the business).

Stock

Stock, or capital stock, represents ownership in a corporation. A share of stock is one unit of ownership. An owner's percentage of all the outstanding shares indicates his or her percentage of ownership. Investors buy stock in order to share in the company's profits. The company issues stock in order to raise money from investors.

Investors affect the finances and direction of a company in several ways:

- An investor purchases a stake in the company's future earnings.

- An investor shares in future earnings in the form of dividends (payments made to stockholders out of the company's income).

- An investor also gets voting rights, meaning he or she can vote on issues that affect the company, such as who'll be on the board of directors and whether the company will be sold to another company.

Note the difference between an investor and a creditor: an investor influences and benefits from the growth and direction of the company; a creditor merely lends money to the company.

A company may issue several classes of stock, each with different features, such as dividend policies and voting rights. The two broad classes of stock are preferred stock and common stock.

MBA ALERT

Creditors lend money to a business; stockholders invest in it. A creditor faces much less risk than an investor. A creditor has a legal right to be paid, which is documented in a sales or loan agreement, or a bond. An investor receives profits, in the form of dividends, only if the business makes enough money to distribute profits. Stockholders can, however, also make money if the stock appreciates—that is, gains value because the company earns profits, even if they are not distributed.

Preferred Stock

Preferred stock pays a dividend at a specific rate, regardless of how the company performs. Owners of preferred stock do not have voting rights. It is called preferred stock because the dividend on this stock must be paid before dividends are paid on the common stock.

Owners of preferred stock do not have a contractual right to a dividend. They get dividends only if the company has earnings to pay them.

Common Stock

Owners of *common stock* have voting rights, but do not receive dividends at a fixed rate. Because holders of common stock share in the future earnings of the company, the value and price of this stock can rise (appreciate) or fall as the company's business prospects change. Most holders of common stock purchase it as much for the potential for appreciation as for future dividends.

Common stock can pay dividends well in excess of those paid on preferred stock. (I cover stocks in more detail in Chapter 16.)

> **MBA LINGO**
>
> Stock comes in different classes or types. The most popular classes of stock are **preferred stock** and **common stock.** Holders of preferred stock have no voting rights, are paid dividends at a fixed rate, and receive dividends before the holders of common stock. Holders of common stock have voting rights and do not receive dividends at a fixed rate.

Additional Paid-in Capital

When a company issues stock, the stock has a *par value*, a value assigned to a share of stock by the company (for example, $1 or $5 or $10 a share). This value does not determine the selling price (that is, the market value) of the stock. The selling price, the price the investor actually pays per share, is determined in the market.

The amount paid to the company in excess of the par value of the stock is counted as *additional paid-in capital*. It is capital paid into the company in addition to the stock's par value. (Additional paid-in capital is also known as paid-in surplus.)

MBA LINGO

Par value is the value assigned to a share of stock by the company. The actual selling price of the stock is determined in the market. The amount paid to the company in excess of the par value of the stock is counted as **additional paid-in capital.**

Retained Earnings

When the company earns a profit for a period, it can do only one of two things with the money: distribute it to shareholders in the form of dividends, or retain it in the company to finance more assets. Any income not distributed as dividends goes into retained earnings. It is thus reinvested in the company and becomes part of the capital that finances the company.

CASE IN POINT

Young, growing companies often go for years without paying a dividend. The stock of these companies is often called a growth stock because the company is growing so fast. Instead of paying a dividend, the company retains all its earnings to finance the growing level of assets it needs to support its rapidly growing sales.

Investors who buy growth stocks understand this and target appreciation of the stock price rather than dividends as their investment goal.

The Least You Need to Know

- A balance sheet shows the values in the company's accounts on a certain date.
- The simple formula for the balance sheet is: Assets = Liabilities + Owners' equity.
- Current assets include cash; marketable securities; accounts receivable; property, plant, and equipment; and intangibles.
- Liabilities include accounts payable, notes payable, accrued expenses payable, taxes, and long-term liabilities.
- Owners' equity includes stock, additional paid-in capital, and retained earnings.

Making a Statement: Income and Cash Flow

In This Chapter

- Using the income statement to understand a company
- A tour through the income statement accounts
- How cash flow shows where the money comes from—and goes

In Chapter 11, you took a detailed tour of one of the key financial statements, the balance sheet. Now let's turn to the other two major financial statements: the income statement and the cash flow statement.

The income statement is as important to your understanding of a company as the balance sheet. The cash flow statement is secondary. What it shows—the sources and uses of the cash that flowed through a company during a period—is important, but it is constructed from the balance sheet and income statement accounts. I include it here because, with any company, large or small, the way cash flows through a business is key.

Introducing the Income Statement

The *income statement* presents the results of a company's operations for a given period, usually a quarter or fiscal year. The income statement shows the company's sales and expenses for that period. It also shows whether the company had a profit or a loss for the period, so the income statement is also called the profit and loss statement, or the P&L.

The simple formula for the income statement is:

Sales – Expenses = Income

Clearly, the higher the sales and the lower the expenses, the greater the income. But the income statement is not quite that simple, because there are various types of expenses (just as there are various types of assets, liabilities, and owners' equity on the balance sheet). Seeing these various expenses on the income statement tells you how the company is spending its money and where management is most and least efficient.

MBA ALERT

As with the balance sheet, the income statements of banks differ from those of nonbanking businesses. That's because banks are mainly in the business of taking deposits and making loans. For example, "sales" is generally expressed as "interest income," and "cost of goods sold" is generally "interest expense."

The balance sheet is a snapshot of the company on a certain date; the income statement covers operations over an entire period. Unlike the balance sheet accounts, those on the income statement began at zero at the beginning of the period. So when you see "Sales" or "Salaries" on an income statement, you are seeing the total dollar amount of sales made or salaries paid during the period.

Let's look at a sample income statement to see what all this means.

Income Statement for Sample Company, Inc., December 31, 2010

	2010	2009
Sales	$22,000,000	$20,400,000
Cost of Goods Sold	$16,400,000	$15,400,000
Gross Income	$5,600,000	$5,000,000
Selling, General & Administrative Expense	$2,800,000	$2,650,000
Depreciation Expense	$600,000	$550,000
Operating Income	$2,200,000	$1,800,000
Other Expenses:		
Interest Expense	$270,000	$300,000
Other Income:		
Interest on Marketable Securities	$100,000	$80,000
Income Before Taxes	$2,030,000	$1,580,000
Provision for Income Taxes	$960,000	$730,000
Net Income (Loss)	$1,070,000	$850,000

Keep in mind these points when examining an income statement:

- As with the balance sheet, you should have at least two years of *income statements* to examine. Trends in sales and income are particularly important to watch. Sales and income growth are management's main responsibilities, so you want to see growth in those areas. Flat or falling sales are usually a sign of trouble.

- Companies are driven to sell because, ultimately, all their money comes from sales. As you see on the statement, all expenses are deducted from sales. Other income or interest income is not part of the company's regular business.

- *Cost of goods sold* captures production expenses, the expenses of producing the products. These are sometimes called direct expenses.

- Selling, general, and administrative expenses capture the costs of selling the products and of operating the administrative functions, such as human resources.

- The accounts "Other Expenses" and "Other Income" record expenses and income not related to operating the business. An example of an other expense is the cost of defending the company against a lawsuit. In contrast, winning a settlement in a lawsuit would generate other income.

MBA LINGO

The **income statement** shows the financial results of a company's operations for a given period, usually a year or quarter. It begins with sales during the period and subtracts all expenses incurred during the period to show how much money the business earned after expenses.

Cost of goods sold is the expense of buying goods and producing the product. They are called direct costs or direct expenses because they are directly associated with making what the company sells, as opposed to the costs of selling the product or administrative costs. The major components of costs of goods sold are materials and labor.

A Tour Through the Income Statement

Let's examine the income statement accounts. Remember, each account started at zero at the beginning of the period (in this case, the beginning of the year) and accumulated the amount shown during that period.

Sales

Sales (also called revenue, revenues, total sales, or total revenue) is the amount of money the company took in, before any expenses, on its operations. This means that sales does not include money the company took in, for example, by selling off old property, plant, and equipment. That would be shown under other income. Nor does sales include interest earned on marketable securities, which would be included under interest income.

> **MBA ALERT**
>
> If you manage a company or department that produces a product, be sure to monitor the individual direct expenses that go into making that product. This includes the cost of materials, parts, and hardware, as well as your labor costs (watch overtime, which adds up quickly) and your costs of operating machinery. Those different expenses are the numbers to watch in order to control your production costs and achieve high gross income. It's just another case of "watch out for the dimes and the dollars will take care of themselves."

Sometimes you'll see a contra account (see Chapter 11) called "Allowance for Returns" that is presented with sales. For instance, you might see "Sales $1 Million Less: Allowance for Returns $20,000." That contra account is set up because manufacturers and retailers know that some percentage of their products will be returned by dissatisfied customers or those who experience breakage or find defects. In this case, the contra account represents 2 percent of total sales ($1 million × .02 = $20,000), which is in the normal range for a manufacturer.

Cost of Goods Sold

For a retailer, cost of goods sold equals the price the retailer paid to suppliers for the merchandise it sells in the stores. This includes the transportation costs of getting the goods into the stores.

For a manufacturer, cost of goods sold equals the total cost of producing its products. The major production expenses include the cost of materials; the wages and benefits of production workers; freight and transportation; and the rent, power, lights, maintenance, and other costs of operating the factory.

Cost of goods sold should capture all the costs directly associated with making (or, for a retailer, acquiring) the product the company sells.

Gross Income

Gross income is the amount of money the company earns on its sales before the selling, general, and administrative expenses, which is the next expense item. Gross income is also called gross profit.

Some income statements don't report income at this level. They don't break out cost of goods sold, but instead deduct selling, general, and administrative expenses and go straight to operating income. To me, that's too bad, because it omits important information. You'll see why in the next chapter.

Selling, General, and Administrative Expense (SG&A)

After a manufacturer makes a product (or after a retailer buys it from a supplier), that product must be sold. That means you have to pay salespeople salaries and commissions. They have to use the phone and Internet, send e-mails and letters, and travel to clients and probably buy them lunch (even drinks and dinner) now and then. All of these expenses, as well as marketing expenses, are included in this account.

On top of that, there are all those support functions—human resources, information technology (IT), accounting, and finance—as well as office space, power, light, supplies, and everything else needed to run a company. The salaries and benefits of managers are also included in SG&A, as it's usually called, since they do not work directly on producing the product.

Depreciation Expense

Depreciation expense is the amount of depreciation charged against sales during the period. This is *not* the same as accumulated depreciation on the balance sheet. Accumulated depreciation on the balance sheet is the total of all the past depreciation expense on the company's existing property, plant, and equipment.

This means that depreciation expense on the income statement for a period is added to the amount of accumulated depreciation on the balance sheet at the beginning of the period.

If you examine Sample Company's balance sheet in Chapter 11 and compare it to the income statement in this chapter, you'll see that the difference in accumulated depreciation between the balance sheet dated 2010 and the one dated 2009 is $600,000. That $600,000 is the depreciation expense charged to operations on the company's 2010 income statement.

Operating Income

Subtracting SG&A from gross income gives you *operating income*, also called operating profit, income from operations, and income from continuing operations.

Note that operating income represents only income directly related to operations. Income from other sources—such as from the sale of a division or the settlement of a lawsuit—is listed separately under other income.

> **MBA LINGO**
>
> **Operating income** equals sales minus the cost of goods sold and minus selling, general, and administrative expenses. This is the amount earned by the company on sales after deducting the direct expenses of making the product and the expenses of selling it and of all other aspects of running the business itself. Operating income is also called operating profit.

Other Expenses

Other expenses include interest expense, plus any extraordinary or nonrecurring expenses, as they are called. Although they are not shown in the earlier statement, other expenses can include costs of litigation, settlements paid in lawsuits, and the expense of closing down a division.

> **CASE IN POINT**
>
> Although they may generally be trivial to most companies in most years, "other expenses" can be significant when they occur. For example, in 2010, the value of the stock of British Petroleum (BP) fell by about 50 percent in the two months following its oil spill in the Gulf of Mexico in April of that year. Analysts estimated the potential cost to BP of the cleanup and follow-up litigation, settlements, and awards as high as $40 billion, with some forecasting bankruptcy. Bankruptcy appeared unlikely, however, given BP's revenues of more than $290 billion for the 12 months ending June 2010.

Interest Expense

Interest expense is counted separately from both operating and other expenses. Interest expense relates fairly directly to doing business, but it varies with both the amount the company borrows and, often, with the level of interest rates. Managers and investors watch interest expense closely because, while there are good reasons to borrow money, too much debt generates high interest expenses that drag on a company's operations.

Other Income

Other income, also called extraordinary or nonrecurring income, is incoming money not generated by regular operations.

Interest income is the most common category of other income. It is counted separately for the same reason that we count interest expense separately. Unless the company is a bank (in which case, interest income actually represents sales), interest income is "gravy"—not a source of income from operations.

Although they are not shown in the sample statement, other sources of income can include money paid to the company in settlement of a lawsuit, money from the sale of fixed assets, or money from the sale of an intangible asset, such as a trademark or patent.

MBA MASTERY

Because businesspeople (like the rest of us) dislike paying taxes, companies have methods—legal ones, of course—of minimizing their pretax income so that they minimize their taxes. In Chapter 14, I show you various accounting methods that affect reported income.

Income Before Taxes

Income before taxes is income from all sources—operations as well as extraordinary items—before the government gets a crack at it. Income before taxes is also called pretax income.

Provision for Income Taxes

Corporate income tax rates can vary from year to year at the federal, state, and local levels. In the sample income statement, I've simply assumed a total tax rate of about 30 percent.

This is called a provision for income taxes because the taxes will be charged against the income earned in this period even if they have not actually been paid in this period. In other words, this account shows the total income tax expense charged to income during the period.

Net Income (Loss)

This is the bottom line you've heard so much about. Net income is what's left of sales and other income after you deduct cost of goods sold; selling, general, and administrative expense; other expenses; and taxes.

If all the expenses exceed sales and other income during the period, the company has a loss for the period. It is *in the red*. (Note that, in the sample statement, parentheses are placed around the word *Loss* in the Net Income line to indicate a negative number.)

MBA LINGO

People say that a company with a loss for a period is **in the red** because losses used to be written in the books in red ink. You'll also hear the expression *red ink*, as in, "If this new product fails, we'll be swimming in red ink."

Get Insights into Income

The income statement represents management's report card for a quarter or a year. Just reading a company's income statements from a couple years will tell you a lot. Here are some of the questions you'll be able to answer after looking at income statements:

- Are sales rising, falling, or just plain flat?

- Are costs rising or falling faster or slower than sales? Or are they keeping pace with the movement in sales?

- How about interest expense? Did interest expense rise or fall from one year to the next?

- Is income keeping pace, or is it changing in relation to sales? How's the bottom line holding up?

- Did the company incur any extraordinary windfalls or charges?

How Are Your Employees Doing?

Sales per employee and net income per employee are two quick measures you can easily calculate from an income statement. They can be quite revealing. To calculate sales per employee, simply divide the sales figure on the income statement by the number of employees in the company. To calculate net income per employee, divide the net income figure by the number of employees.

If either of these figures is on a downward trend, it may mean that the company is not efficiently managing its human resources. You can also compare the results of these calculations with the corresponding numbers for other companies in the same industry to see how your use of employee resources rates.

You'll examine a number of calculations for analyzing both the balance sheet and the income statement in Chapter 13.

The Cash Flow Statement

I wrap up this introduction to financial statements with the *cash flow statement*. This is also called the statement of sources and uses of cash, but, for brevity, let's stick with calling it the cash flow statement.

MBA LINGO

The **cash flow statement** shows the sources and uses of the cash that flowed through the company during a period—typically a year, but always the same period that the accompanying balance sheet and income statement covers. This statement shows where the company's money came from and where it was spent during the period.

Like the balance sheet and income statement, the cash flow statement is presented in a company's annual report. The cash flow statement is important for two reasons:

1. It improves your understanding of what's going on in the balance sheet and income statement, because the cash flow statement is calculated from account values on those statements.

2. It highlights an essential point: cash is king. A company must generate actual cash (dough, jack, Benjamins), and it must generate it from operations instead of through borrowing or by selling off pieces of itself.

A company can have high levels of assets but not much cash. It can have inventory that can't be sold, receivables that can't be collected, and machinery that can't produce what customers want. In those cases, the outfit isn't generating cash, and cash is what you need to pay your bills and distribute dividends.

Easy Come, Easy Go

The cash flow statement shows where the company's cash came from and where it was spent during the period covered by the statement. (This period is the same one covered by the income statement, the period between the beginning and ending balance sheets.)

A cash flow statement shows the increases or decreases in the various accounts and the effects on the cash account. An increase in an asset is a use of cash, while a decrease in an asset is a source of cash. Conversely, an increase in a liability or owners' equity account is a source of cash, while a decrease in a liability or equity account is a use of cash.

For example, if the ending balance in accounts receivable is higher than the beginning balance, that counts as a use of cash, because the company added more in receivables than it collected. Collecting receivables increases cash. Not collecting them decreases cash. (As you saw in Chapter 11, on Sample Company's 2010 balance sheet, receivables are higher than on the 2009 balance sheet. So that counts as a use of cash.)

Conversely, if the ending balance in accounts receivable is lower than the starting balance, that counts as a source of cash. That's because the company collected more receivables than it added during the period. The net effect on cash is an increase, so that's a source of cash.

The cash flow statement also accounts for "noncash" charges—expenses that were recognized on the income statement but did not require a cash payment. Depreciation is the best example of a noncash charge. The actual cash was spent on the fixed asset before the accounting period, but the expense is allocated (as depreciation) to the operating period. Because no cash was spent on depreciation expense, that counts as a source of cash.

A Sample Cash Flow Statement

Here is a cash flow statement for Sample Company, based on the balance sheet in Chapter 11 and the income statement you saw earlier in this chapter:

Sample Company, Inc., Statement of Sources and Uses of Cash for the Year 2010

Cash Flows from Operating Activities:	
Net Income	$1,070,000
Depreciation	$600,000
Decrease (Increase) in Accounts Receivable	($200,000)
Decrease (Increase) in Inventories	$600,000
Increase (Decrease) in Accounts Payable	$120,000
Increase (Decrease) in Notes Payable	($100,000)
Increase (Decrease) in Accrued Expenses Payable	$60,000
Increase (Decrease) in Taxes Payable	$260,000
Net Cash Flow from Operations	**$2,410,000**
Cash Flows from Investing Activities:	
Decrease (Increase) in Marketable Securities	($780,000)
Decrease (Increase) in Buildings and Machinery	($610,000)
Decrease (Increase) in Prepaid and Deferred Charges	($20,000)
Net Cash Flow from Investing Activities	**($1,410,000)**
Cash Flows from Financing Activities:	
Increase (Decrease) in Total Long-Term Debt	(400,000)
Increase (Decrease) in Preferred Stock	——
Increase (Decrease) in Common Stock	——
Increase (Decrease) in Additional Paid-in Capital	——
Dividends Paid	($300,000)
Net Cash Flows from Financing Activities	**($700,000)**
Net Change in Cash	**$300,000**

Keep the following in mind as you examine this cash flow statement:

- The cash flow statement is largely "constructed" from the balance sheet and income statement, so the underlying numbers have to be sound for the cash flow statement to be accurate.

- Like the income statement, the cash flow statement covers only one period (in this case, the year 2010), the period from the beginning balance sheet to the ending balance sheet. It is certainly useful to have two or more years of cash flow statements, but it is not as essential as it is for the other two statements.

- The cash flow statement has three parts: cash flow from operating activities, cash flow from investing activities, and cash flow from financing activities. The most important one is cash flow from operations. A company cannot sustain itself on borrowings or investments (unless it is a financial institution, in which case borrowing and investing or lending are its business).

- The cash flow statement reconciles all other accounts to the change in the cash account that occurred from the beginning balance sheet to the ending balance sheet for the accounting period.

- When more cash comes in from various sources than goes out during a period, cash flow is positive. When the opposite occurs, cash flow is negative.

- The term *gross cash flow* or *gross cash flow from operations* usually refers to net income plus depreciation.

Getting Reconciled

Using the cash flow statement, we can easily begin to *reconcile* the accounts listed on the balance sheet and income statements—that is, analyze how changes in one account affect other accounts.

MBA LINGO

A **reconciliation** of an account analyzes the changes in the other accounts that affect the account.

For example, consider Sample Company's retained earnings shown on the balance sheet in Chapter 11. As you may remember from that chapter, net income goes to one of two places: either it is reinvested in the operation as retained earnings, or it is distributed to the shareholders as dividends. Therefore, what is not retained is paid as a dividend. Since dividends are a use of cash, you have to calculate them for the cash flow statement.

You can easily calculate the amount of dividends paid by doing a reconciliation of retained earnings accounts on Sample Company's balance sheet in Chapter 11.

Beginning retained earnings (12/31/09)	$2,630,000
Plus: Net income for 2010	$1,070,000
Minus: Ending retained earnings (12/31/10)	$3,400,000
Dividends paid during 2010	$300,000

This amount is shown on the cash flow statement under "Net Cash Flows from Financing Activities," because paying dividends on stock is an expense of using stock as a source of financing.

Actually, the cash flow statement is really just one large reconciliation of all accounts to the cash account. If you look back at Sample Company's balance sheets for 2010 and 2009 in Chapter 11, you'll see that cash increased by $300,000. The cash flow statement identifies the changes in the other accounts that led to that $300,000 increase.

The Least You Need to Know

- The income statement, also known as the profit and loss statement, or P&L, is management's report card for the quarter or year it covers.
- Examine at least two years of income statements to see trends in sales and key expense categories.
- Cash flow can be more important to a company and its owners than size, growth, or even profits.
- Use the cash flow statement to examine where money comes from and what it is spent on in a given period in a company.

Financial Analysis

In This Chapter

- The basics of financial analysis
- Measuring liquidity ratios
- Understanding solvency ratios
- Analyzing profitability ratios

In Chapters 11 and 12, I showed you the basics of balance sheets, income statements, and cash flow statements. Simply reading a financial statement will tell you something—but not much. You'll see the dollar amounts of the accounts, and, if you have at least two years of statements, you'll see whether an account increased or decreased.

But to really understand a company, you must analyze its financial statements. Aside from a basic understanding of the accounts, this requires some simple calculations.

In this chapter, you learn basic financial statement analysis—how to look beyond the account values and relate them to one another so you can see into the company's financial structure and performance.

Let's Get Analytical

A ratio is a calculation that shows the relationship between two values. A ratio is nothing more than a division problem with a number on top (numerator) divided by a number on the bottom (denominator).

Financial ratios show the relationship between two financial statement accounts. Ratio analysis enables you to measure a company's performance and creditworthiness (capability to pay its liabilities and take on additional debt). Financial ratios are not the only tool of financial analysis, but they are among the most powerful.

Liquidity Ratios

The following formulas (aside from working capital, which isn't a ratio) are called liquidity ratios. They measure a company's capability to meet its short-term obligations and to convert receivables and inventory into cash. The liquidity ratios we cover are current ratio, quick ratio, A/R turnover, collection period, inventory turnover, and days' sales on hand. But first, let's examine working capital.

Working Capital

Working capital measures a company's capability to pay its current obligations. The formula for working capital is:

Working capital = Current assets − Current liabilities

Current assets and current liabilities are listed on the balance sheet.

MBA LINGO

Working capital measures a company's capability to pay its current obligations. Working capital equals current assets minus current liabilities.

Based on the financial statements presented in Chapters 11 and 12, let's look at the working capital for Sample Company in 2010:

Working capital = $12,000,000 − $5,400,000

Working capital = $6,600,000

For Sample Company in 2009:

Working capital = $11,320,000 − $5,060,000

Working capital = $6,260,000

Working capital improved for Sample Company in 2010, rising by $340,000, or 5 percent ($340,000 ÷ $6,260,000). This 5 percent increase occurred while sales increased by about 8 percent ($22,000,000 − $20,400,000 = $1,600,000, which divided by $20,400,000 = 7.8 percent). Since working capital should grow at about the same rate as sales, this represents good financial management.

Obviously, working capital should, at a minimum, be positive. In general, the higher the working capital, the better. However, positive working capital tells us only that the company's current assets exceed its current liabilities. A ratio can tell us how much greater it is, and a lot more.

MBA ALERT

Be careful when you look at working capital, which can be inflated by useless current assets. A badly managed company often allows poor-quality receivables or obsolete inventories to build up so that its working capital appears strong. Ratio analysis enables you to look beyond raw numbers like working capital to get a better sense of what's really going on.

Current Ratio

The *current ratio*, also called the working capital ratio, shows the relationship between current assets and current liabilities. Here's the formula:

Current ratio = Current assets ÷ Current liabilities

Again, current assets and current liabilities are on the balance sheet.

For Sample Company in 2010:

Current ratio = $12,000,000 ÷ $5,400,000

Current ratio = 2.2

For Sample Company in 2009:

Current ratio = $11,320,000 ÷ $5,060,000

Current ratio = 2.2

In most businesses, a current ratio of 2.0 or better is considered good. It means that the company has twice the amount of current assets as current liabilities. Remember, though, that some assets are more liquid than others. (See Chapter 11 for a discussion of liquidity.) Therefore, we have another measure of a company's capability to pay its current liabilities: the *quick ratio*.

Quick Ratio

The quick ratio, also called the quick asset ratio or acid test ratio, is a more stringent measure of liquidity. The formula is:

Quick ratio = (Cash + Marketable securities + Accounts receivable) ÷ Current liabilities

These numbers are all on the balance sheet. This ratio focuses on the capability of the company to meet its current obligations with its most liquid assets, which are cash, marketable securities, and accounts receivable. Industry norms vary, but a company with a quick ratio of 1.0 or better is usually positioned to pay its current liabilities out of current assets.

For Sample Company in 2010:

Quick ratio = ($900,000 + $1,700,000 + $4,000,000) ÷ $5,400,000

Quick ratio = $6,600,000 ÷ $5,400,000

Quick ratio = 1.2

This quick ratio of 1.2 indicates that Sample Company has a good portion of its current assets in liquid assets rather than inventories.

Let's turn now to a few ratios that measure the quality of the accounts receivable and the inventories.

Accounts Receivable Turnover

The level of accounts receivable tells us little about the quality of the receivables. Here, the term *quality* refers to the collectability of the receivables. If accounts receivable cannot be collected, they are close to worthless.

It's also a bad sign when receivables are "slow," meaning that the company takes longer than it should to collect. In other words, the customers are not paying the invoices when they're due.

MBA MASTERY

If you sell to customers on credit, you are financing them for the time you are waiting to be paid. The slower they pay, the longer you are financing them. If you don't want to finance them for free, have a late charge on your invoices.

This is bad for two reasons. First, if business conditions worsen, slow receivables can become even slower and perhaps uncollectable. Second, the company has money tied up in those receivables, money that it could use to pay off liabilities or invest in marketable securities.

Here's the formula for receivables *turnover:*

$$\text{A/R turnover} = \text{Sales} \div \text{Average accounts receivable}$$

MBA LINGO

Turnover is the number of times the receivables went through a cycle of being created and collected (or turned over) in a period. (In Europe, *turnover* refers to annual sales.)

The sales figure is on the income statement. To calculate average accounts receivable, add the accounts receivable at the beginning of the period (from the first balance sheet) to the accounts receivables at the end of the period (from the second period) and divide the sum by two.

Now, in strictest terms, the numerator should be credit sales instead of sales, but we're assuming that all of the company's sales are on credit. Usually you won't find credit sales broken out from total sales on financial statements anyway. (If you need to, you can calculate this number for your own company with information available from the accounting department.)

For Sample Company in 2010:

$22,000,000

($4,000,000 + $3,800,000) ÷ 2

A/R turnover = $22,000,000 ÷ $3,900,000

A/R turnover = 5.6 times

In general, the higher the turnover, the better, because the faster the receivables are turning, the less money you have tied up in them.

It's particularly useful to compare this ratio with the ratio of other companies within the same industry (known as industry norms). A company in an industry that allows customers to pay within 45 days instead of the more common 30 days, for example, will automatically have a lower turnover.

Collection Period

For an even more complete picture of a firm's accounts receivable, convert the receivables turnover to collection period. This measure is also known as days' sales outstanding. Collection period is the average number of days it takes the company to collect its receivables.

$$\text{Collection period} = 365 \div (\text{A/R turnover})$$

For Sample Company in 2010:

$$\text{Collection period} = 365 \div 5.6$$

$$\text{Collection period} = 65 \text{ days}$$

This means that Sample Company takes an average of 65 days to collect its invoices. This number is "good" or "bad" only in relation to the industry norms and the terms on which the company sells. If Sample Company gives customers 60 days, or even 45 days, to pay, 65 days sales outstanding and 5.6 turns a year is fine. If the terms are 30 days, which is much more common, then Sample Company is not collecting its receivables quickly enough. In practice, virtually no company that sells on credit is paid on time by all of its customers, so the collection period will always be longer than the actual terms on which the sale is made (for instance, 30 days). In most industries, however, a 65-day collection period is not considered good.

Finally, remember that the collection period is one number that sums up all the accounts—those paying quickly and those paying slowly. In other words, it's an average.

MBA MASTERY

To encourage prompt payment, some companies offer terms of "2/10, net 30." This means the customer gets a 2 percent discount if he pays within 10 days of the invoice date, but must pay the full amount if he pays later than 10 days. Whether he takes the discount or not, he must pay within 30 days. Unfortunately, some customers take the discount even when paying beyond 10 days, so be sure to monitor eligibility and to collect from customers who take unauthorized discounts.

Inventory Turnover

Inventory turnover resembles receivables turnover. You want to sell inventory quickly, just like you want to collect receivables fast. The faster your inventory turns over, the less money you have tied up in inventory to support a given level of sales. Here's the formula for inventory turnover:

> Inventory turnover = Sales ÷ Average inventories

The sales figure is on the income statement. Inventories are on the balance sheet.

> $22,000,000
>
> ($5,400,000 + $6,000,000) ÷ 2

To calculate average inventory, add the inventory at the beginning of the period (from the first balance sheet) to the inventory at the end of the period (from the second period) and divide the sum by two.

> Inventory turnover = $22,000,000 ÷ $5,700,000
>
> Inventory turnover = 3.9 times

As with all ratios, you have to judge inventory turns against industry norms. For example, a jewelry store's inventory may turn only once a year because it carries high-priced items with a large profit margin (a measure we discuss later in this chapter) and customers expect a wide selection. However, a grocer may turn over his inventory every three to five days because the prices and profit margins are much lower, many items are perishable, and shelf space is at a premium. A grocer can't afford to carry an item that doesn't sell briskly.

Days' Sales on Hand

As with receivables, it can be useful to convert inventory turns to a measure expressed in days—days' sales on hand. This number reveals the average number of days it takes the company to sell its inventory.

Days' sales on hand = 365 ÷ Inventory turnover

For Sample Company in 2010:

Days' sales on hand = 365 ÷ 3.9

Days' sales on hand = 94 days

This means that Sample Company has an average of 94 days' worth of sales in inventory. Again, this number is "good" or "bad" only compared with industry norms. (Remember, because it is an average, this number includes the fastest-moving as well as the slowest-moving merchandise.)

Solvency Ratios

Long-term *solvency* ratios examine two elements. The first is the proportion of debt the company uses in its financial structure. The second is its capability to pay the interest on the debt (that is, to service the debt).

> **MBA LINGO**
>
> **Solvency** is the capability of a company (or individual) to pay its bills on time.

Debt-to-Equity Ratio

The *debt-to-equity ratio*, also called the debt-equity ratio, is the first of the three long-term solvency ratios we examine. The debt-to-equity ratio measures the extent to which the owners are using debt—that is, trade credit, liabilities, and borrowings—rather than their own funds to finance the company.

Debt-to-equity ratio = Total liabilities ÷ Total owners' equity

Note that total liabilities includes all current and long-term liabilities.

MBA LINGO

The **debt-to-equity ratio** compares the amount of the company's total financing from creditors compared with the amount of money invested by the shareholders. The debt-to-equity ratio is calculated by dividing total liabilities by total owners' equity, both of which are on the balance sheet.

Owners' equity represents the total amount that the owners have invested in the company, both in stock they've purchased and in earnings they've reinvested in the company rather than taken as dividends.

For Sample Company in 2010:

Debt-to-equity ratio = $10,400,000 ÷ $9,000,000

Debt-to-equity ratio = 1.2

Many analysts look for debt-to-equity of 1.0 or less. That means that half of the company's total financing—or less—comes from debt. However, many analysts also do not mind higher proportions of debt in a company's financial structure (the company's financing, as seen on the right side of the balance sheet) as long as they see that the company can handle the interest and principle payments.

Debt Ratio

The *debt ratio* resembles the debt-to-equity ratio. But instead of relating total debt to owner's equity, it measures only long-term debt in relation to all financial resources. This ratio shows the role of long-term debt in the firm's financial structure. The debt-equity ratio is particularly useful to long-term lenders such as banks.

MBA LINGO

The **debt ratio** compares the company's long-term debt to the company's total financial resources. The debt ratio measures the amount of financing that comes from long-term creditors relative to the amount provided by short-term creditors and invested by shareholders. The debt ratio is calculated by dividing long-term liabilities by total liabilities and owners' equity, both of which are on the balance sheet.

The formula for the debt ratio is:

Debt ratio = Long-term debt ÷ (Total liabilities and equity)

The figures for long-term debt, total liabilities, and equity are on the balance sheet.

For Sample Company in 2010:

Debt ratio = $5,000,000 ÷ $19,400,000

Debt ratio = 0.26

This tells us that 26 percent of Sample Company's total financial resources are in the form of long-term debt. Generally, the lower this number, the better. While you must consider industry practices and norms, if this number approaches 50 percent, you want to be sure that the company has a reliable earnings stream.

In this calculation, some analysts would include the current portion of long-term debt in the long-term debt figure (rather than in total liabilities and owners' equity). These analysts believe that although it is part of current liabilities, the current portion of long-term debt should be considered long-term debt because it was provided by long-term creditors. I did not include the current portion of long-term debt in the debt figure, to keep the calculation simple. Either method is correct.

MBA MASTERY

Financial statements are standardized, but different companies use different accounting practices (see Chapter 14). I believe analysts should use the more conservative method of calculating a ratio when there's more than one option. (A more conservative method yields the lower value.)

Times Interest Earned

The *times interest earned ratio* measures the capability of the company to pay the interest on its long-term debt. Here is the formula:

Times interest earned = Operating income ÷ Interest expense

The figures for operating income and interest expense are on the income statement. In this formula, operating income is usually called "earnings before interest and taxes" or EBIT (pronounced *e-bit*). You use EBIT because you want to measure the capability to pay the interest expense out of operating income before you deduct interest out of that income. You use income before taxes because interest is tax deductible.

MBA LINGO

The **times interest earned ratio** measures the capability of the company to pay the interest on its long-term debt out of earnings from operations. Times interest earned is calculated by dividing earnings before interest and taxes (or EBIT) by interest expense during a given period, usually a year.

Don't include "other income" in this calculation. You want to measure the company's capability to service its debt with cash from the operations only.

For Sample Company in 2010:

Times interest earned = $2,200,000 ÷ $270,000

Times interest earned = 8 times

In 2010, Sample Company earned operating income of eight times its interest expense. As always, industry norms will dictate the appropriate value for this ratio. Generally, however, EBIT of at least three or four times interest earned is considered safe.

By the way, times interest earned is often called a coverage ratio, meaning coverage of interest expense.

MBA ALERT

Look twice at any ratio based on earnings. Earnings may be measured by net income, EBIT, or EBITDA (pronounced *e-bit-da*), which is earnings before interest, taxes, debt payments, and amortization and depreciation. Try to judge the quality of earnings by identifying sources of earnings: continuing operations (which is good), new acquisitions (which may be bad if the company paid too much or took on too much debt for them), sales of assets (which may be bad if the company is selling off pieces of itself to pump up earnings), or improper accounting (which is always bad and is discussed in Chapter 14). Be very suspicious if earnings are rising but cash flow is falling.

Profitability Ratios

Finally, let's look at the profitability ratios. These ratios measure the company's earning power and management's effectiveness in running operations.

Gross Margin

Gross margin, also called the gross profit margin, is the first profitability ratio we examine. The gross margin measures the effectiveness of the company's production management.

Gross margin = Gross income ÷ Sales

Gross income and sales are found on the income statement.

MBA LINGO

Gross margin is gross income as a percentage of sales. This ratio measures the effectiveness of production and is calculated by dividing gross income by sales.

For Sample Company in 2010:

Gross margin = $5,600,000 ÷ $22,000,000

Gross margin = 25.5%

Obviously, the higher the gross margin, the better. The values for this number vary widely across industries. Sample Company spends about 75 percent of its total sales on production costs—that is, on cost of goods sold. This means that Sample Company is probably a manufacturer because most retail firms try to keep their cost of goods sold to about 50 percent.

Some businesses have inherently higher margins than others. These "high margin" businesses are often those selling something that customers value highly, particularly if the item can be made cheaply. Designer clothing and other items purchased for their image or status are a good example. For instance, U.S. luxury car models such as General Motors' Cadillac and Ford's Lincoln achieve higher margins than their lower-status products because the luxury models command higher prices for essentially the same components and a lot more sheet metal—and sheet metal is relatively cheap.

Another way to achieve high margins is to add a lot of value to a product. For example, a food-processing company will generally have higher margins than a farmer because the food processor adds more value (through the processing and packaging) than the farmer did by growing it.

Innovative high-technology companies often have very high gross margins—some as high as 70 or 80 percent. That's because a high-tech company with a new solution to an expensive problem can charge almost whatever it wants to those who need that solution. Eventually, however, competitors enter the market with competing solutions, and that drives down the prices of the technology because customers then have a choice. This erodes the gross margin of the innovator, who must usually reduce his price in order to compete. Nevertheless, the first company to introduce a new technology, as Apple did with the iPhone, can make a lot of money before those competitors arise.

Operating Margin

The *operating margin* measures operating income as a percentage of sales. In contrast to the gross margin, the operating margin measures management's effectiveness in the nonproduction areas of the company. It measures the contribution (or lack of contribution) of the sales, administrative, and other nonproduction functions.

MBA LINGO

Operating margin is operating income as a percentage of sales. This ratio measures the effectiveness in the nonproduction areas of the company and is calculated by dividing operating income by sales.

If a company has a good gross margin and a poor operating margin, management is somehow mismanaging the areas that account for selling, general, and administrative (SG&A) expense. Perhaps sales costs are too high. Perhaps lavish offices, luxury cars, and high entertainment expenses are being charged to operations. Perhaps the administrative staff is too large. Or maybe management's salaries are too high—a serious problem at some companies, especially at senior levels.

Here's the formula:

Operating margin = Operating income ÷ Sales

Operating income and sales are on the income statement.

For Sample Company in 2010:

Operating margin = $2,200,000 ÷ $22,000,000

Operating margin = 10%

As is the case with all profitability measures, the higher the operating margin, the better.

Net Margin

The *net margin* measures the bottom line—net income—as a percentage of sales. This shows the percentage of each sales dollar that the company manages to hang on to after production and operating expenses, after interest and other expenses, and after taxes.

Net margin = Net income ÷ Sales

Net income and sales are found on the income statement.

MBA LINGO

Net margin is net income as a percentage of sales. This ratio measures the company's capability to deliver on the bottom line; it shows what percentage of sales the company actually delivers to shareholders as after-tax earnings. The net margin is calculated by dividing net income by sales.

For Sample Company in 2010:

Net margin = $1,070,000 ÷ $22,000,000

Net margin = 4.9%

A net margin in the 5 percent range is common. Interestingly, a number of years ago, nonbusinesspeople were surveyed and asked, "What percentage of a company's sales do you believe wind up as profits?" The researchers got answers ranging up to 25 and even 50 percent! This highlights the general public's lack of understanding concerning business and profits. The public's understanding of business and the legitimate pursuit of profit was eroded further by the financial accounting scandals of the early 2000s and by abuses in the marketing of securities based on subprime mortgages in the late 2000s.

A net margin of around 10 percent would be excellent, particularly if the company could consistently achieve it.

Asset Turnover

As you know, management's job is to use the company's assets to generate cash. Assets must therefore generate sales and profits. The *asset turnover* ratio measures management's effectiveness at using assets to generate sales.

The formula for asset turnover is:

> Asset turnover = Sales ÷ Total assets

The sales figure is on the income statement. Total assets are on the balance sheet.

MBA LINGO

Asset turnover measures sales as a percentage of assets to show how well management is employing the company's assets to generate sales. Asset turnover is calculated by dividing sales by total assets.

For Sample Company in 2010:

> Asset turnover = $22,000,000 ÷ $19,400,000
>
> Asset turnover = 1.1 times

Asset turnover, or asset turns, shows how efficiently management uses assets. A ratio of about 1.0, like that of Sample Company, may indicate either inefficient use of assets or an inherently asset-intensive business—that is, one requiring lots of plant and equipment, such as oil refining or heavy manufacturing.

Return on Assets

Return on assets (*ROA*) measures management's capability to use assets to generate a profit (also known as a return).

Here is the formula for return on assets:

> Return on assets = Net income ÷ Total assets

MBA LINGO

Return on assets (ROA) shows how well management is using assets to generate income. Return on assets is calculated by dividing net income by total assets.

For Sample Company in 2010:

Return on assets = 1,070,000 ÷ 19,400,000

Return on assets = 5.5%

Over time, a decrease in asset turns or return on assets may mean that management is misusing assets somehow. They may be focused on spending money on assets rather than on selling product to customers. They may be growing the asset base faster than they can grow sales. This can also lead to too much debt, because those assets must be financed.

The company could also be acquiring the wrong mix of assets. If it has equipment that could be rapidly superseded by a better technology, for example, management may soon wish they didn't have all those assets.

Return on Investment

This is *the* key measure of return, especially for shareholders and therefore for management. *Return on investment (ROI)*, also called return on equity, measures the return on the money the shareholders have invested in the company.

 MBA LINGO

Return on investment (or **ROI**, also called return on equity or ROE) measures net income against the investment that it took to generate that income. Return on investment is calculated by dividing net income by owners' equity.

This number is critical because management must earn a good return for the owners. If management can't do this, either the shareholders will sell their shares and put their money where it will get a better return, or the board of directors will replace management.

Here is the formula for this important ratio:

Return on investment = Net income ÷ Owners' equity

Net income is found on the income statement; owners' equity is on the balance sheet.

For Sample Company in 2010:

Return on investment = $1,070,000 ÷ $9,000,000

Return on investment = 11.9%

Generally, an ROI of 10 percent or better is considered very good. Investors compare this number to the returns they can earn elsewhere on their money. They look at the returns earned by other companies and at interest rates on bonds and other securities. So management must always be aware of how it is doing, not just as managers of the business, but as stewards of the owners' money.

Keep Your Pencils—and Eyes—Sharp

Now that we've covered the main financial ratios, here are a few tips when doing ratio analysis, particularly if you are analyzing another company's financial statements. Be sure to …

- **Consider the source.** Sound financial analysis depends on sound financial statements. Beware of accounting games and take any red flags (such as increasing earnings and declining cash flow) seriously. Use the 10-Ks and 10-Qs, which are, respectively, the more detailed annual and quarterly reports that public companies must file with the Securities and Exchange Commission. Read about the senior managers and their backgrounds and the companies they have managed before, and weigh the statements accordingly.

- **Look beyond the ratios.** Read the footnotes to the statements and management's discussion of operations in the annual report. Keep up-to-date with company news on management changes, product announcements, and joint ventures.

- **Calculate accurately.** Financial statements can be confusing at first because some accounts, such as depreciation expense and accumulated depreciation, have similar names. Also, the eye can easily misalign numbers and accounts across columns.

- **Calculate conservatively.** Remember that most companies, including completely honest ones, put their best foot forward in financial statements. You can make up for that by being conservative in your calculations.

- **Compare the trend in the ratio over two or more periods.** A ratio from one period can't tell you nearly as much as a trend over two or more years.

- **Cross-check your ratios and look for patterns.** Try to see management's strengths and weaknesses. Do they generate cash? Is their liquidity strong? Do they have too much debt or too many assets? Are they growing the asset base faster than sales? Where are their margins weak or strong?

- **Understand industry norms.** Industry norms place financial ratios in context. Industry norms are published by Standard & Poor's; Dun & Bradstreet, Inc.; and Robert Morris Associates, a national association of bankers.

The Least You Need to Know

- The relationships among various financial statement accounts will tell you about the company's performance and creditworthiness. Financial ratios are the key tools for assessing these relationships.
- The liquidity ratios measure the company's capability to meet its short-term obligations as they come due.
- The long-term solvency ratios measure the company's capability to meet its long-term obligations.
- The profitability ratios measure the efficiency of the company's operations. A strong gross margin indicates efficient production management, while a strong operating margin indicates efficient management of sales and administration.
- When you calculate ratios and find one that's below par, look for patterns. Whenever possible, compare a company's ratios to industry norms.

Look at the Books

In This Chapter

- How accounting ledgers work
- Accounting for inventory
- Calculating depreciation on plant and equipment

Where do financial statements come from? What goes on behind the scenes? What does a bookkeeper do? What decisions go into accounting for various assets, liabilities, and expenses? How do these decisions affect the company's finances?

This chapter answers these questions. It also improves your understanding of financial statements and business. And it prepares you to set up an accounting system for your company or department, or help you understand the one that's already in place.

The Major Ledgers

When you hear someone refer to "the books," it means the company's journals or ledgers or "the books of account." They are set up in books with specially ruled ledger paper or, far more commonly today, in specialized accounting computer software that replicates ledgers in electronic form or in electronic spreadsheets, such as Microsoft Excel.

When setting up an accounting system, you first must decide how often you'll enter transactions into the various ledgers. You can make ledger entries on a daily, weekly, monthly, or quarterly basis. For infrequent transactions, such as purchases of buildings and equipment, you would make an entry when the transaction occurs.

You can enter other transactions on a regular basis. Retail stores or restaurants enter the day's receipts in a daily sales ledger. Assuming that the store or restaurant pays its employees each week, it makes weekly entries in the payroll ledger.

Most companies keep separate ledgers for separate kinds of transactions. They record sales transactions in the sales ledger, payroll checks in the payroll ledger, invoices sent to customers in the accounts receivable ledger, and bills received from suppliers in the accounts payable ledger.

These ledgers do not have to be separate books or spreadsheets. They can be separate sections of a large book or spreadsheet. As a manager, accountant, or bookkeeper, you can choose how to set up your company's books. However, you must follow standard accounting procedures, and your work must be understandable by another accountant or bookkeeper (or, heaven forbid, the IRS).

Most businesses need at least three ledgers: one for cash receipts (that is, cash inflows), one for cash disbursements (that is, cash outflows), and a general ledger. In any system, the various journals or subledgers are *posted* to the general ledger at the end of the accounting period.

MBA LINGO

A bookkeeper or accountant **posts** an account when he or she enters it into the company's books of account. If an amount is transferred from one account to another, that is also called posting.

Posting means "entering an amount." In this case, it means "transferred" to the general ledger, which summarizes all the company's accounts. The financial statements are drawn up from the general ledger.

The Double-Entry System

Bookkeeping in the United States employs the double-entry system. This means that two journal entries are made for each transaction. One entry records the transaction itself, and the other records the description of the transaction. These two entries offset one another so that the net effect on the books is zero. In other words, the books must balance.

The double-entry system requires two entries: one debit and one credit. A debit is simply an entry on the left side of an account. A credit is an entry on the right side of an account.

MBA LINGO

T-accounts represent two sides of an account in a ledger. A ledger may be ruled like a T-account, or the bookkeeper can create T-accounts by using a ruler and a pen to add heavier lines to the ledger paper. Another way to indicate a debit or credit is to write next to the entry the abbreviation "Dr." for a debit entry and "Cr." for a credit entry. (I don't know why it's Dr. instead of Db.)

The following example shows a $1,200 sale recorded by a double entry into two *T-accounts*:

Accounts receivable	Sales
$1,200	$1,200

A sale on credit creates a receivable, which the company will collect later. So we debit accounts receivable and we credit sales. That is, we make a left entry in the accounts receivable account and a right entry in the sales account, because a debit always represents one of the following:

- An increase in an asset account

- A decrease in a liability or equity account

- A decrease in a revenue account

- An increase in an expense account

And because a credit always represents one of the following:

- A decrease in an asset account

- An increase in a liability or owners' equity account

- An increase in a revenue account

- A decrease in an expense account

See Chapter 11 for a description of assets and liabilities.

When the company collects the receivable—that is, when the customer pays his invoice—the following entries are made.

Cash	Accounts Receivable
$1,200	$1,200

Why these two entries? We debit cash because when a customer pays an invoice, the asset called cash increases—and a debit represents an increase in an asset. Meanwhile another asset, called accounts receivable, decreases. We record that decrease with a credit to accounts receivable because a credit represents a decrease in an asset.

MBA ALERT

Some people find the terms *debit* and *credit* confusing at first. Most of us think of credit as something good, as in giving someone credit for something. So it may seem odd that a credit to an asset (like cash) is a decrease, while a debit is an increase. It's best just to think of a debit as a left-side entry and a credit as a right-side entry to a T-account. It might also be useful to remember that when you pay the phone company, they "credit *your* account" (which decreases *their* account receivable).

Remember, in the double-entry system, the accounts must balance. At any time, the sum of the debits must equal the sum of the credits. The debits and credits in a single account do not have to balance, and usually they don't. But the total of all the debits to the various accounts must equal the total of all the credits to the various accounts, because every transaction generates both a debit and a credit of equal amounts.

If every transaction generates two entries of equal amounts, then all the transactions must generate total debits equal to total credits. The double entries thus verify the accuracy of the bookkeeping system. In fact, the accountant can calculate a *trial balance* at any time to ensure that the debits equal the credits.

MBA LINGO

You calculate a **trial balance** by first totaling the debits and credits in each account. Usually there will be a debit or credit balance in each account. Then you total the debit balances and the credit balances to ensure that they are equal. If they are, the books balance.

What About the Financial Statements?

At the end of the accounting period, after all transactions have been recorded, the totals of the various accounts are posted to the general ledger and then to the balance sheet and the income statement. Thus, what you see in the accounts on the financial statements are the account totals, or net balances, after all the entries have been posted and summed.

The Accountant's Opinion

Financial statements for publicly held companies require an opinion written by an independent auditor. The auditor is a *certified public accountant* who has *audited* the company's books and financial statements. For publicly held companies, the accountant's opinion verifies that the company's financial position is accurately represented by the financial statements. If this is not the case, the accountant issues a qualified opinion citing the information that might be inaccurate or incomplete.

MBA LINGO

A **certified public accountant,** or CPA, is licensed by the state in which he or she practices. While requirements vary from state to state, a CPA has acquired a certain level of education, passed certain exams, and accumulated a certain amount of experience. An **audit** is an objective, formal review of the accounting practices and financial records of a company.

If the accountant's opinion is unqualified (that is, the financial statements are approved "without qualification"), then the auditors "found the company's practices and records to be in accord with generally accepted accounting principles (GAAP) and to represent accurately the financial condition of the company," to quote the usual passage.

If the accountant's opinion is "qualified," then the auditors either have discovered a practice or transaction that is not in accord with GAAP or have some other reason to believe the statements do not truly reflect the company's financial condition.

CASE IN POINT

Unfortunately, auditors tend to work with the currently accepted practices, even if they are not completely sound from an economic or financial viewpoint. For example, billions of dollars of highly questionable subprime loans were resold during the housing bubble of the 2000s—and then carried on the books of banks and other financial institutions well after the bubble had burst. The banks that needed a government bailout and the continued support of the Federal Reserve system after the housing bust had been considered "sound" by their auditors and by bank examiners from state and federal government agencies.

Accounting Treatment of Assets

In the chapters on accounting and finance, I've referred to the "accounting treatment" of various items. I've mentioned that accounting treatments can vary and that managers must often decide how to account for certain transactions. And I've pointed out that the accounting treatment can affect the firm's financial statements.

Let's look at two situations in which the accounting treatment of an asset can vary: accounting for inventory and accounting for depreciation.

Accounting for Inventory

In most economies, prices are not completely stable. Inflation occurs in many economies, and deflation—a general decrease in prices—is not unheard of, although it's less common. In addition, even in times of general price stability, prices of specific items can rise and fall.

Because prices change, the way a retailer accounts for the goods it buys and then sells (or the way a manufacturer accounts for the materials it buys) can affect its cost of goods sold and, therefore, its reported income.

Consider what I mean. Suppose a small fuel-oil supplier bought 1,000 gallons of fuel oil in June for $1 a gallon, 1,000 gallons in July for $2 a gallon, and 1,000 in August for $3 a gallon. Suppose in September that he sold 1,000 gallons for $4 a gallon. (These prices are artificially fast moving, just for the example.)

Which 1,000 gallons did he sell in September? Actually, we don't know. Fuel oil is fuel oil. But here's what happens to his gross income under three different scenarios:

If He Sold:	June Oil	July Oil	August Oil
Revenue	$4,000	$4,000	$4,000
Cost of goods sold	$1,000	$2,000	$3,000
Gross income	$3,000	$2,000	$1,000

See how income can change depending on how the inventory is valued? The way most businesses track inventory is to count the items (in units, not dollars) at the beginning of the period, count the items purchased for inventory during the period, and then count the inventory at the end of the period. The total at the beginning of the period, plus the purchases during the period, minus the inventory at the end of the period, equals the amount of units sold.

The formula for cost of goods sold is:

Cost of goods sold = Beginning inventory + Purchases – Ending inventory

Here's how it would work in the fuel oil example:

Inventory (in gallons)

Beginning inventory	0
Purchases	1,000
	1,000
	1,000
Total	3,000
Ending inventory	2,000
Amount sold	1,000

This is fine, but cost of goods sold must be a dollar figure. When we go to put a dollar value on these 1,000 gallons, the question becomes, which 1,000 gallons were sold? The answer depends on how we account for inventories.

FIFO and LIFO

The two main methods of inventory valuation are *first in, first out* (FIFO; say *fife-oh*) and *last in, first out* (LIFO; say *life-oh*). Under FIFO, the company assumes that the first inventory it purchased is the first it sells. Under LIFO, the company assumes that the last inventory it purchased is the first it sells.

MBA LINGO

First in, first out (FIFO) and **last in, first out (LIFO)** are two different methods of accounting for inventories. Under the FIFO method, the inventory that the company purchased first is assumed to be sold first. Under LIFO, the most recently purchased inventory is assumed to be sold first.

Regardless of the accounting method used, following are the actual purchases, in dollars, during the period.

Beginning inventory		0
Purchases: 1,000 @ $1.00/gal.	=	$1,000
1,000 @ $2.00/gal.	=	$2,000
1,000 @ $3.00/gal.	=	$3,000
Total: 3,000 gallons	=	$6,000
Ending inventory: 2,000 gallons	=	$????
Amount sold: 1,000 gallons	=	$????

Let's look at how we would calculate the amount sold using both FIFO and LIFO.

FIFO Effects

Again, FIFO assumes that inventory is sold in the order in which the company bought it. Sticking with our fuel oil example, under FIFO, the 1,000 gallons sold during September are assumed to be the first 1,000 gallons purchased back in June. This means:

Cost of goods sold = Beginning inventory + Purchases – Ending inventory

Cost of goods sold = 0 + $6,000 – $5,000 (the inventory purchased in July and August)

Cost of goods sold = $1,000

Recall that:

Revenue – Cost of goods sold = Gross income

So:

$4,000 – $1,000 = $3,000

FIFO yields a gross income of $3,000.

LIFO Effects

LIFO assumes that the company sells the most recently purchased inventory first. So under LIFO, the fuel oil company would assume that the last 1,000 gallons of fuel oil, purchased in August, were sold in September. That means:

> Cost of goods sold = Beginning inventory + Purchases – Ending inventory
>
> Cost of goods sold = 0 + $6,000 – $3,000 (the inventory purchased in June and July)
>
> Cost of goods sold = $3,000

Because:

> Revenue – Cost of goods sold = Gross income
>
> $4,000 – $3,000 = $1,000

LIFO yields gross income of $1,000.

Which Method Should You Use?

Under FIFO, income equals $3,000. Under LIFO, income equals $1,000. That's a significant swing in income, yet either method is acceptable.

Which one should you use? Unfortunately, the answer is, "It depends." Consider these points when you're trying to decide:

- If your firm buys and sells inventory, you *must* choose a method of accounting for inventory. Either FIFO or LIFO is permitted for income tax purposes, but once you choose a method, you must stick with it or ask the IRS for permission to change.

- Each method has a different effect on income. When prices are rising, FIFO produces a higher ending inventory value and therefore a lower cost of goods sold and higher income. When prices are rising, LIFO yields a lower ending inventory value and therefore a higher cost of goods sold and lower income.

- Each method has pros and cons. FIFO users believe that it better represents the way a business actually moves inventory. They see FIFO as valuing inventories at closer to their replacement cost in times of inflation. (The stuff in inventory was purchased most recently, so it's closer to current market prices.)

- Fans of LIFO believe their method better matches current costs (as in cost of goods sold) to current prices. If costs are rising, they believe that the higher-value (more recently purchased) inventory should be shown as the inventory that was sold.

However, the choice of which method to use mainly depends on the effects on income. In times of rising prices, which is most of the time, FIFO yields a higher income figure—and therefore a larger tax bite—than LIFO. Meanwhile, LIFO yields a lower income figure—and therefore a smaller tax bite. Since businesspeople want to minimize their taxes, LIFO is often the choice.

However, most managers want to show high income to current owners and to prospective investors and lenders. Therefore, FIFO is also often the choice. If raising money is a priority, FIFO may make more sense than LIFO, because you want to show investors and lenders that you can generate high income.

MBA ALERT

In 2014 or 2015, publicly held U.S. companies will very likely be adopting International Financial Reporting Standards (IFRS) rather than GAAP as their guidelines to preparing financial statements. IFRS is used in Europe and much of the rest of the world, and adopting IFRS will enable global companies and international investors to work with a single set of accounting standards. One feature of IFRS is that it does not permit the use of LIFO. Instead, inventories are generally valued at cost or at realizable market value.

Accounting for Depreciation

The cost of a fixed asset—a piece of equipment or machinery, or a computer or a vehicle—is allocated over the productive life of the asset. Actually, businesses would prefer to *expense* the cost of these items in the period they were purchased because that reduces reported income and thus income taxes by that much more.

MBA LINGO

To **expense** an item means to recognize the full cost in the accounting period in which the money was spent.

From an accounting standpoint, there is excellent reason to depreciate an asset over the years of its life rather than to expense it in the year it is purchased. If the asset is depreciated, its cost is recognized and written off over the period during which it is producing revenue. The accounting principle here is that of matching costs and revenues. If an asset is going to have a productive life of five years and produce products and sales over that period, it only makes logical and economic sense to recognize some of the value of that asset during its productive life.

The matchup between the amount of cost and revenue in any particular year, however, does not have to be perfect. That's just as well, because it would be impossible to account for depreciation this way. There are just too many assets purchased at different times to allow for that. But several methods of accounting for depreciation do work well for what they are supposed to do, which is allocate the cost of the asset over the life of the asset.

Let's examine the three most common depreciation methods:

- Straight-line
- Double declining balance
- Sum of the years' digits

Don't let these names throw you. The calculations involved are at the grade-school level. In examining these three methods, we assume that the company is buying a piece of equipment for $10,000 with a productive life of four years and no *salvage value*. We assume no salvage value purely for convenience.

MBA LINGO

Salvage value, or residual value, is the value of the asset after its productive life. Most fixed assets have some salvage value, although it may be minimal.

When salvage value exists, just subtract that amount from the asset's full cost to get the depreciable cost (the amount to be depreciated).

Straight-Line Depreciation

In the straight-line method of depreciation, you simply divide the cost of the asset (or the depreciable cost, which is the same thing in our example) by the asset's years of life.

Thus, you calculate straight-line depreciation on the machine in our example, as shown in the following table.

Year	Depreciation Expense	Accumulated Depreciation
1	$2,500	$2,500
2	$2,500	$5,000
3	$2,500	$7,500
4	$2,500	$10,000

Straight-line depreciation is *not* a method of *accelerated depreciation*. It does not generate higher depreciation in the early years of ownership and does not lower income in those years. Therefore, many companies choose one of the two following methods of accelerated depreciation. The IRS permits both for tax calculations.

MBA LINGO

Accelerated depreciation allows a company to allocate more of the cost of the asset to the early years of ownership. The more costs a company can charge against current revenue, the lower the income—and therefore the lower the taxes.

Double Declining Balance

The double declining balance method allows you to calculate depreciation by multiplying the *book value* (undepreciated value) of the asset by twice the straight-line rate. In our example, the straight-line rate is 25 percent per year, so the double declining balance rate would be 50 percent a year. This 50 percent is applied to the asset's book value in each year of its life.

MBA LINGO

For a fixed asset, **book value** means the undepreciated value of the asset. Recall that an asset is carried on the books at its original cost, less accumulated depreciation. The original cost minus accumulated depreciation equals the book value.

The following table shows how to calculate depreciation on the machine in our example using the double declining balance method.

Year	Remaining Value	Depreciation Expense	Accumulated Depreciation
1	$10,000	$5,000	$5,000
2	$5,000	$2,500	$7,500
3	$2,500	$1,250	$8,750
4	$1,250	$625	$9,375

They don't call it accelerated depreciation for nothing. With this method, 75 percent of the value of the asset in our example is charged to depreciation in the first two years of its life.

Keep in mind two points about the double declining method. First, you don't consider salvage value, even if it exists. At twice the straight-line rate, the asset is depreciated to a negligible value by the end of its life. Second, the IRS allows you to switch over to straight-line depreciation one time in the life of the asset. In our example, the logical point to do so would be in year 3.

If you do switch to the straight-line method, you must then consider salvage value. So if the salvage value were $250 and the company switched over in year 3, the calculation would look like this:

To figure book value at start of year 3:

$10,000	Original cost
– $7,500	Accumulated depreciation
– $250	Salvage value
$2,250	Book value

Then, dividing the book value by two (for the two years left in the asset's life) yields straight-line depreciation of $1,125 in years 3 and 4. The company gets a bit less depreciation in year 3 than if it continued using double declining balance, but it gets a lot more in year 4.

Sum of the Years' Digits

The sum of the years' digits method, also called the sum of the digits, calculates depreciation on what may at first seem an odd basis. (At least it seemed odd to me at first.)

In this method, you first add the numbers of years in the life of the asset. Then you use that number as the denominator (the bottom one) in fractions that you apply to the depreciable cost of the asset.

Confused? I don't blame you, but here's how it works. For an asset with a six-year life, you add the numbers $1 + 2 + 3 + 4 + 5 + 6 = 21$. That 21 is your denominator. The numerator goes in the reverse order of the years, meaning that the first year's depreciation is 6/21 of the asset's value, the second year's depreciation is 5/21, the third year's is 4/21, and so on. These fractions are applied to the asset's original cost (*not* to the book value).

Let's use this method in our example, which you'll recall is a $10,000 asset with a four-year life and no salvage value. The sum of the years' digits is $1 + 2 + 3 + 4 = 10$.

Year	Value ×	Fraction =	Depreciation Expense	Accumulated Depreciation
1	$10,000	4/10	$4,000	$4,000
2	$10,000	3/10	$3,000	$7,000
3	$10,000	2/10	$2,000	$9,000
4	$10,000	1/10	$1,000	$10,000

The sum of the years' digits method depreciates the full value of the asset by the end of the process (unlike double declining balance). Also unlike double declining balance, it first deducts salvage value if there is any.

Comparing the Three Methods of Depreciation

The method you choose will depend on your goals. As with inventory valuation, you have to consider the effects on income and taxes.

Let's compare depreciation expense from our example under the three methods. (In the double declining balance method, we are not switching to straight-line depreciation.)

Annual Depreciation Expense Under the Three Methods

Year	Straight-Line	Double Declining	Sum of the Balance Years' Digits
1	$2,500	$5,000	$4,000
2	$2,500	$2,500	$3,000
3	$2,500	$1,250	$2,000
4	$2,500	$625	$1,000

The sum of the years' digits is not quite as accelerated a method, but in our example, it still charges off 70 percent of the value in the first two years. This is comparable to the double declining balance rate.

Thus, under the double declining balance method, first-year income would be $2,500 lower than under the straight-line method. Under the sum of the years' digits method, income would be $1,500 lower than under the straight-line method.

You might be asking, "What about the later years? What about the years when things 'flip over' and the straight-line method yields the lower reported income?"

Those are valid questions, but for now, just take the "least and latest rule" of taxes on faith: you want to pay the least amount of taxes you can and pay them as late as you can.

Matching Depreciation to Productive Life

Aside from the income and tax effects, there's the issue of matching depreciation to the life of the asset. Fans of accelerated depreciation point out that an asset is more productive in its early years. In those years, machinery incurs less downtime and requires less maintenance, so there's an economic argument for accelerated depreciation.

Fans of straight-line depreciation believe that the asset is productive throughout its life, so you may as well allocate its cost equally over that time. Also, perhaps they prefer to show higher income in the early years, just like users of FIFO inventory accounting. Again, investors and lenders like to see high income. As with inventory valuation, the choice of depreciation method is up to you, considering your tax and income situation.

Clearly, a lot goes into financial statements, and the better you understand accounting systems and practices, the better you'll understand financial statements.

If you're in a position to make these decisions, you will certainly need to understand the effects of these choices. In fact, no matter what your position, your efforts to look behind financial statements will always be repaid. Understanding the financials is the only way to know what's really going on in a company.

Number Games

The goal of financial statements is accurate reporting of the company's financial condition and performance. This is often referred to as transparency—nothing should be hidden from investors or lenders, who are, after all, committing their funds and the funds of others to these companies. Transparency goes hand in hand with the rule of disclosure, which states that a public company must divulge all information—positive and negative—that could affect an investor's decision to buy, sell, or hold the company's stock.

Chapter 27 examines the ethical issues involved in business. However, even aside from the ethical issues, attempting to improve a company's performance by falsifying its financial statements is like trying to cure cancer by touching up the patient's X-rays. Even certain legal practices, such as some forms of *off-balance-sheet financing*, can harm a company because managers often act as if the lack of reporting means the situation (that is, the debt) doesn't exist when, in fact, it does.

 MBA LINGO

Off-balance-sheet financing includes certain loans, leases, partnerships, and other means by which a company can raise funds without creating a liability that must be reported on the balance sheet. These methods are usually legal and often must be reported in the footnotes to the financial statements. However, although off-balance-sheet financing has its uses, it can easily be subject to abuse, as was the case with Enron's myriad off-balance-sheet partnerships.

As noted in Chapter 4, every relationship rests on trust. Trust cannot exist in an atmosphere of accounting games. Therefore, any manager who employs them essentially dooms his company and himself to failure in the long run, no matter how well the games seem to work in the short run.

CASE IN POINT

Much of the financial crisis of 2008–2009 was generated by accounting games. Lax regulation of the banking system and tolerance of off-balance-sheet entities allowed companies to hide the amount of risk that they were actually incurring. When the housing bubble burst and subprime borrowers were unable to pay their loans, markets lost faith in virtually all mortgage-backed securities (securities made up of payment streams from mortgage borrowers). This led directly to the demise of the investment banks Bear Stearns and Lehman Brothers, and to the "bailout" of AIG.

The Least You Need to Know

- Because you can use various accounting treatments for certain transactions, you must often decide which one will provide greater benefit to your company. The flip side of this is that if you are looking at a company from the outside, you must be aware of which accounting treatments were used—and of their effects.

- A transaction generates a debit and a credit. A debit is an entry to the left side of an account, and a credit is an entry to the right side.

- A debit represents an increase in an asset account, a decrease in a liability or equity account, a decrease in a revenue account, or an increase in an expense account. A credit represents a decrease in an asset account, an increase in a liability or equity account, an increase in a revenue account, or a decrease in an expense account.

- Methods of accelerated depreciation, such as double declining balance and sum of the years' digits, allocate more of the asset's cost to the early years of its life than straight-line depreciation. Therefore, accelerated depreciation yields lower income in those early years of life.

- Faith in the financial markets depends on honest accounting and transparency regarding risks. Otherwise, investors cannot know what they are investing in and will ultimately lose faith in certain companies or, as was the case with mortgage-backed bonds, classes of securities.

Making Investment Decisions

In This Chapter

- Recognizing the time value of money
- Understanding major investment decisions
- Analyzing a business investment in three ways
- Deciding whether to lease or buy an asset

Major investment decisions are among the most important—and difficult—decisions you will face as a manager. They involve large sums of money and affect the company's long-term future. These decisions also affect people's jobs.

They can even affect *your* job. Company shareholders and boards of directors take an extremely dim view of poor investment decisions.

Decisions with so much at stake require careful analysis. This chapter shows you how to analyze major business investment decisions. But first you need to know some basic concepts.

Time Is Money

The key concept in investment analysis is the time value of money. The time value of money refers to the fact that a dollar you receive today is worth more than a dollar you receive a year from now. It's also worth more than a dollar you receive two years from now. It's worth more than a dollar you receive at *any* time in the future.

Why is that? After all, it's still the same amount, right? Well, the dollar you receive today is worth more because you can invest it at some interest rate for one year or two years (or for however long you want to invest it). You can't invest the dollar you'll receive next year today.

Let's look at this another way. Suppose you do not have a dollar right now; instead, you have an absolute guarantee that you will receive a dollar in one year, or two years, or five years. What exactly is that dollar worth today? In other words, what is the *present value* of that dollar?

Financial professionals have the answer: the present value of that dollar is an amount that, when multiplied by the proper interest rate, becomes a dollar in the time allowed.

Here's what I mean: At a 10 percent interest rate, that dollar you have coming to you in one year is worth 90.9¢ today. Why? Because 90.9¢ multiplied by 1.10 (for the 10 percent interest) equals $1.00.

At 15 percent interest, that dollar you have coming to you in one year is worth 87¢ today. That's because 87¢ × 1.20 equals $1.00. At 5 percent interest, that dollar is worth 95.2¢ today; at 1 percent, it's worth 99.9¢.

These interest rates I'm using are called *discount rates*. We call them discount rates because we're using them to discount the value of the future payment to its present value.

MBA LINGO

Present value is the current value of an amount to be paid in the future. The **discount rate** is the interest rate an analyst uses to calculate the present value of future cash payments. This rate is chosen by the analyst making the evaluation.

Believe it or not, this is the essence of investment analysis: you discount future payments (that is, future cash flows) produced by the investment to their present value. Then you compare these cash flows to the amount you have to invest to produce those cash flows. Then you ask yourself, "Is this worth it?"

A Present Value Table

The following table shows the present value of $1.00 for the years and discount rates indicated. For example, the present value of $1.00 discounted at 10 percent for five years is 62.1¢.

This table is hardly exhaustive. Complete tables give more interest rates (for example, from 1 percent to 40 percent) and cover every period from 1 to 50 years or more.

The interest rates and periods in this table are enough for our purposes. You can find extensive present value tables in finance textbooks. In fact, you can find books with nothing but present-value tables. (Talk about bedtime reading!)

Present Value of $1.00

Years	5%	6%	7%	Interest Rate 8%	9%	10%	11%	12%	15%
1	.952	.943	.936	.926	.917	.909	.901	.893	.870
2	.907	.890	.873	.857	.842	.826	.812	.797	.756
3	.864	.840	.816	.794	.772	.751	.731	.712	.658
4	.823	.792	.763	.735	.708	.683	.659	.636	.572
5	.784	.747	.713	.681	.650	.621	.593	.567	.497
6	.746	.705	.666	.630	.596	.564	.535	.507	.432
7	.711	.665	.623	.583	.547	.513	.482	.452	.376
8	.677	.627	.582	.540	.502	.467	.434	.404	.327
9	.645	.592	.544	.500	.460	.424	.390	.361	.284
10	.614	.558	.508	.463	.422	.386	.352	.323	.247
12	.557	.497	.444	.397	.355	.319	.286	.257	.187
15	.481	.417	.362	.315	.271	.239	.209	.183	.123
20	.377	.312	.258	.214	.178	.148	.124	.104	.061

You'll see how to use this table a bit later in this chapter. For now, just know that it's best to evaluate major investments with a method that considers the time value of money. Before we look at these methods, let's look at the kinds of investments we're talking about.

Major Business Investment Decisions

The investment decisions we need to evaluate concern *capital expenditures*. These are investments in new plant and equipment, improvements to existing capacity, or perhaps the acquisition of another company.

MBA LINGO

A **capital expenditure** cannot be charged as an expense in the current accounting period. It must be recognized over time because the asset associated with the expense will last longer than one year. (This resembles depreciation.) Instead, a capital expenditure must be capitalized, which means placed on the balance sheet as an asset, with its cost to be allocated to subsequent accounting periods.

Investment in Plant and Equipment

An investment in new plant and equipment is the classic investment decision for a manufacturer. Adding capacity is a serious move because it's expensive and affects future costs. The company must spend its cash, borrow money, or issue stock to raise cash. So management had better be sure that the added sales and profits will make the investment worthwhile.

Every investment takes money, but building new capacity (like a new factory) is a long-term decision. It's hard to say after a year or two, "Gee, this wasn't a good idea. Let's sell this factory we just built." You can't unload it like a bad stock. You probably won't get the true value of the assets, and costs will be associated with disposing of them.

Major improvements to existing plant and equipment require similar care and analysis. Many companies expand their current operations or lease additional space in response to rising sales. And many of these find that when sales decrease or level off (typically with the arrival of the next recession), they are saddled with expensive, upgraded equipment or office space that they cannot easily unload.

Expand carefully and get all you can out of assets already on the books. Study your asset turnover and return on assets (see Chapter 13 for more on ratios) before adding new capacity. Seriously consider your growth prospects when analyzing any investment in plant and equipment.

Acquisition of a Company

The acquisition of another company is even more complex. The acquiring company must have a plan for either integrating the acquired company into its operations or leaving it as a separate business unit. Both of these choices have their own complexities (which we won't go into here).

CASE IN POINT

It is essential to factor the possibility of economic recession or other business difficulties into expansion plans, especially when debt is used to finance the expansion. A number of major U.S. companies, including two of the Big Three U.S. auto manufacturers (General Motors and Chrysler), had to file for bankruptcy in the 2008–2009 recession. (The car companies then received federal government assistance.)

Other companies declaring bankruptcy in those years included Six Flags, Circuit City, Fortunoff, Linens 'n Things, and Ziff Davis Media. Excessive debt—that is, more than the company can handle—plays a role in virtually every bankruptcy. (Six Flags carried a whopping $1.8 billion in debt at the time it filed bankruptcy.)

Large investments in expansion and the debt required to finance them can appear reasonable during an economic expansion but can quickly become untenable when a recession reduces revenue and cash flow. This is a good reason to finance expansion with earnings or with capital from investors, rather than with debt, when possible.

A company can pay for an acquisition with cash, stock, or a mix of cash and stock. Accounting for acquisitions is a field unto itself. Nonetheless, the decision to acquire a company—and, for that matter, the price that should be paid for that company—should be based on the present value of the future cash flows. (Note, however, that, when financing capital investments, those future cash flows have to be *estimated* future cash flows.)

A merger, in which two companies combine their operations, requires analysis on the part of each party to the deal similar to the analysis needed for an acquisition.

GIGO, Once Again

You've probably heard the expression GIGO (pronounced *gee-go*). (No, it's not another method of accounting for inventory.) GIGO is a saying from computer professionals. It means garbage in, garbage out. If you put bad data into a computer, you'll get bad information out. Similarly, when you analyze an investment, the accuracy of your result depends on the reliability of the numbers you use. You need solid estimates of future cash flows and the best possible fix on the discount rate to use in the analysis. We'll examine ways of choosing the discount rate after we look at the investment analysis methods.

Three Ways to Analyze Investments

We will examine three methods of analyzing business investments:

1. Net present value

2. Internal rate of return

3. Payback period

The first two, net present value and internal rate of return, consider the time value of money. The payback period does not.

Net Present Value

In the net present value (NPV) method, you calculate the net present value of all future cash outflows (the money you'll invest) and cash inflows (the money the investment will produce). *Net* here means you subtract the outflows from the inflows. If this net amount is positive—if the discounted cash inflows exceed the outflows—then the net present value is positive and the investment may be worth undertaking.

The discount rate you use is your *required rate of return*—that is, the return you need to achieve on the investment.

 MBA LINGO

The **required rate of return** on an investment is the rate that the company or person doing the analysis and making the investment has defined as the rate that they must achieve for the investment to be worthwhile.

Calculating NPV

Suppose you're a regional manufacturer based in Phoenix. You see an opportunity to expand into the Southeast by building a production and distribution facility near Atlanta. Building the facility requires a $22 million investment.

You have a five-year *horizon* for the investment because, after five years, you may, for personal reasons, sell the entire business. But you're not sure. So one way or another, you want this deal to work as a five-year investment.

MBA LINGO

The investment **horizon** refers to the length of time of the investment. The horizon is either the natural life of the investment (for example, a bond that matures on a certain date) or the time you want to take your money out of the investment.

Over the next five years, you estimate the income from the new facility as follows:

Year 1	$2 million
Year 2	5 million
Year 3	7 million
Year 4	8 million
Year 5	10 million
Total	$32 million

You thus have a total of $32 million in future cash inflows associated with this investment.

Let's say you need at least a 10 percent return on investment for this deal to work. That 10 percent is the discount rate you'll use to calculate the net present value of the investment.

You don't discount the initial $22 million investment because it's an outflow now, not in the future. It's the amount of the investment. However, if you had to invest more money over the investment horizon—for example, another $5 million in Year 3—you would discount that amount at the 10 percent rate using the value in the earlier table for 10 percent at three years (that is, .751).

To discount the future cash inflows, you do the following calculations (the amounts in column three, "Present Value of $1.00," are from the present-value table presented earlier in the chapter):

Year	Cash Inflows	Present Value of $1.00	Present Value of Cash Inflow
1	$2,000,000	× 0.909	$1,818,000
2	5,000,000	× 0.826	4,130,000
3	7,000,000	× 0.751	5,257,000
4	8,000,000	× 0.683	5,464,000
5	10,000,000	× 0.621	6,210,000
			$22,879,000

Again, that $22,879,000 is just the present value of the future cash inflows. To calculate the *net* present value of the investment, you subtract the initial investment (the outflows) from the discounted inflows:

Present value of inflows	$22,879,000
Minus initial investment	– 22,000,000
Net present value of investment	$879,000

This $879,000 is the net present value of the investment. It is the current value of the money that the investment will make.

Seeing the Time Value of Money

To see the impact of discounting—and the importance of the time value of money—consider how this investment would look if you didn't discount the cash inflows and outflows:

Undiscounted cash inflows	$32,000,000
Initial investment	– 22,000,000
Net undiscounted return	$10,000,000

Because the time value of money is real, not theoretical, it would be quite wrong to think that this investment is worth $10 million today. There's a big difference between $10 million and $879,000. That's why it's best to think in terms of rates, not just dollars, when considering investments.

You'll make over a 10 percent return on the investment. Since 10 percent is your discount rate and the net present value of the investment is positive at that discount rate, you would say yes to this investment (purely on the basis of this analysis).

If you were analyzing more than one investment opportunity with the NPV method, you would choose the one (or the ones) with the highest net present value. (For the purposes of this analysis, we are ignoring other, nonfinancial factors that would affect the decision, such as the strategic fit with the business and the ease or complexity of managing the opportunity.)

Internal Rate of Return

The internal rate of return, or IRR, also considers the time value of money. However, the approach and calculations differ slightly from those in the NPV method.

The internal rate of return on an investment is the discount rate that brings the present value of the future net cash flows to zero. In other words, you must find the discount rate that will make the future cash inflows equal to the up-front cash outflow. In this method, you don't know the discount rate. You must find it by trial and error.

The discount rate that makes the future net cash flows equal zero is the internal rate of return on the investment. When you find that rate, you compare it to your *hurdle* (target) *rate* (another way of saying your required rate of return). If the internal rate of return exceeds your hurdle rate, you say yes to the investment.

By the way, it's called the *internal* rate of return because it's the rate of return that the investment itself produces. The investment has only three components—the cash outflow, the cash inflows, and the number of years. Those three items are all you need to calculate the investment's internal rate of return.

Figuring the Internal Rate of Return

Let's stick with the example of the manufacturer with the five-year horizon expanding into the Southeast and assume that our hurdle rate is still 10 percent.

To calculate the internal rate of return, let's start by discounting the same estimated cash flows at 12 percent (again, the values in the present value column come from the present-value table earlier in the chapter).

Year	Cash Inflows	Present Value of $1.00 of Cash Inflow	Present Value
1	$2,000,000	× 0.893	$1,786,000
2	5,000,000	× 0.797	3,985,000
3	7,000,000	× 0.712	4,984,000
4	8,000,000	× 0.636	5,088,000
5	10,000,000	× 0.567	5,670,000
			$21,513,000

Discounted cash inflows	$21,513,000
Minus initial investment	– 22,000,000
Net amount	($487,000)

(Remember: In finance and accounting, a number in parentheses is usually negative.)

This tells us that the internal rate of return is *below* 12 percent, because 12 percent discounts the net cash flows to less than zero. So the internal rate of return is a bit lower than 12 percent. Let's try 11 percent.

Year	Cash Inflows	Present Value of $1.00	Present Value of Cash Inflow
1	$2,000,000	× 0.901	$1,802,000
2	5,000,000	× 0.812	4,060,000
3	7,000,000	× 0.731	5,117,000
4	8,000,000	× 0.659	5,272,000
5	10,000,000	× 0.593	5,930,000
			$22,181,000

Discounted cash inflows	$22,181,000
Minus initial investment	– 22,000,000
Net amount	$181,000

Because 11 percent yields a positive net amount and 12 percent yields a negative net amount, the internal rate of return on the investment is between 11 and 12 percent. In this case, it looks like it's a bit above 11 percent, meaning closer to 11 percent than to 12 percent.

We don't need to calculate the internal rate of return out to one or two decimal places—especially because our hurdle rate is 10 percent. In that case, an investment with an IRR a little over 11 percent would be acceptable.

As with NPV, if you are evaluating several competing investments, you would choose the one (or ones) with the highest internal rate of return. (Again, we are ignoring other, nonfinancial factors that might affect the investment decision.)

Payback Period

The payback period does not consider the time value of money. This makes it a lot easier to "do the numbers" but produces numbers with a lot less value.

The payback period is simply the amount of time that it will take to earn back the original amount invested. The amounts involved are not discounted.

In the example we've been using, the amount invested is $22 million. The following table shows the annual returns.

Year	Cash Flow	Cumulative Return
1	$2 million	$2 million
2	5 million	7 million
3	7 million	14 million
4	8 million	*22 million*
5	10 million	32 million
	$32 million	

The payback period is exactly four years. After four years, the original $22 million investment will be recouped. If the payback period fell between any two years, you could divide the return in the final year of the payback period by 12 months and *prorate* the return, to come up with a period expressed in years and months.

MBA LINGO

You **prorate** an amount any time you apportion it in some mathematical manner. Depending on the situation, you may prorate an amount by the months in the year, by contractual share, or by some other means. For example, in a liability suit, a judge may prorate the damage award according to the plaintiffs' share of the suffering.

Aside from ignoring the time value of money, the payback period has another serious drawback: it doesn't consider returns after the payback period. For instance, let's say you're comparing two five-year investments: one with the returns in our example, and one with the same returns in the first four years, but with $15 million instead of $10 million in the fifth year. The payback period doesn't take that fifth year into account.

So what good is the payback period? It's most useful for short-term investments, meaning those of a year or less, where you can measure the payback period in months.

Also, you might calculate the payback period for longer-term investments as extra information to use along with net present value or internal rate of return, or both.

Pick a Rate, but Not Just Any Rate

You have two good ways to choose the discount rate you apply to future cash flows in the NPV method or the hurdle rate you use for comparison with the internal rate of return:

1. You can use the opportunity cost.

2. You can use your cost of capital—or, more properly, your incremental cost of capital.

Let's examine each of these methods.

Using the Opportunity Cost

In general in investment analysis, the opportunity cost is the return you could earn on the next-best investment. Here, "next-best investment" refers to one you could actually make and earn that return on. "Opportunity cost" means the cost of forgoing the opportunity.

One good way to think of opportunity cost is to use the rate you would get by investing in an interest-paying security, such as a bond. If you can invest in a bond with 8 percent interest instead of pursuing a business investment with a similar return, why not just buy the bond?

If you have a next-best investment and you know its return, you can use that rate in your NPV and IRR calculations.

CASE IN POINT

I've seen a number of business investments that didn't work out well. Often, after they didn't work, someone would say, "You know, we could have done better just putting the money into Treasury notes." Those people were referring to the opportunity cost, and it was something they should have considered more carefully beforehand.

Of course, that's easy to say *after* the investment sours. The trick is to consider it before investing. Far too many companies make investments with marginal or risky returns. Sometimes they kid themselves into thinking the returns are higher or more certain. But other times they fail to ask themselves, "What could we get by just investing the money in securities until we find a great opportunity?"

Using the Cost of Capital

The cost of capital is a good rate to use in investment analysis because it is "the price you pay for money" and you can calculate that from your balance sheet. A company's cost of capital is a weighted average of its cost of debt and its cost of equity. These, as you know, finance long-term (as opposed to current) assets.

Of course, the company must have cash to invest over on the asset side of the balance sheet, or be willing to sell some assets and invest the proceeds in other assets. In other words, the actual cash to be invested is not in the debt and equity accounts, but rather in the cash and marketable securities accounts. Or the company must raise the cash from lenders or investors.

MBA ALERT

As with other costs a company faces, the lower the cost of capital the better. If the company's cost of capital is low, then it will not only have a larger range of investments to choose from (because of its lower hurdle rate), but also will make more money on an investment with a given return. In other words, a company with a cost of capital of 8 percent will make more on an investment with a 14 percent return than will a company with a cost of capital of 10 percent. Savvy financial managers, particularly in large companies, are always on the lookout for less expensive capital from sources such as foreign investors and competitive banks.

To calculate the weighted average cost of capital, first multiply the company's cost of debt by the percentage of debt in its long-term financing; then multiply the company's cost of equity by the percentage of equity in its long-term financing. Then add up the results.

The following table shows you what I mean.

ABC Company Liabilities and Owners' Equity

Source of Funds	Cost	Amount on Balance Sheet	Percent of Total Capitalization
Bank Loan	prime +1%	$1,000,000	10
Bond	8%	2,000,000	20
Total Long-Term Debt		**$3,000,000**	**30**

continues

ABC Company Liabilities and Owners' Equity (continued)

Source of Funds	Cost	Amount on Balance Sheet	Percent of Total Capitalization
Preferred Stock	5%	$1,000,000	10
Common Stock	???	3,000,000	30
Retained Earnings	???	3,000,000	30
Total Owners' Equity		**$7,000,000**	**70**
Total Capitalization		**$10,000,000**	**100**

ABC Company has 30 percent of its capitalization in long-term debt and 70 percent in equity. More specifically, the company gets 10 percent of its capital from a bank loan at *prime* plus 1 percent, 20 percent from a bond on which it pays 8 percent interest, 10 percent from preferred stock, and 70 percent from common stock and retained earnings.

MBA LINGO

The **prime rate** is the interest rate that major banks charge on loans to their most creditworthy corporate customers. Loans to less creditworthy customers are usually priced a "prime plus X percent" where X is 1 percent or more. The prime rate is published in *The Wall Street Journal* and other major news sources.

What's the Cost of Equity?

You may be wondering why I've shown question marks rather than the cost of common stock and retained earnings in the earlier table. That's because the cost of common equity and retained earnings is often not precisely known.

Common stock promises no guaranteed return. And retained earnings simply represent profits that were reinvested in the company rather than distributed as dividends.

The calculation of the "cost" of common equity is complex and subject to theory. The complexity concerns the rate of return required by equity investors in the market as a whole and in the company in particular. Because the return on common stock has two components—dividends and price appreciation—and both are uncertain, the calculation of the cost of equity is controversial.

So let's just say that, for ABC Company, the cost of equity is 12 percent. This doesn't mean the company has to pay 12 percent to stockholders the way it pays interest on the bank loan and the bond. Instead, it means that its investors expect a return of 12 percent on their investment over the long term.

Calculate the Cost of Capital

In any event, assuming the costs presented in the earlier table and a prime rate of 6 percent, the weighted average cost of capital for ABC Company is calculated as follows:

ABC Company Weighted Average Cost of Capital

Source of Funds	Cost	Percent of Total Capitalization	Weighted Cost
Bank Loan	.07	× .10	= .007
Bond	.08	× .20	= .016
Preferred Stock	.05	× .10	= .005
Common Stock and Returned Earnings	.12	× .60	= .072
Total Weighted Average Cost of Capital		.100	= 10%

The total weighted average cost of capital for ABC Company is 10 percent. This would be a good rate for the company to use as its discount rate or hurdle rate.

Why? Because if the company's cost of capital is 10 percent and it can get more than that on an investment, then it will be making money on that investment.

About Leverage

In the world of investment, you will often hear about *leverage*. Essentially, leverage is a strategy for using debt to boost the return on an investment. It doesn't mean every kind of borrowing, nor does it just mean being in debt. Leverage means using debt to increase the rate of return you can earn on a given investment.

MBA LINGO

Leverage is the financial strategy of borrowing money at a lower rate than you will earn by investing that money, so you can raise the rate of return that you earn. It's called leverage because it raises the rate of return beyond what it would be if you used only your own money.

Consider a simple example. Let's say you buy shares of stock for $100,000 using your own money, and you sell them one year later for $120,000. You've made a return of 20 percent on your investment (20,000 ÷ 100,000) in one year. Congratulations!

Now let's bring leverage into the deal. Let's say you do the exact same deal, only you *borrow* half of the money you invested, or $50,000. You still earn $20,000, but your return on investment (ROI) increases to 40 percent (20,000 ÷ 50,000). Double congratulations!

However, this leaves out the interest you had to pay on the borrowed money. So let's say that over that year you paid 10 percent interest, or $5,000, on that borrowed $50,000. That reduces your $20,000 return to $15,000 (20,000 – 5,000), *but* your ROI still increases from the original 20 percent to 30 percent (15,000 ÷ 50,000).

A lever enables you to lift something higher than you could with your own strength. Similarly, financial leverage—or OPM, for other people's money—lifts your rate of return. For this to work, you need two things: the ability to borrow money, and investment opportunities with rates of return higher than the interest you must pay on that money.

Using leverage is a legitimate method of increasing the rate of return on an investment, whether it is an investment in business expansion or in financial assets. However, problems occur when a company becomes overleveraged—when it takes on more debt than it can pay the interest on and repay, particularly if business conditions somehow worsen. Problems also occur when companies (or individuals) use debt to finance speculation or questionable or marginal investments.

MBA ALERT

Be very careful when using leverage. In the Great Recession, many households used leverage in the form of money borrowed against the equity in their homes to finance the purchase of second, or even third, homes. These deals were speculative because they depended completely on the prospect of continuously rising home prices. When home prices stopped rising, the entire rationale for these deals fell apart, and many of these "investors" found they could no longer make their payments. A number of financial companies, including Bear Stearns and Lehman Brothers, were also overleveraged when the subprime crisis hit, and both went bankrupt.

Beyond the Numbers

When analyzing investments, look beyond the numbers. Use these practical guidelines:

- Many investments look great on paper but fall apart in reality. Be sure you understand the operating and technical aspects of an investment, not just the financial aspects.

- Think for yourself. Don't let competitive threats or senior management's enthusiasm lead you astray. You should find creative ways to "make the deal work," but apply that creativity only to deals you believe in.

- The more good choices you have, the better. In my experience, most companies don't develop enough really good investment alternatives.

- Seek projects that can be self-funding to at least some degree. The investment itself should throw off money that can be used to fund the project as it proceeds.

- Remember that *not* investing is always an option. If there are no good opportunities, invest in securities or buy back your stock, which can be a good move. It can be a good move because it generally raises the market price of your stock by decreasing the number of shares available in the market.

The problem with investment analysis is that the amount you must invest is certain, but the returns are not. Take all reasonable precautions. But remember, you must invest to get a return.

The Lease-Versus-Buy Decision

You can often finance property, plant, and equipment through a lease rather than a purchase. There are two major types of leases: financial and operating.

A financial lease goes on the balance sheet as an asset, to record the fixed asset being financed, and as a liability, to record the payments due under the lease. The lessee (the party getting the equipment) assumes the maintenance, insurance, and taxes. The lessor just provides financing. According to generally accepted accounting principles, these leases must be capitalized (that is, shown on the balance sheet), because they are contractual obligations and usually cannot be canceled.

An operating lease doesn't go on the balance sheet, but is usually shown in the footnotes to the financial statements. The lessor usually remains responsible for maintenance, so this is often called a service lease. These leases are mostly used for equipment, such as vehicles, computers, and copiers, and may have cancellation provisions.

I won't go into the calculations for a lease-versus-buy decision. Basically, they involve examining the total cash inflows and outflows if you were to buy the asset and comparing them with those if you were to lease it. Then you consider service arrangements, tax implications (due to depreciation), and the likelihood of the equipment becoming obsolete (if it might, an operating lease may be better).

The Least You Need to Know

- The time value of money refers to the fact that a dollar you have now is worth more than a dollar you would receive in the future. That's because you can invest the dollar you have in hand and earn a return on it.
- Two major investment-analysis tools—net present value and internal rate of return—consider the time value of money. Thus, they are better than the other major analytical tool, the payback period.
- For net present value or internal rate of return analyses, use the discount rate that most accurately reflects your cost of capital or required rate of return.
- Always look beyond the numbers, even if your job is to "just do the numbers." A project must fit the company's strategy and be suited to its people if it is to succeed.

Ups and Downs: The Financial Markets

In This Chapter

- Key financial markets
- Major types of financial securities
- How the markets work
- Interpreting market activity

The financial markets have always played a key role in business, and in recent years that role has become even more important. Despite occasional (and inevitable) market turmoil, more companies are issuing an ever-broader range of financial instruments to an ever-broader base of investors. As a result, the financial markets now affect every business on some level. In addition, over the course of your career, you will probably be investing your company's money or your own, if you aren't already doing so. Moreover, the financial markets are barometers of business psychology and economic trends.

You don't need deep knowledge of the financial markets to understand their impact, or even to invest wisely. But you do need to understand the overall workings of the markets and the characteristics of the major types of securities, and you will gain that understanding in this chapter.

What Are the Financial Markets?

Broadly, the financial markets are organized forums for buying and selling securities and other financial instruments, such as foreign currencies. Securities are documents that evidence ownership in a company (stocks) or debts owed by a company or government entity (bonds). Although the financial markets include physical markets in actual buildings, such as the New York Stock Exchange and the Chicago Board of Options Exchange, the financial markets actually comprise millions of buyers and sellers linked by national and global telecommunications networks.

A financial market provides mechanisms for ensuring that transactions occur in an orderly manner and are accurately reported and tracked. An exchange is such a mechanism. For example, the New York Stock Exchange (NYSE) reports the prices of stocks that are listed on that exchange. The NYSE, the oldest stock exchange in the United States, maintains certain listing requirements—including minimum levels of income, shares outstanding, and total value of shares—for companies traded on the "Big Board," as the NYSE is commonly called. To maintain order, the NYSE can halt trading of a particular stock or of all stocks, as it did after terrorist attacks on the World Trade Center and the Pentagon on September 11, 2001.

The Players in the Market

Aside from the exchanges, several other parties play key roles in the financial markets:

- **Institutional investors** include insurance companies, commercial banks, mutual funds, pension funds, and other financial institutions that invest as part of their business. For instance, insurance companies invest a large portion of policyholders' premiums in stocks and bonds (and in real estate). Institutional investors are often collectively referred to as the "buy side."

- **Individual investors** are people who invest their own money in securities to meet their financial goals.

- **Investment banks** enable corporations to issue and sell stocks and bonds to institutional and individual investors (in contrast to commercial banks, which take deposits from and make loans to businesses and individuals). Investment banks often employ traders of stocks and bonds, who facilitate the sale of securities in the *secondary market.*

- **Brokers** act as intermediaries between buyers and sellers of securities. A registered representative (or registered rep or account executive) is licensed by the Securities and Exchange Commission (SEC) and represents clients who trade stocks, bonds, and other investment products.

- **Dealers** buy and sell securities for their own or their employer's account (rather than facilitate transactions for buyers and sellers). Most brokerage firms employ brokers and dealers, and when the firm sells securities out of its own inventory, the buyer must be notified of that fact. Collectively, investment banks and brokerage firms are known as the "sell side" because selling securities is their main line of business.

MBA LINGO

Secondary markets are where securities are bought and sold after they are issued. They are issued in the primary market, where the issuing entity sells them to the public and receives the proceeds. The proceeds of sales in the secondary market go to the seller, not the issuer, of the security.

Other key players include the Securities and Exchange Commission, which I cover later in this chapter, and, of course, corporations and other issuers of securities.

Why Companies Sell—and Investors Buy—Stock

As we discussed in Chapter 11, there are two broad classes of stock: common and preferred. Common stock represents ownership shares in a corporation, and holders of this stock vote on proposed members for the board of directors and receive dividends (when the company pays them). Preferred stock pays dividends at a specified rate, and holders of this stock receive their dividends before dividends can be paid to holders of common stock. However, preferred stock usually carries no voting rights. Convertible preferred stock, a hybrid of the two, can be converted to a specified number of common shares.

A company sells shares to the public to raise capital. Buyers of stock actually buy a share in the future earnings of the company, to be paid as dividends. (In the language of Chapter 15, they are buying a share of those future cash inflows.) Investors buy and sell a stock based mainly on differing estimates of the company's future earnings. Those differing estimates are based upon each investor's view of the company's industry, management, operations, finances, products, and strategy, all of which determine future earnings. The higher an investor believes those earnings will be, the more he will be willing to pay for the stock.

Thus, when a company announces a new product that's expected to be wildly popular, investors bid up the price of the stock. They expect the new product to generate higher sales and earnings than they expected before the announcement.

In practice, the stockholder expects something in addition to a share of future earnings. He expects the price of the stock to appreciate as the company grows and increases its earnings. Higher earnings command a higher stock price. In fact, many investors buy stocks more for expected appreciation than expected dividends, and that generates some of the more fascinating dynamics of the stock market.

The Price/Earnings Ratio

Before we look at those dynamics, let's examine the relationship between a company's earnings and its stock price. The *price/earnings ratio* neatly captures that relationship and therefore is widely used in equity investing and reported in newspapers' listings of stocks.

The price/earnings ratio, or P/E ratio, is just what it sounds like: the ratio of the company's stock price to its earnings—actually, *earnings per share.* A company's earnings per share is calculated by dividing its total net profit for the most recent 12 months by the number of shares of common stock outstanding. Thus, if the company earned $50 million last year and has 50 million shares outstanding, it earned $1 per share.

Now, if a stock with earnings per share of $1 is selling at $10, its P/E ratio (or *multiple*) is 10. If the stock were selling at $20, it would be selling at a multiple of 20.

MBA LINGO

The **price/earnings ratio** (P/E ratio) equals the price of one share of stock divided by earnings per share. **Earnings per share,** a widely reported measure of a company's performance, equals total net income divided by the number of shares of common stock outstanding. The P/E ratio is commonly referred to as the stock's **multiple,** meaning the multiple of earnings per share at which the stock is selling.

Why would the stock of Company A with earnings per share of $1 sell for $10 and the stock of Company B with the same earnings per share sell for $20? Because investors believe that the *future* earnings of Company B will be higher than those of Company A. Remember, investors in common stock are buying a share of the future earnings.

From 1965 to 1995, before high-technology and dot-com stocks drove average stock prices to unsustainably high levels, the average multiple for the U.S. stock market as a whole was about 14, with a range from about 7 to 20. In the late 1990s, the overall P/E ratio for the S&P 500 rose into the 20s, then decreased into the mid- to high teens in the early 2000s after the dot-com and tech-stock bubble burst. Then it rose to almost 18 in the mid-2000s before plummeting as the Great Recession hit the markets hard. In the second half of 2010, it returned to the 17 range.

Stocks with extremely high multiples—for instance, 40, 60, or 80 times earnings and higher—are considered growth stocks. Investors purchasing these stocks expect the future earnings—or, more realistically, future earnings and appreciation—to justify those multiples. Investors who won't purchase those stocks don't believe that those multiples (that is, those prices) are justified.

Stocks selling at low multiples—for instance, in the single digits—are viewed by most investors as either slow-growth stocks or "dogs" (stocks in troubled companies). However, some investors search for stocks with low multiples in an effort to find and buy undervalued stocks or those with "slow and steady" performance.

CASE IN POINT

Some investment professionals believe that the P/E ratio has become less relevant than it once was. Some believe it never was or is very relevant. The P/E ratio's reputation took a beating during the bull market of the 1990s as the stocks of dot-coms with little-to-no earnings reached stratospheric levels. Then the accounting scandals of the early 2000s cast suspicion on reported earnings, and the P/E is based on earnings.

It's true that companies' earnings reports vary depending on the accounting they use. Yet the P/E ratio for a given stock is still useful data. Ignoring the link between earnings and stock prices causes trouble for individuals and markets. Also, if a company's income figures can't be trusted, what's the point of buying its stock?

Bulls, Bears, Bubbles, and Crashes

An investor is bullish on a stock if he believes the price is going to rise and is buying it. He's bearish if he believes the price will fall and is selling the stock. Investors are said to be bullish on the stock market if they are buying stocks—bidding up prices—and are said to be bearish if they are selling stocks—sending prices lower. Hence, the popularity of the terms *bull market* and *bear market*. (Bulls stampede; bears hibernate.)

Again, as in all markets, the dynamics of supply and demand determine prices. In the short run, the supply of stock in a company and in the overall market is fairly fixed.

Publicly held companies don't frequently issue new stock (which would increase the supply) or buy back existing stock (which would decrease it—yes, as noted in Chapter 15, companies do buy their own stock).

MBA LINGO

A **bear market** is usually defined as a 20 percent decrease from the previous high in the market averages. A **bull market** is usually defined as a period of at least a few months of generally rising stock prices and high trading volume. (Less widely, it is described as a 20 percent increase in overall stock prices.)

You might also think that demand for stock should be fairly stable. After all, events in a company or the economy that could change the earnings outlook for a stock, let alone for the market as a whole, don't happen every day. Therefore, demand should be fairly stable. In reality, however, demand for a stock and for stocks in general can vary wildly, even in the short term, based on market psychology.

Market psychology moves the overall market—which is measured by various market averages that I'll explain later in this chapter—up or down as often as expectations about earnings change.

When market psychology becomes too optimistic, a bull market can turn into a bubble. When "the bulls run loose on Wall Street," they can bid up the prices of stocks too far, too fast. If this goes on long enough or the prices go up high enough, a bubble results. In a bubble, the overall market or a segment of it (for instance, technology stocks) becomes highly overvalued. Prices become too high relative to potential future earnings and the stocks' collective multiple rises to historically high levels.

When prices become too high, demand falls (as it will in any market), and when demand for stocks falls, market psychology—which feeds on itself—becomes pessimistic. If market sentiment becomes pessimistic enough for long enough, "the bears take over" and a sell-off occurs. Investors sell in order to lock in, or realize, the gains they made on paper when the price of their stocks rose in the bull market. Or they sell to limit their losses. A massive sell-off signals falling demand, and prices spiral downward. If prices fall far and fast, it's called a crash.

A bear market ends and recovery from a crash begins when investors see that the prices of stocks are low relative to expected earnings and start buying again.

MBA MASTERY

The main U.S. market averages are the Dow Jones Industrial Average, the S&P Composite Index of 500 Stocks, and the NASDAQ-OTC Price Index, each of which has a shorter nickname. "The Dow," a weighted average of 30 large-company stocks, is the most widely reported market average. The S&P 500, based on 500 stocks selected by the financial information company Standard & Poor's, obviously represents a broader measure of the market's performance. The NASDAQ (National Association of Securities Dealers Automatic Quotations system) is a broad average of stocks of smaller companies traded "over the counter." These OTC stocks aren't listed on a major exchange, but are nonetheless bought and sold through brokers.

Information and the Market

Information is, and has always been, the lifeblood of the financial markets: information on the companies issuing securities, on current and historical prices and returns, on buying and selling activity, and on economic and market trends. As noted in Chapter 14, the principles of disclosure and transparency underlie financial statements. Those principles also underlie the financial markets because a truly free market can exist only when buyers and sellers have equal access to information. Of course, the conclusions they draw from the information will vary, as will the information they actually employ. However, that information enables them to judge potential risks and returns and to make informed, useful investment decisions.

Efficient financial markets depend on open access to information. In fact, the efficient market theory holds that the market price of a stock reflects all known information about the stock and the collective expectations of all investors. According to the theory, any new development that affects the stock will be immediately assessed by millions of market participants, who will, through the market mechanisms of selling and buying, correctly assign a new price to the stock.

The efficient market theory has been debated for decades. Supporters believe that information spreads so quickly and investors respond so rapidly that it's impossible to "beat the market." Detractors believe that inefficiencies in the distribution of information and investors' varying analytical skills and judgment render the theory only theoretical. Although the theory may not perfectly describe reality, the stock price is set by the market, which is the sum total of millions of buy and sell decisions.

The most widely used print and online sources of information for investors include the business news, investment newsletters, brokerage-house analyst reports, and research services such as Standard & Poor's and Value Line. The company's financial statements (which are almost always available at their websites) are essential sources and form the basis for much of the other information that firms such as Value Line and Standard & Poor's issue on a company's stock. These statements are required of all public companies by the *Securities and Exchange Commission (SEC)*.

> **MBA LINGO**
>
> The **Securities and Exchange Commission (SEC)** regulates the securities markets and specifies the type and frequency of the information that companies issuing securities in the United States must make available to the public.

The SEC is the U.S. federal agency charged with protecting investors from fraud, supervising the exchanges, and regulating the process by which companies issue securities. The SEC requires that detailed quarterly and annual financial statements (the 10-Q and 10-K, respectively) be filed with the SEC and made available for public distribution. The SEC's rule of disclosure calls for the release of all information, positive or negative, that would affect an investor's decision.

> **MBA ALERT**
>
> One of the best print sources for definitions of financial terms is the *Dictionary of Finance and Investment Terms,* by John Downes and Jordan Elliot Goodman (Barron's Educational Series, 8th Ed., 2010). In my opinion, it is *the* best source.

Types of Investors and Traders

Investing entails a longer-term commitment than trading, which aims for gains on short-term price appreciation. In addition, there are various styles of investing and trading.

Value investors seek companies with strong management teams, earnings histories, and balance sheets. (A strong balance sheet has little to no debt, high levels of equity capital, and valuable, productive assets.) They often use a *buy-and-hold* strategy, which aims for returns from dividends and long-term appreciation. Although some value investors sell when they believe the stock has reached a peak, others hold it as it goes down (and even buy more, at the lower price) because they expect a higher peak further in the future.

A **buy-and-hold** investment strategy seeks to identify companies with above-average long-term growth prospects and to make money from dividends and long-term price appreciation.

So-called bottom-feeders look for undervalued stocks. These stocks often have some characteristics of value stocks, such as strong balance sheets, but their prices may be depressed by current conditions or lack of investor interest. Bottom-feeders expect to reap gains when conditions change, the companies turn around, or investors rediscover the stock.

Growth-oriented investors seek growth stocks, typically those of companies with new technologies or products, vigorous expansion plans, or both. Growth investors are willing to forgo dividends, which growth companies usually do not pay, for the prospect of high short- to long-term appreciation. They often hold stocks for shorter periods than buy-and-hold investors. Although some growth investors purchase stocks for long-term appreciation, most prefer to sell when the stock reaches a cyclical peak or a target level they had set, and then to invest that money in the stock of another, newer company with prospects for more dramatic growth and price appreciation.

Unlike investors, traders hope for very short-term gains—within hours, in the case of day traders. In general, traders try to profit from very short-term inefficiencies in the market by closely following news and events that could affect the company's business. They sometimes play their hunches, in effect betting that the stock price will rise when the event occurs.

Investors, particularly short-term investors, and traders must factor transaction costs into their profit and loss calculations. Transaction costs include brokerage fees, taxes, and any other out-of-pocket expenses directly associated with the purchase or sale of a security.

In short selling, a short-term investor or trader believes that a stock is going to go down. He borrows (rather than purchases), say, 100 shares of the stock from a broker, sells them immediately, and sets that money aside in a bank account or other risk-free vehicle. Then, when the price of the stock has fallen, he buys 100 shares and repays the broker with those shares. The successful short-seller pockets the difference between the price of the stock when he borrowed and sold it, and the price when he purchased it and repaid the broker. However, if the stock goes up rather than down, the short-seller loses because, to repay his broker, he must buy the 100 shares on the open market at a higher price.

Short selling is a good introduction to stock options, which also involve judgments about the price of a stock in the near-term future.

Options: Puts and Calls

In general, an option gives a person the right to purchase or sell something in the future. For instance, when a Hollywood producer options a best-selling novel, he or she pays the author an amount of money—for instance, $25,000—for the right to buy the book as the basis of a movie, at a certain price (let's say $500,000) within a certain period of time (usually one to two years).

An option has value because it locks in the price of an item for a certain period of time, as well as the right to buy it. The price of the option is usually a small fraction of the price of the item. Also, an option is not an obligation to buy or sell something. The decision to buy or sell remains with the holder of the option (which is why it's called an option rather than a purchase or sale agreement).

Puts and calls are both stock options. A put gives its holder the right to *sell* a specific number of shares of a specific stock at a specific price—known as the exercise price (or "strike price")—by a certain date. A call gives its holder the right to *buy* 100 shares of a stock at a specific strike price by a certain date. Puts and calls are sold by the person or institution that owns the underlying stock. Companies do not sell options on their own stocks, which, in effect, would be "betting" on the price movements of its own stock when their focus should be improving the value of the stock.

Calls

Let's start with call options. The buyer of a call option hopes that the price of the stock will rise above the strike price before the option expires. The buyer of the option wants to buy the stock at a (strike) price *below* its market value before the option expires, and then sell the stock at the market price and pocket the difference. For this to be profitable, the difference between the strike price and market price must be greater than the amount paid for the option.

Example: Say you have an option to buy stock in XYZ Inc. at a strike price of $50, and you paid $5 per share for that option. If the price rises to $55 before the option expires, you make no money if you exercise the option. That's because if you exercised the option, you would buy 100 shares at the strike price of $5,000 and sell them for $5,500—but you paid $500 for the calls, and therefore you would make nothing. (In fact, you would lose money because of transaction costs, which are omitted here to simplify the calculations.) Thus, you would not exercise the option if the price rose to $55 a share or less, nor, of course, would you exercise it if the stock fell (or remained) below the strike price of $50.

However, if the price of the stock were to rise to, say, $60, you would definitely exercise the option. You would buy the 100 shares at the strike price of $50, promptly sell them for $6,000, deduct your costs of $500 for the option and $5,000 for the 100 shares, and pocket a $500 profit.

What's so great about call options? You just made $500 on an investment of $500—a return of 100 percent on your investment!—in a matter of a few weeks or months.

Yes, this is a simplified example, and, true, options are a sophisticated investment vehicle in which money can be lost as easily as it is gained (perhaps more easily). Moreover, most options are not exercised before the expiration date because the stock price is such that the holder allows them to expire (because the price of the stock vis-a-vis the strike price of the options would not allow the holder to make any money by exercising them). However, the fact that calls enable an investor to profit from a rising stock price without actually buying the stock is the underlying logic and motivation for buying them.

CASE IN POINT

The incentive stock options given to managers and employees at start-ups or to senior executives at large, established companies as part of their compensation are essentially calls. The holders have the right to buy shares in the company at a certain price. The intent is to give the holders of the options added motivation to work hard and make the stock price as high as possible.

In practice, however, stock options can give senior managers incentives to pursue short-term earnings rather than to build the long-term value of the company. For instance, a focus on this year's bottom line can lead to reductions in short-term expenses and in long-term investment, which can harm the company in later years.

Puts

Again, a put option gives its holder the right to sell a stock at the strike price to the seller of the put (known as the "writer"). (In other words, the writer of the put agrees to buy the stock at the strike price from the holder of the put by the strike date.) The buyer of a put is betting that the price of the stock will *fall* before the option expires. He makes his profit by buying the stock on the open market at a price below the strike price and then exercising the option, which forces the writer of the put to buy the stock at the strike price from the holder of the put.

Example: Suppose you hold an option to sell 100 shares of ABC Company to Joe Smith (the writer of the put) at a strike price of $50. Suppose, again, that you paid $5 per share for the option. If the price of the stock falls to, say, $40, you would buy 100 shares on the open market and then exercise the put. That put option compels Joe to buy 100 shares from you at the strike price of $50 a share, for a total price of $5,000. You make $500, which is the $5,000 Joe paid you, minus the $4,000 you paid for the stock on the open market and minus the $500 you paid for the option.

As with call options, the difference between the strike price and the stock price must exceed the price of the put (plus transactions costs), or there is no point in exercising it. If the holder does not exercise the put option, then, as with calls, he loses the amount he paid for the option. Finally, as with calls, puts offer the *possibility* of high returns.

Meanwhile, the writer of the put is hoping that the stock price rises, remains the same, or falls by less than the price of the put. If any of those things occur, then the put is not exercised and the writer of the put, Joe Smith in our example, does not have to buy the 100 shares. Smith's profit on the transaction is the $500 paid to him for the put.

Again, both puts and calls enable investors to profit on the movement of a stock's price—upward in the case of calls, downward in the case of puts—without having to buy the stock itself. This limits the potential loss to the amount paid for the options.

Fundamental Analysis vs. Technical Analysis

No discussion of stocks would be complete without touching on the two major schools of equity analysis. All analysis aims to develop enough information about a security so that a wise investment decision can be made. Fundamental analysis deals with information about the company that has issued the stock. Technical analysis deals with information about the stock's price, particularly its historical levels and trends.

Fundamental analysis focuses on the company's "fundamentals"—including its record of sales and earnings, the strength of its balance sheet and cash flow, the quality of management, and the health of its industry—and uses these to determine the company's prospects for profitable growth. Fundamental analysts judge the company's quality of earnings—for instance, how much profit comes from operations and how much from selling off assets—and its levels of debt, R&D spending, and exposure to lawsuits. They also use techniques (such as forecasting earnings per share over the next year and applying the stock's multiple to that EPS figure) to forecast the stock's price.

The goals of fundamental analysis are to assess the company's prospects and to decide whether the stock is overvalued, undervalued, or fairly valued. If the stock is over-valued, fundamental analysis says to sell it, because sooner or later the fundamentals will always affect the stock's price. If the stock is undervalued, it should be purchased. Fairly valued stocks may be bought, sold, or held, depending on the investor's goals and preferences.

MBA ALERT

Completely ignoring a company's fundamentals can be dangerous. When practiced widely enough, this approach results in wildly overvalued companies and entire markets, as in the dot-com bubble of the late 1990s. Ignoring housing market fundamentals led to the housing and mortgage-backed securities bubble of the late 2000s.

Technical analysis ignores financial statements and instead focuses on the price, past prices, sales trends, and trading volume of the stock itself. Using mathematical formulas, graphic analysis, and computing firepower, technical analysts (or technicians) chart the supply and demand for a stock based on past patterns and trends. Important concepts in technical analysis include the stock's resistance level (its previous high price), support level (its previous low), horizontal price movement (fluctuations within a narrow range over time), and correction (usually downward and temporary reversal of direction in a trend). Most technical analysis is geared to the short to intermediate term.

Although fundamental and technical analysis each have their fans, the wise investor considers the company's financial performance *and* the stock's price movements.

Corporate Bonds: Big IOUs

Corporate bonds represent long-term borrowings on which the company pays interest and principal at regular intervals. At maturity, the bondholder redeems the bond and receives any interest due and the remaining unpaid principal. Bondholders are lenders rather than owners of the corporation (who are shareholders) and have no voting rights. They do, however, have a written agreement to be repaid in the form of the bond.

Key features of corporate bonds include the following:

- Bonds may be secured or unsecured. An unsecured bond, also known as a debenture, is backed only by the creditworthiness of the issuer. A secured bond is backed by collateral, financial or physical assets that may be sold by the bondholders in the event of *default*.

- Asset-backed securities are bonds that "package" the future payments of interest and principle on credit cards, auto loans, mortgages, or other loans. Because the loans are bundled into securities, they are "securitized"; the process of creating these bonds is "securitization."

- Bearer bonds pay the interest and principal to whomever holds the bonds. Registered bonds pay interest to the owner who is registered in the company's records.

- A convertible bond can be exchanged for other securities, usually preferred or common stock.

- Bonds may be purchased at the time they are issued or in the market after they are issued. Over the bond's life, its price will fluctuate with supply and demand, interest rates, and investors' judgments about the creditworthiness of the issuer.

The interest rate on a bond is a function of the length of the maturity, the creditworthiness of the issuer, and the bond rating. Generally, the longer the *maturity* and the lower the creditworthiness, the higher the interest rate, because both factors increase the risk for investors, who must be compensated with a greater reward.

MBA LINGO

A company is in **default** when it cannot pay the interest or principal on a bond or loan when it is due. Long-term **maturities** are those of one year or longer, and short-term are those of up to one year.

There are three major bond-rating services: Standard & Poor's, Moody's Investors Service, and Fitch's Investors Service. These companies assess the creditworthiness of companies that sell bonds to the public by analyzing their operations and finances. Then they assign letter grades that range from AAA (highly unlikely to default) to D (in default). (The letter grade systems vary slightly among the three services.)

Only bonds rated B or higher are considered investment grade. Bonds rated lower are considered noninvestment grade, also known as high-yield bonds (because they carry high interest rates) or, less charitably, junk bonds. Regulations usually stipulate that insurance companies and other financial institutions cannot invest their customers' funds in junk bonds.

In general, bonds are considered more conservative investments than stocks because of the agreement to pay a fixed amount of interest. (Incidentally, bonds are also referred to as "fixed-income" securities.) Before we look more closely into bonds, let's quickly examine a common and important type of corporate investment.

CASE IN POINT

Bond-rating agencies are paid to rate the bonds by the companies that issue them. This creates a conflict of interest, given that the rating agencies do not have the same professional standards as auditors, who are paid to audit financial statements by the companies that issue them.

This, and perhaps the rating agencies' lack of expertise, contributed to an erosion in quality in mortgage-backed securities in the mid-2000s, as securities that mixed prime and subprime mortgages were given ratings that did not fully reflect their risk.

Commercial Paper

Commercial paper is issued by large, extremely creditworthy corporations and financial institutions with short-term borrowing needs. These IOUs, with maturities ranging from 2 to 270 days, are traded among large corporations and financial institutions in the commercial paper market.

Commercial paper has several advantages for both issuers and buyers. The market is active and the issuers are creditworthy, so commercial paper can be issued, bought, and sold relatively easily. Issuers like the flexibility of the maturities and the rates they pay on the paper, which are lower than the prime rate. Buyers like the range of available maturities, the ease of purchase, and the ability to "park" excess cash in a security offering a higher return than a bank account or short-term government securities, but comparable levels of safety and liquidity.

Government Securities

The U.S. federal government issues securities of varying maturities to finance the public debt. These securities are negotiable and are backed by the full faith and credit of the U.S. government, which, if it has to, can raise taxes or print money to pay its debts. The interest earned on government securities—also known as government obligations and "treasuries" (because they are issued by the U.S. Treasury)—is exempt from state and local, but not federal, taxes.

MBA ALERT

The U.S. government can always issue securities to finance budgetary shortfalls created when it spends more than it collects in taxes, fees, and other revenue. However, when the government issues securities, it is borrowing money that could be used by private industry. This can create a phenomenon known as crowding out, because the government's demand for funds "crowds out" private-sector borrowers.

The government can also print money to pay its debts, but that can contribute to inflation. Structural (as opposed to cyclical) deficits occur when the populace of a nation continually demands more in government services than it pays for in taxes.

The most common U.S. treasury issues are the following:

- **Treasury bills,** known as T-bills, have maturities of one year or less and are sold at auction at specific intervals and traded in the secondary market. T-bills come in denominations of $10,000 and up.

- **Treasury notes** carry maturities of 1 to 10 years and are sold at auction or in exchange for outstanding or maturing treasuries. Treasury notes come in denominations ranging from $1,000 to $1 million and up.

- **Treasury bonds** carry maturities of at least 10 years and come in denominations of $1,000 and up.

Because they are backed by the U.S. government, treasuries are viewed as a "risk-free" investment. As such, they carry interest rates lower than those of corporate bonds or commercial paper, or other types of government securities.

Other Government Securities

A variety of U.S. government agencies, such as the Federal Home Loan Bank, issue bonds. Although these are relatively safe investments, they are backed not by the U.S. Treasury, but rather by the creditworthiness of the issuing agency.

State and municipal governments and government agencies also issue bonds to finance their operations and manage their budgets. These securities, known as "munies," are relatively low-risk investments because they are backed by the taxing power of the state or local government or (often, but not always) a reliable source of income, such as highway tolls. However, they are not risk-free; therefore, unlike treasuries, they are rated by the rating agencies. Munies are usually free of federal, state, and local taxes if they have been issued solely for a public purpose rather than for one that also benefits private parties.

How Bond Prices Fluctuate

Bonds are issued with a face value and a stated interest rate. Corporate bonds are generally issued with a face value of $1,000, federal government bonds for $10,000, and municipal bonds for $5,000. Face value is also known as par value.

Bonds also carry a stated interest rate, and interest is paid at that rate, applied to the face value of the bond. However, each time a bond is sold, its price may be more or less than the face value. The price of the bond fluctuates in this manner because of changing interest rates and changes in investors' judgment of the creditworthiness of the issuer.

Therefore, if a bond issued by XYZ Inc. has a face value of $1,000 and pays 10 percent, that means each year the company pays the bondholder $100. Now if the price of the bond falls and XYZ continues to pay whoever owns the bond $100, then the effective interest rate on the bond has risen. For example, if you purchased this bond in the market for $950, the effective interest is $10\frac{1}{2}$ percent (= $100 ÷ $950).

Conversely, if the price of the bond rose and you paid $1,050 for it, the effective interest rate falls to $9\frac{1}{2}$ percent (= $100 ÷ $1,050).

In this way, the bond market and the mechanism of supply and demand adjusts the price of the bond to reflect investors' judgments about the company's creditworthiness and the prevailing level of interest rates. A bond can gain or lose value, and the investor can see price appreciation or erosion, although usually not of the magnitude customarily seen in equities.

The following key factors affect bond prices:

- If investors sell off stocks and move into bonds, which are inherently safer, demand for bonds increases and bond prices will rise as the buying continues.

- Conversely, if investors move into stocks because they seem more attractive, demand for bonds decreases and bond prices will fall.

- Bond prices are also affected by the general level of interest rates. If interest rates are generally high relative to the effective yield on stocks (dividends plus appreciation), investors will buy bonds, driving up demand for them and their prices. In a low-interest-rate environment, investors normally seek the higher returns offered by the stock market.

This is not to say that the stock and bond markets move in opposite directions. However, investors seeking healthy returns have a limited number of securities in which to invest. Therefore, the markets for stocks and bonds *tend* to behave in complementary ways.

The Risk/Return Tradeoff

Purchasers of financial securities assume a degree of risk that the value of their investment will decrease. Even treasuries can lose value if inflation runs high, although the United States now issues Treasury Inflation Protected Securities (TIPS), which are indexed to adjust the returns for inflation. Investors take this risk expecting a return on their investment in the form of dividends or interest plus appreciation. The actual degree of risk and the actual return are unknown because they lie in the future. Yet historical performance and the features of various securities provide a general guideline regarding the risks and returns associated with them.

For instance, stocks are riskier than bonds because a stockholder owns a share in the company's future profits and those profits might not materialize. But a bondholder is a lender whose money must be repaid whether or not the company earns a profit. For accepting more risk, the stockholder expects a higher return. Stockholders expect the company to earn a profit and expect to share in those profits in the form of dividends. They assume greater risk in expectation of a greater return. Yet a stockholder is *not owed* a portion of the profits. In fact, the company may choose not to pay any dividends and instead reinvest the money in the company.

Bondholders also expect the company to earn a profit. An unprofitable company will eventually go bankrupt and be unable to pay its debts in full, including those owed to bondholders. But bondholders typically have a lower tolerance for risk than an equity investor. Thus, they accept a known, fixed return at a lower level of risk than stockholders, who choose a potentially higher but riskier return.

Other Financial Markets and Investment Vehicles

Although the markets for stocks, bonds, and treasuries are the basic ones for most investors, there are others:

- **Commodities markets,** where buyers and sellers trade contracts to deliver agricultural staples such as wheat, corn, soybeans, and pork bellies. The spot market deals in goods for immediate delivery, while the futures market deals in goods for delivery on a future date. Oil is also traded in spot and futures markets.

- **Foreign exchange markets,** where buyers and sellers trade currencies. Foreign exchange (or FX) futures are also traded, with the goal of reducing the risks inherent in future currency fluctuations.

- **Precious metals markets,** where metals such as gold and platinum are traded. A "goldbug" is an investor who invests relatively heavily in gold as a hedge against inflation or because he or she believes that a depression or other disaster lay ahead.

Other investments include those in tangible assets rather than financial securities or precious metals. The most popular of these by far is real estate, followed by a huge range of collectibles, including art, antiques, vintage automobiles, coins, and memorabilia. While real estate has proven itself as a reliable long-term investment, collectibles are generally purchased as much for their aesthetic value and emotional appeal as for their investment value. In other words, if you love Elvis buy Elvis memorabilia, but don't count on it to fund your retirement.

MBA MASTERY

Gold has traditionally been viewed as an extremely safe and conservative investment, but not one noted for high returns. For this reason, a rising price for gold indicates investor pessimism about the economic or political future, and a falling price signals optimism.

The Least You Need to Know

- The financial markets are organized forums for buying and selling securities and other financial instruments, such as foreign currencies.
- Common stock provides an ownership share in a company and the potential for dividends and price appreciation. Bonds are IOUs from a company, government, or government agency and offer returns mainly in the form of interest payments.
- U.S. government obligations, or treasuries, are essentially a risk-free investment because they are backed by the full faith and credit of the U.S. government, which has both taxing authority and the ability to print money.

Managing Marketing for Maximum Sales

Everything you do as a manager comes down to the customer. All your work is for nothing if customers don't buy what your business sells. People in marketing and sales spend their working lives focusing on the customer. Who is the customer? What does the customer want? What will the customer pay for it? When is the customer satisfied? Where can we find new customers? How can we beat our competitors in the fight for customers?

Because customers make or break a business, the human factor dominates marketing and sales more than any other area of business. This makes these areas the most exciting part of business to many people. But marketing and sales are also where business competition can be toughest.

So hang on as we charge into the battle for markets and the quest for customers.

Ready, Aim, Sell

In This Chapter

- The difference between marketing and sales
- How marketing and sales work together
- Basic concepts in marketing and sales

Recall from the income statement in Chapter 12 that a company's financial health starts with sales. Every company must sell its products or services to make money to pay its bills and earn a profit.

This makes marketing and sales two of the most important functions in a company. Their job is to find people to buy what the company sells. In most businesses, this isn't easy. When it *is* easy, it doesn't stay that way, because competitors quickly come along. So marketing and sales offer some of the most challenging work in business. But it's some of the most satisfying and financially rewarding work as well.

In this chapter, we examine marketing and sales, and how they serve the company and its customers. We also cover some basic marketing and sales concepts.

Marketing, Sales—What's the Difference?

Think of marketing as selling to groups of people, while selling is done one-on-one. Advertising and direct mail are great examples of "selling to groups." But marketing goes beyond advertising and direct mail to include many other activities, including web-based ones. Marketing raises people's awareness of a product and generates interest in buying it. However, it takes selling to get an individual to hand over money or a check. Selling means getting a person or a company—a customer—to pay for your product or service. But selling goes beyond "pitch the product" and "ask for an order."

In most organizations, marketing exists to support the salespeople. That's good, because selling is the toughest job in business. Most people will not part with their money, or their organization's money, without a good reason. The marketing and sales departments are there to supply those reasons.

Marketing is a staff activity, usually located at the company's headquarters. Selling is a line activity, and salespeople are said to work "in the field." Marketing also tends to be *strategic*, while sales tends to be *tactical*. This flows from the idea that marketing supports sales. That support often takes the form of planning and guidance. For example, marketing identifies groups that appear to need the company's products. Then salespeople go to individuals within those groups to try to meet those needs with the company's product. (In this chapter and throughout Part 5, *product* generally means "product and/or service.")

MBA LINGO

Strategic initiatives operate on a larger scale than **tactical** initiatives. Managers craft a strategy to achieve a goal. For instance, to achieve the goal of increased sales, management may adopt a strategy of pursuing a new market. To implement that strategy, the company will have to develop the right tactics, which might include developing new products. In general, tactics implement strategy.

People in marketing and sales approach business a bit differently. Marketing people tend to view their work in more intellectual and abstract terms than salespeople. The issue of "selling to groups" insulates marketing people from the hurly-burly of face-to-face selling. A marketing person researching product features faces less difficulty than the salesperson phoning busy people for appointments or trying to persuade a reluctant buyer.

There is often some tension between marketing and sales. Marketing can view salespeople as mere tools in its grand strategy, existing simply to execute the wonderful plans hatched by marketing geniuses. Meanwhile, sales can view marketers as hopelessly out-of-touch "staff-types" who would starve to death if they had to actually make sales. People in marketing and sales must either eliminate this tension by fostering mutual respect or at least manage it creatively.

MBA MASTERY

To get marketing and salespeople to understand one another, force them to work together. Be sure marketing includes salespeople in its planning process and decisions. Be sure salespeople tell marketing about competitors and problems they face in the field. Get salespeople to take marketing people on sales calls now and then, just so they can observe the process. Get marketing people to solicit ideas from the salespeople about how marketing can best support them.

Marketing Strategy Basics

Companies compete largely on price and quality. Basically, a company can deliver either high quality at a high price (like Mercedes-Benz) or lower quality at a low price (like Hyundai). The economics of our planet will not allow a company to manufacture a car with the quality of a Mercedes for the price of a Hyundai.

So the first strategic decision for a company is to choose the basis on which it will compete: price or quality. Then marketing delivers that message to the marketplace. John's Bargain Store says, "Come here if you want to pay a low price and get commonplace goods." Neiman Marcus says, "Come here if you can pay top dollar for the very best."

There's another dimension: service. Here, *service* means everything not included in price and quality—selection, post-purchase support, warranties, and so on. In some businesses, service can be as important as price and quality. And other elements are involved, including novelty, design, and ease of use.

Of course, I've simplified things considerably, but essentially the goal of marketing strategy is to have a competitive advantage and to get word of that advantage out to the marketplace.

Sales Tactics, Summarized

After marketing strategy identifies markets, prospects, and a competitive position, sales must win customers. So after marketing gets the word out and customers come to the store, salespeople help them find what they want, explain how the products work, and so on. In retail, the sales challenges are typically lower than in industrial sales because the customer comes to the store. And customers don't go to John's Bargain Store looking for gold cuff links or to Neiman Marcus to buy clothespins.

In many businesses, the salespeople must go prospecting for customers. They must telephone them for appointments and make sales calls. Then the salesperson guides the prospect through the sales process, which I show you in Chapter 21. A sales call is a visit or phone call a salesperson makes to a customer or prospect in order to sell something.

Commercial vs. Consumer Sales

In business, there's a distinction between consumer and commercial—or business-to-business—marketing and sales. If the person is buying the product or service for himself or herself as an individual, we're talking about *consumer sales.* If the person is buying it for his or her organization, we're talking about *commercial, corporate, industrial,* or *business-to-business sales,* which all mean the same thing.

MBA LINGO

In **consumer sales** (also called business-to-consumer, or B2C sales), the customers buy the product or service with their own money for their own personal use. In **commercial sales** (also called **corporate, industrial, business-to-business,** and **B2B sales**), the customers buy the product or service with their organization's money for professional use by themselves or others on the job.

The product or service usually dictates the type of sales. For example, breakfast cereal and toothpaste are sold to consumers. Meanwhile, office supplies and photocopiers are business-to-business items. But it gets tricky. For example, the boom in home-based businesses over the past 20 years created a whole new market for personal computers and office supplies. This market has characteristics of both the commercial market and the consumer market.

Each type of sale—consumer and commercial—presents its own challenges, which we examine as they arise in this part.

Translating Sales Goals into Marketing Plans

Every company wants to grow, which means that the dollar volume of sales should always be higher next year. You can achieve a sales increase in several ways:

- Increase your prices
- Sell more existing products to current customers

- Sell new products to current customers

- Sell existing products to new customers

- Sell new products to new customers

Let's briefly look at each of these strategies.

Increase Your Prices

A price increase might seem to be the simplest way to increase your sales. All you have to do is raise your prices 5 percent, then sell the same amount of product next year as you did this year, and your sales increase by 5 percent. Great, huh?

There's only one problem: *price resistance.* That's MBA-speak for customers not wanting to pay a higher price. When they see higher prices for the same products, they look for other places to buy or they try to get along with less of it, or without it. They also bargain harder with your salespeople.

MBA LINGO

Price resistance refers to the fact that customers who face high or increasing prices for a product or service will generally seek cheaper alternative products or services, try to get a lower price from the seller, or go to a different seller with lower prices.

If you have the market power—that is, if you face few competitors and your customers have no options—your price increase may "stick." But it's not a strategy you can count on for long. A product that commands constantly increasing prices will quickly attract competition. Also, customers often learn to live without companies they perceive as gouging them.

The other four goals all involve selling more units of product rather than selling the same amount of product at a higher price.

Sell More Existing Products to Current Customers

This comes down to "pushing product," and it can work. It is based on the reasonable idea that your best prospects are your current customers.

This strategy can work if your current customers are underserved, your product line is broad, or both. If you have only scratched the surface of your current customers and you have a broad product line to sell, you have ample opportunity to *cross-sell* them—that is, sell them other products that you offer.

MBA LINGO

Cross-selling means going to a customer who is buying one kind of product from you and selling him another kind, too. The question "Would you like fries with that?" is surely the most common example of cross-selling.

You can also offer volume discounts and find ways of binding the customers closer to you, perhaps by setting them up on an electronic system for automatic purchasing and billing. Anything you can do to make doing business with your company easier can help.

Sell New Products to Current Customers

New products are so vital that Chapter 22 is devoted to new product development. Even if you have what you think are satisfied customers, someone is out there working on ways to satisfy them even better or more cheaply. So you must always be improving your current products and developing new ones to meet your customers' needs.

Current customers can be your best prospects for new products, particularly products that solve problems you learned about when selling them old products.

CASE IN POINT

Many companies know how to use the Internet to bind customers to them, or at least to keep them interested. The most effective ways of doing this are to deliver well-targeted information about promotions and new products. Careful targeting is key, or customers soon see the communications as annoying or irrelevant.

Sell Existing Products to New Customers

Some companies get into a rut by just serving the same old set of customers. When you have a successful product or service, constantly ask yourself, "Who else might buy this? Who else can use this?"

You should never stop searching for new customers. Even the most successful companies lose at least some customers each year. Even your best accounts may leave you, for any number of reasons—a better product or price from a competitor, a snafu with your technology, or a simple desire for change. Also, any potential customer that you don't approach is one that a competitor will probably win. Why give away business without a fight?

CASE IN POINT

New markets for existing products can even give rise to entirely new businesses. For example, the office-supply retailers Staples and Office Depot didn't exist before the home-office boom. But then the need arose.

Companies selling office supplies commercially were not about to start calling on consumers. However, consumers, who are used to going to a store when they need something, have no problem going to one for paper, toner, or folders.

Sell New Products to New Customers

When sales of your product begin to slope off—often in the phase of *market maturity* or *saturation*—you have three choices:

1. Close up shop or sell the business

2. Try to survive on repeat and replacement business

3. Sell new products to new customers

The third choice is the best—provided you want a growing business. But don't make the mistake of waiting until your markets are saturated with your old products before developing new ones.

MBA LINGO

Market maturity means that the product has achieved wide acceptance and that growth in sales has leveled off. **Saturation** means that every potential customer who wants, needs, and can pay for your product already has one. It can be hard to know when your product has saturated its markets, because it depends on the true market potential for the product. (See the product adoption curve later in this chapter.)

Selling new products to new customers can be the most powerful of the five growth strategies. However, new products for new markets can be the hardest to develop. Even if you stay close to your main business (and generally you should), it's tough to come up with something new for a new market. That's why companies usually develop new products for their current markets, even when they enter a new business. For example, Disney entered theme parks in the 1950s. That was different from films, but Disney was already established in family entertainment. Nike and Adidas moved from athletic shoes to active wear, but their target customers were already buying their athletic shoes.

Most senior managers and all marketing and salespeople think constantly about ways to increase sales. These five strategies can move those thoughts in practical directions.

Product Differentiation

Product differentiation means making your product different from the others like it. Successful products offer customers a difference, something better. Even products that compete mainly on price should offer some difference.

Marketing plays a big role in making and highlighting product differences. In the following sections, I discuss certain proven ways of achieving product differentiation.

Improved Performance

Performance improvements actually make the product better. The Japanese challenge to U.S. automakers in the 1970s was one of improved performance. Gas mileage, durability, and value for the price improved dramatically in Japanese cars during this decade.

Improved performance may strike you as a manufacturing rather than marketing issue. But product improvements must be announced and "made real" in the marketplace, and that's a marketing challenge. It's not enough to build a better mouse trap. You have to show and tell people how and why it's better.

A company can decide to improve the performance of its product in various ways, including ease of use, durability, freedom from maintenance, economy of operation, and characteristics such as speed, weight, or water resistance. As you will learn in Chapter 25, many consumers (and companies) now evaluate the products they purchase at least partly on the basis of their health, safety, and social and environmental impacts. These are indeed aspects of product performance.

One caution: Worthwhile performance improvements are those that people want and will pay for. If you make improvements that customers don't care about, you're not differentiating your product in a meaningful way. The result is often "a gold-plated crowbar." You get nothing but added production costs, which are the last thing you need.

Improved Appearance

Modern society is visually oriented. Today the appearance of a product can be as important as its performance. Therefore, design—the blend of form and function that dictates the appearance of a product—is now a powerful product differentiator.

CASE IN POINT

Some products have succeeded largely on their design. For instance, the Best Made Company, which began by selling well-made, beautifully designed axes (of all things) and employing excellent public relations, soon transformed these usually prosaic tools into objects of desire, even among people with little need to fell trees or chop wood.

Improved Image

In our society, many people define themselves at least partly by what they buy and use. Thanks to advertising, television, and movies, products convey certain images, both to ourselves and to others. These images involve wealth, youth, status, sophistication, sexuality, health, caring, environmental consciousness, power, and danger (and, in some cases, a social critic would surely add, stupidity).

Product images pervade our culture. Consider the various images cultivated by products as diverse as Marlboro cigarettes (rugged and manly), Chivas Regal scotch (smooth and sophisticated), Sears Kenmore appliances (sensible and reliable), Campbell's soups (wholesome and comforting), Kellogg's Corn Flakes (pure and simple), *The New Yorker* magazine (urbane and literary), Harley-Davidson motorcycles (big and American), and the MGM Grand Hotel in Las Vegas (entertaining and swingin').

These images often go beyond mere product qualities. They attempt to create an experience for the customer that says, "When I buy this product, I am saying that I value these qualities, and that I have them myself."

Marketing Basics

Like every area of business, marketing and sales have their own ways of describing things. In the rest of this chapter, we cover several major concepts in marketing and sales that are worth knowing.

Who Drives Your Company?

A market-driven company looks to the market—to groups of customers—to learn what it should be doing. A market-driven company listens to customers to learn why and how customers use what they sell. A market-driven firm watches trends in the marketplace in technology, pricing, packaging, and distribution (where and how it sells its products). It also watches competitors.

A customer-focused company also listens to customers for cues on what it should do. However, the term *customer-focused* emphasizes an effort to make each customer's experience satisfying. A customer-focused company believes that every customer is important and tries to ensure that each customer is treated as an individual. These companies tend to be very accommodating when they face customer requests, taking a "can-do" approach. Many companies say they're customer-focused, but few truly are.

Sales-driven companies are focused on the top line. They want sales. I'm not saying that they ignore their markets and customers. No company can do that. I'm saying that those are not the main priorities. Increasing sales is the main priority.

Technology-driven companies tend to focus on innovation as their major source of growth and competitive advantage. Apple may be the best example of a company that—without sacrificing a focus on markets, sales, or customers—has continually used technological and product innovations to grow and, actually, to outdo itself.

MBA ALERT

The concept of the customer experience developed in the 2000s. Although some companies get carried away with the notion, the concept recognizes that engagement with customers extends beyond the product or service. The customer experience encompasses the entire process in which customers consider, buy, use, maintain, and dispose of the product. It considers every interaction between company and customer in every medium, and aims to make each one satisfying for the customer. The goal is to build long-term customer loyalty (measured as repeat business).

Of course, all companies want increasing sales. But sales-driven companies take a very direct route to this goal. They hire salespeople who "push product" rather than discover and satisfy needs. They take a "get-the-money" approach to customers, which can close sales but fail to win long-term customers.

The Product Adoption Curve

The product adoption curve states that a successful new product will be adopted by various categories of buyers in a predictable order. That's because not all buyers are willing to try something new. Many people need to see other, more innovative buyers adopt the product first. The product adoption curve and the categories of buyers are shown in the following figure.

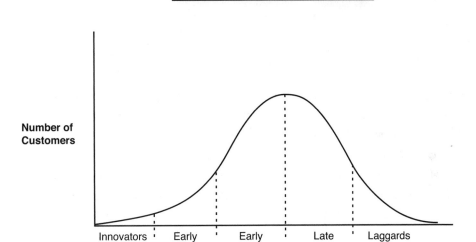

The product adoption curve.

By definition, the following percentages apply to each category of buyer:

Innovators	=	The first $2\frac{1}{2}$ percent of buyers
Early adopters	=	The next $13\frac{1}{2}$ percent

Early majority	=	The next 34 percent
Late majority	=	The next 34 percent
Laggards	=	The final 16 percent

These categories present different marketing and sales challenges. Innovators have to be located, which can take some doing, and then persuaded to try something new and unproven. Early adopters present similar challenges, but at least you have some earlier customers to point to as success stories.

You have to get to the early majority quickly, because you're soon going to face competitors if the product is successful. You may have to broaden your marketing effort and increase the size of the sales force. The late majority will probably require discounts and other inducements, such as service plans. At this stage, you're in a battle for market share. You'll also be trying to find completely new markets for the product, perhaps overseas.

By the time you're selling a product to the laggards, the challenge has shifted to controlling your sales and manufacturing costs, and squeezing all the profitability you can from the product while it's still alive.

The product adoption curve is also called the technology adoption curve because it applies to a technology (such as the VCR or personal computer) as well as to new products.

MBA MASTERY

Different types of customers respond differently to different marketing messages and sales approaches. For example, innovators and early adopters get excited when they hear that something is new and different. In contrast, you have to sell the late majority on the reliability and wide acceptance of the product.

The Product Life Cycle

Like people and organizations, products have lives. They are conceived, they are born, they grow, they have a period of maturity, and they go into decline. The product life cycle was developed in the 1960s to describe the predictable phases in the life of a product. Those phases are as follows:

- Introduction
- Growth
- Maturity
- Decline

Usually these phases are shown on a curve that plots sales over time, as shown in the following figure.

Each phase presents a different marketing and sales challenge. In the introductory phase, the challenge is "missionary work"—spreading word of the new product and finding the first customers. During growth, the challenge is to beat competitors, who introduce similar products when they see one that makes money, and win as many customers as possible. In maturity, the challenge becomes controlling sales costs, fighting for market share, and developing variations of the product. In decline, the challenge is deciding what to do with the product: Can it be revitalized? Is it still profitable enough for you to sell?

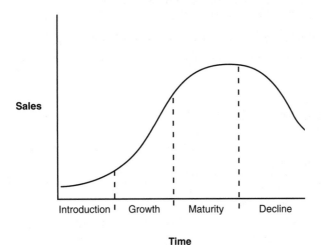

The product life cycle curve.

MBA MASTERY

Few things in business are predictable, but the product life cycle is one of them. Unfortunately, the *timing* of the phases is not very predictable. The key is to watch the sales trend. When sales are slow early in the product's life, it is in the introductory phase. When sales rise sharply, it is in the growth phase. When sales growth levels off for an extended time, it is in maturity. And when sales decrease, it is in decline.

The length of any particular phase can vary for different products. A fad item such as a video game can have a life of a few years, with some phases measured in months. A car brand like the Ford Mustang can take off rapidly, moving quickly from introduction to rapid growth, and then enjoy a long maturity and gentle decline with periods of revitalization. The product life cycle can be applied to entire product categories such as healthy frozen dinners (now in maturity) or steam locomotives (now defunct).

Occasionally, a product or category can go into decline and then stage a comeback. Large-engine, gas-guzzling cars and vans bounced back from their 1970s decline with the economic boom of the 1990s, then declined again in the late-2000s recession.

By the way, the product life cycle applies only to successful products. Those that don't make it past the introductory phase are product failures (products that are introduced but do not win market acceptance). Such failures are more common than most nonbusinesspeople realize.

The Least You Need to Know

- Since companies basically compete on price and quality, a company must first decide where it wants to be in terms of price and quality. Then it must establish and reinforce that position through its products and marketing message.
- Several strategies can increase sales: increase prices, sell more existing products to current customers, sell new products to current customers, sell existing products to new customers, or sell new products to new customers.
- Successful products go through a life cycle from introduction, to growth, to maturity, to decline. Each phase of the life cycle presents a different marketing and sales challenge.
- A product usually is adopted—either rapidly or gradually—first by innovators, then by early adopters, then by the early majority, followed by the late majority, and finally the laggards.

Who Are Your Customers, Anyway?

In This Chapter

- The purpose of market research
- The characteristics of market segments
- How to conduct a market research study

The better you know your customers and their wants and needs as they relate to your products or services, the better for your business. Only when you understand their wants and needs can you fulfill those wants and meet those needs more effectively than your competitors. But how do you learn what they are? There are a number of ways, and market research—by various means—is among the best.

This chapter examines the goals and tasks of market research. It also tells you how to plan and launch a good market research study.

What Is a Market?

A *market* is a group of customers or potential customers for a product or service. A company focuses its market research on its particular market. Coca-Cola studies the soft drink market. Merrill Lynch researches the market for financial services. Sony wants to know about the entertainment and home electronics markets. You research a market to get practical information your company can use in its sales, marketing, and product-development efforts.

Most companies think of their markets in two ways. First is the broad market the company serves, such as the soft drink or financial services or home electronics market. Second are *market segments*, which are specific markets within markets.

MBA LINGO

A **market** is a group of customers or prospects—usually a group made up of individual people or organizations with certain shared characteristics, if only a need for a certain product or service. **Market segments** are parts of a market that have some characteristic in common. For example, the market for personal computers has two broad segments—homes and businesses.

Divide and Conquer: Market-Segmentation Strategies

A market segment is a section or a slice of a broader market. Market segmentation recognizes that different customers have different needs and motivations. A number of standard market segments exist, such as the baby boomer and Hispanic markets. However, most companies also define their own market segments using one or more of the following segmentation strategies:

- **Geographic segmentation** divides the broad market into regional or local markets. Managers in a company using geographic segments will talk about the "Northeast market" or the "Dallas–Fort Worth market."

- **Demographic segmentation** classifies the broad market by customer characteristics such as age, gender, income, and race. Television shows, radio stations, magazines, and other media aim for specific segments (such as males 18–34 years old, working mothers, senior citizens, or African Americans). This helps companies *target* these demographic segments with their advertising messages.

- **Product segmentation** divides the broad market by the products the company sells. For example, the automotive industry deals with the markets for luxury, midsize, compact, subcompact, and sport utility vehicles.

- **Sales-channel segmentation** divides the market according to how a product is sold. For instance, the sales channels for Coca-Cola include grocery stores, restaurants, stadiums, movie theaters, and vending machines.

MBA LINGO

Targeting refers to the practice of developing specific advertising, promotions, products, or services for specific markets. These markets are referred to as target markets.

Large companies can use several segmentation strategies at once to better target their markets. For example, combining geographic and product segmentation enables General Motors to approach the California luxury car market. Combining demographics and sales channels lets Coca-Cola divide the working mother segment into working mothers who buy beverages in grocery stores, at restaurants, and from vending machines.

By segmenting markets, a company can better understand customer needs, motivations, and behavior. That understanding is also the goal of market research.

Why Do Market Research?

Broadly, market research includes all activities that aim to gather and analyze information on customers and the characteristics, attitudes, and behaviors that affect their buying behavior as it relates to your product. Market research aims to understand customers, because the better a company understands its customers, the better it can serve them.

Most market research focuses on one or more of the following types of information:

- **Demographic characteristics** include descriptive information about the customer. In consumer markets, *demographic* data includes age, gender, income, education, race, marital status, housing, and number of children. In business markets, it includes industry classification, annual sales, number of employees, number of locations, and years in business.

- **Buying behaviors** are the ways in which customers buy (such as retail stores and websites), frequency of purchase, and influences in the buying decision (such as advertising or recommendations from friends).

- **Customer satisfaction** is the buyer's happiness (or disappointment) with the product or service. Components of satisfaction include perceived value for the price, ease of use and maintenance, product defects, most and least important features, desired features, and likelihood of repeat purchase.

- **Attitudes and lifestyle,** often called *psychographics*, are relatively new concerns for marketers. These include hobbies, participation in sports, frequency of dining out, vacation plans, favorite magazines and television shows, time spent on the web or with *social media*, concerns for the future, political leanings, religion, and even personality traits and sexual orientation.

MBA LINGO

Demographics are characteristics of a market or market segment. These characteristics are usually statistical information such as age, gender, income, and so on. **Psychographics** are characteristics of a market or market segment that usually focus more on attitudes (such as political affiliation) and lifestyles (such as attendance at sporting events or museums). **Social media** are ways in which individuals and organizations can communicate with groups and individuals through self-generated text, photos, videos, and sound enabled by the Internet and telecommunications technologies. MySpace, YouTube, Facebook, and Flickr are key examples.

Among the newest identified lifestyle segments is the gay market. Since many gay people are urban dwellers without children, some marketers target them as prospects for leisure-time services such as vacations and fine dining. Companies in fields such as financial services and consumer packaged goods are developing specific ways to approach this market segment.

Who Needs Market Research?

Companies vary in their need for market research. For example, large companies tend to do more market research than small ones. Small companies often see research as costly and feel they already know their customers.

Often companies that shun market research sell *commodity* products (products such as coal or grain that are indistinguishable across companies that sell them) and believe their customers care only about low prices and fast service. Others have a *homogenous market*, meaning that they sell to only one type of customer. For example, manufacturers of professional dental equipment sell only to dentists, and defense contractors sell only to governments.

Firms that don't do market research on this basis may have a point, but often research can discover something new that would help them *differentiate* their product or further understand their customer. If nothing else, they might find ways to improve their service by learning how their customers use their products or how they can make their lives easier. For example, a cement company improved its sales after its research showed waiting times for customers' trucks were a barrier to selling more. They computerized and streamlined the process for picking up premixed loads and eliminated paperwork to move trucks through the process and out to construction sites faster.

MBA LINGO

A **commodity** is a product whose characteristics and performance are indistinguishable across the companies that sell it. Petroleum products, coal, and grain are examples of commodities. A **homogenous market** is one where all the customers and prospects share most characteristics. If you sell only to government agencies, you have a homogenous market. Product **differentiation** presents real or perceived product differences as beneficial to customers.

Some companies avoid market research because they feel that their sales force does a good job of reading their customers. Some managers don't believe that market research yields accurate or useful results.

These attitudes are understandable. However, most companies benefit from at least occasional research on their customers and prospects.

The Two Types of Market Research

The two broad types of market research are primary market research and secondary market research. Primary market research usually means asking people prepared questions in telephone, web-based, or in-person surveys. This includes questions included in hard-copy and web-based warranty registration forms, such as "Where did you by the item?" and "What is your household income?" Secondary market research gathers data and information on markets and customers from published material, such as websites, newspapers, magazines, and books. For example, a company might go to the U.S. Census Bureau's website to gather information on household incomes, buying patterns, education levels, and ethnicity in order to judge the size and other characteristics of one or more markets.

This chapter focuses on primary market research, but secondary research has its place. It will give you a good overview of a product or service. This can help you focus your primary research, particularly in an area completely new to your firm. Secondary research is also faster and cheaper than primary research.

In primary research, you go directly to sources of information. This usually means surveying customers or prospects (or both). Sometimes primary research is essential. Only someone who has used a product can discuss customer satisfaction. Only a prospect can tell you whether he'd buy a new service you're offering. Specific information directly from the source is the main advantage of primary research. But this comes at a price: primary research costs more than secondary research of comparable scope.

Primary research delivers very structured information. Since you design the questions, you can use primary research to develop *quantitative* (numerical) or *qualitative* (verbal) responses. Also, the web now enables companies to conduct market research without the expense of mail or telephone surveys and with easy capture and analysis of the results. On the downside, however, web-based surveys must usually be kept quite short or respondent fatigue (and frustration) quickly arises.

The rest of this chapter focuses on how to conduct a primary research study, regardless of the medium.

MBA LINGO

Quantitative information involves numbers and data that can be analyzed mathematically. For example, "29 percent of the survey respondents said the Mighty Vac was an excellent value" is quantitative information. **Qualitative** information tends to be verbal and less subject to mathematical analysis. For example, "The Mighty Vac lets me clean in hard-to-reach places" is qualitative.

Creating a Market Research Study

Let's say you've decided to prepare a market research study in order to uncover primary information about your customers. A market research study has five steps:

1. Define the goal of the research.

2. Design the study.

3. Develop the questionnaire.

4. Field the survey.

5. Analyze and present the results.

How well you carry out each step determines the quality of the results of your study. Let's consider each step in turn.

Define Your Goal

Good market research—either primary or secondary—starts with a goal. Your goal may be "to assess customer satisfaction with our Mighty Vac vacuum cleaner" or "to develop a profile of our customer base."

In defining your goal, consider how you will use the results. Think about the behaviors and attitudes you want to understand about your customers and prospects. Think ahead to the analysis phase and the final presentation, and gear the research accordingly.

MBA ALERT

People tend to load market research with too many goals. They'll often say, "As long as we're doing a survey, let's be sure to cover X, Y, and Z." This makes the questionnaire too long and can muddy the results. If people try to overload your survey, explain the goal and point out that you can explore other issues in the next round of research. Try to stick with one goal.

Design the Study

Study design results from a series of decisions about who you will survey, how you will conduct the survey, and what questions you will ask.

Who you survey depends on what you want to learn. If you want to know why you have lost customers and how to win them back, you must survey former customers. If you want to know how young single people perceive your company, you must survey young single people.

Who you survey also depends on the size of the sample you intend to survey. A cable-television company trying to learn why people do not subscribe doesn't have to ask every nonsubscriber in the area. It merely has to ask a sample of them.

The medium you use—mail survey, telephone interviews, in-person interviews (either through informal methods, such as "sidewalk surveys," or through more structured *focus groups*), or the Internet—depends on the budget, sample size, and goals of your research.

MBA LINGO

A **focus group** is a panel of 5 to 10 individuals brought together to respond to questions requiring in-depth discussion. Issues range from a company's service or image, to reactions to new product ideas, to feelings about political matters. Respondents are paid for their time (from $50 to $150), and the session is run by an experienced facilitator. Managers from the company often observe the session from behind a mirrored wall (with the participants' knowledge), and most sessions are taped for later viewing.

Let's briefly consider the pros and cons of each medium.

Survey Structure

Survey Medium	Benefits	Disadvantages
Mail	Relatively inexpensive.	Yields low response (many surveys get thrown out).
	Ideal for conducting a large survey (with easily answered questions) on a tight budget.	Those who do respond may have extreme feelings on the subject, leading to a skewed sample.
		You cannot control how readers respond (they may skip questions, answer incoherently, and so on).
		You cannot ask for more information.
Telephone	Generally yields better response rates than mail surveys.	Far more expensive than mail surveys.
	You control the order of the questions and can ask for more information.	
	An excellent choice for in-depth data on customers' experiences with your products.	
In-person	Best if your sample can be reached at a certain place (such as a health club or supermarket).	Getting interviewees can be difficult.
	Yields in-depth information.	Extremely expensive for large samples.
	Necessary if you have a product prototype that must be demonstrated in person.	
Internet	Inexpensive survey method (assuming an established website and straightforward programming).	Requires a website with a good volume of activity.
	You control the order of the questions and can make the respondent answer before proceeding.	Not good for in-depth questions or long questionnaires.
	Best for conducting surveys with respondents you do business with on the web.	

Finally, during the study design phase, you must decide how you will handle the mechanics of getting the questions answered. The main decision is whether to do it in-house (with company employees or independent contractors) or to use a market research firm (or "vendor").

Obviously, you may want to use a vendor if you don't have the in-house time or resources to complete the survey. Also, certain research subjects are best left to market research firms. If the subject is sensitive or will elicit negative comments, a vendor may get more honest answers. Many people will withhold negative comments about your product if they're speaking with someone from your company.

You might also hire a vendor if you want outside, independent research on issues that affect key company decisions, such as whether to enter a new market or where to place a large retail chain store. If you need totally objective information about a thorny subject, use a vendor. Whether research is done in-house or jobbed out, someone at your company must closely supervise the project from start to finish and ultimately be responsible for the costs and the results. And however you choose to handle your survey, you have to make sure your company can afford it.

Develop the Questionnaire

Questionnaire design is a field unto itself. The guidelines here will enable you to either write a questionnaire or work well with the person who is writing it.

First, list the issues you want covered and the questions you want asked. Brainstorm. Write down anything that may be pertinent. Include identifying questions such as name, address, and general characteristics (such as "education" for consumers, and "industry" or "annual sales" for companies).

Here are the major kinds of questions and their uses, along with some examples.

Open-ended questions cannot be answered "yes" or "no," nor do they prompt for a specific response. Open-ended questions are particularly good for eliciting opinions, attitudes, and feelings. They tend to get honest answers, because without prompting, the respondent has no choice but to say what he or she thinks (or refuse to answer). Examples of open-ended questions include the following:

- Which features of the Mighty Vac are most important to you?

- What is your opinion of the service you receive from Acme Industries?

MBA MASTERY

Many market research firms will offer to do an analysis, a written report, and even a presentation of the results. Although many of them do very good work and they have the advantage of objectivity, in my experience, it is best for in-house managers to conduct the analysis. They know the company, product, customers, and internal politics best.

Closed-end questions can be answered "yes" or "no," or they prompt for a response. They can be standardized so the answers are easy to compile and compare when you do your analysis. Closed-end questions are also easy for respondents to answer. Here are some sample closed-end questions:

- Which of the following features of the Mighty Vac are important to you? (Check all that apply.)

  ❏ Extra-long hose

  ❏ Extra-long power cord

  ❏ Extra-high horsepower

  ❏ Square head

  ❏ Other *(Please specify)* _____

- How would you rate the service you receive from Acme Industries? (Check one.)

  ❏ Excellent

  ❏ Good

  ❏ Fair

  ❏ Poor

With closed-end questions, you must often give directions to the respondent (such as "Check one" or "Please rate from one to five, with five being the best").

Identifying questions ask the respondent to verify name, title, address, and similar information. These questions make good icebreakers for telephone or personal interviews. Qualifying questions are asked early in a survey when you must determine whether the person is qualified to take part in the survey. For example, a customer-satisfaction survey requires a respondent who has actually used the product ("Have you ever used the Mighty Vac?" is a qualifying question).

Follow-up questions, also called probing questions, ask the respondent to add more to the answer he or she gave to the previous question. These questions let you dig deeper into a subject. For example, you might first ask a respondent for her opinion of the service she received from Acme Industries. Whatever her response, you then ask why she feels that way.

Don't overuse follow-up questions, or you'll fatigue the respondent and eventually produce cursory answers. Don't waste a follow-up question asking the obvious (such as, "Why do you prefer a low price?").

Once you've brainstormed a list of questions, pare the list to the necessary questions. Keep questionnaires short; long surveys annoy or fatigue respondents. Ask only what you need to ask, and you'll get a better response rate and more accurate information. A written questionnaire should be kept to one page (two, at most), if possible. Telephone questionnaires should ideally be kept to five minutes. You can go over these limits, of course, but your response rate will fall.

> **MBA MASTERY**
>
> Often on a rating scale with five elements (such as 1–5 or Excellent, Very Good, Good, Fair, or Poor), many respondents just check the middle value. You may force a more positive or negative answer if you give the respondent a choice of only four ratings. This forces the respondent to make a positive or negative judgment.

Do's and Don'ts of Questionnaire Design

Consider some general guidelines for questionnaire design:

- **DO** think ahead to the analysis phase and ask questions that will produce answers you can compile and analyze.

- **DO** keep the survey as short as possible, while asking all questions pertinent to your goal.

- **DO** try to ask important questions early in the survey, in case the respondent chooses not to finish it.

- **DO** be careful when you give instructions for answering the survey.

- **DO** leave enough space for respondents or interviewers to write answers to open-ended questions.

- **DO** write a one-page cover letter that politely tells a respondent to a mail survey why the survey is important.

- **DON'T** be afraid to ask sensitive questions if they're important to your goal. The respondent always has the right to refuse to answer.

- **DON'T** let others load up the survey with questions that don't relate to the goal.

- **DON'T** crowd the questions to fit them onto a certain number of pages.

- **DON'T** expect a huge response. And don't rule out making a second request of those who haven't replied to a mail survey after three weeks.

- **DON'T** go to the same sample too often. They will lose interest and may become hostile.

MBA MASTERY

Be absolutely certain to test your questionnaire before you field it. See which questions work and which don't. Modify or omit any confusing questions. (And don't blame the respondents. If they say it isn't clear, it isn't clear.)

Fielding the Questionnaire

If you have handled the first three steps properly, actually fielding (conducting) the survey should be straightforward. However, depending on your particular study, there will be details to oversee. For example, mail questionnaires must be sent on time, and at a time free of predictable distractions, such as after the winter holidays. Telephone interviewers need up-to-date lists of phone numbers. They should also be instructed to schedule a specific time later with any respondent who is busy but will agree to be interviewed at another time.

Be reasonable in your expectations and don't become overly excited or disappointed by the early responses. It's often a good idea to not look at early results very closely (except to ascertain that the surveys are being properly completed).

In this step, your goal is to get the target number of completed surveys (or "completes"). This can take more time and effort than you originally thought. If glitches occur (okay, *when* they occur), work with the interviewers or others, such as your mailroom or mail house, to resolve them. You may even have to enlarge the sample. As you work to resolve problems, just be sure to project an air of calm confidence. Ultimately, you'll get to your target number of completed surveys.

Analysis and Presentation of Results

I have always found analysis of results to be the most interesting part of any market research project. It's investigative work and it brings out the detective in most of us. If your study and questionnaire were properly designed—and if the questionnaires were properly completed—you'll have the information that you set out to capture. Now you merely have to make sense of it.

Here are some guidelines:

- **Be as objective as you can.** We all like to believe that we approach research results with an open mind, but most of us would prefer a certain outcome. Be sure you're aware of your biases and those of others on your team, and trust the survey respondents to tell the truth as they see it.

- **Look for patterns in the answers.** The more you see an answer, the more likely it is to be true.

- **Don't be swayed by wildly positive or negative answers to open-ended questions.** Especially if they are, uh, colorfully worded, it's easy to latch on to them. Unless they're part of a pattern, they represent only one person's opinion.

- **Consider who is saying what.** Often you must evaluate responses in light of the characteristics of the respondents. If the opinions of newer customers diverge from those of longer-term customers, if those of city dwellers differ from those of suburbanites, if those of your customers in financial services don't match those of industrial clients, that may tell you something.

- **Think back to the goal of the research and evaluate the results in light of that goal.** If the research was done to support a decision—for example, to pursue a new market or change a product—what did the respondents tell the company to do? If the research was done for purely informational purposes— for example, to compile a profile of your clients—what are you hearing? These conclusions will make up your major findings.

- **Given the research results, decide what recommendations you would make.** Most market research (actually, most research of any kind) should produce "actionable results." That is, the results should point to some kind of action the company should take now that this information has been unearthed.

Various statistical tools beyond the scope of this book are available for analyzing research results. However, provided that the base of respondents is large enough for your purposes, simple percentage readings of various responses (that is, the percent that answered this way or that) will typically tell you what you need to know. Most political poll data reported in newspapers, such as approval ratings and voters' positions on issues, are based on simple percentages.

Use common sense when analyzing market research results. If most respondents say something and your common sense supports their view, you can safely believe that most of the population represented by that sample feels similarly.

Powerful Presentations Pack a Punch

In presenting the results of market research, you have powerful information to announce: the opinions of customers and prospects. With that kind of ammunition, it's best to let the results—good, bad, or otherwise—speak for themselves to the extent possible.

Here's a general outline for a written report of typical market research results:

- **Executive summary:** A one- to two-page summary of the study and its goals, findings, and recommendations.

- **Purpose:** The first section of the body of the report. This should mention the goal and scope of the study and when it was conducted.

- **Major findings:** How the survey respondents answered the key questions.

- **Secondary findings:** How the less important questions were answered.

- **Recommendations:** What actions the company should take in light of the findings.

- **Appendix 1:** Methodology of the study, telling how the study was conducted and how the sample was developed, and showing a sample questionnaire.

- **Appendix 2:** Respondents to the survey.

This outline is only an example. An actual report of research results might easily contain more, fewer, or different sections.

Market research represents one of the best foundations for making decisions available to a company. It can also be tailored to very precise needs and can be conducted on virtually any scale.

Whatever your needs and resources, market research often spells the difference between flying blind and following a clearly lighted course.

Voice of the Customer

Voice of the customer (VOC) is a term for highly detailed research efforts used mainly in Six Sigma and other quality-improvement methodologies, which you learned about in Chapter 10. Their main goal is to learn the customers' requirements for the product—what customers expect in terms of performance, quality, features, price, and other relevant characteristics.

There's no set formula or format for VOC projects, but they do systematically gather information on customers' needs and wants. They also systematically prioritize those needs and wants. The overall aim is to learn what customers value in terms of quality and performance and then, to the extent possible and practical, to deliver those things in the product.

VOC projects often originate with the quality department, but marketing can also initiate them and should always participate. These projects rely on both active and passive information collection. Active collection includes surveys, interviews, and focus groups. Passive collection entails gathering relevant data from customer complaints, sales and service reports, warranty claims, and similar information. This data must be compiled, analyzed, and presented in ways similar to information gathered in regular market research surveys.

The most common flaw in VOC efforts is that they tend to focus on product specifications rather than on the entire customer experience. To improve your VOC efforts—or any market research efforts—always look to the problems your customers are trying to solve and the benefits they aim to enjoy when you design, analyze, and consider market research. That way, you will learn more about your customers and about your products and services.

The Least You Need to Know

- Be clear about the goal of a market research study and gear the survey accordingly.
- The five major steps in a market research project are to define the goal, design the study, develop the questionnaire, field the survey, and analyze and present the results.
- The quality of the sample often dictates the quality of the research. Unless you are doing "quick and dirty" research as a simple double-check, be sure that your sample is representative of the population.
- If you see the budget for a market research project going too high for the value of the information you seek, reduce the number of questions. Or try doing half of the survey first, and then do the second half only if it would add useful information.
- If your company doesn't believe in market research, patiently try to sell the idea. Meanwhile, conduct secondary research, which costs relatively little, to learn as much as you can about your markets and customers.

The Five P's of Marketing

In This Chapter

- Understanding the marketing mix
- Using product, pricing, packaging, place, and promotion properly
- Thinking about product positioning

How do they do it? How do companies like Nike, Absolut, Disney, Toyota, Kraft, EverReady, McDonald's, Coca-Cola, and American Express sell so much to so many people year in, year out? You might at first say, "They advertise like crazy." But advertising is just one piece of the marketing mix, and a company has to get most of the pieces right.

The term *marketing mix* refers to the combination of elements that a company uses to market its product. It takes work to combine them to create the best marketing mix for a product. You have to gauge both the market (your prospects and customers) and your competitors properly. You must then gear the mix to the actual customer experience that you can and will deliver.

This chapter explains each element in the marketing mix. All five of them can help you gain a competitive advantage, if you know how to use them. Let's learn how.

The Marketing Mix Made Easy

The Five P's of marketing are as follows:

- **Product:** The product or service you are selling. For a product to succeed, it must be well conceived, it must be well executed, and it must fill a customer need.

In most companies, marketing and sales play a big role in any decision affecting the company's products. That's because they understand market trends and customer needs, and they know what makes products or services sell.

- **Price:** After the product itself, price is the key element in the marketing mix. Price affects the rest of the mix and can generate strong responses in customers and competitors. Your pricing strategy is quite important.

  Although a purely mathematical approach might work in setting your price (for example, you might choose to set your price 10 percent below your nearest competitor's or 30 percent above your costs), there really is as much art as science in pricing decisions.

- **Packaging:** A product (particularly a product as opposed to a service) needs a package. A package must protect your product and present it in the best way. Attractive, efficient packaging is so important (and difficult to design) that entire design firms focus exclusively on this area of marketing.

- **Place:** In the marketing mix, place really means *sales channels*, which relate to *distribution*—the specific means through which you get your product to your customers. (But "distribution" begins with the letter *D*, not *P*, and these are the Five P's, not the Five D's, of marketing.) A product needs the right distribution to reach the right customers in the right way.

- **Promotion:** Promotion is what most people think of when they hear the word *marketing*. Promotion, which includes publicity and advertising, is how you choose to get the word out about your product and the inducements you provide to prompt purchase decisions.

The rest of this chapter examines each of the Five P's in more depth. Put them all together, and you have the marketing mix.

MBA LINGO

Distribution refers to the ways you get your product into the customer's hands. It can even include the methods of transportation by which you ship your products. In the marketing sense of the term, however, distribution focuses mainly on sales channels. **Sales channels** (also called distribution channels) are the specific means of getting the product to customers. These include retailers, wholesalers, telemarketers, direct-mail campaigns, websites, and so on.

Product Is Paramount

Some people believe that great marketing can overcome a product's flaws. That does happen, but I believe it's rare and almost never works in the long run. Most truly successful products do fulfill their purpose for those who buy them.

You will see how to develop great products in more detail in Chapter 22. For now, your product must have these characteristics to succeed in the marketing mix:

- Ability to fulfill a customer need

- Ease of use

- Quality in keeping with the price

- Minimal (or positive) health, safety, and environmental impact

- A good "fit" with the rest of your company's business

Now, any of these characteristics—such as ease of use or quality—can be pitched to customers in your marketing messages and sales presentations. However, the way you pitch them can make a real difference. That's because most customers are more interested in *benefits* than *features.*

MBA LINGO

A **feature** is a characteristic of a product—for example, its color, size, power, or something it can do. A **benefit** is what the customer receives because of the product and its features.

A product should have features—such as a convenient size, a special technology, or an appealing color—that distinguish it from other products in its category. These features should not be included in your product for the heck of it. (What's the point of producing a pocket-sized waffle iron, for example, if portability isn't a feature anyone wants in waffle irons?) Rather, every feature you include in your product must deliver a benefit to the customer. You must focus on that benefit when you market and sell your product.

Consider the difference between a feature and a benefit: a feature is a characteristic or quality of your product; a benefit is the way that feature helps your customer. For example, consider the following features and benefits for a sports car.

Feature	Benefit
420-horsepower engine	Fast cruising and easy passing
No tune-ups for 50,000 miles	Money in your pocket; more time to enjoy your car
Huge 18-inch wheels	Staying upright in your seat on sharp turns
Candy-apple-red exterior	Drawing attention and projecting a fun-loving image

Customers care about benefits, not features. A feature that doesn't deliver a benefit is useless from a marketing standpoint.

If you're a marketing pro, you must always think in terms of the customer. If you can make your product smaller, you, the marketer, must tell customers what that means to them. Does it make the product easier to hold? Easier to store? More portable? More compatible with something else? If your product is more durable, what should you tell the customer? That he or she will never have to buy another one? That he or she will save money in maintenance cost? Find the benefit, and market it. Try to work with engineering, research and development, product development, and senior management to always improve products in ways that are important to your customers. Ask yourself, is it really an improvement if nobody will pay extra for it?

 CASE IN POINT

Some companies are tempted to develop ways of drawing more money from customers for products that are essentially the same as the previous model or that add only marginal value. For instance, *planned obsolescence* is the tactic of making your product "outdated" (which Microsoft does with each successive operating system it issues) or building it to last for an artificially short time (which U.S. automakers were accused of doing before the Japanese quality challenge of the 1970s).

Deceptive or confusing pricing schemes are another popular way of parting customers from their money without adding value. Many financial services companies lead customers on with a low base price (for a credit card, loan, or mortgage), but then add arcane fees and charges that more than make up the difference.

Consistently successful companies put their energy into creating products and services that customers want, and then marketing them aggressively but honestly.

Pricing Problems

Pricing mistakes can kill a good product—and even a good company. The first requirement for a "proper" price is that you must be able to make money at the product's *price point*. If the product costs more to make than you are selling it for, there's almost no sense in making it. (I say "almost" because you may be able to use the product as a *loss leader*—that is, a product that doesn't make a profit but lures customers to try other products.)

You must be able to sell the product at a competitive price. If your competitors can underprice you on a product of similar quality, how will you get business? Don't rely on your relationships with customers or the skill of your sales force to overcome prices that are above the competition's. There are, however, other ways to justify high prices that deliver the high profits we all crave.

MBA LINGO

Price point means price level or price in relation to the prices of similar products. A **loss leader** is a product on which a manufacturer or, more commonly, a retailer does not make a profit, but carries to attract customers.

Pricing Strategies

Companies use three basic pricing strategies: competitive pricing, cost-plus pricing, and value pricing. Let's examine each one.

If your product sells at a price lower than your competitors' prices, you are practicing *competitive pricing*. Your prices certainly *don't* have to be the lowest to succeed in the marketplace. (Just look at the price of a Mercedes.) But low prices are one way to compete effectively.

Sometimes competitive pricing is essential. For instance, in a commodity business— where the products are basically the same no matter who sells them—the outfit with the lowest price usually succeeds. That's because when the products themselves are not differentiated, price becomes the differentiator. Iron ore, coal, lumber, rice, and many other products drawn from the earth are commodities.

Competitive pricing isn't just for commodities, however. In retail, plasma-screen televisions aren't a commodity, but once a customer decides to buy one, price plays a big role in where to buy and which brand to buy. So competitive pricing is common in retail. In fact, some retailers offer to beat any other advertised price.

In general, the success of a competitive pricing strategy depends on achieving high volume and low costs.

In *cost-plus pricing*, you look at the cost of what you sell (that is, your costs) and then add on the profit you need to make. That's your price. Cost-plus means "cost plus profit." So if a stereo equipment retailer buys a Sony television for $180 and he needs to make a gross margin of 40 percent, then he has to sell the television for $300 (because $300 – $180 = $120 and $120 ÷ $300 = 40%). (You can figure out your price using cost-plus pricing in various other ways, but all are based on clearing a certain level of profit above your costs.) This method is straightforward and ensures that you will make money on what you sell. Unfortunately, it doesn't ensure that you will sell it.

MBA ALERT

Cost-plus pricing can be particularly useful in labor-intensive service businesses such as consulting. However, the costs in these businesses can be more difficult to estimate than those in manufacturing businesses. You can lose money unless you closely figure the labor needed on each project beforehand, add your profit, and keep your costs within the budgeted amount.

The success of this pricing strategy depends on your not being underpriced by a competitor. It also depends on controlling your costs and targeting a "reasonable" profit.

Value pricing is the alternative to basing your prices on your competitors' prices or on your costs. Instead, you base your prices on the value you deliver to customers. In this strategy, you deliver as much value as possible to your customers—and charge them for it. With this strategy, you can charge a high price and justify it by delivering high value. Value pricing is common in high-technology and luxury items, such as clothing, restaurants, and travel.

MBA LINGO

A company engages in **competitive pricing** when it attempts to price its products below the prices for similar products from competitors. In **cost-plus pricing,** a company assesses the total cost of producing the item or of delivering the service that it sells, and then adds what it believes to be a reasonable profit. In **value pricing,** a company charges a price that reflects the value of what it is delivering to the customer. This is the alternative to competitive and cost-plus pricing.

If you sell aspirins, competitive pricing says to charge a lower price than competitors, cost-plus says to charge what it cost to make them plus a profit, and value pricing says to charge what the customer will pay to have his or her headache gone.

Value pricing works well for new, high-tech products. When a new technology either has very high appeal or solves an expensive problem, it has extremely high value. In other words, if customers really want it or need it, they will pay a high price for it.

You will notice that after a technology is established, the price falls. This pattern is now well established, as demonstrated by personal computers, video recording devices, plasma-screen televisions, global positioning systems (GPS), and many other product classes. In fact, it is common when a new technology is released to hear people say, "I'm going to wait until the price comes down."

In other words, the technology doesn't have enough value to them to warrant the high price. But other customers, who are less price sensitive or who really want or need the new technology, will buy it first. For example, mobile phones (for automobiles) have been around since the late 1960s, but only people who would benefit greatly from them, such as real estate contractors or highly successful salespeople, would pay the thousands of dollars they cost at the time.

Value pricing in other markets depends on the ability to deliver value and the perception of value. Service is one way to create value. Many outfits justify high prices by servicing their customers like crazy. Another way is to be "the best" in terms of quality, materials, construction, and features. This then delivers benefits such as long life, high performance, and freedom from maintenance.

Often the perception of value can be as important as—or more important than—actual product qualities. Value is in the eye of the buyer. Does a Hermes silk scarf really deliver 10 times the value of a $75 silk scarf? Does Johnnie Walker Black deliver three times the value of Passport Scotch? The buyers seem to think so.

This leads to an odd situation in some product categories: the higher the price of your product, the more you sell. This phenomenon is called the Veblen Effect, for the American economist who identified it. The Veblen Effect runs contrary to normal price theory, which states that the lower the price of your product, the more you will sell. Veblen saw that some products sold in greater amounts if their price was increased. In other words, high prices can create the perception of value.

Mix Pricing Strategies

In practice, you must consider all three pricing strategies. You have to consider your competitor's prices, even if you're not competing on price. You also have to consider your costs, or your profits will suffer. You must consider the value you deliver because, no matter what you sell, customers want value for their money.

There's a dynamic aspect and an element of trial and error inherent in successful pricing. Pricing is dynamic because your products, customers, and competitors often change, and your prices often must change in response. Pricing involves trial and error because your prices affect your sales, income, and growth. So you must monitor the effects of your prices on these measures and then decide what do to next.

Packaging Presents Your Products

Packaging includes all aspects of the package that holds your product. Your product's package must be practical and promotional. Issues of engineering, design, graphics, distribution, and marketing enter into packaging decisions.

Different products present different packaging challenges. For fragile products, protection during shipment is the key consideration. For retail products, the ability to attract customers in the store is paramount. Many retail products also must vie for overcrowded display space, and packaging can impact the retailer's decision on where to place the product. The cost of packaging is always a consideration, too.

In the past two decades, three new packaging issues have emerged: environmental concerns, safety concerns, and what I call "packaging as product."

Environmental, or "green," concerns drive an ever-growing segment of the U.S. population's purchase decisions. This segment tends to place high value on environmentally friendly products. These products are made from or packaged in recyclable or biodegradable materials, or can otherwise claim to be "earth-friendly." For example, Wal-Mart mandated that suppliers of products must reduce their packaging by an aggregate amount of 5 percent over a five-year period.

Safety concerns arose after several product-tampering cases and scares in the 1970s and 1980s. Tamperproof packaging is now standard for many foods and consumer packaged goods. We also now have childproof caps for prescription and over-the-counter medicines. However, this new packaging strategy had an unintended consequence: elderly people or others whose hands are weak or arthritic often find childproof caps on medicines difficult or impossible to open.

MBA ALERT

Surveys have revealed that health, safety, social, and environmental concerns are playing an increasing role in consumers' buying decisions. A 2010 United Nations study titled "Trends in Sustainable Development" found that environmentally friendly consumer behavior increased in 13 of the 14 countries that had been surveyed in 2008 and 2009.

In "packaging as product," the package becomes integral to the product and acts as a differentiator. This can work well in commodity-like product categories. For example, unrefrigerated milk packaged in boxes has found broad acceptance in Europe, although it's been a tougher sell in the United States. However, juices in boxes have proved quite successful in the United States.

At its best, packaging provides physical protection, attractive display, and ease of use, as well as product differentiation and a form of competitive advantage. Like every part of the marketing mix, packaging demands thought and effort.

A Proper Place Produces Profits

Today there are more places to sell your product than ever before, including these:

- **Direct sales force:** Salespeople who are employees of the company and sell only the company's products.

- **Wholesalers:** Companies that sell the products of other companies to outfits that will resell them. Wholesalers are sometimes called "middlemen" because they are between the maker of the product and the business that sells it to the customer. For example, a food wholesaler buys food from the food-processing companies and sells it to the grocery stores.

- **Retailers:** Stores that sell to individual and (sometimes, but much less often) business customers. A retail chain is a company that owns more than one location of the same store, such as Macy's or CVS.

- **Original equipment manufacturers (OEMs):** Companies that assemble and sell equipment made from components and products made by other companies. OEMs operate mainly in computers and other high-technology businesses.

- **Independent sales reps:** Salespeople who sell products for a company without being employees of the company and who generally work purely on commission.

- **Direct response:** Selling only through the mail or by means of advertisements in magazines or on television or radio, asking customers to mail or phone in their order.

- **Telemarketing:** Technique that involves calling lists of people and selling to them over the telephone.

- **Internet:** The World Wide Web has established itself as a full-fledged sales channel across virtually every product and service category. Even for products and services that cannot be ordered or delivered via the web, the technology plays a key role in providing potential customers with information and in facilitating customers' purchases. Every business must understand the unique advantages of the web—information delivery, interactivity, continual updating capabilities—and the ways in which customers use the web to educate themselves, compare products, and place orders.

- **International:** For a business in any country, foreign markets are becoming increasingly important. The web is one driver of the global marketplace, but for products and services that must be physically delivered (unlike, say, information and software), companies still face the issue of exporting. Although exporting can be a complex and costly means of selling, the U.S. Department of Commerce in Washington, D.C., offers businesses lots of free information on how to go about it.

- **Joint marketing agreements:** One company supplying a product for another (usually larger) company to sell.

MBA ALERT

Visit the U.S. Department of Commerce exporting portal at www.export.gov for information on how to go about initiating or expanding exports in your business.

These are all distribution channels. How many of them you can use depends on your product, pricing, and target markets. But try to use all that you profitably can.

When formulating a distribution strategy, ask yourself these questions:

- What am I selling?

- Who are my prospects?

- Where are they?

- How can I reach them?

- How does the distribution channel work?

- What does it cost to sell through this channel?

- How many channels should I use?

Answering these questions will help you choose the right sales channel—however, there may be no single "right" channel. The choice may be which two or three to use (or at least try) and whether to start using them together or one at a time in a certain sequence.

CASE IN POINT

As marketers seek to reach customers through a variety of sales channels, the issue of channel management arises. Channel management entails matching the sales channel to your goals and products and minimizing "channel conflict."

For example, a window manufacturer with a line of windows ranging from economy to quality to specialty, employs a variety of sales channels—and brands. The economy model is sold through major chains, such as Home Depot, under one name. The quality model is sold under another name to large contractors by the company's sales force. The specialty (or super-premium) windows—for instance, skylights that change their degree of tint for sunrooms in expensive homes—are sold to architects through distributors and the sales force.

Channel conflict arose in the specialty category when distributors found themselves competing with the company's sales force for sales to certain architects. When distributors complained, the company agreed to pay a commission to any distributor who had called on the architect in the previous 12 months, even if the distributor didn't make the sale. The company felt it was worthwhile and fair to pay a distributor a commission even though a company salesperson had made the sale, to keep the distributor happy and reduce channel conflict.

Promotion Boosts Purchases

Defined narrowly, *promotion* means ways of creating awareness or inducing people to buy. Tactics include cents-off coupons, limited-time offers, rewards programs, and special events, such as sponsoring concerts or athletic competitions. *Premiums*, which include standard promotional items such as pens, T-shirts, calendars, and coffee mugs, are another example of a promotion. (I discuss premiums more in Chapter 20.)

More broadly, promotion includes these tactics, along with everything you do to tell the market about your product—most important, advertising, web-based efforts, and public relations.

Because most markets are crowded, good promotion can make or break a product. Its importance is underscored by the existence of advertising agencies and public relations firms, which help companies promote their products and themselves.

We look at advertising, promotion, and public relations more closely in the next chapter.

The Role of the Web

The web has affected every one of the Five P's of marketing, in the following ways—and more:

- **Product:** The web has transformed information and software to the point that they are themselves web-based products. An ever-increasing percentage of books is now not only sold via the web, but also delivered via the web to electronic readers. Even products that cannot be encrypted, delivered, and updated on the web have been transformed because of the way the medium enables companies to present products and services and build their brands.

- **Price:** The web has driven down prices in certain areas where it is a critical part of the selling and delivery process, notably books and certain financial services, such as brokerages. Because it shifts certain selling costs downward, the web can enable smaller companies to compete on a more equal footing with larger ones.

- **Packaging:** The effect of the web on physical packaging depends on the product, but in general, people develop a tolerance for primarily functional packaging when they purchase a product on the web. (After all, when something is being delivered in a brown box from a brown truck by a man or woman in a brown uniform, we've lowered the bar a bit.) The actual "packaging" occurs mainly on the web, in terms of how the site is structured and designed, how users interact with the site, and how products are presented and pictured.

- **Place:** The web *is* a place in the marketing sense of the term. It is a sales channel. By shifting distribution costs downward, web-based technology can enable smaller companies to compete on a more equal footing with larger ones in the virtual world. A virtual storefront costs a tiny fraction of what a physical storefront costs, whether you're a Fortune 500 company or you're operating out of your home. Bear in mind, however, that the web is a "place" people visit, not just a series of pages that they read.

- **Promotion:** The web is revolutionizing promotion, and not just advertising, which it already has revolutionized. It has created an environment in which finding and comparing products, obtaining recommendations, and bypassing sales messages is as easy as clicking a mouse. The real key to successful web-based promotion is to learn and target the true interests of your customers and to nurture a relationship with them based on those interests. It's really one-on-one marketing.

To get the most from web-based marketing efforts, a business must think through every aspect of its product and the customer experience. It must understand how customers will use the web to learn about the product, compare it with similar products or substitutes, and develop opinions about the various sellers of the product. Then it must make life as easy as possible for the customer to do those things, because customers flock to the companies that do and avoid those that don't.

Proper Positioning Prevents Poor Performance

All the Five P's add up to one final piece of the program—positioning, which refers to the position of the product in relation to others in its category and in the minds of prospects and customers. Positioning is linked to quality and price. In most categories, there are two extremes—high-quality, high-price offerings and low-quality, low-price offerings—and various spots in between.

Please understand that every company would like to be able to deliver high quality at a low price. Unfortunately, it's just not economically possible, so individual companies have to decide where they want to be. Mercedes decided to produce high-quality cars at a high price. Hyundai decided to produce lower-quality cars at a lower price.

Essentially, positioning hinges on two elements of your business:

- Your target market
- Your operating costs

A target market of lower- or middle-income people with a lower demographic profile dictates different positioning than a higher-income target market.

And, again, you have to be able to make money on the product, which goes back to your costs. If your costs dictate a high price, you cannot position your products as low-price, lower-quality offerings. You will lose money and ultimately fail.

Thus, positioning grows out of the strategic choices underlying the entire enterprise: Who are your customers? What business are you in? What are you selling? What are your financial objectives? We examine these decisions more deeply in Chapter 23.

From the marketing standpoint, every element in the mix must establish or reinforce the product's positioning. The product itself, its price and packaging, the places that sell it, and the way it is promoted all play their role in positioning the product.

The Least You Need to Know

- The marketing mix has five elements: product, price, packaging, place, and promotion.
- The best marketing is generally in service of the best products. Marketing can do the best job on products that meet a genuine customer need reliably, effectively, and economically.
- When pricing your products, consider competitors' prices, your costs, and the product's value to customers.
- Packaging must ensure that the product gets to the store or customer in one piece. But it can also help the product competitively.
- Promotion is the essence of marketing.
- The web has affected most components of the marketing mix in ways that call for more than just putting up a website with product information.

You Can Understand Advertising (and That's a Promise!)

In This Chapter

- Developing advertising messages that work
- Creating an advertising budget
- Determining where you should advertise

Advertising is everywhere. None of us can escape it, even if we want to—and many of us do. Yet despite criticism, which has been around as long as advertising itself, the volume of ads in any medium continually increases over the long term.

Why? Because advertising works well enough to encourage companies to keep doing it.

This chapter gives you a general overview of what makes advertising work and why so many companies use it in so many different forms. You also learn a bit about public relations, another method of business communication.

What Is Advertising and What Does It Do?

Advertising is a positive message about a product, service, or organization in a communication medium that is paid to carry the message. In any advertisement, the sender of the message is identified. (Note that the sender does not have to be a business. Many nonbusiness outfits, including the military and nonprofit organizations such as the American Heart Association, use advertising, as do individuals, such as political candidates buying television time and people selling their cars on Craigslist, although the latter is free of charge.)

The major advertising media include broadcast media (television in broadcast, cable, and satellite forms, and radio), print media (magazines and newspapers), outdoor media (billboards and mass transit), and, most recently, web-based media. The web has already overturned the traditional advertising models of broadcast and print media because it is far less expensive and more targeted, and results can be tracked more effectively. The web has also changed how people get their information and entertainment—we've shifted large chunks of the time we used to spend on broadcast and print media to online media. Technology such as TiVO and other digital recording devices (and even the remote control channel changer) have reduced TV advertising viewership.

People's dislike of advertising is deeply rooted. Since the rise of television advertising in the 1950s, critics have said that advertising manipulates people. The manipulation allegedly takes the form of using constant repetition, overpromising benefits, preying on people's insecurities, and hiding products' disadvantages. Other criticisms are that advertising uses bad grammar and, worst of all, bad taste to appeal to the lowest common denominator. Finally, some people oppose advertising on the grounds that it needlessly raises the price of the products being advertised.

MBA MASTERY

Advertising Age and *Adweek* are weekly publications that cover trends and issues in the advertising industry. If you're interested in influencing your company's advertising strategy, they may be worth a look. They're available at large newsstands, by subscription, and at many libraries; you can find selected material at http://adage.com and www.adweek.com.

Defenders of advertising point out that consumers realize that advertising is self-serving, so they view it skeptically. Defenders also believe that people's purchase decisions are influenced by many factors besides advertising: recommendations from friends; their own experiences and observations; and elements such as salespeople, service, warranties, financing, and, of course, price. A lot of advertising deserves criticism, but no one has proven that it forces people to buy products. The challenge to businesspeople who want to use advertising in their marketing mix is to make it as effective as possible. *Effective* means that it boosts sales.

Advertising's place in the marketing mix is simple: it is part of promotion, the fifth P (discussed in Chapter 19). It plays a role in establishing and reinforcing the product's positioning. As a marketing tool, advertising supports the sales force.

Advertising, and any advertising campaign, works with the other elements in the mix to present the product to prospects, along with reasons to buy. Advertising cannot make up for failings in the product or in other parts of the marketing mix.

CASE IN POINT

Over the past several years, direct-to-customer (DTC) advertising of pre-scription medications has generated controversy. Print and television DTC advertising creates awareness of medications among consumers, who ask their doctors to prescribe them. Until recently, these drugs were advertised only to physicians.

Opponents of DTC advertising contend that it raises the marketing costs and thus the price of medications. They also believe that this advertising prompts consumers to request the newest, most expensive medications. The pharma-ceutical companies counter that consumers have a right to know about all available medications and that the more users there are for a given medication, the lower its price becomes (as increased volume spreads development and manufacturing costs over a wider customer base). As usual in such controver-sies, both parties make valid points.

Components of Advertising

Many questions arise in any advertising decision. The major ones center on these areas:

- **Message:** What should you say in advertisements?
- **Money:** How much should you spend on advertising?
- **Media:** Where should you run the advertisements?

Let's examine these one at a time.

Ad Messages: Say What?

There are three basic types of advertising messages: creative messages, selling mes-sages, and messages that try to sell creatively.

A creative message tries to capture the audience's attention by standing out from the clutter (advertising overload). Advertisements that rely on humor are good examples of creative messages. So are most MTV- and YouTube-influenced television ads. Whether they use talking infants, hyperkinetic movement, intense music, or some combination of these and other elements, they aim to get attention.

These approaches are sometimes called image advertising, because they aim to create a feeling, an image, and an attitude around a product rather than to sell it on its features, benefits, or competitive merits. Jeans could be sold on their merits. In fact, Levi's once were, showing their durability with a picture of two mules trying to pull the pants apart. Soft drinks and luxury cars could also be sold on features and benefits, and sometimes are. But creative messages tend to ignore standard descriptions of features and benefits, and instead focus on getting attention and generating an attractive product image.

Selling messages are more matter-of-fact in their approach and are oriented toward features, benefits, and requests for action ("Buy now and save up to 30 percent on any Black and Decker power tool").

Slice-of-life commercials for detergents, cleaners, headache and indigestion remedies, and diet products are good examples of selling messages. You know the kind I mean: a woman suffering from a cold can't get to sleep. She gets out of bed, goes to the medicine cabinet, opens it, and takes some NyQuil. Next, she is sleeping soundly. This is straightforward and, for these kinds of products, effective advertising.

Most advertisers want either image-oriented ads that create an ambiance of luxury or "hipness," or reality-based pitches that tout a benefit ("Get better checkups with Crest") or incite customers to action ("Only three days left in the Toyota sell-a-thon"). At the same time, a major goal of almost all advertising is to establish or reinforce a *brand*.

MBA LINGO

A **brand** is a company name (Levi's, Chevrolet) or product name (501 jeans, Corvette), together with its logo (that is, a distinctive graphic associated with the name) and any other identifiers, which can even include the shape of a bottle (as for Perrier water).

The best advertising aims to combine the factual information of a selling message with the humor or visual appeal of a creative message. This is extremely hard to do. In addition, one other consideration pertains mainly to broadcast advertising and, to a lesser degree, print advertising: you must consider the web.

Many, many broadcast ads also aim to drive viewers to the web. Tactics include contests, special offers, and exclusive information available only at the site. When you have a viewer on your website, the goal changes slightly to one of informing the visitor, encouraging repeat visits, obtaining data on the visitor, and prompting purchases. The grand slam on the web is for your ad to find a second life as a "viral video" or a frequently viewed YouTube video.

Hot Copy

The kind of message you use depends on your product, its positioning, the audience, and the medium you're using. So does the content of your message. Various guidelines developed over the years offer hints on developing ad *copy*. Two of the most famous, which I find useful, are the AIDA formula and the unique selling proposition.

> **MBA LINGO**
>
> **Copy** narrowly refers to the text in a print ad or the words read by an announcer. More broadly, it means the total ad as presented to the audience. This includes not only the text, but the color, graphics, photos, video, and so on. Copy strategy refers to all the choices you have to make in developing an ad.

The AIDA formula helps you remember the four key things that good copy must do: get attention, capture interest, create desire, and request action. Let's briefly examine each of these goals:

- Getting **attention** is essential because people are busy, clutter is everywhere, and you can't sell to people until you have their focus. Humor, color, movement, design, offbeat situations, and astonishingly attractive models are major tools for getting attention.

- After the audience notices the ad, you have to get them **interested** in it. Copy that starts with a provocative question ("Can you afford to die?") or statement ("Don't throw money away") is a trusty tactic. Others include dramatizing a problem, offering an escape, or using a celebrity endorsement—which can also get attention.

- A good ad must create **desire** for the product. Appeal to the heart, the head, the stomach, the wallet, the whatever. Tell customers about the money they'll save, the fun they'll have, or the affection they'll win with your product.

Show the luscious turkey, the happy family, the headache-free worker, the beautiful lawn—whatever your product or service offers. Make them want it.

- Then you ask for **action.** Tell your customers what they have to do to quench this flaming desire you've created. Sample actions you can suggest include these: "Call now." "For a limited time only." "Send no money." (No money??) "Operators are standing by." "Be the first on your block." "Saturday only." "Don't let this once-in-a-lifetime opportunity slip through your fingers."

Another excellent concept for developing a message—or a theme for an entire campaign—is the unique selling proposition (or USP). As the name indicates, the USP is the unique thing about your product or service that provides a motivation for people to buy it.

This can be something real, such as Federal Express's "Guaranteed overnight delivery," or something made up, such as "Wonder Bread builds strong bodies 12 ways." (I say that this is made up because no one in the target audience can name even 3 of the 12 ways—and that doesn't matter.)

A really great USP isn't just a memorable tag line, like Sprite's "Obey your thirst." Instead, it's something unique about the product that provides motivation to buy. The USP can begin in the product-development process. "Guaranteed overnight delivery" is a feature, benefit, product, and selling proposition—all in one. And when FedEx started, it was unique.

If you can't create a USP around a wonderful and intrinsic feature of your product, you have to come up with something almost as good. McDonald's "You deserve a break today" was great because it reminded people who are too tired and overworked to cook that there's a fast way to get a tasty meal. It's not unique in itself—any fast-food outfit can make that claim—but through advertising, it became unique because it was McDonald's message.

Money: Your Advertising Budget

The advertising budget is part of the marketing budget. It's the amount the company will spend on paid messages in the media. This includes any ad agency fees and money spent on the media itself. If your account is large enough, the advertising agency works for 15 percent of the bill for *media buys*. If not, the agency bills you directly for its services.

The advertising budget can include the direct mail budget, since technically direct mail is an advertising medium. The budget must include website design and maintenance, *search engine optimization* (*SEO*), and other web-based advertising initiatives.

MBA LINGO

A **media buy** is the purchase of space (in print media), time (in broadcast media), or placement or clicks on websites, portals, and search engines for running your advertisement.

Search engine optimization (SEO) refers to tactics and technologies that increase the likelihood that people using search engines such as Google and Bing to find a solution to their problem or a business like yours will find your website. Essentially, SEO attempts to put your website location higher on the lists of search results. It's also worthwhile to speak with Internet advertising agencies.

You can set your advertising budget in several ways. One easy way is just to set the amount of the ad budget as some percentage of sales. If you do well spending 5 percent of total sales on advertising, do that. Or move it higher. Or lower. This method has the advantage of tying this cost to revenues, but it does little else.

Other approaches are to just pick a number (yes, this is done), or to spend the industry average, or to spend a bit above or below the industry average. Many advertisers fall into habits, believing that since they've always advertised in certain media, they should continue to do so. Habit is a bad way to budget.

MBA MASTERY

If you're shopping for advertising or you're curious about a particular media's demographics and audience, call and ask for a rate card, which details the prices for various ads. Most media sales departments can also send you a media kit that provides even more information, including demographics.

You can use a more thoughtful approach: decide what you want to achieve and then see how much you must spend on advertising to get there. This could result in spending either more or less than you did as a percent of sales last year or compared with the industry average. However, it ties the expenditures to what you're trying to accomplish. You may not have the money to do all you'd like to do—but at least you can then back off the "ideal" number and spend where you believe it will do the most good.

Please understand, however, that an element of risk accompanies advertising expenditures. Advertising is an inexact medium, in that no message is guaranteed to work and the correlation between expenditures can vary. There's also the issue of luck. A massive distraction, such as a natural disaster, snowstorm, or major trial on television can distract people or even keep them from buying. For instance, warm winters hurt ski resorts, even though they can make snow and usually have temperatures cold enough to ski. People just don't think about skiing as much during a warm winter.

If you've hired an advertising agency to handle your advertising budget, a media planner in the agency will help you determine the best use of your money. He or she will calculate the cost per thousand—that is, the cost of reaching 1,000 people—for the media being considered. Cost per thousand (CPM) places the costs of various media on an equal basis.

Cost per thousand enables you to compare the costs of media that deliver different-size audiences at different prices. Be careful, however: a low CPM is of no value unless the audience being delivered is *your* audience.

Media: Who's Watching?

As you develop your advertising message, you have to consider which media you will use to deliver that message to your target audience. Again, the major media you have to choose from are print, broadcast, and online. More specifically, they include the following:

- Magazines
- Newspapers
- Broadcast television

- Cable television
- Radio
- Internet

Other media include these:

- Direct mail
- Outdoor advertising (billboards, posters, mass transit)

Different media have varying potential for displaying your product, explaining its uses, and dramatizing the satisfaction customers will get from it. Some products, such as exercise machines, benefit from live demonstration, which television and online video provide. Others, such as mutual funds, benefit from printed charts and graphs, and newspapers, magazines, and online media work well for that. Still others benefit from a quick reminder to customers that you're always available. A billboard can generate that kind of *awareness*.

> **MBA LINGO**
>
> **Awareness** is a major goal in advertising. On one level, it means that people know your product exists. On another, it means they think of your product when making a purchase. (This is called top-of-mind awareness.) On another, very specific level, awareness means that people recall seeing your ad. Market research can measure these kinds of awareness. However, awareness has minimal value unless it leads to purchases.

Before you choose the media in which to run your ad, you have to decide what you're trying to do with your ad. Are you demonstrating? Dramatizing? Explaining? Displaying? Motivating an immediate purchase? Then you must consider the media's ability to help you do that.

Consider the Demographics

The demographics of a medium are the demographics of the audience that the medium delivers to the advertiser. (I covered demographics in Chapter 18.) The desirability of a medium's demographics depends on your target market or markets. In other words, it depends on what you are selling and to whom you are selling it.

It's no coincidence that you'll find rock 'n' roll CDs advertised in *Rolling Stone* and investment CDs in *Money*. Movies are advertised during television shows for 18- to 34-year-olds because they are the most frequent moviegoers.

These examples may lead you to believe that choosing the right media for your target market is a no-brainer. It often isn't. First, there's the issue of cost: getting your ad in a major national magazine or during prime-time TV can be expensive. Second, the psychographics (see Chapter 18) can be impossible to determine. Third, there's the chance that your target audience won't even see the ad, due to clutter (too many ads competing for attention) or "channel surfing."

CASE IN POINT

As the effectiveness of web-based advertising came to be questioned, experts in the field took up the challenge of making it more effective. Random banner and pop-up ads have fallen off. Many advertisers found they were ineffective unless they tapped an extremely broad and intense need in a creative way, as certain mortgage lenders were able to do in the housing bubble of the 2000s.

Search engine optimization, methods of targeting customers' interests (as Amazon tries to based on past purchases), and strategies for actually helping people are developing rapidly. Many advertisers of prescription drugs fall into the latter category. They not only provide deep and rich information and special offers, but some even help people with serious illnesses, such as rheumatoid arthritis, to form online affinity groups with other sufferers so they can share experiences and find support.

Other Media Characteristics

When deciding where to place your ad, you must also consider some other—somewhat technical—media characteristics, specifically these:

- **Reach** is an inexact number that attempts to quantify how many people or households have been exposed once to a single ad. Reach calculates the number of people using the media (that is, the number who read a publication, watch a particular television show, or listen to a particular radio station at a certain time of day) when the ad ran in that media. Reach tells you the number of people who were *potentially* exposed to the ad, not the number who actually saw it or can recall it.

- **Frequency** is the number of times these people will see or hear the advertisement. There's a way to measure frequency. Let's say that a monthly magazine has 500,000 readers. Let's also say that, in a month, 200,000 will see the ad once, 200,000 will see the ad twice, and 100,000 will see it three times. The ad's frequency would equal 1.8, as calculated here:

$$(200{,}000 \times 1) + (200{,}000 \times 2) + (100{,}000 \times 3) = 900{,}000 \div 500{,}000 = 1.8$$

This number, which is more precise than the value for reach or measures of impact, can be compared with the frequencies of other media to evaluate them as potential advertising venues. In general, the higher the frequency, the better.

- **Impact** determines whether the advertisement is remembered and communicates what it's supposed to. Ultimately, impact should be evident in increased sales. However, the connection between advertising and sales can be fuzzy, since factors other than advertising, including the competition and even social trends, can affect sales. Impact can be assessed by market research designed to measure ad recall and even purchase behavior after recall.

- **Internet metrics** are unique to the online medium and aim to determine the effectiveness of specific pages, messages, and offers. Because the number of visitors and their movements through the site can be tracked, these metrics are far more precise than those of print or broadcast media. Any good website hosting service can provide metrics such as visits, clicks, click-through rate, conversions (to requests for more information or a sales call or to actual orders), and conversion rate.

Before choosing the correct media for your ad campaign, you must compare media on reach, frequency, and impact, as well as on cost and demographics. Then choose. After that, await the market's response.

Promotional Tools

Promotional items have their place: you've probably got several corporate coffee mugs in your cabinet, or T-shirts and tote bags emblazoned with company logos in your closet. These and similar *premiums* carrying the name of your company or product should be part of an advertising or marketing campaign—but just a part.

MBA LINGO

A **premium** is a token item such as a coffee mug or tote bag that features the company name and logo. Premiums are given away either free or with a purchase. The goal of a free premium is to get your company name out there.

Other tools of promotion include these:

- Discounts
- Coupons
- Incentives and rebates
- Rewards and customer loyalty programs
- Affiliate programs
- Free samples and demonstration models
- Contests
- Special events

Briefly, discounts, coupons, incentives, and rebates all have one goal: to get people to buy your product. A discount, coupon, or rebate reduces the price, usually for a limited time. Technically, incentives are any inducement to buy, but they more narrowly include items such as optional features, related products, or special services offered for a limited time.

Rewards and customer loyalty programs are essentially either a means of providing cash discounts or specific discounts (via coupons) to customers, or a means of providing other incentives, such as airline miles or "points" redeemable for products and services. Affiliate programs are more like cross-selling or cross-promotion efforts you engage in with a company that sells a complimentary or noncompetitive product or service, or that pursues prospects similar to those you pursue.

Free samples can be very effective with consumer packaged goods such as cereals, snack foods, mouthwash, and candy. Demonstration models (demos), such as a test drive for a car or a "demo disc" for a video game, let people try a product when free samples are impossible.

Contests work in three ways. First, they attract attention and associate your product with an exciting experience. (A chance to win concert tickets if you buy a CD is one example.) Second, those who enter the contest become more bonded with your product by having taken the trouble to enter. Third, by collecting entry forms, you are getting the names of potential prospects.

Sponsoring special events can take many forms. These include sporting events or teams, racing cars, marathons, or parts of an event (such as the half-time report for NBA or NFL games) or even the stadiums themselves. These are not incentives to buy, but rather a means of advertising and associating the product or company and the event in the minds of the target market.

Of course, these promotional tools should reinforce one another and your advertising. For instance, a promotional tie-in with a movie combines premium items (figures of the characters), a special event (the release of the movie), and advertising (for the movie and the promotional item).

Public Relations Programs

Public relations (PR), broadly defined, includes nonadvertising communications aimed at the company's existing and potential customers and shareholders, and at the general public. In many businesses, especially consulting, financial services, and health care, PR aims to establish the company's people as experts whom the media can call for interviews. These spokespeople boost the name recognition of the orga-nization and represent the interests of the company and its industry to the public.

More narrowly, public relations focuses on developing article ideas for editors of print media and ideas for segments for producers of broadcast and cable media. These should, of course, place the company, its products, and its people in a positive light.

Even more specialized areas of PR include working to influence critics, reviewers, and other opinion leaders who can influence your target markets' purchasing decisions. This can be quite important in the software and video game industries. Internet-based PR is another subset of PR, which focuses on web-based opinion leaders such as online authorities, bloggers in specific areas, and ratings services.

Public relations services also include writing speeches and press releases. Another key service is assisting executives in dealing with reporters and interviewers, especially in times of a company crisis.

Depending on your industry, good PR can be more powerful than advertising. People realize that an advertisement is a paid announcement intended to sell. But a positive story about your company or its people or products is generally viewed as fact; there-fore, it builds credibility in a way that is close to impossible with advertising.

The Internet as Game-Changer

The Internet has changed the game in advertising and public relations in ways that few people foresaw even 10 years ago, and social media are close behind. Both enable people to quickly and broadly share positive and negative experiences they've had with companies, products, and services.

Online reviews and ratings can make or break movies, books, restaurants, hotels, and a host of other products and services. Unfortunately, the anonymous nature of the Internet can enable rapid transmission of false or negative information planted by unethical competitors, irrational customers, or irate current or former employees.

The nature of the web can make it difficult, but every company should do its best to actively influence its image in online and social media. This begins with being truly dedicated to delivering the value implied by your messaging and pricing, and being as transparent as possible in your dealings with all stakeholders. It then extends to cultivating good relationships with experts and others who influence your customers and prospects, and to affiliating with like-minded complementary organizations.

Finally, it's important to deal with genuine mistakes, difficulties, and negatives in a forthright and honest manner. Even if it means a short-term setback, the long-term value of your business may well depend on your willingness and ability, in your online and social media messages, to be transparent, to apologize, and to explain how future problems will be avoided.

The Least You Need to Know

- Advertising is a paid-for, positive message in a communication medium. The sender of the message is identified. Advertising doesn't force anyone to buy a product, although getting people to buy is its ultimate goal.

- The best way to set the advertising budget is to decide what you want to achieve, then see how much you must spend on advertising to achieve it, and then look to your costs and your competition to reach a final figure.

- Ad copy must get attention, capture interest, create desire, and request action.

- Advertising media can be viewed in terms of reach, frequency, and impact. These three measures, plus cost per thousand and demographics, enable you to use similar measures to compare different media.

- Various promotional tools can reinforce advertising and help prompt people to buy. Public relations can build credibility in a way that advertising cannot, and good PR is essential during a company crisis.

- The web and social media are transforming advertising and public relations and enabling companies and customers to communicate in new ways. The best response is continual evolution of your online strategy, along with dedication to your customers' well-being.

Selling to Customers and Keeping Them Happy

In This Chapter

- The critical mission of the sales force
- How the sales process really works
- Customer service that shines

Salespeople play several crucial roles in a company. First, they are the primary source of revenue. Star salespeople are often called "rainmakers." In traditional cultures, a rainmaker could conjure the clouds to produce rain to grow the crops and put food on the table. Salespeople put food on the table for a company. They bring in the money.

Second, salespeople are the link between the company and its customers. On one hand, prospects and customers know the company mainly through its salespeople. On the other hand, the company knows its customers mainly through its salespeople.

Finally, the sales force represents the company's frontline offense and defense. They are the foot soldiers in any business. They are directly exposed to the pressures of finding prospects, solving problems, making deals, handling complaints, and beating competitors.

Given these critical roles, a company must do all it can to develop and support the best possible sales force. This chapter shows you how to do that.

Types of Sales

Sales can be characterized in several ways, which I discuss over the following pages. Consider a few.

- Order-taking occurs at a movie theater or sporting event. The customer asks for a ticket and the vendor sells one. It occurs when a delivery person (for example, for a brewery or bakery) takes the order for the next delivery from a restaurant or store. In order-taking, the customer either approaches the company or is purchasing a steady stream of product on a schedule.

- Active selling, on the other hand, involves prospecting, presentation, problem solving, and persuasion. In active selling—the focus of this chapter—the salesperson approaches the customer, and to some degree, the customer resists purchasing. Thus, active selling involves overcoming *sales resistance*.

  You'll sometimes hear a salesperson mocked as an "order taker." This means that the salesperson is supposed to be actively selling but isn't. Instead, he or she is getting by on current accounts, going for easy sales, and avoiding the hard work of prospecting and persuasion.

- Inside sales refers to selling done mainly by telephone. This may include telemarketing, but also allows for situations in which the customer comes to the salesperson's place of business. Inside sales usually does not mean retail sales, which is yet another type of selling.

- Outside sales involves going to the customer and starts with getting appointments to meet with businesspeople or to see consumers in their homes.

MBA MASTERY

Sales resistance takes various forms, including delay, evasiveness, indecisiveness, budgetary excuses, and simple reluctance, plus, in commercial sales, bureaucracy.

The Sales Process

The sales force has two goals: selling to current customers and finding new ones. Every company and salesperson must strike a balance between the two, but let's focus on winning new customers because it includes all three parts of the sales process:

- Prospecting

- Problem solving and presenting the product

- Persuading

I explain these steps in the following pages.

Prospecting: On the Hunt

Prospecting involves finding people to sell to, and there are various ways of doing this. *Cold calling* means picking up the phone and calling people that you don't know for appointments (or trying to sell products to them on the phone).

> **MBA ALERT**
>
> For absolutely first-rate advice on the mental, emotional, and tactical aspects of cold calling, see *The Complete Idiot's Guide to Cold Calling*, by Keith Rosen (Alpha, 2004).

Most salespeople have a strong preference for cold calling *leads* or *referrals*—people who have already been identified as prospective customers. Leads are identified in various ways by salespeople, their assistants, or the marketing department. Public records at courthouses (for example, for recent home purchases) are one source. The newspapers are another (for example, for people recently promoted), as is the Internet with its news stories and databases of companies and contacts.

> **MBA LINGO**
>
> **Prospecting** is the act of finding prospects for the product or service you sell. A **cold call** is a telephone call or (much less often) a visit to someone who does not know you. A **lead** is the name of a person who has been identified as a potential prospect. A **referral** occurs when a current customer refers the salesperson to a friend or acquaintance who may be interested in the product.

Many companies generate leads through advertising and, of course, through inquiries coming in by telephone or mail. (For example, frequently targeted leads involve new businesses or people who recently bought a home, got married, or had a child.) In those cases, it is still a cold call, since the salesperson doesn't know the person he's calling. But, as with the weather, there are degrees of coldness.

After making contact, the salesperson must qualify the prospect early in the sales process. This means somehow getting the answer to two questions:

1. Does the prospect have a need for or an interest in the product or service?

2. Does the prospect have the money and, in commercial sales, the authority to buy the product?

If the prospect doesn't meet these two criteria, most salespeople move on to the next prospect. But there's a judgment call here: will the prospect qualify at some later point? For example, you may not need a new car now. Maybe you can't afford one. Maybe you just bought one. But next month, if you get a raise or total your car, you may be in the market for one. So most salespeople keep a file of active prospects—people who may buy in the future—and contact them regularly.

Problem Solving and Presenting: Show and Ask

Assuming that a prospect qualifies, the salesperson moves to problem solving and presenting the product. The salesperson must explore the customer's problems—the ones that relate to the product, that is—and show how the product or service will solve these problems.

Customers buy solutions rather than a product or service. For this reason, the best professionals in both consumer and industrial sales frame much of their sales presentation in terms of questions.

Let's take an example of a salesperson selling a desktop-publishing system to a business account. Useful questions to pose in the sales presentation might include these:

- What volume of desktop publishing do you do in your shop?

- What system are you currently using?

- How are the original documents created (for example, in WordPerfect or Microsoft Word)?

- What problems do you encounter most often?

- How much training do new people need on the system?

- What complaints do you hear most often about your current system?

- Do you have a maintenance contract for the system? What are the key terms of the contract?

- Which features of your current system do you like best?

- How does this system perform during crunch times?

- Would you be interested in a system that can reduce your costs and manpower requirements while delivering better quality in less time?

And so on. Questions like these work as well for a lawn-care service or personal trainer as they do for a computer networking or advertising firm. With the answers to these questions, the salesperson can finish the job that marketing began—proper positioning of the product.

> **MBA ALERT**
>
> In some product categories, the web has supplanted some of the salesperson's function of supplying information. Although not all prospects take the trouble to educate themselves before a salesperson calls, many do. Those who do often have little need for (or patience with) basic sales presentations. Instead, they will understand your product, and its pros and cons and those of competitive products beforehand. So your salespeople have to be prepared to deal effectively with these prospects.

Persuasion: Overcoming Objections

Most people think of persuasion when they think of selling. But today the *hard sell* (use of high-pressure sales tactics) turns off many prospects. This is not to say that it's not used or that it doesn't work. It is, and sometimes it does. But it produces a lot of wear and tear on salespeople and customers.

> **MBA LINGO**
>
> The **hard sell** employs high-pressure sales to close sales. This pressure can include large discounts (often on inflated prices) for acting now, aggressive questioning of resistant prospects ("Can't you make a simple decision?"), and ways to wear down the prospect by not leaving his or her premises.

However, persuasion is often necessary to close a sale. The professional approach is to use questions to lead the prospect to a logical conclusion: I should buy, now. These questions center on the problem, the product, and the solution. As the salesperson forges these links—a process called "tying down" issues such as cost, operating requirements, and installation—he or she uses questions to keep the prospect involved and moving toward the close.

But logic isn't the only tool. Good salespeople appeal to the emotions as well as to reason. Motivators such as being up-to-date, doing the smart thing, joining a select group of companies, and so on can be just as important as the cost-benefit analysis.

CASE IN POINT

You'll see a startling array of personality types and selling tactics in sales. I've known salespeople who've told customers that they need this sale—or they'll lose their jobs. One guy I knew would pull out a photo of his three kids and tell the prospect they needed shoes. I've known salespeople who literally wouldn't leave a prospect's office without a signed contract. Others would directly question the sanity of resistant prospects.

But I've also known great sales pros. Several even told me their product wasn't really for me, given my needs. Others fought their companies to get me a better deal, faster delivery, or higher quality. These people win business—and referrals.

A sales force, like any other department or resource, must be actively managed. This means the salespeople must be properly organized, motivated, compensated, and supported. Let's examine these issues in more detail.

Organizing a Sales Force

The two major issues in organizing a sales force are these:

- Size of the sales force
- Alignment of the sales force

Let's look at both.

Sales Force Size: When Is Bigger Better?

Remember the law of diminishing returns? It says that more of a good thing is good, but only up to a point—the point of diminishing returns. So one way to get the right-size sales force is to add salespeople until the last one does not produce more in sales than he or she earns. In other words, add salespeople as long as they profitably add sales. This is actually one sensible method of sizing the sales force.

However, there's another consideration: the proper workload. The average salesperson's workload should also guide decisions about the size of the sales force. You have to think about this carefully, because sometimes small accounts require more sales effort than large ones. Large accounts are often large because they routinely place an order every month.

The sales force has to be large enough that each prospect and customer receives adequate *coverage* (communication and attention). Management, even the sales manager, can quickly lose track of how well accounts are being serviced, especially if the poor coverage is masked by growing sales. Poor coverage is an open invitation to competitors.

MBA LINGO

Coverage means regular sales calls and other forms of communication, and enough service to keep the account from ever feeling neglected.

To judge the workload properly, the sales manager must carefully analyze how many tasks the salesperson must complete to cover his or her accounts, prospect properly, and solve the inevitable problems that arise every week or month. Then the manager must examine the number of working hours in the week or month and adjust the number of salespeople accordingly.

Sales Force Alignment: Three Choices

The alignment of the sales force refers to the way in which the sales force is organized in relation to who and what it is selling. You can align the sales force in three ways:

- By territory
- By product
- By customers

Alignment by territory divides the company's market into geographical areas. For a regional company, this might mean by city. For a national company, it might mean by state. An international company may divide its markets by country.

However it's done, alignment by territory has the advantage of simplicity. A salesperson or sales team sells all the company's products to consumers or companies in their territory. The disadvantage is that a company with lots of product lines may find that *product knowledge* suffers. The next type of organization addresses that issue.

MBA LINGO

Product knowledge includes everything the salesperson has to know about the product. First-rate salespeople can answer virtually every question about the product they sell: its construction, use, installation, and maintenance. They also know how their product differs from competitive products. In some businesses, especially high-tech businesses, this is too much to ask of a salesperson, so the salesperson teams with a technician who has complete product knowledge.

Alignment by product means that each salesperson or sales team specializes in a product or product line. For example, an office-supply company might have one sales group for computers and related equipment, another for general office equipment, and another for furniture and fixtures.

The advantage of this arrangement is that each salesperson offers deep product knowledge and total coverage of each customer. The disadvantages are a potentially too-large sales force and numerous salespeople calling on the same customer. The best way to handle this may be to have an overall account manager who then calls in a product manager or a brand manager for a particular product line.

Alignment by customers calls for coverage of certain types of customers by certain salespeople. Alignment by the customer's industry is quite common. Many commercial banks have account teams for specific industries, such as consumer-packaged goods, telecommunications, high technology, and so on. This reflects the customer's desire for account managers who "understand my business."

Customer characteristics other than industry can also be used: a common one is size. Many banks have special account reps for "high-net-worth individuals" in their retail (that is, consumer) divisions. In commercial sales, various levels of sales volume move an account to a different sales team. And many companies have national account reps who sell to corporate customers with nationwide operations.

Companies often use more than one of these methods of aligning their sales forces. A company can even combine all three methods, having sales teams for different product lines covering different-size customers by geographical territory. The idea is to get the best alignment for both the company and the customer.

Compensating and Motivating Your Sales Force

We look at the issues of compensating and motivating salespeople together because most salespeople are heavily motivated by money. Their compensation has to reflect this.

Salespeople can be compensated by straight commission, straight salary, or salary plus commission. Salespeople on straight commission are paid a percentage of the amount of each sale they make. They are paid only their commission; they get no salary, although they may receive a draw (advance against future sales). Salespeople on straight salary receive a salary but no additional commission based on sales. Salespeople on salary plus commission get paid a base salary (also called the "base") plus some percentage of the sale. Benefits as well as bonuses can be added to any of these compensation systems as well.

Commission plans are often structured so that the salesperson makes a certain percentage on the first, say, $100,000 of business he or she sells, then a higher percentage on the next $100,000, and then an even higher percentage on sales above that.

The big advantage of a commission plan—particularly straight commission—is that it ties pay directly to performance. It also ties sales costs to sales. What's more, commissions can be tweaked in various ways to focus the sales force on particular goals. For instance, many firms pay a higher commission on new business than on repeat business. Some pay higher rates on sales of new products.

There are also disadvantages to commission compensation. First, these systems can be complex and costly to administer. Second, some salespeople get so focused on selling that they resent anything that cuts into selling time and any initiative they see as "fiddling with their income." Third, if sales decrease (which may or may not be their fault), they may become depressed or desperate when their incomes dwindle. Finally, while most people are honest, there is greater temptation to abuse a commission system.

CASE IN POINT

When their incomes depend on how much they sell, some people resort to an aggressive hard sell that can alienate customers. Salespeople may also be more prone to dishonestly report sales in ways that generate higher commissions. One way this is done is to report sales they'll make in January as December sales, to pump up the current year's revenue.

It gets worse. Sales teams have moved business around among salespeople to manipulate commissions and then shared the artificially high payments. There are also illegal "kickbacks"—bribes paid by dishonest salespeople to dishonest customers out of their commissions.

Straight salary is easy to administer and not prone to abuse, but most salespeople do not find it very motivating. Most companies shoot for the best of both worlds: a base salary plus a commission on sales.

Surveys have shown that money is the biggest motivator for most salespeople. However, there are other ways of motivating salespeople, some of which relate to money and some of which do not.

Sales quotas (the amount of revenue an individual salesperson or team is budgeted to bring in) tend to work, provided they are neither too high nor too low. They work because financial rewards such as higher commissions and most bonuses are tied to quotas. If they're too high, they frustrate and anger the salesperson. If they're too low, the company will overpay for the amount of sales it gets. That's because commissions are usually based on the salesperson making his quota and then exceeding it by various amounts. Quotas have another built-in advantage: you can terminate salespeople who consistently fail to meet their quotas.

MBA MASTERY

A good portion (say, 30 to 50 percent) of a salesperson's salary should be in commissions or bonuses. This is critical for small firms, which really can't afford to pay nonproducers.

Sales meetings, particularly off-site meetings that include golf, tennis, and banquets (and, yes, cocktails), are popular with salespeople and build camaraderie (to put it mildly).

Sales contests work for many companies, even companies that think they might be "too sophisticated" for them. The winners usually must beat their quotas significantly and are ranked by performance for the grand prize—usually a vacation at a nice resort on company time or a cash payment—and subsidiary prizes. Structuring these contests takes skill. For example, there can be monthly winners and various ways of qualifying for the grand prize, to keep the sales force pumped up for the entire year.

Some relatively inexpensive (and less impressive) motivators include plaques, awards, membership in the "CEO's Roundtable," and so on. Access to senior management in meetings or special luncheons and inclusion on special task forces are useful, inexpensive rewards that are generally underused.

Finally, the opportunity for advancement can be a powerful motivator. But watch out. Many a first-rate salesperson has found managing others, not to mention meetings and paperwork, boring and worse than what he or she was doing before. I've heard a few salespeople promoted to sales manager or product manager yell, "Give me a bag and put me back on the road!" after two months.

Supporting a Sales Force

Salespeople are "out there," exposed, competing, and facing daily rejection. To do their job, they need the best support a company can give them.

This support starts with the best products, service, and marketing that the company can deliver. The products have to be the best in their class and price range. The service has to have one goal: total customer satisfaction. The marketing has to be connected with the real world of customers and their problems and buying motives.

Support also means a sensible and (key point) consistent credit policy and good credit management. Having a salesperson break his or her neck to make a sale only to have it killed by the credit department makes no sense. It helps if the credit policy is predictable and if salespeople can get an early reading on a prospect's creditworthiness (with a call to the credit department, for example).

Support includes good management. Unfortunately, some sales managers believe fear and threats are motivational. Maybe firing the three lowest producers is a good idea, but doing it publicly is not. Salespeople, like everyone, need trust and the authority to make decisions. And more than most people, they need minimal paperwork and bureaucracy, and the freedom to manage their own time.

Finally, rapid resolution of customer complaints about quality, defects, and delivery is essential. That's where a good customer service department comes in handy.

Customer Service

Many companies of all types have customer service departments separate from the sales function. They usually report to sales or to marketing (the best ones work closely with sales). They deal mainly with customers—people who have purchased the company's products—but some also answer inquiries from prospects.

Customer service has two goals: to keep customers happy (or make them happy if they aren't) and to do it without burdening the salespeople. That second function is essential. Everyone in a company wants the customer to be happy, especially the salespeople. But the time that salespeople must spend resolving disputes, answering routine questions, and fielding requests for price lists and product literature erodes selling time.

So customer service should be staffed with individuals who have people skills (including patience), product knowledge, and an understanding of what can be done operationally, procedurally, and legally to resolve customer complaints.

Customer service can be a great training ground for future salespeople. In fact, if they develop leads that later become customers, they should get some kind of compensation or recognition. It's a small price to pay to someone with the sales orientation that keeps a company growing.

MBA MASTERY

Be sure to give your customer service people the authority they need to resolve problems. Customers find it extremely irritating to deal with people who can't help them. Some companies get customer service right, while others seem to use it as an obstacle to service. Hire good people for this function and let them do their jobs. Dissatisfied customers can hurt your company far worse than competitors.

A Few Words on Sales Training

Too often, new salespeople are given product literature to read, taken on a couple of sales calls, and then given a desk, phone, and phone book. Some outfits view salespeople as cannon fodder and hire ten for every one they figure will make the grade.

Smart companies take a different approach. They do their best to hire smart. When they seek experienced people, they take the time to locate good performers who will fit in well. When they seek entry-level people, they hire just as carefully and train them in sales. They also train everyone, new or seasoned, in the company's products and procedures.

General sales training can be valuable, and any good-size city has firms that provide it. But I believe that the training will help only those people who have that special motivation that real salespeople have: they are competitors. When they sell, they win—and they hate to lose. More than being outgoing or gregarious or "a people person," that motivation, plus an interest in solving customers' problems, makes a true salesperson.

The Least You Need to Know

- Salespeople are a company's source of revenue, link to customers, and frontline offense and defense. They find prospects, solve problems, make deals, handle complaints, and fight competitors, so they need lots of support.

- The major parts of the sales process are prospecting, problem solving and presenting the product, and persuading prospects to purchase.

- When figuring the best size for a sales force, consider the incremental sales of each additional salesperson, as well as workload per salesperson. A sales force can be aligned by territory, product, or customer—or all three.

- In most businesses, salary plus commission is the best way to compensate salespeople.

- A customer service department can make life easier for salespeople while perhaps delivering better service than a busy salesperson might. It can also generate leads and be a training ground for future salespeople.

Product Development: Pioneers at Work

In This Chapter

- How to develop successful products—and quickly kill the duds
- Where to get ideas for great new products
- Why new products are the key to growth

As I'm sure you've noticed, in our economy, new products are introduced with amazing frequency. At times it seems that if a product isn't new or improved—or new *and* improved—then it isn't worth selling. This focus on new products is driven by market demand, competitive concerns, and our ability to improve products with better technology.

New products are the lifeblood of many companies. Remember that, aside from raising prices, you have only four ways to increase sales, and two of them involve new products: you can sell new products to current customers or you can sell new products to new customers. The other two ways involve existing products.

In most companies, the marketing department plays a key role in new product development. This chapter examines that role and shows you how to develop successful new products. (In this chapter, as in the rest of Part 4, you should consider the term *product* to include service, so this chapter is also about how to develop new services.)

The Value of Cross-Functional Teams

Until fairly recently, product development was done by various departments within an organization that didn't work closely together. Marketing might dream up a product concept and then throw the idea to the design people, who designed the product and then threw it to the engineers. The engineers made a *prototype* (sample model). Production then manufactured it. Then the salespeople started selling. This process not only was time-consuming but often created products that nobody would buy.

MBA LINGO

A **prototype** is a model of how a product looks. A working prototype also shows how the product would work, although it might not include every function.

Today managers recognize that development is best accomplished with a *cross-functional* approach. A cross-functional team (which you learned about in Chapter 5) includes someone from every department that will deal with the product. That way, each department has input at each stage of development. This helps the company minimize problems and secure support for the new product at each step.

The Product-Development Process

Managers have a process for product development that involves six steps:

1. Idea generation
2. Concept testing
3. Prototype and product design
4. Product testing
5. Market testing
6. Product launch

Each step plays an important role in the process; you can kill a product that isn't succeeding at any time. Therefore, you don't start this process with the fixed goal of seeing it through. Instead, you view each step as a hurdle that the product must get over in order to get to the next step. There's no point in launching a product that didn't make it through the previous steps.

Let's examine each of these steps in turn.

Step One: Get a Good Idea

Product ideas come from a variety of sources. The best source is the marketplace. The market never stops generating product ideas, because that's where the problems are—and the best products are the ones that solve problems.

Listen to Your Customers

To get product ideas, listen to your customers. Welcome their complaints; they can point the way to new products. Market research should also periodically seek the answers to questions like these:

- What do customers want to see the product do?
- How do customers use the product?
- How does the product fit into customers' operations?
- What problems do customers have with the product?
- What would make customers use the product more?

Many customers will only tell you, "Just lower the price," but others will tell you things that you'd never know unless you asked—things that can lead you to new products. Some of these will be product line extensions, essentially variations on the basic product. These can range from the fairly mundane, such as the many versions of food products, like Cool Ranch, Fat-Free Cool Ranch, Cool Ranch with Lime, Fat-Free Cool Ranch with Lime, and so on. But you can sometimes learn things that lead to more original products by asking more penetrating questions, such as these:

- What do you want to accomplish with this product?
- In what other ways do you try to accomplish it?
- Without this product, how would you accomplish it?

You can get customer input by sponsoring a customer council or user group. A customer council consists of 6 to 10 customers who devote time to discuss your products and service, how to improve them, and how you might meet unmet related needs. A user group can be larger and more informal. User groups are often used in high-tech companies, where they're sometimes formed by users themselves.

MBA ALERT

In too many companies, there's an invisible "wall" between marketing and sales. The two departments don't communicate. If you're in marketing, talk to everyone you can in sales. If you're in sales, talk to marketing. It's the best way to develop good products and marketing programs.

Ask Your Salespeople

Your salespeople are out there in the market dealing with problems. Their biggest goal is selling more product. If you're in marketing, you should regularly ask your salespeople these questions:

- What are the biggest barriers to a sale?
- How could you sell more?
- What product modifications do customers ask for?
- Do you see any "holes" in our product line?
- What competitive products beat us to the sale?

Watch Your Competitors

Let's face it: sometimes the other guy has a better idea. When he does, grab it, if you can. Better yet, improve on it.

Patent laws protect true inventions, yet many products are not inventions, but just new ideas, and you can't patent an idea. In the beverage industry, a new flavor can be readily copied. In consumer goods, many packaging ideas can be copied. So can most styles in the clothing, home furnishings, and entertainment industries.

Outright copying, which results in products known as knockoffs, is rampant in consumer foods and beverages, consumer packaged goods, film and broadcast entertainment, banking, consumer products, fashion, and the automotive industry.

Sometimes regulations drive new products. Home-equity lines were developed after interest on credit-card debt was no longer tax deductible. Trends and fads generate products (for instance, the national obsession with health and fitness has spawned products ranging from organic TV dinners to nicotine patches); so do safety concerns and technology, particularly in automobiles and home entertainment.

Copycat or *parity products* are often developed by *reverse engineering*. It is fairly easy to copy successful products and to "twist" their design or operation slightly, to bring out a competitive one.

MBA LINGO

A **parity product** (or "knockoff") copies a competitor's product or service more or less directly, to give you parity (that is, equality) in the market. In **reverse engineering,** your engineers take apart a competitor's product to see its materials, assembly, and workings, and then replicate the design.

I prefer creativity over copycat tactics, and I'll talk about that later in this chapter. But you may someday need a parity product to stay competitive, so it's silly to rule them out.

Finally, technology itself can drive new products. In some industries, such as medical equipment, application of technology to improve diagnostic and treatment generates new products. In others, such as personal telephones and digital assistants, the technology itself—the ability to send messages and pictures, access the web, and navigate roadways—meets needs that most people barely knew they had. I'm not denigrating technology-driven product development, which is the tendency to create a product because it's possible (the "if we build it, they will buy it" approach). Technology-driven development often works; however, often it does not, and those are the products we tend not to hear about. Yet many products that set out to meet a widely known need also fail, so there's no single "right way" to go about generating product ideas.

Step Two: Test the Concept

When you have a product concept, it's essential to test it among potential prospects for the product. These prospects may or may not be among your company's current customers.

Concept testing is market research for getting reactions to a product idea. This can be done by just describing the product idea in detail and then asking the respondents a set of structured questions about the concept. Or you can build a prototype and get reactions to that, also with structured questions.

With or without a prototype, typical questions to ask in a concept test include the following.

- Do you understand the product and what it would do?

- How do you now accomplish what this product would do?

- What would you change about the product?

- Would this product solve a large, costly problem?

- How frequently would you use this product?

- What products do you see as competitive with this?

You may be tempted to ask the prospects how much they would pay for the product, but it's very hard to get a good reading on price at this stage. You may as well ask, but take the answers with a grain of salt.

In most cases, your company will benefit by concept-testing product ideas. Yet in some situations you should probably limit or even omit concept testing. For instance, if the idea represents a small change (such as introducing a low-fat version of an existing line of snack foods), you can omit testing the idea and go directly to the product test, particularly if you know you need that product offering to stay competitive.

MBA MASTERY

The prototype needed for a concept test varies with the industry and budget. In the magazine business, you can do a mock-up to show how the cover and pages would look. In a web-based business, you can show what visitors would see, without doing any programming. For tools, appliances, or cars, you can use clay models, computer simulations, or actual working models.

Step Three: Design the Prototype and Product

Of course, you also need to address the matter of developing the actual product or service. This stage calls for marketing's input, but not much hands-on involvement. Rather, this is when designers, engineers, materials specialists, programmers, and others with the technical skills to bring the product to life go to work.

Marketing must make sure that any barrier to making, selling, or using the product is eliminated at the design stage. So ease of use and installation, freedom from maintenance, and control of manufacturing costs are all considerations for marketing to discuss with those making the prototype and the product.

Step Four: Test the Product

When the product or service exists—ideally, before it's ready to go into production—a product test should be conducted jointly by marketing and the design and production team with actual users.

The product test is often lumped in with the next step, the market test, but if possible, keep these two steps separate, because they address two distinct issues. The product test addresses product issues: Does it work? Can customers use it? How do they use it? What would they change? Do they like it? Does it fit into their operation? The market test addresses marketing issues.

In many businesses, product tests involve recruiting *beta-site* customers for the product who agree to act as guinea pigs and provide feedback by field-testing the product. Some companies do their own field testing—for example, in their own company's offices—which is fine. But only objective parties using the product under real conditions can pass final judgment.

MBA LINGO

A **beta site** is an organization or individual (usually a customer) who uses a product and reports the experience to the company developing it. Beta sites are used mainly for industrial products and most often for high-tech products such as equipment and software. Many businesspeople call a product test a *beta test.*

By the way, beta-site participants are not motivated simply by the joy of helping a company develop a product. They are typically innovators or early adopters (as described in Chapter 17) who want exposure to something new that may give them a competitive advantage. You may also have to give them discounts or free usage for some period of time, even beyond the beta test.

Step Five: Do a Market Test

By this time, you should have a good fix on the product's positioning. You do a market test to learn whether that positioning is correct so you can adjust whatever isn't. You want to get reactions to your advertisements, sales pitches, and product literature. These can all be in close-to-final form, but not written in stone. They may need fine-tuning or more.

A market test gathers information about the customer as a buyer, rather than user, of the product. To the extent possible, a market test should gauge buying behavior. The major issue to nail down is pricing, which may be a fuzzy issue even at this stage, particularly if the product is completely new.

You can test various price levels in several ways. One of the best ways is to start high and then slide the price downward during the market test to see if lower prices boost sales. An even better way is to try two or three different prices in various customer samples. These samples can be subsets of customers divided by geography, industry, or size.

Avoid introducing a new product at a price that's too low. You may be stunned by the high volume of business, but if the price is too low, you're leaving money on the table. Also, due to customers' price resistance and expectations, it's far tougher to raise prices than to lower them.

Aside from pricing, the main considerations to study are purchase motivations, buying patterns, frequency of purchase, favorite features and benefits, and customer satisfaction.

MBA ALERT

Be sure to include difficult prospects as well as easy sales in the market test. Going only to innovators and early adopters, particularly if they like your other products, will skew the results. If you intend to reach the masses with the product, include some early and late majority types. Doing so will help you identify their objections and may help you gauge how long it will take to win them over.

Step Six: Launch the Product

A product launch, or rollout, can be done in various ways. It can be gradual, starting with several cities or states. It can also be a broad regional or even national rollout.

Successful product launch depends upon having a marketing mix that supports the effort. Essentially, a launch needs the Five P's of marketing—product, pricing, packaging, place, and promotion. Developing the product and pricing are part of the product development process. For that matter, so is packaging. It's important that your distribution and sales channels (*place* in the Five P's) understand the product and are prepared to sell it, and that your promotion of the product supports them in those efforts.

Provided you've done the first five steps of the product development process properly and have geared up production and shipping, in this final step the main tasks left are to execute the promotional program and to support the sales force and any sales channels. This is easier said than done, but it represents a set of tasks you should be prepared for if you have conducted the previous five steps and arranged the Five P's properly.

Know When to Stop

As I mentioned earlier, a product can be killed at any one of these stages. Clearly, if a product is going to be a loser, the earlier you figure that out, the better. Of course, that's because the sooner you stop, the less time, effort, and money you've spent on it. But the issue goes a bit deeper.

The more time, effort, and money a company spends on something, the more likely it is to continue on that path. People find it hard at the product test or market test phase to say, "Well, this isn't working. Let's bag it." After all, they've gone through the idea generation, concept testing, prototype development, and some development of the actual product. The further you proceed, the more you have invested, in ego as well as money, in a product.

So rigorous idea generation and concept testing are essential. If the concept does not address a real customer need, what good will the product be? If customers are lukewarm in the concept test, how can they be thrilled when they're asked to pay for it? Kill bad product ideas early.

MBA ALERT

True innovation may require you to lead customers to products and pastimes that they didn't even realize they wanted. This is key in the entertainment and technology industries, where most prospective customers would barely understand a product concept like social media until they experienced it.

Extending Your Line

The process I've presented will help you manage product development in an orderly way. However, you may find that this much structure isn't always necessary. For example, a simple product-line extension might not call for several steps. In fact, going through the steps might cost more than just slinging the product into the market and seeing if it works.

Product-line extensions are less risky and don't call for as much creativity. They may be necessary from the competitive standpoint—for example, to address a competitor's product or to offer a complete selection. However, product-line extensions rarely, if ever, lead to a breakthrough—an entirely new product line or category—that will transform a business or even establish an industry. The automobile, airplane, telephone, computer, credit card, microwave oven, microcomputer, World Wide Web, VCR, cellphone, and DVD are examples of breakthrough products.

Only genuine creativity will develop a breakthrough. There's nothing wrong with leaving the development of breakthroughs to other companies. But a real breakthrough can raise a company and its shareholders to an entirely new level of wealth.

CASE IN POINT

Companies that invent new products, or product categories, can grow so large so rapidly that they virtually invent—and dominate—an entirely new industry. Federal Express invented overnight delivery. Microsoft invented the disk operating system (DOS) for microcomputers. Amazon invented, or at least revolutionized, online shopping, as Google did online information search.

These and other firms became leaders because they had the creativity and discipline to address problems that others didn't see or couldn't solve. And these companies continue to reap the rewards to this day.

What About R&D?

R&D—research and development—refers to a more technical function than product development. A true R&D function, which may be called product development in some companies, is usually staffed by scientists and technicians rather than marketers.

The *R* in R&D—research—creates the need for scientists. Many companies in high-technology industries such as aerospace, chemicals, pharmaceuticals, telecommunications, medical instruments, and materials conduct basic research in the hope of a breakthrough. Basic research is a long-term, intellectual activity with frequent failure as part of the process.

Yet product development (the *D* in R&D) is a shorter-term, profit-oriented activity that seeks to minimize failures. Often these failures occur in attempts to commercialize a technology—that is, to find useful products that rely upon the technology. So managing R&D calls for understanding the interaction of research and development. It requires faith in both processes. Researchers must understand that they are pursuing knowledge not for its own sake, but for commercial reasons. Product developers must understand that research is a trial-and-error process with a long-term payoff.

CASE IN POINT

Apple CEO and founder Steve Jobs realized, after his company introduced its iPod music player, that Apple would have to deal with cellphones and personal digital assistants (PDA) that could play music.

He charged Apple's engineers with applying touchscreen technology to a cellphone that could access e-mail and the web, and download and play music. That was a challenge, but as reported by Fred Voglestein in the January 9, 2008, *Wired,* an even greater one would be wresting control of the cellphone business from the wireless companies.

Voglestein reports that after a precursor to the iPhone, the ROKR, developed with Motorola, failed, Jobs decided that Apple must develop its own phone. That required an investment of some $150 million and cutting a deal with AT&T (then Cingular) to shift market power from wireless providers to device manufacturers. Apple's Jobs did a deal limiting its exclusive with AT&T to five years and getting a share of AT&T's subscription revenue.

Often the best way to manage R&D is to get it away from the rest of the organization. That way, the scientists can be free to pursue research, and when they come up with something the company can develop into a product, they can hand it off to the right people.

Because markets and technology move so quickly today, a company can gain a major competitive advantage by being able to develop new products quickly.

The Least You Need to Know

- A cross-functional product-development team includes someone from every department who will deal with the product. This gives each department input into the process, which minimizes problems and gets everyone's buy-in at each step.

- The product-development process has six steps: idea generation, concept testing, prototype and product design, product testing, market testing, and product launch.

- You can save time, energy, and money by quickly eliminating bad ideas. Be tough when judging product ideas, and be sure the concept test reveals enthusiasm for (not just interest in) the product.

- A product test ensures that the product operates the way it should. The market test ensures that customers respond to it the way you thought they would. The market test also helps you fine-tune the product's positioning.

- The best products meet a need or solve a problem. There's nothing wrong with product-line extensions or parity products. But the really huge returns go to companies that come up with breakthrough ideas.

Steering the Business into the Future

When you steer a car, you're not supposed to focus on your dashboard or even on the car in front of you. Instead, you're supposed to look at what driving instructors call the big picture.

So it's time to look up from your desk and gaze out on the big picture. Think about strategy and the course you're plotting for your company. Ponder the nature of business information and how to use it to your advantage. Think about the risks that must be managed and about the health, safety, social, and environmental impacts your business generates. Also consider your company's legal obligations and your role as an ethical manager.

If you've set your sights on a senior management position in a large company—or if you're an entrepreneur starting or managing a small company—you need to understand the big picture to do your day-to-day job. This part shows you how.

Charting a Course with Strategic Planning

In This Chapter

- The role of strategic planning in the future of your company
- How to assess threats and opportunities
- Classic business strategies and action steps

All the activities and tools we've covered so far have to serve the larger needs of the company. All the jobs of finance, accounting, marketing, and sales must be coordinated so they work together smoothly.

This calls for a long-term strategic plan. You need a plan to give managers the framework for making good decisions. That plan must relate to the major goals of the whole company, and management's decisions must serve those goals.

This chapter explains long-range strategic planning, which is usually just called strategic planning. It tells you why you need a strategic plan and covers steps and techniques that will help you create one. (Chapter 26 covers the business plan, a document that explains the operations, finances, and marketing goals of a small business or a business unit.)

What Is Strategic Planning?

Strategic planning typically involves five steps:

1. Define the company's goals.

2. Analyze the company's environment.

3. Consider the company's resources.

4. Identify actions that will move the company toward its goals.

5. Implement the actions and monitor progress.

Through the rest of this chapter, I explain each of these elements.

Define the Company's Goals

The company must have a large, unifying goal that will organize the thinking and activities of everyone in the business. The most widely accepted goal of a company is to maximize long-term *shareholder value*—that is, to improve the worth of the company.

 MBA LINGO

Shareholder value is the investment of the owners of the company. The most common measure of this is the stock price multiplied by the number of shares of stock outstanding. The higher the stock's price, the higher the shareholder value.

Unfortunately, having the goal of maximizing shareholder value does not tell you *how* to maximize shareholder value. So most companies need one or more other strategic goals that will help them do that.

Your goals should help you direct the assessments of the environment and your resources. They can be broad ("to increase sales and operating profits by 10 percent") or more specific ("to increase European sales of the Mixmaster to $3 million next year").

Later, you may find that these goals are too low or too high. Or you may find that you can develop several specific goals that would support one overall goal. For instance, you might identify product lines that can increase sales and profits by more than 10 percent.

In setting a corporate goal, you must do the following:

- Define your business in the broadest terms possible
- Make your goal measurable
- Consider the basic sales-growth strategies

Let's look at each of these guidelines.

Define Your Business Broadly

Many companies have gotten themselves in trouble by defining their business too narrowly. Management consultant Peter Drucker used the example of the railroads to illustrate this. Before the development of air travel, the senior managers of railroads believed they were in the railroad business. If they had seen themselves in the transportation business instead, they would have been prepared to compete when airplanes came along. In fact, they may well have entered, or even developed, the airline industry.

Although it hardly guarantees success, looking at your business broadly will open your mind to possibilities you might otherwise miss. For example, if you're in training or consulting, think of yourself as being in the information business. This may open up possibilities in publishing and software. If you're in the restaurant business, think of it as food services or entertainment. You may find that corporate catering, cooking classes, or dinner theater are avenues of growth for you.

> **MBA MASTERY**
>
> Many companies fail because they are one-product firms. For long-term success, virtually every company needs a "second act."

How Will You Know You've Arrived?

To be "real," a goal must be measurable, as noted in Chapter 2. Vague goals don't motivate people. Be precise. Define a goal in numerical terms, if possible. Useful measures include revenue and profit gains, number and size of accounts, market share in certain product and customer groups, and percentage of sales and profits in certain areas of the business. These goals are measurable. And if you fail to achieve them, at least you'll know how close you came.

Consider the Sales-Growth Strategies

The key strategic question that recurs every year is, "Where will growth come from?" As a starting point, consider the sales-growth strategies covered in Chapter 17 (increasing prices or selling new or existing products to new or existing customers).

Thinking about these strategies as goals—for example, to sell new products to existing customers—will help you identify markets, customers, products, and price sensitivities as you assess the environment and your resources.

Analyze the Company's Environment

The company's environment includes the economy, market, competitive landscape, physical environment, and regulatory and social climate. You have to analyze each of these aspects, because threats and opportunities can emerge in any one of them. Most companies make a strategic plan every year or two because the environment changes—and as it does, so do the threats and opportunities.

Nonetheless, many companies have been blindsided by change, succumbing to competitors they failed to take seriously and missing opportunities that once stared them in the face.

CASE IN POINT

The complexity and connectedness of systems have increased the amount and pace of change in business. For example, aging, immigration, and ethnic patterns have increased demographic change. Technological change has transformed people's use of information, which itself has increased change. Economic change—at least, negative economic change—increased in the 2000s due to high risk, high debt, and lower middle-class incomes. Environmental change may be accelerating, with stronger storms, expanding deserts, and decreasing animal habitat in various locales.

Such forces, along with the human "pursuit of happiness," drive social change, which has also accelerated. The push and pull of progressive and conservative social and political forces operates in all cultures and affects businesses and their customers in various ways.

Let's talk about the different parts of your environment that you need to continually monitor.

Customers and Prospects

Any sales-growth strategies you suggest must take into account your customers' needs, satisfaction, price sensitivity, and alternative product choices. Be sure to get the views of the sales force on these issues. Market research and the business press can also be good sources of information on consumer preferences and habits.

Competitors

You must closely monitor your competitors and—key point—your *potential* competitors by analyzing annual reports, reading announcements of personnel changes, examining new products, keeping up with acquisitions and alliances, and even speaking with former employees or customers to gain insight into competitors' plans and operations.

Suppliers

Keep an eye on your suppliers, because they can affect your future. If they plan to increase their prices or phase out a product, it could impact your business. Plan accordingly. Pay special attention to the financial condition of your major suppliers.

To monitor suppliers, talk—and listen—to their salespeople and read the business press. Read the annual report of any supplier upon whom you depend heavily. Suppliers don't always warn customers of adverse changes. The sooner you know of any, the sooner you can respond.

> **MBA MASTERY**
>
> Find "promontories" from which to scan the environment for change. You can monitor competitors through your salespeople and customers, their websites, and their presentations at conferences. More generally, suppliers, outspoken consultants, and new companies in your industry often provide early indicators of future developments. Also, have someone watch for emerging technologies that could affect your business.

Regulatory and Social Change

The strategic-planning process must include an analysis of changes in regulations that affect your business. Regulatory changes are often driven by social change. Cigarettes are a good example of a product affected by both regulatory and social change. Since the 1960s, when television commercials for cigarettes were banned, the tobacco industry has seen increasing restrictions on its business.

Deregulation—the full or partial lifting of restrictions on business activity—can change the landscape, too. Deregulation of power generation, for example, has created an environment of change and competition in a business that had been stable and predictable. Similarly, deregulation (and product innovation) in financial services helped to create and exacerbate the recession of the late 2000s.

> **MBA LINGO**
>
> **Deregulation** occurs when an industry that had been operating under close government restrictions sees those restrictions loosened or removed.

Your local, state, and federal representatives and your trade association can help you keep abreast of regulatory change. In large, publicly held companies, this is the job of the government affairs or legal staff.

Economic Trends

Depending on your business, the major economic factors you should consider might include interest rates; housing starts; consumer confidence; consumer spending; monetary and fiscal policies; and local, state, regional, and national (and perhaps international) growth trends. Look beyond the surface reports on the business cycle to see any local and regional effects it may have on your business and what you can do in response.

As noted in Chapter 6, economic information, including news of the latest statistics and forecasts, is continually reported in the business press. Many large banks and investment firms make forecasts available to their customers. There are also consulting firms that sell economic forecasts and data, with IHS Global Insight and Moody's Economy.com among the most prominent.

Add It Up

After you assess the environment, you must examine each development you have identified and decide whether it is a threat or an opportunity. The following table shows how this kind of assessment might look for a U.S. auto manufacturer.

Development	Threat	Opportunity	Comment
Customers			
Larger vehicles have fallen out of favor	✓		We get X% of profits from mid- to large-size cars and sport utilities.
Desire more comfort and performance in smaller cars	✓	✓	See above, but we can respond by repositioning our compacts.
Spending lower percentage of income on transportation	✓		May hurt sales and profits. Stress economic benefits of our cars?

Development	Threat	Opportunity	Comment
Competitors			
Several new competitive subcompact models	✓		We must distinguish our lower-end models, perhaps by adding luxury features.
Lower-priced smaller cars added to Mercedes and BMW lines	✓		We can deliver luxury in a small car at a much lower price.
Introduction of hybrid, electric, and microcars (such as Smart car)	✓		We can start to compete in these markets, but how should we go about it?
Suppliers			
Rising steel prices	✓		Can we nail down low prices in contracts now?
Small firm has a new accident-prevention technology		✓	Should we test it? Can we get an exclusive? At what cost?
Economic			
Growth will slow in the next few years	✓		This will make it hard to match past sales levels.
Rising interest rates ahead	✓	✓	Threat to sales volume, but can benefit our financing subsidiary.
Regulatory/Social			
Environmental groups more visibly opposing large vehicles	✓		Marketing must stress environmental friendliness.
Possibly higher gas prices		✓	Could work in favor of our economy models.

As you see, some developments pose both a threat and an opportunity. This is often the case because changes in various areas actually open up opportunities while posing a threat. (Remember, the Chinese character for *crisis* combines the symbols for *threat* and *opportunity*.)

Consider the Company's Resources

Most companies do a decent, if incomplete, job of considering their resources. In assessing your company's resources, you must consider the resources you need, as well as those you have. These needs are dictated by the company's goals and by the threats and opportunities in the environment. Your most important resources include these:

- Product profitability and growth

- People

- Productive capacity

- Other resources

Let's examine each of these.

Profitability and Growth

Regarding the profitability of current products, you must answer these questions: Which product lines and activities are making money? Which are not? How do we create more money-making ones? How do we phase out unprofitable ones?

Regarding growth, you must answer these questions: Which product lines and activities are growing the fastest? Which are stagnant or declining? How can we boost the growing products and eliminate the others?

A straight accounting analysis will tell you a lot about the profitability and growth of your company or products. This means that you need accurate numbers from your accountants that clearly identify revenues and costs.

MBA ALERT

To protect themselves, some managers don't want their financial results to be very clear. They usually construct complicated systems, keep poor records, and argue about whose costs are whose. Senior management must insist that accounting staff work with department managers to develop clear, accurate, comparable numbers that fairly reflect their performance.

An excellent tool can help you evaluate the relative strength and profitability of your products or product lines: the growth-share matrix. The Boston Consulting Group (BCG) developed the growth-share matrix (or growth/market-share matrix) to help managers of multidivisional companies classify their subsidiaries. However, it also helps managers of a single company or division to classify products and product lines.

The classification system works along two dimensions: market growth and market share. Basically, growth is a measure of how much investment—that is, cash—the company or product requires. High growth requires lots of cash; low growth needs less cash. Market share is a measure of the company's or product's position in its market, which can range from dominant to weak. In general, the larger the market share, the more cash the company or product should be generating for the owners.

Here's how the growth-share matrix looks:

Market Growth	High	Star	?
	Low	Cash Cow	Dog
		High	Low

Market Share

Here's how to read the growth-share matrix:

- A star has high market share in a rapidly growing market. It needs a high level of investment, but it can generate lots of cash. That's why it's a star. To manage a star, invest whatever you can in it, because if you have a high share of a growing market, you're going to make money.

- A cash cow has high market share in a slowly growing market. This kind of company or product should yield lots of cash, particularly if the market is large, yet requires relatively little investment. That's why it's called a cash cow. Invest only what you need to invest to keep a cash cow healthy. It should be a net source of cash.

- A question mark is a product in a high-growth market, but it has not achieved high share of that market. Like the star, it requires investment to expand capacity to win high share. The question is, if you make the investment in more capacity, will the product or division win high share? If you believe you can move it into the star area, you should invest in it. Otherwise, you shouldn't.

- A dog offers the worst of both worlds: low market share in a low-growth market. On one hand, it doesn't require much investment. On the other hand, it's not going to generate much cash. It's a dog. A dog should be sold or phased out.

People Are the Company

At most companies, the resource assessment tends to be incomplete in the area of human resources. That's because the assets on the balance sheet are easier to inventory than the knowledge in people's heads. However, certain human resources can give a company a competitive edge that physical resources cannot.

In considering your resources, consider the skills, education, expertise, and experience of your employees. Consider knowledge they could apply to your business, as well as what they are now applying.

Many companies with sophisticated human resources departments use a knowledge and skills inventory of their employees. A formal knowledge and skills inventory asks employees to list their skills, education, experience, languages, and other characteristics, often for entry into a computerized database. This kind of inventory can help managers make sure they are making the most of their employees.

Productive Capacity

To determine your true productive capacity, you need to look beyond the fixed assets on your balance sheet. You need to understand everything about your equipment: downtime, maintenance requirements, ease or difficulty of operation, amount of training required, and productivity of the machinery and the people using it.

You must go to the machinery operators and their managers to get this information. These people have the information you need to assess productive capacity realistically.

Also consider the potential to outsource specific operations or functions, or parts of them, to vendors or other providers. Outsourcing can enable a company to expand its capacity quickly and then, if necessary, to decrease it. It minimizes investment in fixed assets and permanent staff. However, it can lead to lower quality, increased risks, and generally decreased management control. (Also, it's not a great deal for employees.) Yet sensible outsourcing should at least be considered in most strategic plans.

Other Resources

Other resources to consider are less tangible—and perhaps lie outside the company—but they can be important nonetheless. These include …

- Patents, trademarks, and brands.

- Sales channels and distribution systems.

- Alliances or joint ventures with other companies.

Importantly, the potential to develop these kinds of resources can often point toward useful ways of acquiring resources that the business currently lacks. In fact, developing these resources is often among the action steps that emerge from a strategic plan.

Add It Up Again

As you consider the company's resources, you must decide whether they are adequate to meeting the threats and capitalizing on the opportunities posed by the environment. The following table shows how this assessment might look for a U.S. auto manufacturer.

Resource	Strength	Weakness	Comment
Profitability & Growth			
Minivan and SUV lines are aging (cash cow).		✓	Lines continue to be profitable, but we haven't invested in them recently and we don't want to.
Midsize sedan line is losing ground (dog).		✓	Competitors have overtaken us in midsize market because we placed our bets on vans and SUVs.
Our new high-performance sports coupe has sold well (question mark).	✓		We may be able to capitalize on this key product strength to build a line of high-performance small cars.
People			
Our dealer network has not been happy but remains committed to us.		✓	We must improve dealer relations by helping them improve their profits.
Our unionized workforce is aging, as we have emphasized production in Mexico.		✓	We cannot function without a solid, well-trained U.S. workforce.

continues

continued

Resource	Strength	Weakness	Comment
Productive Capacity			
We have large amounts of capacity, but we have not updated it in some time.	✓	✓	This reflects our investment in minivan and SUV capacity, which we may need to retool for sedans.
Outsourcing has left us dependent on two major suppliers of key components.		✓	This exposes us to price increases that can be difficult to resist. We must bring some of this work back inside.
Other Resources			
We have filed a number of patents that we haven't used or exploited in any way.	✓		We must look into commercializing these inventions by applying them ourselves or licensing them to other companies.
Our financial structure remains strong.	✓		Although we have new products, our reliance on cash cows has left us financially underinvested.

As with environmental developments, a resource can now and then represent both a strength and a weakness. Also, the preceding list represents a sample of resources to be considered. In reality, an automobile manufacturer would have many more resources to consider in every category, and perhaps several other categories as well.

What's SWOT?

From time to time you will hear the acronym SWOT, another example of MBA-ese. SWOT stands for an analysis of strengths, weaknesses, opportunities, and threats. Thus, SWOT also sums up the second step (analyze the company's environment) and the third step (consider the company's resources) of the strategic-planning process presented here.

That is, the product of step 2, analyzing the environment, should be an assessment of the threats and opportunities that the company faces in the marketplace. And the product of step 3, considering the company's resources, should be an assessment of its strengths and weaknesses.

Although SWOT is widely used, it's only part of the strategic-planning story, which many managers forget. I believe that a SWOT analysis works best when performed *after* the company sets at least a preliminary goal. I also believe that it's best to analyze the environment (opportunities and threats) *before* you consider the company's resources (strengths and weaknesses). That way, you can evaluate the resources in light of the opportunities and threats you must address.

In sum, SWOT is an excellent mnemonic, but the process it represents must occur in context. Company goals provide that context. Also, if you literally follow the SWOT sequence and analyze strengths and weaknesses before identifying opportunities and threats, you are, in a sense, putting the cart before the horse.

It is also essential to identify risks to the company, its existing assets, and the achievement of its goals. In a sense, the weaknesses and threats identified by SWOT and those in the sample analysis I've provided for the U.S. auto industry are indeed risks. But you have to consider risks more closely and manage them aggressively, so I cover risk management separately in Chapter 24.

Any strategic plan worthy of the name must include actions that will move the company toward its goals, our fourth step.

MBA MASTERY

A staggering amount of information on goals, environmental developments, and resources can go into a strategic plan. Several software packages have been developed to assist the strategic planner. These range from cheap to pricey, and new packages and updates of existing packages are always being introduced. The key features to look for are the ability to handle various types of information—that is, text as well as columns of numbers—and to create alternative planning scenarios easily.

Alternative scenarios might include those based on assumptions of slow, medium, and fast economic growth. Or a resource assessment might be based on optimistic, pessimistic, and best-guess levels of sales or market share. Software enables the planner to change the assumption and automatically generate new figures for any value tied to that assumption (such as equipment or number of people needed). In this way, the effects of different assumptions about the future can be considered more realistically.

Identify Actions

On the basis of the information resulting from the first three steps, you should now be positioned to decide what action the company should take to move toward its goals. These actions must do the following:

- Neutralize or eliminate threats

- Capitalize on opportunities

- Exploit existing resources and develop or acquire needed resources

Actions are the heart of the strategic plan. The result of this step should be the actual "to do" items that operations, marketing, sales, finance, and other departments must undertake. Examples of general action steps for key departments that would typically come out of a strategic plan include the following:

Marketing

Develop new products.

Develop a new marketing campaign.

Replace advertising agency.

Reposition existing products.

Identify new markets.

Develop new sales channels.

Sales

Explain price increase to customers.

Employ new sales tactics.

Restructure sales-force alignment.

Restructure sales territories.

Restructure sales compensation.

Improve customer service.

Finance

Secure debt financing.

Issue stock.

Refinance debt.

Adjust capital structure.

Improve financial controls.

Start a cost-cutting effort.

Secure international financing.

Production

Expand capacity.

Improve product quality.

Increase productivity.

Outsource production tasks.

Find new suppliers.

Improve inventory methods.

General Management/Human Resources

Expand certain areas of the organization.

Develop hiring or downsizing campaigns.

Increase use of independent contractors.

Form business alliances or joint ventures.

Merge with or acquire another company.

Of course, this list is not exhaustive, nor would all of these steps be taken at once.

Implement the Steps

If you're new to business, you may be surprised to learn that strategic plans are often created, presented to management, and even approved—but never implemented. This occurs most often in companies with strategic planning functions that are isolated from the company's real business and operating managers. These "ivory tower" planners typically either are too removed from the business to create a relevant plan or are seen by operating managers as useless, or both.

To lessen the chances of this, you must get input from all managers before the plan is formulated. Then, after it is completed, you must tie their individual goals to the plan and tie their raises, bonuses, and promotions to those goals. Both of these tactics will make the plan much more relevant to them.

Also, the management and leadership skills covered in Part 1 are essential to implementing strategic plans. For instance, managers must communicate the plan and its goals throughout the entire organization. Effective leaders link the strategic plan to the organizational vision. They focus people on the tasks that will get the plan implemented and hold them accountable for taking action and achieving the goals of the plan. They also ensure that the organization is aligned with the plan, and they take the time to coach and mentor people in the context of the plan.

Many strategic plans fail not because they're poor plans, but because they're poorly implemented. Implementation is the toughest step in the process, yet in a sense, it lies outside strategic planning. That's because strategic planning is largely an analytical function, while implementing is a management function—getting things done through others.

Throughout the planning process, and especially when you're crafting the action steps, be sure that you can implement the plan. The plan is not an end in itself, but rather a tool to move the company toward its goals. It can do that only if the goals, analysis, and action steps are rooted in reality.

Strategic-Planning Guidelines

No part of strategic planning is easy, but some guidelines, as well as tools and techniques, can help you in the process. Let's turn to them now.

Set a Time Frame

The most common time frame for a strategic plan is one year and five years—that is, you have a plan for the coming year and for the coming five years. Most companies prepare the plan for the coming year in detail. Businesses vary in the detail they go into for the subsequent four years. An alternative is more detailed one-, two-, and three-year plans.

Get Everyone Involved

A plan that originates with senior management and is then dictated to the troops is called a top-down plan. A bottom-up plan begins with input from the department managers, who may, in turn, get input from their employees.

Top-down and bottom-up represent two extremes. In reality, if senior managers try to impose a plan they develop unilaterally, they'll have trouble implementing it because they won't have buy-in from those who must implement the plan. On the other hand, if senior managers rely only on the input of departmental managers as the basis for the plan, they may miss a major development outside the day-to-day operations that are the main focus of the departmental managers. So a mix of the two approaches works best.

Who Needs a Plan?

Virtually every business of any size needs a strategic plan if it plans to be around for more than a year. Poor planning and lack of planning are repeatedly cited among the top reasons for business failure.

There's no valid excuse for not planning. Attempting to perform the basic managerial functions of organizing and controlling the company is difficult or impossible without a good plan. Planning brings the future into the present so that you can think about it more clearly and more productively than you can when it comes hurtling toward you. Remember, proper planning prevents poor performance.

The Least You Need to Know

- A long-term strategic plan gives managers a framework for making good decisions that serve the long-term goals of the company. A strategic plan can ensure that day-to-day decisions and tactics move the company toward its major goals.

- A strategic plan should start with a goal, even if that goal will be modified as more information is gathered during the planning process.
- Since companies are affected by the business environment, you must assess the environment for threats and opportunities.
- Use Boston Consulting Group's growth-share matrix to examine your company's divisions (or products) for growth rate and market share, and to assess current and future profitability.
- Be certain that the identified actions can be carried out by those who will be accountable for doing so. Align your incentives and communicate management's support of those who carry out the plan. Use management and leadership skills to implement the plan.

Managing Risk in a Risky World

In This Chapter

- Why risk management has become so important
- Types of risk businesses face
- Tools of risk analysis and risk management
- How to discuss risks so that colleagues will listen

Risk management has become a topic of great concern to managers at all levels in companies large and small. That's because organizations face more, and more severe, risks than in the past.

Risk management doesn't mean avoiding all risks. Risk management cannot eliminate risks, nor can it prevent all disasters, failures, and bad outcomes. But it can minimize the chances and effects of bad outcomes and can accelerate an organization's recovery from disasters.

This chapter explains how. It examines the nature and practices of risk management and the types of risks businesses face. It explains senior executives' risk-management responsibilities, discusses specific tools of risk management, and provides examples of risk management. It also explains how to begin risk-management efforts by identifying and assessing risks.

What Is Risk and Risk Management?

Today's business world is extremely interconnected, which means that a risk that affects one industry or organization can affect many others. The global scope of major companies also exposes them to more risks. Consider all the effects of poor risk management by mortgage originators during the U.S. housing bubble of the mid-2000s. Unscrupulous mortgage professionals made and resold loans to unqualified homebuyers, which led to a global recession, the bankruptcy of Iceland, and the end of several major banking organizations, which also had poor risk management.

Risk management calls for understanding business risks in general, as well as the specific types of risk an organization faces based on its industry, goals, strategies, and activities. Before looking at specific types of risk, I want to make a few general points about risk in business.

In general, risk is the possibility that the organization or one of its business units or activities will fail to achieve its objectives or will create or encounter an unintended negative outcome.

Risk cannot be eliminated, so it must be managed. Many organizations try to avoid risk by sticking with what they do best and repeating the strategies that made them successful in the past. These companies are invariably outflanked by those willing to take risks. In other words, trying to avoid risk can be … risky.

Risk can be managed. The risk of investing in financial instruments can usually be quantified, particularly if the issuing company has a track record. The amount of property at risk, say, in case of a fire, is usually limited to its historical or replacement value. Other risks can be harder to quantify, but they can be analyzed, measured, and managed using tools I discuss later in this chapter.

People in business take on risk in anticipation of rewards. Usually, those rewards are monetary, but they come as a result of, for example, launching successful new products, increasing market share, and acquiring other businesses. Those activities have potential rewards associated with them, as well as risks.

Finally, although the major risk is the risk of failure, that is too general to be managed. Therefore, executives and *risk managers* break risk down into discrete types, which enables them to manage risk more effectively.

MBA LINGO

Risk managers are specialists who work with senior executives, business unit heads, and employees to identify, measure, monitor, and mitigate risks created in the course of the company's business activities. Many major companies have a chief risk officer, the senior executive in charge of risk management.

The practice of risk management includes the following key activities:

- Identifying the risks the organization faces

- Assessing the size and likelihood of those risks

- Having the right risk-management tools and the skills needed to apply them

- Developing a culture in which everyone feels responsible for risk management

Risk management comes under senior executives' general management responsibilities and the board of directors' corporate governance responsibilities (which I explain in Chapter 27). It is management's responsibility to manage risk, with guidance from the board of directors. To manage risk, managers must understand the types of risk that the organization faces.

Top 10 Types of Risk

The number of risks that an organization faces can appear overwhelming. However, classifying risks makes them less overwhelming. Doing so also helps people develop, choose, and use the right risk-management tools.

Organizations face these key types of risk:

- **Financial risk:** Money invested in a project could be lost, or returns could be less than expected or less than another investment would offer.

- **Currency (or foreign exchange) risk:** An investment or stream of payments may lose value due to currency fluctuations.

- **Credit risk:** A company or lender might not be paid for goods sold on credit or for money loaned to a customer.

- **Security risk:** The company faces threat of fraud, theft, embezzlement, or misdirection of funds, goods, or other company assets.

- **Property risk:** Company property could be destroyed due to fire, flood, earthquake, storms, war, terrorism, or similar causes.

- **Regulatory risk:** A domestic or foreign government agency could find the company to be in noncompliance with requirements or regulations.

- **Legal risk:** Customers, suppliers, employees, competitors, investors, or other parties could launch lawsuits, or the company could break the law.

- **Information technology (IT) risk:** The company's IT systems could be breached or misused.

- **Country (or political) risk:** A foreign government could appropriate or nationalize a business or its assets, or otherwise create losses.

- **Reputational risk:** Statements or actions of employees or the company's agents or spokespeople could harm an organization's brands or reputation.

Not every organization faces every risk. A company doing no international business need not concern itself with currency risk or country risk. However, every company faces some risks. That means every management team must engage in risk management, to some extent. The extent depends on types of risk and the potential losses posed by the risks, which are determined in a risk assessment.

MBA ALERT

Risk management gained importance for most executives and board members after the financial crisis of the 2000s and resulting bank failures and business difficulties. Also, cases of financial fraud, such as the Bernie Madoff scandal, closer regulatory scrutiny, and the threat of terrorism, have increased management's awareness of risk.

Risk Assessment

A risk assessment begins by identifying all the risks the organization and its business units and functions face. It then moves on to measuring the magnitude and likelihood of the potential losses associated with those risks (or the *risk exposure*). The company must allocate risk-management resources only to the risks that warrant them; you don't buy flood insurance if you live in the desert.

MBA LINGO

Risk exposure is the potential monetary losses that could occur if a risk became a reality. So if a bank has loans to Russia totaling $2.5 billion, management would say, "Our total exposure in Russia is $2.5 billion."

Let's examine a three-step process of identifying risks and measuring their size and likelihood.

Identifying Risks

You identify risks by considering the organization's strategies and activities and asking these questions: What can go wrong? What types of failures or events could negatively affect this strategy, initiative, activity, or product?

Potential answers may include these:

- Human errors or failures, such as inattention or confusion

- Hostile human action, such as theft, embezzlement, or other crimes

- Process or product failure, or failure of materials or systems

- Market and cultural forces, such as bad publicity or changing styles

- Government or regulatory actions, such as changes to laws or to tax, trade, or economic policy

- Natural or manmade disasters, such as earthquakes, storms, fires, terrorism, and war

To identify risks, you look for the possibility of these events within each strategy, initiative, process, and activity. The more familiar you are with the types of risk in the previous section, the more precisely you can identify risk. For example, if your company plans to introduce a new product, you can see how a specific failure, such as a botched advertising campaign, could generate various risks. A botched advertisement might, for instance, lead to financial risk, because of money invested in the product; regulatory risk, because of laws regarding product claims; legal risk, because of product-liability suits; and reputational risk, because the company's brands may be harmed.

This raises a point. Often when you prepare to manage one risk, such as regulatory risk, you also manage other risks, such as legal risk and reputational risk. It's not as if you have to manage every risk separately with its own specific tool, although sometimes you do. Rather, you must identify every risk so that you know you have managed it, even if only as a side effect of managing another risk. For example, disaster-response plans, which maintain or restore communication and other systems, usually work regardless of the type of disaster.

Also, be sure to identify risks that arise due to actions by other parties, such as suppliers and customers. It's important to do business with people who share your approach to risk management and to be sure that they understand and cooperate with your risk-management policies.

MBA ALERT

Many employees are unaware of their companies' disaster-recovery plans, even when such plans are in place. Whether as a manager or an employee, you must understand what you're supposed to do in various emergencies. If plans are not in place, you can assist your company by helping to develop them.

Measuring the Size of Risk

Measuring the size of a risk means assessing the potential effect on your company. This can include direct monetary losses due to property destroyed (which is what insurance companies pay for) and from the effects on your customers, suppliers, employees, and other stakeholders (which might not be insurable).

You have to ask questions such as these:

- What if our largest customer shut down its operations? What would be our lost revenue and profits?

- In a terrorist attack or hurricane scenario in which one or two of our locations were partly destroyed, what would be the time for repair and the potential costs of repairs and lost business?

- If interest rates were to rise by 50 percent in a two-year period, how would our borrowing costs be affected?

- If a new technology were to supercede our technology in three years, what losses might we incur?

In measuring the size of a risk, you often develop a range rather than a single number. This range might be a percentage, say, of revenue or profits, rather than a monetary amount. However, percentages can usually be converted to amounts. If you are a $10 million company and the loss of a major customer would be 20 percent of your revenue, you know that is $2 million.

Once you have gauged the magnitude of a potential risk, you then turn to the likelihood of the risk occurring.

Measuring Likelihood

Measuring the likelihood of a risk can be straightforward or difficult. It is fairly straightforward for routine risks for which the company has experience and data. One good example is credit risk. Banks and companies have a good idea of the delinquency and default rates that their credit policies will generate. A bank knows that when it lends money to someone with a certain credit score, income, and employment history, in a certain percentage of cases, the money will not be repaid. A company selling on credit can obtain a credit rating from an agency, such as Dun & Bradstreet, and have a good idea of the probability of being repaid.

The likelihood of other risks, such as the risk of an economic downturn, are far more difficult to measure. Most difficult to measure is the likelihood of the extraordinarily bad but relatively rare situation such as natural disasters, financial crises, industrial accidents, and terrorist attacks.

In cases for which there is little data and thus little chance of predicting likelihood, many managers dismiss the risk as highly unlikely. However, "highly unlikely" does not mean impossible. Responsible managers prepare for highly unlikely risks when those risks could result in huge losses for the company.

For example, suppose you're a small company and you supply a component to a major company, like Hewlett-Packard (HP). Let's say that company is 60 percent of your business. You might think it's impossible that anything would happen to HP, but something could. Moreover, even if nothing did, they might still find a substitute for what you sell or discontinue their need for it.

This means that you must do some scenario planning and develop contingency plans as part of your risk management.

CASE IN POINT

Many executives dismiss relatively rare events as "impossible" when such events actually occur fairly frequently. Before the 2010 British Petroleum (BP) disaster, there had not been an oil-rig disaster in the Gulf of Mexico in more than 40 years. BP failed to account for the fact that drilling deeper increased the risks if a blowout were to occur and that repair would be difficult and costly.

About Risk Appetite

At the highest level, the organization has a certain approach to risk management. Some companies believe it is in their interest to accept high risk in the pursuit of high returns. Such companies often develop new products and markets and invent new approaches. Apple is a good example of a company that takes risks that usually—but not always—pay off.

In contrast, a company may believe that "pioneers go running off cliffs" and that taking more risk will not generate consistent, growing returns. They then would take fewer risks and stick with time-tested approaches. IBM has generally been such a company. IBM did not invent the computer, the minicomputer, or the microcomputer, but it has succeeded by using these inventions in disciplined ways.

In practice, this means that different companies have different risk appetites. Risk appetite is the company's willingness to take on risk in the pursuit of its goals. Risk appetite can be defined numerically, but in many companies, it is "understood" as being high, medium, or low. A numerical value would be the amount of capital the company can invest in a strategy and lose without going bankrupt. It's up to management to set the risk appetite.

There's no correct or incorrect risk appetite, as long as management and its stakeholders are aware of it and manage risk accordingly. A high appetite for risk is fine, but the shareholders and employees must understand that the company has that appetite. Management cannot present itself as conservative and take high risks behind everyone's back, and still claim to be honest.

Another key to risk management is monitoring risk in various areas and reporting the level of risk, and increases or decreases, in specific areas. For example, the risk in a specific business or division, such as the retail division, may increase due to economic or market trends, while the risk in the commercial division may be decreasing, for similar or different reasons.

MBA MASTERY

Risk management extends to suppliers and business partners, and those efforts should be formalized whenever possible. Every large company needs a suppliers' code of conduct, as well as a rigorous process of choosing suppliers. Contracts should consider the risks the supplier might pose, then mitigate those risks or designate which party will be responsible for managing them or compensating the other for them.

Risk-Management Tools

As discussed shortly, some risks can be managed by using standard tools, such as insurance against property risk and options contracts to hedge against currency risk. Other risks must be managed through ethical codes and behavior standards. For example, reputational risk can be addressed by "morals clauses" in contracts between companies and the sports or entertainment stars they hire as spokespersons.

These are the most common risk-management tools:

- **Prevention and safety procedures:** Wearing hard hats in construction areas, keeping borrowing to reasonable levels, and insisting that passwords not be shared are all ways to manage risk. The Occupational Health and Safety Act (OSHA) specifies safety procedures in many work environments, but management must enforce them and develop procedures for activities not covered by OSHA.

- **Control environment:** The control environment is the overall set of policies and procedures that apply to transactions, accounts, and financial and other information. A control environment can be strong, weak, or in between. In a strong control environment, two or more people must approve certain transactions, passwords are updated often, and people who audit transactions are not the people who execute the transactions. Also, management should receive regular reports on the key controls.

- **Monitoring:** Risks must be monitored because they can change. Changes in the industry, media, regulatory, or economic environment can increase or decrease levels of risk. Also, changes in certain accounts, Internet traffic, and customer or supplier behavior can signal increased or decreased risk. For example, the mid-2000s housing bubble was apparent when 25 percent of condos in some areas were being bought as investments. That should have told experienced real estate professionals to get out of the market before the bubble burst.

- **Insurance:** Property and casualty, life, health, and other types of insurance all work on the same principle. The insurer agrees, in exchange for premium payments, to pay the insured a certain amount or up to a certain amount to compensate for a loss arising from a specific type of risk. The insurer creates a pool of insured people or entities that share the risk (the "risk pool"). The insurer determines the premiums based on the size and likelihood of the losses and the supply and demand for the insurance.

- **Hedging:** Hedging is used to offset financial and currency risk. A hedge is usually a contract to purchase or sell a security, currency, or commodity for a specific price on or by a specific date. For example, a contract that gives a company the right to purchase 50,000 gallons of heating oil for a certain price per gallon next winter is a hedge against prices increasing by more than that amount.

- **Response plans and resilience:** Response plans enable an organization to recover from a risk event. Contingency and backup plans help to ensure the *resilience* of operations and systems. These plans focus mainly on physical facilities, operational capabilities, communication and distribution systems, and IT systems.

MBA LINGO

Resilience in this context is the ability of operations, systems, and employees to recover from a disaster. All stakeholders, particularly customers and investors, depend on management to have contingency and recovery plans in case of disaster or attack.

It takes time, money, and expertise to develop and deploy the tools of risk management. Not every organization needs every tool, and not every tool is effective in all cases. Thus, management must decide which tools are necessary and cost effective, and how they should be used.

The tools themselves are neither magical nor foolproof. Controls must be tested and adjusted periodically. Insurance must be purchased from reputable companies. Hedging contracts must be carefully worded. Recovery plans must be practiced before a disaster occurs.

In addition, everyone in the organization must know when it is and isn't appropriate to take risks, which risks are worth taking, and which are prohibited. They must also know how to recognize and report increasing risk, and how to respond to risk events.

MBA ALERT

It's essential to understand how risks evolve and change. For instance, sophisticated cybercriminals can now enter IT systems using the very passwords that are meant to keep them out. Then they can act as if they were authorized users. These criminals aim to steal millions, yet most IT security efforts do not focus intensely enough on them.

Risk Management in Practice

To show you how risk management works in practice, I use the example of credit risk in a company that sells its products to other businesses on credit. (Recall the material on the credit department in Chapter 9.) When a company sells on credit, it incurs credit risk. The key activities in addressing credit risk are as follows:

- Setting credit policy
- Assessing credit risk
- Monitoring credit risk
- Managing credit risk

Setting Credit Policy

Setting credit policy means defining the company's tolerance for losses generated by uncollectible accounts. Credit policy can be loose or tight. A loose credit policy usually calls for selling to less creditworthy customers (along with more creditworthy ones), while a tighter credit policy calls for selling only to more creditworthy customers. A looser credit policy permits more uncollectible accounts.

Credit policy can be set fairly precisely because the company can usually forecast the level of losses. For instance, a company can set the expected level of losses at 2 percent of sales. These losses are viewed as a cost of doing business and are built into the company's prices. The company needs the infrastructure—a credit department, a credit approval process as described in Chapter 9, and a collection department—to support its credit policy. Also, the sales force must understand the credit policy so they don't waste time on the wrong customers.

Credit policy—like every risk-management policy—must be made clear to the relevant parties, implemented with discipline, and periodically reviewed.

Assessing Credit Risk

Assessing risk requires information, expertise, and time, so it's important to gear the assessment effort to the level of risk being contemplated (that is, the credit limit). In decisions involving selling on credit, this is a straightforward analysis. Many companies simply approve any sale below $500 to another company. For sales between $500 and $2,500, they might get a credit report and do a brief analysis. For sales above $2,500, they might request a financial statement and two references from other companies that have sold to the customer on credit.

In this way, the company expends reasonable resources on the assessment and has a good idea of the probability of being paid. The company then either approves the sale or not, or approves it for a lower credit limit and demands, say, partial payment in cash and the balance in 30 days.

Monitoring Credit Risk

After the sale, the credit department monitors customers' payment behavior. If the customer pays on time, no action is taken. (The credit limit may even be increased.) If the customer fails to pay on time, collection efforts begin. The credit department also monitors the overall risk of the accounts-receivable portfolio. If more customers fall behind—for example, due to an economic recession—they may consider tightening the credit policy.

Credit policy would be changed only in consultation with sales and management. Tighter credit policy might make it more difficult for salespeople to sell, which might affect marketing, production, and distribution. In other words, if the company starts rejecting more sales as potentially uncollectible, it may see a loss of business. Risk management cannot be done in a vacuum, because it usually affects other areas of the business.

Managing Credit Risk

Companies manage credit risk mainly through the collections department, through collection efforts like those described in Chapter 9. If a customer is seriously past due, a company usually does not sell additional goods on credit and insists on cash payment. If the customer is completely unable to pay, the company typically charges off the amount as a loss. But when long-standing customers fall temporarily behind, most companies try to work with them and perhaps make some adjustments. Many companies have retained customers and built loyalty by helping them through a rough patch.

That shows how broad risk-management considerations can become. The risk of losing the customer, the likelihood of his becoming solvent again, and the likelihood of losing money in trying to help him must all be considered. Similarly broad considerations often arise in other types of risk management.

Companies take a broadly similar, if more complex, approach to managing financial, currency, country, legal, and other risks. Note that, in most areas of risk management, information technology (IT) plays an essential role.

The Role of IT in Risk Management

Most businesses run on their computer systems. They conduct some or most of their marketing, purchasing, accounting, bill paying, investment tracking, internal and external communicating, and other business on their computer systems, on external systems, and on the Internet. This exposes them to security risks due to hackers and cybercriminals, privacy risks arising from mistakes involving customer or employee data, and risks due to technology becoming outdated or compromised (say, by disruptions to the power grid).

IT plays a huge role in monitoring and controlling risks. Most accounting systems are IT based. Most payments to and from the company flow through the system. Although systems generate reports, they vary in their relevance to risk management. For instance, reports on accounts receivable are usually quite relevant in managing credit risk. Reports on employees' use of company resources are often less so in managing property risk (because when property is stolen, thieves usually conceal that fact). The best IT systems provide control and monitoring capabilities that support sound risk management.

IT security is paramount. Major cases of personal data being compromised regularly occur, and many are never even discovered. Cybercriminals are the fastest-growing major criminal class. If you are an IT professional or intend to become one, you know the importance of cybersecurity. If you are a general manager or intend to become one, be sure you understand the risks posed by IT and the measures your IT department takes to address them.

Backup IT systems are essential. Sound risk management calls for capabilities that embed back-up and security precautions into the system. To the extent possible, non-IT people should not have to worry about IT security or disaster recovery. They should know that the IT department has done all it can to ensure the security of company data and continuity of operations. The latter calls for reliable offsite backup of data and systems in remote locations, and regular tests and reviews of backup systems and procedures.

IT security is a field unto itself. General managers and entrepreneurs must ensure that their IT people understand the importance of risk management and their roles in it.

MBA ALERT

Many executives—and politicians—ignore experience and common sense. After the 1993 terrorist bombing of the World Trade Center, New York City's "response team headquarters" was located in, yes, the World Trade Center. Similarly, after two 1970s oil crises originating in the Mideast, the United States *increased* its dependence on foreign oil.

Creating a Culture of Risk Management

As with quality improvement, risk management cannot be performed as an afterthought or viewed as an optional activity. Instead, risk management must be embedded in the ways people do their jobs. Employees at all levels must understand risk-management policies and procedures and incorporate them into their daily job-related activities.

Senior executives are responsible for creating the corporate culture. They do so by the goals they set, the decisions they make, and the policies and procedures they institute. In those ways, management sets the tone of the organization and dictates the level of excellence in risk management that people aspire to and achieve.

The Least You Need to Know

- Risk management has risen in importance because the number, severity, and interconnectedness of risks has increased.
- Broadly, risk is the probability that a strategy, initiative, activity, or process will fail or that some outside event will cause it to break down or generate losses. Risk management is the activity of identifying, assessing, and mitigating the risks the organization faces.
- Key types of risks that businesses face include financial, currency (or foreign exchange), credit, security, property, regulatory, legal, IT, country (or political), and reputational risk.
- IT systems play a major role in risk management, given the exposures that IT systems create and the capabilities that IT has for identifying, assessing, monitoring, and controlling risks.
- Responsibility for risk management resides mainly with senior executives and risk managers, but it's also the responsibility of every manager and employee.

Achieving Corporate Responsibility and Sustainability

In This Chapter

- What corporate responsibility and sustainability means
- The "triple bottom line" of profits, people, and planet
- Key tools in achieving sustainable operations

Back in the 1960s, a popular bumper sticker read, "Ecology—The Last Fad." It drew a few smiles at the time, but it may still turn out to be true. Scientists have determined that if every one of the roughly six billion people presently living on Earth lived like the average American consumer in terms of their consumption of energy, food, water, and other resources, it would be the equivalent of some 70 billion people living on Earth. No one believes that the planet could sustain anywhere near that many people.

And that's the point of this chapter: some lifestyles and business practices are sustainable, and some are not. That issue is now being addressed in boardrooms, offices, supermarkets, and showrooms around the world. In this chapter, we define sustainable practices and examine ways in which companies go about adopting them.

What Is Sustainability?

Sustainability refers to practices that enable companies to do business and continue to grow without sacrificing opportunities for future generations to do the same. This does not mean that all future generations will have the exact same opportunities in the same industries as those of us who are now alive. Rather, it means that we will not have depleted resources to the point that the opportunities we enjoy are closed off to future generations. It also means that certain resources, such as national parks and clean air and water, will be available to them.

Many people think of sustainability as relating only to environmental impacts such as air and water pollution and depletion of resources such as timber and oil. However, sustainability encompasses the full range of health, safety, social, and environmental impacts. For example, all of the following are considerations in sustainability:

- Waste of water and materials in production and in packaging

- Excessive energy use, including all fossil fuels and electricity

- Pollution of water (including groundwater and runoff), air, and soil, as well as soil erosion

- Waste created by disposal of packaging and products (especially batteries and computers)

- Illnesses or injuries caused by the product or in its production or decomposition

- Distribution of products, including fuel usage and vehicle maintenance, storage space, and wear and tear on roads and other infrastructure

- Climate change due to greenhouse gas emissions

- Exhaustion of resources, such as timber and oil, and reduced *biodiversity* due to overfishing or other human intervention

- Impact of large-scale agriculture and food production on animals and on food quality and safety

- Effects of labor practices on the health, safety, and well-being of workers, particularly in underdeveloped nations

Over the past 20 years, consumers, particularly in Europe and North America, have become more conscious of these impacts. Many consumers now factor these impacts into their purchase decisions and into their satisfaction with products. They are also becoming increasingly sensitized to companies' reputations in these areas.

MBA LINGO

Biodiversity refers to the variations of life forms in an ecosystem. In the context of sustainability, concerns usually focus on the exhaustion or elimination of plant, animal, fish, or insect species, or the potential effects of creating or eliminating a bacteria or virus.

Also, many companies that once pursued environmentally or socially sound policies to garner "good citizenship points" now see substantial business benefits to sustainability. These companies tend to view sustainability in terms of the "triple bottom line" of people, planet, and profits. That means that they value stakeholders as people as well as in their roles as customers, employees, suppliers, and investors. They value the planet and want to pass on its resources to future generations. They value profits because they are in business, but they don't seek profits at the expense of the well-being of people or the planet. It's a welcome development.

About Corporate Responsibility and Sustainability

To set sustainability in a larger context, businesspeople often think in terms of corporate responsibility and sustainability (CR&S). CR&S sums up sustainability and the entire issue of health, safety, social, and environmental impacts. Other names for this area of business include green practices, greening, environmentally sound practices, eco-friendly practices, sustainable practices, sustainable management, and social responsibility.

A broad view of CR&S considers the total health, safety, social, and environmental impact of the company's processes, policies, practices, products, and services. The entire issue of CR&S falls within the responsibility of senior management and the board of directors. Like risk management, CR&S comes under senior executives' general management responsibilities and the board of directors' corporate governance responsibilities. (Again, I explain corporate governance in Chapter 27.) Management is responsible for managing the company in a sustainable (and, given environmental regulations, legal) manner, with guidance from the board of directors. The board exercises governance by overseeing management's practices in all areas, including CR&S.

Speaking of risk, CR&S issues can pose a number of risks. Regulatory risk is an obvious one. However, as the tobacco industry learned in the 1990s when they lost a number of large product-liability lawsuits, CR&S issues can also hold legal and financial risks. Other risks include the potential loss of value of your brands and the company's reputation. Indeed, a product or company's reputation can be quickly damaged or undone even by rumors, let alone the reality of unhealthy, unsafe, or unsound practices or products.

Thus, it is important to consider the risks posed by waste, emissions, fuel, and other resource use, as well as labor practices and other aspects of sustainability. When you consider the CR&S impacts, also consider your customers and how they use, maintain, and dispose of your products and the CR&S practices of your suppliers and distributors.

Managers use a number of methods and tools to understand the impact of their processes, products, and services and to reduce that impact. We even do this as individuals. You and people you know probably don't purchase or use specific products, eat certain foods, or patronize certain companies because of real or perceived CR&S issues, which can include supporting certain political positions.

CASE IN POINT

Burger King and several other major companies stopped using Indonesian palm oil when they learned that deforestation in that nation was a side effect of producing it. Whole Foods stopped carrying foie gras due to controversy over the treatment of the geese. Some food companies limited or avoided use of high fructose corn syrup when news articles were thought to claim that it contained more calories than sugar. (Most stories actually focused on the "hidden calories" it can add to foods.)

Many major companies, including retailer Wal-Mart and furniture manufacturer Herman Miller, have committed to significant sustainability initiatives. For products it carries, Wal-Mart is developing a sustainability index, which considers energy use, materials efficiency, natural resources, societal impacts, and disposability. The Herman Miller website states that, by 2009, it had reduced volatile organic compound (VOC) air emissions by 93 percent, water use by 77 percent, hazardous waste by 95 percent, and solid waste by 88 percent. The company also has other goals that it has publicly committed to achieving by 2020.

Other examples of more focused initiatives include Nestlé phasing out polyvinyl chloride (PVC) in all its bottled water brands; Genecor increasing the concentration of liquid detergents to save packaging, weight, and space; and UPS eliminating left turns on its delivery routes to save fuel and reduce emissions.

MBA ALERT

Check out the websites of major companies that you are interested in to keep up on their sustainability programs. For example, Wal-Mart reports on its CR&S initiatives at http://walmartstores.com/sustainability/. Shell Oil does so at www.shell.com/home/content/environment_society/.

Challenges in Managing Sustainability

Most businesspeople prefer to produce completely safe products with minimal negative CR&S impacts. Yet they face barriers to doing so.

Understanding What Needs to Be Done

Every company can take some "no-brainer" steps to reduce their impact, but it takes serious effort to get beyond that. Most companies are already trying to minimize their electricity and fuel usage and waste of water and materials, if only to minimize costs. The real challenges are threefold: first, to inventory and analyze all of the impacts; second, to decide which ones present the greatest risks to the company and other stakeholders; and, third, to calculate the costs and benefits of addressing them. Also, various stakeholders, including consumer activists, employees, suppliers, investors, and regulators, often have competing interests.

Obtaining Accurate Measurements and Useful Standards

The universal measure of performance in business is money, which is why accounting systems are very highly developed. But CR&S impacts are measured in illnesses (which may have unclear causes), injuries (which involve human error), gallons, kilowatts, and parts per million rather than dollars, euros, or pesos. Methods for tracking these impacts are rudimentary compared with accounting systems. In addition, various standard-setting organizations (in addition to government agencies) issue a raft of standards that are always in flux.

The Cost/Benefit Tradeoff Can Be Unclear

Partly due to the measurement challenges, the cost/benefit tradeoff can be difficult to gauge. Worse, it can threaten the company's basic business model. For instance, if a company in an industrial nation imports materials or products from a nation with high pollution and low labor standards, what should it do? Start importing goods from a higher-cost location, which might make it less competitive and even drive it into bankruptcy? What would be the impact of that on the foreign workers or their nation? Unfortunately, the right thing to do is not always clear.

The Returns on Investment Can Be Long Term

Ideally, CR&S investments pay for themselves. Indeed, if you save fuel and electricity, reduce waste, and improve distribution logistics, you will probably save money. But over what time horizon will you save it, and what are your competing investments and *their* returns? For many companies, the choice is not whether to invest in CR&S or leave the money in the bank. Rather, it is to invest in CR&S or a new product line or new marketing program, or to expand operations and hire more workers. The returns on CR&S initiatives can be not only longer term, but also more uncertain than investments in more traditional business strategies.

Despite these four factors, most major companies in high-impact industries in Europe, Canada, and the United States (with Europe leading the way) do have formal CR&S programs. Many of these companies have responded to government mandates, but they have also responded to other stakeholders, including customers, investors, and *nongovernmental organizations* (*NGOs*).

How, exactly, do companies implement CR&S initiatives? One of the major methods is product footprinting.

MBA LINGO

A **nongovernmental organization (NGO)** is a usually national or international nonprofit enterprise that is unaffiliated with a government and excludes government representatives. Generally, an NGO works to achieve an environmental, social, or humanitarian goal. Examples include Oxfam, which assists victims of famine; Amnesty International, which works for the release of political prisoners and to end torture; Doctors Without Borders, which deploys physicians to areas of need (often to assist civilians injured in wars); and Greenpeace, which works for a clean environment.

Getting Grounded: Product Footprinting

Product footprinting, also known as product lifecycle analysis, is a method of examining the total sustainability impact of a product. It is not so much a formal methodology as it is a collection of tools for defining, assessing, and improving CR&S impacts while maintaining or improving the quality, performance, and value of the product.

Note that last point. It is important not to sacrifice product quality and performance to achieve CR&S goals. Most consumers won't purchase products they see as inferior just because they are "green." (This is among the major issues in developing an electric car.) However, many consumers are concerned about sustainability and will pay more for products that address those concerns while meeting their normal expectations. Although they still account for a minority of the market, those consumers see sustainability as part of the value of certain products and are willing and able to pay more for them. Companies like Whole Foods Markets and those selling hybrid automobiles target these customers. These companies seriously consider product footprint, as every company should.

Product footprint should cover every phase of the product's lifecycle. Those phases include materials, production, distribution, packaging, and storage, as well as customers' use, maintenance, and disposal of the product. At every stage, product footprint should consider the health and safety of everyone who produces, handles, and uses the product.

Analyzing product footprint is useful because it does the following:

- Reduces CR&S issues to a manageable level. A company can't change the world, but it can improve its products.

- Extends backward to suppliers and forward to distributors, as well as to customers.

- Examines the process for making the product, as well as the product's contents or ingredients.

- Quantifies revenue, costs, and profits so you can consider various products and invest where returns will be highest.

- Can be rolled up for all of a company's products, to develop a total footprint.

Product footprinting is useful for businesses just beginning their CR&S efforts and for those going beyond their initial initiatives, such as reducing fuel usage. Footprinting generates specific projects that can be planned, implemented, and evaluated. Then, when a project succeeds, the company can replicate it across the business and share it with suppliers. For instance, if the goal is to eliminate polyvinyl chloride (PVC) from products and packaging, and the company locates a good substitute, it may be able to use that substitute in all of its products and packaging, and help its suppliers to do the same.

Steps in Footprinting

Product footprinting begins with an inventory of impacts. This may call for help from an external engineer or consultant with experience in product footprinting, although internal experts may offer good initial estimates of certain impacts. Here are some questions to ask when examining a product's footprint:

- What is the approximate usage of fuel (such as gasoline or oil) and energy (such as electricity) across the footprint?

- What materials are used, and where are they from? How are they produced, transported, stored, and handled, and with what impacts?

- What about the product's size, weight, and packaging? What are the reasons behind these characteristics (such as ease of use, water content, or cost factors)?

- What types and levels of air, water, and ground pollution are created across the footprint? What are the specific causes of these impacts?

- What health and safety dangers and potential liabilities do these products pose to our workers, suppliers, distributors, and customers?

- What have employees, distributors, or customers reported in the way of complaints, injuries, illnesses, or CR&S concerns?

- What changes have we made in materials or in production or distribution process over the years? Have these increased or reduced the footprint?

After taking this inventory, ask what you can do to minimize or mitigate these impacts. Also ask who might have ideas about how to reduce the product footprint. Be sure to consider competitors and what they have done to address these issues. I'm not suggesting that you illegally obtain proprietary information on competitors' practices. However, copying ideas or unpatented processes is a legal, practical, cost-effective way to reduce footprint and serves the greater good. For example, although UPS may have been the first major company to eliminate left turns on delivery routes, there's nothing to stop other delivery operations from doing so.

Getting Departments Involved

When you discover the impacts and where they originate, you can develop ways to address them. This usually means reducing the product footprint in specific ways, which may involve initiatives ranging from simple changes in procedures to entirely new product lines.

It may also involve several areas of the business, most notably these:

- **R&D and product development:** R&D and product development can work to develop safe and sustainable materials, processes, and products, from concept and design through production. These may be product line extensions, such as green versions of existing products, or new or substitute products that reduce CR&S impacts.

- **Operations:** Many companies have realized gains by altering policies, practices, and procedures in production, storage, and distribution. Especially as formerly inexpensive resources such as fuel and water become more expensive, significant savings can result from energy efficiency and lower usage. Looking to suppliers can help operations find ways to reduce footprint.

- **Purchasing:** Does your company monitor the contents of the materials, components, products, and packaging you purchase? It should. As I explain shortly, standards and certifications can provide peace of mind regarding the impact of your supply chain. Also, if your purchasing department has these standards, it can work more effectively with suppliers to strengthen your CR&S program.

- **Sales and marketing:** Salespeople should be aware of customer preferences regarding the CR&S impacts of your products. Marketing should monitor competitors' plans and initiatives. Customer service should track warranty claims and customer comments to learn how customers actually use and dispose of products. (You may be unpleasantly surprised.) Sales, marketing, and customer service must understand that many customers factor CR&S considerations into purchase decisions. Also, the zealots among them can strongly influence purchase decisions of friends and acquaintances.

Product footprinting can be initiated in small ways. A change that works on a pilot basis can generate huge impact when implemented across the organization. However, the greatest impact will be realized when product footprints are assessed and reduced in systematic ways across the organization and up and down the *value chain*. This often means working with suppliers to reduce their contribution to your product footprint.

MBA LINGO

The term **value chain** refers to the entire process by which your products and services are produced and delivered. It includes all activities that add value to the product in any way, and extends to suppliers and to all functions within the organization that affect the product, including sales and marketing. The term was developed by consultant Michael Porter in the 1980s and has endured. A related term is the supply chain, which commonly designates all suppliers of materials and components outside the company (as in "supply chain management").

Working with Suppliers

Suppliers of materials and components inevitably contribute to your product footprint. That means they can help you reduce it. But how do you go about that?

Essentially, you talk with them about it in a spirit of collaboration. It is best not to force changes on them, although in some cases you may have to, if your company is in a position to do so. Insisting that suppliers change is justified if your company faces costs or risks if suppliers do not change their approaches. Of course, you can also switch to suppliers that share your company's approach to CR&S.

In fact, relations between companies and their suppliers have become highly collaborative over the past two decades. That was one outcome of companies adopting quality-improvement methods such as Total Quality Management and Six Sigma (discussed in Chapter 10). Just as suppliers can help you improve the quality of your products, they can help you reduce their footprint.

In addition, suppliers who adopt sustainable practices realize benefits in addition to retaining and perhaps expanding the amount of business they do with your company. They can also better serve the ever-growing population of companies seeking suppliers who can address CR&S impacts. In addition, if their processes and practices become more sustainable, they will probably lower their risks and costs, along with those of your company.

Going back to the quality- and process-improvement methods covered in Chapter 10, programs such as Total Quality Management and Six Sigma and Lean can be used to work with suppliers. Just as you can ask for changes to a supplier's processes or materials for quality reasons or to enhance your productivity, you can request changes geared to helping you reduce your footprint.

For example, these might include the following:

- Changes to less wasteful or time-consuming packaging or delivery schedules

- Elimination or reduction of hazardous ingredients or materials

- Movement to suppliers with humane workplace policies

- Joint efforts to develop new products with minimal footprints

Many major companies have formal supplier certification, management, and review programs, with guidelines, checklists, and rating systems for maintaining "preferred supplier" status. These supplier programs can be used to set expectations and monitor suppliers' performance in sustainability. Although these programs can be used to enlist suppliers in reducing product footprint, this presumes that such a program is in place and working well, and that the program can accommodate product footprint reduction. Unfortunately, many companies often do not monitor suppliers closely enough.

MBA ALERT

It's essential to know what your suppliers are doing—and not doing—in terms of CR&S. You don't want to find out through a product-liability suit or in the media that a supplier uses hazardous ingredients, exploits child workers, or despoils the environment, particularly if they do so in producing something that goes into your products. In other words, your suppliers' risks can become your risks.

Another tool is a supplier code of conduct, which sets forth certain practices. Companies use these to set expectations and to cite standards of their own or those of standard-setting organizations. Some codes are developed by industries. For example, the Electronic Industry Supplier Code of Conduct was developed by companies in the electronics industry to address the areas of labor, health and safety, environment, and ethics.

CASE IN POINT

Key organizations that set CR&S standards include the Global Reporting Initiative (GRI, at www.globalreporting.org) and AccountAbility (www. accountability.org). GRI issued G3, the sustainability reporting framework most widely used by large companies. AccountAbility has also issued a standard for companies preparing CR&S reports (Accountability 1000 Principals Standard). In addition, Social Accountability International (SAI, at www.sa-intl.org) sets standards for workplace and employment practices.

In working with suppliers, as in every area of business, be sure to set your priorities and proceed systematically. First, identify the suppliers who contribute the most to your product footprint. Then identify the ways in which they contribute the most. Even before you speak with them, review changes that they have made or that you have requested regarding product content or their production or delivery processes. (Be careful if you will be asking them to change something you originally asked them to do.) Then try to get a fix on the potential costs and benefits of the changes you might request.

Ultimately, efforts to reduce product footprint help your suppliers for the same reason that they help you. If suppliers don't see that, they may pose risks to your company that should be considered in purchasing decisions. Of course, many factors go into your choice of suppliers, including costs, quality, and relationships. But it makes sense to do business with suppliers who share, or at least understand, your sustainability concerns.

Small or Large CR&S Efforts?

Realistically, a company's CR&S efforts will be geared to the health, safety, social, and environmental impacts that it produces. A global oil company is going to produce more impact than a local retailer. That oil company will also be subject to regulations and will receive more scrutiny from activists and the media. It also has shareholders, who will be concerned about their investment in the company.

However, even a local business can generate significant impact. These impacts can seem deceptively small, as was the case when most people thought of high-tech industries as "clean," only to learn later about certain hazardous materials in computers. Also, like every consumer, every company generates waste and uses water, fuel, and electricity.

What can every business do?

Start Small

Begin with the obvious—reducing your company's fuel and electricity consumption, decreasing your water usage, increasing recycling and use of recycled paper and plastic, and disposing of batteries and computers properly. Take baseline measures in these areas so you can measure and report your progress. With a basic effort in place, you can then measure other impacts and get to work on reducing them.

Ask Around

A formal survey of your employees, customers, suppliers, and other stakeholders regarding their sustainability concerns can be quite useful. You may be surprised at what you can learn from this low-cost exercise. Also, once you have a baseline measure of people's concerns and priorities, you can address them and then conduct a survey to measure the progress they perceive.

Build a Program

There's nothing like a formal program to pull together your initiatives into a coordinated effort with measurable results. A senior manager should be responsible for the program, have a budget, and report on the program's performance (the costs and gains). The gains should include not only gallons saved or pounds of paper recycled, but also the dollars spent and saved. See what competitors and companies in other industries are doing, and keep abreast of regulatory changes and reporting requirements.

Produce Feedback

Be sure to tell all stakeholders about the gains you achieve, but don't "*greenwash.*" Instead, report honestly on your efforts, challenges, and progress. Also, be sure to meet all regulatory reporting requirements. However, think twice before publicly announcing goals, which can backfire. Many companies do announce goals, but they almost certainly ascertain that they are achievable before they do, although some appear to announce "stretch" goals to challenge themselves.

MBA LINGO

Greenwashing refers to a company's efforts to portray itself as more environmentally or socially conscious than it is. (It's a variation of the term *whitewashing,* which means covering up the truth.) Greenwashing ranges from exaggerating CR&S efforts or accomplishments to flat-out lying about the sources, ingredients, or hazards of a product.

Getting to Sustainability

Sustainability is here to stay. Forces such as diminishing natural resources, climate change, and emerging middle classes in China and India (and their adoption of higher-consumption lifestyles) will see to that. Government regulations, liability suits, activist organizations, and the media will continue to pressure companies to adopt sustainable practices.

The best approach is to embrace sustainability rather than try to avoid it. View CR&S as a set of opportunities rather than a bunch of costs. Yes, CR&S practices involve extra costs. But the benefits include reduced regulatory, legal, and financial risk, as well as increased customer loyalty and, often, revenue. Not all customers are willing or able to pay extra for green products, but many are.

In addition, CR&S practices are generally the right thing to do. I'm not saying that all other practices are wrong; there are many gray areas. For example, "factory farming" brings nutritious food to mass markets at relatively low prices. Also, converting every product to zero-footprint would be overwhelmingly costly in the short run and perhaps impossible even in the long run.

Yet unsustainable practices, by definition, do not represent a long-term strategy for success for most companies or for any society. So be aware of the health, safety, social, and environmental impacts of your company's products and services. And then make informed decisions that consider those impacts and ways to reduce them.

The Least You Need to Know

- Sustainability goes by a number of names, including sustainable, green, environmentally sound, and eco-friendly practices, and by the more formal corporate responsibility and sustainability (CR&S).
- In general, sustainability refers to practices that recognize and minimize negative health, safety, social, and environmental impacts, or that improve positive impacts.
- Sustainable practices include reducing fuel and electricity usage, reducing water usage, recycling and using recycled paper and plastic, engaging in fair labor practices, product footprinting, and reducing product footprint.
- The type and size of a company's sustainability program depend on its size, industry, and impacts; whether it is a public company; and the extent to which it is regulated.
- Sustainable practices can increase certain costs, but they yield benefits such as reduced risks, reduced costs in other areas, enhanced brand image, increased sales, and greater customer and employee loyalty.

Entrepreneurship and Small Business Management

In This Chapter

- Creating a great business plan
- Finding funds to start a business
- Buying an existing business
- Predicting problems in growing a business

Being an *entrepreneur* differs sharply from being an administrator. An administrator assumes responsibility for an established department or function within a larger organization. An entrepreneur must create a business from scratch and with very limited resources. Although MBA stands for Master of Business Administration, most business schools have established or expanded their course offerings for those who want to become entrepreneurs. This recognizes that many students would rather start a company or join a small company than work for a large corporation. They would rather be entrepreneurs than administrators.

But it also recognizes that many large companies want to hire people capable of managing entrepreneurially. These companies realize that sometimes they can compete in a market only by starting a totally new business, apart from or within the larger organization. They have also learned that developing these new businesses calls for approaches different from those required to manage their traditional, established businesses. Thus, they seek entrepreneurial managers for certain areas of the business.

This chapter examines the process of starting a business and managing the growth of a small business. It also touches on ways in which large companies tap entrepreneurs.

Big Plans

An entrepreneur faces three broad tasks. He or she must finance the business, produce the product or service, and bring it to market. Clearly, there are other tasks, such as finding suppliers and setting up an accounting system, but financing, producing, and marketing the product are the big ones.

These tasks are also linked in chicken-and-egg fashion. How do you market a product if you haven't produced it? How do you produce a product if you don't have much money? How do you raise money if you don't have a proven product?

The business plan answers these questions. A business plan describes the product or service, its market and its production and distribution requirements, the background and qualifications of the entrepreneurs, and the amount of money that the business will require.

The business plan is a blueprint for the business, as well as a sales tool. (The business may be a *start-up* or an existing operation, but I discuss plans in terms of start-ups.) As a blueprint, a business plan guides the entrepreneurs through the steps necessary to get the business up and running. Therefore, the business plan must be complete and realistic. As a sales tool, it tells potential investors and lenders about the company's business, prospects, and financial requirements. Therefore, it must also be positive and optimistic.

MBA LINGO

An **entrepreneur** organizes resources into an enterprise that brings a product or service to people who need it, while making a profit for both the entrepreneur and the investors. A **start-up** is a new business created to bring a product or service to market. Most start-ups begin with one product or service, or an idea for one.

Outline for a Business Plan

Although the exact section titles and their order may vary, every business plan must include the following information:

- Table of Contents
- Executive Summary
- Business, Products, and Services

- Market Analysis

- Management Team

- Operations

- Financial Projections

A business plan should be written in plain English and answer the major questions that prospective investors, lenders, employees, and suppliers have about the enterprise:

- What is the product?

- How large and needy is the market?

- Who are the managers of the business?

- Can this business make and sell the product?

- What are the potential sales and earnings?

Don't load up the main sections of the plan with too much detail. That material should go into appendixes. The outline presented here works for a proprietorship, partnership, or corporation, but it assumes that the business is a corporation seeking equity investors.

Describe the Business, Products, and Services

Describe the location, nature, industry, and history of the business, as well as its current products and services and those in development. Mention brand names, trademarks, service marks, and patents, as well as any licensing arrangements, alliances, or joint ventures. Although financial information will be covered later, it's good to note sales and profits, and the proportion of sales and profits derived from key products and services, in this section. Also note any trends and government regulations affecting the business.

Particularly if the only products are still in development, briefly describe the underlying technology and the functions it performs and customer needs that it meets. Note the stage of development. For example, is there a prototype? Has it been tested? How will the product be produced, packaged, distributed, serviced, and maintained?

This section is also where basic data on the company—year founded, locations, facilities, number of employees, and so on—should go.

Analyze the Market

Market analysis is a key section of the plan and one of the hardest to write for a business with no track record. In those cases, the analysis depends almost solely on market research, which should be conducted in each major target market (and which you learned about in Chapter 18).

It's not enough to determine that a good portion of the respondents say they "like" the product concept or are "likely to purchase" it. Survey respondents often give positive answers just to be agreeable. Therefore, the research must ascertain how and how often they would use the product, how they are currently addressing the need the product addresses, and how much money they would make or save by using the product. These questions prompt respondents to relate their needs and behavior to the product.

Market research can also bolster the case for products already in the marketplace. In those instances, the research should substantiate that there is still a large, untapped market for the product even though it is already available.

Finally, the market analysis should describe existing and potential competitors and substitute products. Take care with this section, and never assume that your business will face no competition. Even if it has no competition in the beginning, if the business succeeds, it soon will have plenty.

CASE IN POINT

Research isn't necessarily the last word on a product's feasibility. When a product or service is totally new, a company may just have to launch it to build a market. For example, Citibank developed and introduced the ATM (automatic teller machine) even though survey respondents said they would never use it. People said they needed a live teller, they wouldn't trust a machine, and they feared being robbed. Today, however, most people could barely get along without ATMs.

Note, however, that although Citibank acted in a highly entrepreneurial manner, it was at the time the nation's second-largest bank. Its branch network and its base of accounts positioned it to win customers over to the new technology.

Marketing and Sales Strategy

Many start-up companies fail not because they have a poor product, but because they cannot sell it or get it distributed. The business plan must therefore present realistic marketing, sales, and distribution strategies (see Part 4). Also mention any firm orders you have for your products or services, along with the expected delivery date.

Introduce the Management Team

Investors and lenders must know the qualifications and track records of the business's senior managers. If the product or service depends on technology, they need the same information on the key technical people.

At a minimum, the business needs an experienced general manager, a sales or marketing professional who can close sales, a production manager, a manager of information systems, and an office manager. Perhaps one person can cover two of these functions, but attempting to attract financing without the right people on board is foolhardy.

The plan should include the resumés of key employees and emphasize each individual's qualifications for the role. If any key positions have not yet been filled, mention that and a time frame for filling them.

Describe the Operation

The plan must describe how the company's products will be produced and how its services will be delivered. When and how will the production facilities be built, leased, or purchased? What equipment will be necessary, and will it be leased or purchased? If production will be done by a *contract manufacturer*, describe that outfit. What are its capabilities? What is its track record? Mention any details, such as packaging, shelf life, and other product characteristics, that affect production, distribution, and storage. Also identify major suppliers and their record of quality and reliability.

MBA LINGO

A **contract manufacturer** produces products to the specifications of another company, which has designed the product and handles the marketing, sales, and distribution. In other words, an entrepreneur can outsource manufacturing to a contract manufacturer. This allows the entrepreneur to minimize his investment in plant and equipment.

Discuss the staffing requirements in the various operating functions, and the qualifications and sources of any highly specialized personnel (for instance, software engineers).

Here are some other questions to address at this point:

- Which distribution channels will be used for the product? Who are the wholesalers, retail chains, or other middlemen involved in the process?

- What are the product's transportation and storage requirements?

- Are there seasonal variances in the sales and production cycles of the business?

- What are the anticipated needs for facilities, equipment, staff, and distribution?

Analyze the Financial Needs and Potential Returns

For an established business, the plan should include historical financial statements for the past five years through the most recent quarter. It should also include *pro forma* statements for the next five years. Present monthly projections for the next two years and quarterly projections for following three years.

MBA LINGO

Pro forma financial statements project the values for the various accounts on the balance sheet, income statement, and cash flow statement. Underlying the pro forma statements are assumptions about future sales growth, financial requirements, and other factors. Thus, the believability of the pro forma statements depends on the believability of the assumptions, which should be included as footnotes to the statements.

If the company has not yet opened for business, only pro forma statements can be presented. However, an accounting of the money invested so far by the founders and other investors should be presented. How much has been invested and raised? How has it been used? How much cash is on hand? Mention other investors who have backed the business or made firm commitments to back it. Note the current distribution of the company's stock and the effect that new investors will have on that distribution.

The financial section should also include the owners' compensation plan and benefit plan (if any) and those of other employees. Most important, this section must explicitly state how much money you are trying to raise and the uses to which that money will be put.

Keep It Short and Substantive

Some business plans are long on sales pitches and short on substance. Although many insubstantial plans did raise money in the 1990s and even in the 2000s, today's business plans must be true plans rather than sales pitches. That does not, however, mean that a plan should bury the reader in information. Investors "get it" very quickly and can decide whether they are interested on the basis of the two-page executive summary. If they are interested, they will want to meet with you and will request more detailed information.

Incidentally, the planning process may reveal that the business would not, in fact, become successful. If that happens, that's good. You have just saved yourself (and others) huge amounts of time, energy, and money by avoiding a situation that was destined to fail.

Finding Financing

A new venture offers investors an equity stake in the business. If the business grows, they will receive a share of the proceeds when the company goes public or a share of the sales price if the company is sold to a larger company or to new owners.

Where do you find venture investors? These are some of the traditional sources of funds for new businesses:

- **Managers of the business and their relatives and friends:** Typically, the founders—the senior managers—of a business first use savings, personal bank loans, and even credit cards to raise money for their business. Then they go to family members, relatives, and friends. This can be uncomfortable and must be handled in a businesslike manner.

- **Wealthy individuals, known as "angels":** Angels invest directly in the business and are typically savvy businesspeople with a background in the type of businesses they back. Entrepreneurs locate them through personal contacts and plain old networking.

- **Small Business Administration (SBA):** The SBA is an agency within the U.S. Department of Commerce that supports small businesses through information, advice, training, and loan programs. It has far too many loan programs to list here, so it's best to check out its website at www.sba.gov.

- **Venture capital firms:** A venture capital (VC) firm manages funds that invest money gathered from individual and institutional investors in early-stage companies. The average venture capital firm receives about 100 business plans for every 10 it seriously considers, and then invests in only 1 of those 10.

- **Large corporations, suppliers, and other sources:** Some large corporations realize that the Next Big Thing could be launched by a very small business. Therefore, some of them are open to investing in or forming an alliance with a new or small business with a high-potential product that fits their business. Suppliers rarely invest in a new company, but it does happen. More often a supplier extends favorable terms to a start-up with the potential to grow into a large customer, particularly if the start-up agrees to use the supplier as its sole source for a key component of its product.

MBA MASTERY

Venture capitalists almost always want a substantial block of stock, a seat on the board of directors, and a role in major decisions. In other words, you give up some control when a venture fund invests in your business. Yet good venture capitalists bring more than money to the table. They bring experience, contacts, and expertise that can help the company grow faster and larger than it otherwise could. A venture capital firm also knows how to go about taking a company through its initial public offering (IPO), meaning the first offering of a corporation's stock to the investing public.

Managing Growth

No matter how well a business has been planned, things rarely proceed according to that plan. After the business begins operating, entrepreneurs generally face one of two problems: growing too slowly or growing too quickly.

If the business is growing too slowly, you should consider the following tips:

- Evaluate your salespeople and sales process to ensure that both are able to close sales rather than just generate interest. New businesses need "missionaries" and "rainmakers"—enthusiastic people who can close sales.

- Adjust your marketing message by examining each of the Five P's, which I covered in Chapter 19, and experimenting with different combinations.

- If you have a new product, be sure you've identified and reached the relevant innovators and early adopters.

- Find out, through informal and formal research, why customers aren't buying, or aren't buying repeatedly—and address those issues.

- Learn whether the company is delivering as promised. Great sales efforts must be backed up by great products and service. Early customers will tolerate a few glitches from a new company with a new product. But sloppy service or unsolved problems will inevitably generate bad word of mouth.

- Get the resources you need to grow the business. If the business could grow more quickly with more money, people, and other resources, work hard to get them.

In some cases, patience and persistence are the keys to surviving a slow start. But you must learn why things are starting slowly and remedy the situation.

If the business starts growing too quickly, you have another set of problems. You may be thinking, "We should all have such problems," but business history is filled with companies that grew too fast and flamed out as a result. If the business is growing too fast, look to these solutions:

- Exercise leadership to motivate people through the long hours and high demands that growth imposes on a rapidly growing company. Let them share in the rewards of growth (for example, through bonuses).

- Collect your accounts receivable as quickly as possible. Booking sales without collecting the cash will not enable you to pay your employees and suppliers. To speed up your cash flow, consider using the receivables to secure a loan or line of credit.

- Do all you can to expand production without compromising quality. Make and ship product as fast as you can, but when quality problems arise, fix them fast, even if it costs a lot. A disappointed customer—particularly a large disappointed customer—can quickly spread the word that you don't have your act together.

- If you're strapped for resources, outsource some of the production, installation, and even customer service instead of expanding permanently and increasing your fixed costs.

- Keep your investors informed about your success and your problems. They may well be willing to invest more money in what now looks like a success, if that money will help you grow. This would also be a good time to meet with your banker about a loan or line of credit.

- Get all the advice you can from your board of directors; your network of advisers; and your accountant, suppliers, and industry association.

- If production, quality, delivery, or financial problems overwhelm the company, seriously consider hiring a competent operating executive to put the right management systems and controls in place.

Never underestimate the power of systems and controls, which are necessary in every company. Management systems provide vital information on the needs and performance of the business—for instance, on sales, expenses, inventory, time usage, customers, transactions, and other aspects of the business. Controls involve understanding the contribution that each activity makes to the business, and creating policies and procedures that cut less productive activities and increase the more productive ones.

Systems and controls also send employees, customers, investors, and other stakeholders the message that this is a true business, not a fly-by-night operation. Most of all, systems and controls, especially financial controls, keep management in touch with reality.

MBA MASTERY

Data must be developed into information by cross-referencing, examining trends, and identifying patterns. For example, data on customers—who they are, where they are, how much they spend on which of your products, how they heard about your company, their creditworthiness, and so on—can be used to develop customer profiles.

A customer profile can enable marketing to target and tailor your company's message to the most promising prospects. It can also help sales understand how best to close deals with them. And this is just one type of information that can be developed from the data generated by good systems.

Policies and procedures distinguish a well-managed business from a seat-of-the-pants outfit. A business needs policies and procedures to guide people in areas such as accepting deliveries, using overnight delivery, purchasing materials, handling customer complaints, and responding to emergencies—to name a few.

This means that, in the midst of all the production and sales activity, someone must see to the administrative side of the business. In the early stages, the business may get by with an office manager, a bookkeeper, and a sales assistant, and perhaps with a few people performing multiple functions. However, as the company grows, it will need specialists and even more sophisticated systems.

For instance, when enough money is flowing through the business (the amount varies by industry and company size), an on-staff accountant or controller becomes necessary. In many jurisdictions, once a business has a certain number of employees, it must begin complying with a new level of regulation and perhaps institute an employee benefits plan. At that point, a knowledgeable head of human resources may become necessary. To get to "the next level," a company may need a seasoned vice president of marketing or sales, or even a new CEO. Many companies flounder when an entrepreneur can't let go of the company he or she founded even though he or she is not equal to the managerial demands.

Financing Growth

As the saying goes, it takes money to make money. Start-up capital is only the beginning. It takes money to grow a business, and that money can come from only two places: inside the company or outside the company.

Internally generated funds—the earnings generated by the business—are the cheapest source of growth capital. They carry no interest rate and no promise of future dividends. Internally generated funds also enable the founders to maintain the most control over the company.

Yet insisting that the business stick to self-funding may hamper its growth. If the company is growing—or is positioned to grow—faster than it can fund itself, then it's quite likely that external financing is necessary to bring the company to its greatest potential.

To finance growth, the business must usually locate additional financing from the original investors, new investors, or one or more banks. At a certain point, most truly successful companies at least consider the ultimate step in gaining access to capital: going public.

The IPO

A successful initial public offering provides long-term capital at a lower cost than borrowing. An IPO also usually gives the early investors in the company—management, angels, venture capitalists, and so on—the opportunity to reap substantial returns on their investment.

An IPO comprises a series of steps, which include working up in-depth information on the business and its history and plans (in the form of a prospectus), notifying the SEC of the owners' intention to sell stock to the public, registering the securities with the SEC, setting a price, and deciding how the stock will be sold and distributed.

An investment bank usually guides the owners through this process. Aside from providing the legal and financial expertise to make the IPO happen, the investment bank has the distribution network needed to sell the stock to investors. The investment bank is compensated with a fee, at least some of which is tied to the amount of money raised by the IPO.

A successful IPO, meaning one that raises the targeted amount of capital or close to it, often identifies the issuer as a growth company in the minds of investors. As noted in Chapter 16, these investors expect any profits to be reinvested in the business to finance its growth. For that reason, and for the ability to raise additional capital in the public markets if necessary, going public is the ultimate in financing strategies.

Buying a Business

The image of the entrepreneur starting in his or her kitchen or garage and going public several years later may be the popular one, but many entrepreneurs prefer to buy a business. It may take a bit more creativity to start a business from scratch than it does to buy a going concern, but the business challenges are quite similar.

Anyone buying a business, whether it's a small retail store or a division of a large company, must understand its products and services, market and customers, facilities and operations, and financial history and prospects. Understanding the impact of current legal actions, tax matters, and regulatory issues on the company is also part of the *due diligence* required when you purchase a business. Rather than deal only with the owners or brokers of the business, speak to key employees, customers, suppliers, and lenders about their history with the business and their role in its future.

MBA LINGO

Due diligence refers to the process of discovering and understanding all aspects of the business and all the factors that could affect the prospects of the business. Due diligence must be undertaken by brokers representing securities for sale, managers, and investment bankers involved in a merger or acquisition, and anyone buying a business.

In addition to the sources of financing already mentioned in this chapter, the buyers of the business may be able to use a leveraged buyout (LBO) to raise some or most of the funding. In a leveraged buyout, the new owners use the assets of the company to finance the purchase of the company. The borrowings are then repaid out of the company's future cash flow. If the current managers of a company are buying the business from the owners, the transaction is often referred to as a management buyout.

MBA MASTERY

Leveraged buyouts can be used to take a public company private. The company's senior managers (or other purchasers of the company) pledge the company's assets as collateral for the loans to finance the purchase of the stock. Then they use the proceeds of the loan to buy the stock from the existing shareholders, usually at a premium over the current market price.

However they finance the purchase, people buying a company must understand the business, develop a plan to keep the company growing or boost its growth, and avoid paying too high a price. Any key employees—and, for that matter, the former owners—should be available in at least a consulting capacity to see that the new owners get off to a good start. This is particularly important for buyers of a service business, where the relationships and skills of the former owners probably played a big role in the success of the business.

As always, the watchwords are *caveat emptor* (buyer beware). It's easy for a buyer to overpay for a successful business. Savvy founders are motivated to sell when the value of the company has peaked. They may know that competitors are entering the market, that the company's technology is about to be superceded, or that the fad that drove their success is about to end. It's difficult to know these things if you're not in the industry. In other words, there's almost no way to overdo due diligence.

MBA ALERT

If you buy a business, try to structure the deal so that part of the purchase price depends on the future earnings of the company. This can be tough to do, because the seller wants his or her money and doesn't want payments to depend on your competence. Yet to the extent that at least some of the price can be linked to certain contingencies (for example, continuance of a contract with a major account), you, as a buyer, have some protection.

Corporate Ventures

Many major companies understand the value of entrepreneurial behavior and realize that their organizations are too large and rigid to encourage such behavior. Although these companies need the entrepreneur's creativity, drive, and willingness to take risks, most true entrepreneurs do not want to work for them. The standard salary structures and bonus policies of most large companies don't offer the entrepreneur the earnings potential of starting a company, particularly one that might go public. Bureaucracy stifles entrepreneurs, and they lack the patience to sit through unproductive meetings, deal with the chain of command, and have their ideas reviewed, altered, and perhaps killed.

Recognizing this, a number of large companies have launched efforts called corporate venture programs or business development programs to find and tap into entrepreneurial businesses in their industry. Others try to give their "home-grown entrepreneurs" the environment and compensation they require.

A corporate venture program looks for new businesses, solicits and reviews business plans, and provides financial, distribution, and other resources needed by a small company. As noted, the deals may range from distribution or licensing agreements to direct investment in the smaller company.

Efforts to grow in-house entrepreneurs are often related to product development, R&D, or business-development efforts. The company forms a small team under the leadership of a creative executive with both technical and business skills, and gives it a mission. Ideally, the team is cut off geographically from the rest of the company; provided with extra financial incentives; and given funding, a goal, and freedom to find ways of reaching that goal.

However, true entrepreneurs put their own capital at risk and want complete autonomy. Thus, it is difficult for a large company to create and hold on to true entrepreneurs, because that element of risk (and extraordinary reward) cannot really be duplicated in a large, relatively secure organization. Yet large companies can encourage a certain amount of entrepreneurial behavior, and some have had some success in doing so.

MBA ALERT

For entrepreneurial guidance and inspiration, read *Creativity in Business,* by Michael Ray and Rochelle Myers (Main Street Books, 1988). Based on a course at Stanford University's Graduate School of Business, it's still one of the best books on the topic.

Entrepreneur Away

Not everyone is suited to the entrepreneurial way of work. It takes dedication, high energy, tolerance for risk, willingness to fail, and the ability to form relationships and get things done with minimal organizational structure. That last item is key. Most of us spend most of our early years in structured environments—family, school, scout troop, baseball or soccer team, band or debating squad, college, and military service. In contrast, entrepreneurs must function with very little structure. They make it up as they go along.

That ability to improvise—to make it up as they go along, and to do it productively and profitably—may be the signal characteristic of true entrepreneurs. That is difficult to learn. But many entrepreneurs have learned how to improvise, if only because they had to in response to the demands of the market and their business. Moreover, very few entrepreneurs would change their way of working. Most people who "go out on their own" never regret it, and that even includes the ones who fail.

The Least You Need to Know

- An entrepreneur identifies a need and organizes the financial, productive, human, and other resources required to fill that need, and then, if he or she succeeds, fills it profitably.
- Entrepreneurs either buy a business or start their own. The latter is the more challenging undertaking, but both require a true entrepreneurial approach.
- Successful start-up companies are built around a product or service that meets a genuine need, by founders with management skills; access to financing; and the means to make, market, deliver, and distribute the product or service.
- A business plan is the sales tool for the entrepreneur seeking investors.
- Sources of financing include the founders themselves, individual investors (or "angels"), large companies, venture capital firms, and sometimes banks.
- Large companies that have tried to encourage entrepreneurial behavior have a mixed record, but those that have succeeded have reaped rewards.

Doing Well by Doing Good: Business Law and Ethics

In This Chapter

- How business and society interact
- Key areas of the law that concern managers
- The importance of business ethics

The financial accounting and stock trading scandals of the early 2000s revealed a high level of greed and self-dealing among senior managers of some companies. Enron, Global Crossing, Qwest, Computer Associates, and AOL were subject to criminal investigation. Executives at Arthur Andersen, WorldCom, Tyco, Adelphia Communications, and Imclone Systems were charged with crimes ranging from fraud to obstruction of justice. Merrill Lynch paid a $100 million fine to New York State for violations of securities law.

During the rest of that decade, greed and malfeasance concentrated itself in the U.S. financial sector, particularly in the mortgage origination, lending, and securitization industry. (I explained securitization, the process by which mortgages or other loans are bundled into bonds, in Chapter 16.) Major financial institutions completely ignored risk management and even basic credit policy, for two reasons: they wanted rapid growth in profitability, and they believed someone else would get stuck with the bad loans they resold. These activities helped create the financial crisis of 2008–2009 and exacerbated the late-2000s recession. One result was the multibillion-dollar government bailouts of the institutions that caused these troubles.

Of course, wrongdoing and greed occur in all institutions and professions, so business and banking did not corner the market on legal trouble and ethical lapses. Yet given the scale of wrongdoing and greed that seems to permeate business (and politics), it's clearly time for businesspeople to understand their legal and ethical responsibilities.

This chapter aims to assist you in developing that understanding by providing an overview of the major legal and ethical issues in business.

Society, Business, and the Law

Any society worthy of the name has laws. Laws form the very basis of society, and modern societies have extremely elaborate systems governing both criminal behavior and civil matters.

Society—through government institutions—makes laws to reasonably govern people's behavior. The criminal code, the set of laws that define criminal behavior, simply forbids certain behavior. The civil code governs property rights and the rights of organizations and individuals. Each of us has a right to buy, own, and enjoy property, and to live without suffering because of someone else's negligent behavior. Similarly, each of us has an obligation to act responsibly, and that includes acting responsibly in our business dealings.

> **MBA ALERT**
>
> Please understand that I am not an attorney, nor am I dispensing legal advice. I'm just pointing out pertinent areas of the law for managers and underscoring the value of ethical behavior in business.

Business Law

Business law governs the conduct of people and organizations engaged in business. Major areas of business law include the following:

- Antitrust
- Consumer protection
- Product liability
- Bankruptcy
- Business organization
- Contracts

- Real estate and insurance
- Employment
- Intellectual property
- Securities regulation
- Uniform commercial code
- Taxation

Let's look at the legal issues surrounding each of these areas.

Antitrust

The antitrust laws attempt to ensure that competition remains fair. The *monopolies* of the late 1800s in industries such as railroads, oil, and steel prompted Congress to pass the Sherman Antitrust Act in 1890, named for Senator John Sherman, its chief architect. Antitrust laws prohibit companies from merging with or acquiring one another to form monopolies.

> **MBA LINGO**
>
> A **monopoly** exists when there is only one supplier of some product or service. The monopoly can usually charge whatever prices it wants to, because it has no competition.

Restraint of trade can include monopolistic practices, such as price fixing and other attempts to limit competition in an industry or business. For instance, an agreement that "punishes" customers for doing business elsewhere would be an attempt to restrain trade.

Some controversy surrounds antitrust law. The main issue has to do with whether attempting to halt mergers and acquisitions will lead to small, inefficient companies. Given the prevalence of large companies despite the perils of large size (for example, banks and auto companies that are "too big to fail"), this concern may be misplaced. In any event, the government appears to have focused antitrust efforts more on preventing monopolistic business practices than on limiting mergers and acquisitions.

> **CASE IN POINT**
>
> In 2010, in a case brought by the U.S. Department of Justice (DOJ), Panasonic Corp., and Embraco North America Inc., a Whirlpool subsidiary, agreed to plead guilty and to pay a total of $140.9 million in fines for their roles in an international conspiracy to fix the prices of refrigerant compressors. These devices are used in commercial and home refrigerators and freezers.
>
> Price fixing and other forms of collusion aimed at stifling competition are prohibited by law. Visit the DOJ Antitrust Division website at www.justice.gov/atr/ to keep abreast of the department's efforts in this area.

Consumer Protection

Consumer-protection laws are regulations regarding products, services, and credit practices. Some of these laws (such as the ban on cigarette advertising on television) are federal, while others (such as those covering smoking in bars and restaurants) are local or state laws.

Consumer-protection laws arise as the need demands. For example, automobiles are so expensive and their quality so important that purchasers of new automobiles in many jurisdictions are protected by "lemon laws." These laws specify certain remedies—for example, that the dealer has three chances to fix a recurring problem or defect before the buyer can obtain a refund or a different vehicle. (These laws vary significantly across jurisdictions.)

Opponents of these laws believe that it is the buyer's responsibility to carefully inspect all purchases before buying (summed up in the saying *caveat emptor*, or "let the buyer beware"). However, regulatory authorities believe that the seller makes certain *implied warranties* about the products offered for sale. At the minimum, for example, the product should serve its intended purpose and be safe to use.

MBA LINGO

Implied warranties are not explicitly stated by the seller but can reasonably be assumed by the buyer to exist. For instance, consumers should be able to assume that food is safe and that a car has working windshield wipers.

Product Liability

Product liability comes under consumer protection, yet there have been so many lawsuits in this area, with some resulting in awards against companies well into the millions of dollars, that it warrants separate mention.

Essentially, case law in this area says that a company cannot knowingly sell a product that it believes will be unsafe or harmful when it is used for its intended purpose. This logic underlies the investigations of the tobacco companies to discover when, if ever, management knew that smoking caused life-threatening diseases. Those investigations culminated in the multibillion-dollar Master Settlement Agreement between the major U.S. tobacco companies and 46 states. In that settlement, the companies agreed to pay more than $200 billion to reimburse states for tobacco-related health-care costs and to curtail certain marketing practices in exchange for exemption from liability suits.

Most product-liability suits seek to prove either that the company knowingly sold an unsafe product or that the outfit's negligence in manufacturing created a dangerous defect. Or the plaintiff—the party bringing the lawsuit against the defendant—tries to prove that the company should have issued warnings about the product's dangers.

CASE IN POINT

Product-liability suits are the reason for the warnings we see on everything from coffee-cup lids ("The beverage you are about to enjoy is very hot") to children's sleds ("Wear a helmet and use in an open area under adult supervision").

Many people believe product-liability suits have gotten out of hand. They see a "victim culture" in the United States and believe juries are manipulated by attorneys. Defenders of the suits believe that safer products and useful warnings are the result.

Bankruptcy

The bankruptcy laws let a company that is having serious financial problems "seek protection" from the demands of creditors so that they can either *reorganize* or *liquidate* the business.

You might hear about Chapter 11, as in, "If this doesn't work out, we're headed for Chapter 11." This refers to Chapter 11 of the bankruptcy code, the chapter of the code that regulates liquidation. Chapter 7 of the code regulates reorganizations.

MBA LINGO

The term **reorganization** more commonly refers to major changes in the way a company is structured. In connection with bankruptcy, it means a court-supervised procedure to reorganize the business while its creditors wait for payment. **Liquidation** means closing the company and selling its assets to pay creditors. The expression "10¢ on the dollar" refers to the notion that creditors usually wind up getting about 10¢ for each dollar they are owed, although the actual figure varies.

Business Organization

Laws govern the formation of businesses such as partnerships and corporations. As you learned in Chapter 3, a corporation is a "legal person," and this means it has certain rights, such as the right to purchase and own property, and responsibilities, such as paying taxes, just as a person does.

Contracts

Contract law is complex and constantly evolving. Many people find it hard to understand how two parties who have agreed to a transaction can then spend even more time and money on the details of the contract. But the days when business was done "on a handshake" are gone.

MBA ALERT

In all your business (and personal) dealings, be very careful when you sign a contract. Many naïve people have unwittingly signed away valuable rights. Have an attorney, or at least a very knowledgeable person, review any contract that you are about to sign but do not fully understand.

A lot of the complexity of contracts comes from the terms and conditions that people (especially attorneys) put into them. These terms and conditions govern every aspect of the contract, such as "right to terminate" and so on.

Most lawsuits over contracts occur when one party fails to perform, or is seen as failing to perform, as agreed. This is called "breach of contract," and the usual remedy, if you cannot negotiate, is to sue the nonperforming party.

Real Estate and Insurance

Both real estate and insurance broadly come under contract law. However, these contracts can become extremely complex. For example, real estate transactions involving legal structures such as condominiums and cooperatives can become quite intricate. And insurance attorneys spend a lot of time, effort, and money deciding whether a major claim under an insurance policy is valid.

MBA MASTERY

If you are a hiring authority or manage others, know your responsibilities under employment law. For example, it is illegal to ask certain questions in a job interview, such as those relating to age or child-bearing intentions. In most companies, the human resources function can advise managers of their responsibilities in this area. But it is your responsibility to request assistance.

Employment

Employment laws regulate the hours and conditions under which people work and who can work. For example, the child-labor laws prohibit the hiring of children. The minimum wage sets a minimum level of hourly pay. Among the most significant employment laws at the federal level in recent decades was the Americans with Disabilities Act (ADA) of 1990. This law expanded the rights of disabled people in employment.

Employment laws, including those against racial, religious, age, and gender discrimination, impact most managers' day-to-day activities.

Intellectual Property

Intellectual property includes innovations, ideas, know-how, methods, processes, and other intangible elements of the business. Intellectual property rights are protected by copyrights, trademarks, and patents. These devices are key to protecting your business and to establishing ownership in the event that someone else tries to exploit these rights.

Intellectual property law has grown in importance in recent years due to several factors. One major factor is the realization that brands and proprietary processes, such as those used to deliver certain business services, can have tremendous monetary value. Another is that piracy of intellectual property has grown substantially as digital technologies have made such piracy increasingly easier. Also, a number of large companies have lobbied for stronger intellectual property laws, such as longer copyright and patent protection. This area of the law, like most, is a field unto itself. If you need a specialist in this area, hire one.

Securities Regulation

One hundred years ago, securities fraud was common. Bogus stocks and bonds, dishonest investment schemes, and various forms of market manipulation (running up the price of a stock) were common. The U.S. government realized that an honest, open, regulated securities market was essential to a capitalist economy, so it created the Securities and Exchange Commission (SEC), which you learned about in Chapter 16.

The SEC has the ongoing job of policing all players in the financial markets. Among the most common and challenging situations the SEC faces are these:

- Insider trading, in which managers, board members, and other people with information not publicly available buy or sell stocks on the basis of that information

- Stock price manipulation, such as "pump-and-dump" schemes in which a group of investors trade a stock among themselves and then sell it to other, unsuspecting investors

- Improper financial reporting by publicly held companies, or accounting practices that deliberately hide risk

- Improper and illegal practices at brokerage firms, including overcharging customers, appropriating customers' funds, and "pushing" stocks that the firm wants to unload

CASE IN POINT

During the 2000s, Bernard Madoff ran a classic Ponzi scheme, bilking investors of tens of billions of dollars. In a Ponzi scheme, the criminal uses money from investors to pay what appear to be healthy dividends to new investors, without making actual investments.

What's particularly disturbing about the Madoff case is that the SEC didn't dig deeply into Madoff's scheme after repeated complaints from skeptics. It's equally disturbing that at least one major bank became suspicious and refused to do business with Madoff years before the scandal broke, but didn't report its suspicions to regulators.

Uniform Commercial Code

The Uniform Commercial Code, or UCC, is a set of laws governing business transactions. Areas governed include sales of goods, commercial paper, bank deposits, and shipping and delivery of goods. The UCC was prepared by the National Conference of Commissioners on Uniform State Laws and has been adopted by all 50 states except Louisiana, which has adopted most of it.

This body of law does what the name implies: it standardizes the laws that govern business transactions across all the states, which makes it easier to do business.

Taxation

The federal tax code, as you probably know, is one of the most lengthy, complex, and impenetrable documents ever created by political, legal, and accounting minds (and that's saying a lot). Major companies employ batteries of attorneys and accountants to interpret tax law and, if necessary, to defend the company's decisions in tax court, where differences with the IRS are decided (unless they are settled before going to court).

Rules and Regulations

In addition to all of these areas (and some I haven't mentioned, such as maritime law, which governs shipping and other matters regarding the seas), businesses must cope with regulations issued by federal and state agencies.

Some of the more important federal agencies include these:

- The Food and Drug Administration (FDA), which regulates the quality of products for human consumption

- The Environmental Protection Agency (EPA), which regulates air and water quality

- The Federal Aviation Administration (FAA), which regulates air transportation

- The Federal Reserve Board (the Fed), which regulates banks

- The Equal Employment Opportunity Commission (EEOC), which enforces antidiscrimination laws

A company's involvement with any particular agency depends on its size and industry. Pharmaceutical companies such as Eli Lilly must deal with the FDA. American Airlines has to be concerned with the FAA. Merrill Lynch has the SEC to think about.

If you're in a large company in a regulated business, you'll become familiar with the major regulatory requirements and how they affect your job. But what about other managers and other laws? What do managers generally have to be concerned about in the law?

What Does This Mean to Managers?

As a manager, it's not your responsibility to know the tiny details of the law in every area. However, it is your responsibility to comply with the law. Here are some general guidelines for doing so, from one businessperson to another:

- Use common sense and think before you act. Most of us have learned the difference between right and wrong. For instance, if someone offers you a kickback if you'll do business with them, you don't need an attorney to tell you to refuse it and to take your business elsewhere.

- When in doubt about whether you need legal advice, ask for help. Your boss, legal department, or attorney can advise you, but only if you ask.

- Be very careful about what you sign. If an attorney drew up a contract of more than a couple of pages, have your attorney review it before you sign it.

- If the other party has an attorney, you should probably have one, too. If the other party brings an attorney to a transaction, you should have yours along.

- If you're ever accused of a crime, such as fraud, or of serious negligence, get an attorney. Say as little as possible until you get legal advice. Many innocent people have blurted out something that "sounded bad" or was misinterpreted, and wound up in serious trouble.

Finally, conduct yourself as ethically as you possibly can on the job.

About Business Ethics

Ethics are moral guidelines that tell you right from wrong. Business ethics tell you what is right or wrong in a business situation, while professional ethics tell you the same thing regarding your profession. Ideally, there should be no conflict between your personal ethics and your business or professional ethics. However, ethical conflicts can arise when what might be best for the company is wrong morally or professionally.

Here's a real-life example of what I mean. Your ethics probably tell you that child labor is wrong. Yet in some countries, children are put to work at a young age, and often in poor working conditions. They have no choice in the matter, and from our point of view, they are being exploited.

Suppose that your company purchases well-made, inexpensive products from a foreign company that uses child labor. The good quality and low price help your company stay competitive. But is it right to purchase these products?

This is an ethical dilemma, particularly because no law is being broken. The foreign nation does not prohibit child labor, and the United States does not prohibit these imports. It may be legal, but is it right?

The child-labor situation has other complexities. Suppose you believe that the purchase is wrong because children are being exploited, but the families of these children need their income for food and shelter. Is it still wrong? Under the circumstances, perhaps buying those products provides a *greater good*.

Sometimes your professional or personal ethics may conflict with your business ethics. From the business standpoint, you are paid to further your employer's interests. But you also have professional and personal ethics to uphold. To minimize moral and psychological conflict, it's best to work in a business that reflects your ethics, and to live up to your own highest ethical standards.

MBA LINGO

The **greater good** in a situation is the outcome that provides more benefit, at the expense of sacrificing an ethical standard or a smaller benefit to another party. For example, murder is wrong, but the state sanctions killing in war because the defense of our nation is the greater good.

Many people believe in having two sets of ethics, one for their business lives and one for their personal lives. They see business as a game in which honesty and fairness are relative terms and in which money made or lost is the only measure of value. A few of these people actually are honest and fair in their personal, as opposed to business, dealings. But people who behave unethically on the job have corrupted business and eroded the public's faith in business institutions.

Business sometimes does pose genuine ethical dilemmas. In those situations, each of us must do what our conscience tells us is right. This may well involve overcoming the "business reason" that we give ourselves or that someone else gives us for going against our conscience.

Perennial Legal and Ethical Topics

You should be particularly aware of several "hot topics" that often come up in discussions of modern-day business ethics:

- **White-collar crime** is a fact of business life, so be on the lookout for it. Billions of dollars are lost annually due to fraud, embezzlement, theft of equipment and supplies, false insurance claims, bribery, kickbacks, and various schemes. Customers, suppliers, shareholders, and everyone else pays a price for this. If you learn of such activity, bring it to the attention of your company's chief of security or legal services.

- **Whistle-blowing** refers to going to the authorities or the media with proof that your company is engaged in wrongdoing. Some people see whistle-blowers as "squealers," while others see them as heroes. Extreme situations call for extreme measures, and whistle-blowing usually serves an important purpose.

- **Conflicts of interest** arise when you must play two conflicting roles in a situation. For example, if you are part-owner of a company that could become a supplier to your current employer, you have a conflict of interest. How can you be objective regarding who should become the supplier when you stand to gain from the decision? When you face a conflict of interest, it's best to inform someone responsible about the situation or to relinquish one of your roles.

MBA ALERT

Most companies and agencies of the federal government, as well as most other levels of government, do not allow employees to accept gifts of any kind. I've seen a high-ranking U.S. government official return a $79 pen he received in appreciation for a public-speaking engagement for which he was not paid. Accepting gifts is prohibited because it could create a conflict of interest. Most companies also forbid giving gifts—for example, to customers or suppliers—for the same reason.

- **Fiduciary responsibilities** are typically those that an attorney, financial adviser, or executor of an estate has toward a client. In a fiduciary relationship, you must put your client's interests ahead of your own because the client has placed significant trust in you and your professional abilities. You must never harm the client's interests, you must remove yourself from serving him or her if you judge yourself not fully competent, and you must protect the client's rights at all costs.

- **Privacy** is everyone's right and should be respected to the greatest extent possible. This is obvious—and a matter of law—in industries such as health care and investing. But the privacy of all employees, customers, and suppliers must be respected. This is important, given threats to privacy posed by certain uses of technology and by government intrusion in private matters.

- **Sexual harassment** is defined as unwanted repeated or aggressive sexual commentary or advances of a sexual nature toward another person. It is wrong, and it can amount to professional suicide.

- **Discrimination** based on race, religion, ethnicity, gender, age, marital status, or sexual preference is to be avoided on legal and ethical grounds. Most of us understand that we all have prejudices to some degree; the goal is to be aware of them and not let them affect our behavior or relationships, especially on the job. In fact, companies increasingly see the benefits of developing a diverse staff, if only because such a staff can best serve their increasingly diverse markets.

- **Business and politics** have become linked in ways that distort the behavior of people in both institutions. When legislators accept corporate campaign contributions and then support bills that benefit the contributors, the legislators and contributors erode trust in government and business. Abysmally low trust in business and government stems at least partly from self-dealing, cynical behavior by leaders in business and government.

MBA MASTERY

You may have heard that the *customer* is always right. That's a good policy, but the fact is that the *client* is not always right. An attorney, accountant, financial adviser, or consultant must tell the client when he or she is wrong. The client relies on the professional's judgment, even if the client doesn't like it or disagrees.

Governing the Corporation

Heightened risk and the financial crisis of 2008–2009 moved corporate governance into the spotlight. The term *corporate governance* refers both to the policies by which a company operates and to the system of controls and oversight that enables the company to operate according to those policies.

Policies are broad guidelines for behavior and decisions. For example, many companies once had a "no-layoffs" policy (none do today). In tough times, they might have asked employees to take a pay cut, but they didn't lay anyone off. Some companies' financial policies call for them to minimize their debt, while others believe in using relatively high debt in their financial structures. Some companies have a policy of promoting diversity, while others do not.

MBA LINGO

Corporate governance refers both to a company's policies and to the system of controls that enables the organization to operate according to those policies. Ultimately, corporate governance is the responsibility of the board of directors, which oversees the company at the policy level. **Policies** are broad guides for acceptable behavior and decisions in specific areas, such as financial policies and human resources policies.

As you learned in Chapter 3, the ultimate authority over the corporation rests in the board of directors, who are elected by the shareholders. Thus, ultimate responsibility for corporate governance rests with the board.

The board, which includes some members of senior management (who are the "inside directors"), governs the corporation through two major means: quarterly meetings to discuss, review, and advise management on major developments and decisions; and various committees that oversee specific aspects of the organization.

Sound corporate governance demands that board meetings be substantive debates about developments and decisions. Boards with outside directors who rubber-stamp every management decision are useless and don't represent the shareholders effectively.

Good corporate governance also calls for board-level committees that can act forcefully. Typical oversight committees include the finance committee, which oversees major financial decisions; the audit committee, which oversees audits of the company's financial statements; the compensation committee, which reviews and approves executives' pay and bonuses; and the legal affairs committee, which deals with matters such as lawsuits.

Although it will take time for corporate governance in the United States to improve, it will almost certainly do so. Large shareholders, which include major pension funds, have the power to demand change, and they are demanding it. The erosion of investor confidence and the public's outrage over management abuses of power virtually guarantee that improvement will occur. But again, it will take time.

Act with Integrity

The word *integrity* has the same linguistic roots as the words *integrate* and *integral*. With various shades of meaning, all of these words indicate states of being whole and undivided. Thus, a manager with integrity does not have one set of ethics for business and another set for the rest of his life. Nor does he hold one set of ethics for all areas of his life, which he then betrays when he can profit by doing so.

The manager with integrity has one set of sound ethics based on honesty, fairness, and decency, and applies them to all aspects of his or her life, including—make that especially—business dealings.

Big businesses are often reviled by people outside business as being greedy, corrupt, and impersonal. But that can be true only to the extent that people in business—people like you and me—walk away from doing what we know to be fair and right. Millions of businesspeople—the vast majority of whom are never covered by the media—have proven that you can do well by doing good in business.

The Least You Need to Know

- Society makes laws to govern people's behavior. Business law governs business transactions, such as contracts, as well as issues such as monopolistic practices, employment, and taxes.
- In the United States, laws can be created by legislatures, which write codes and statutes, and by courts, which create case law.
- Key areas of the law for most managers to be concerned about include consumer protection, contracts, employment, and product liability.
- As a manager, you don't have to be a legal expert, but you must use your common sense, distinguish between right and wrong, and act with integrity. Also get legal advice when you need it, be careful what you sign, and use an attorney if you feel you need one or if the other party has one.
- Although some managers see conflicts between business goals and ethical behavior, conducting business ethically is good from a business and financial perspective.

Index